The New Political Geography
of California

The New Political Geography of California

edited by
Frédérick Douzet
Thad Kousser
Kenneth P. Miller

Berkeley Public Policy Press
Institute of Governmental Studies
University of California, Berkeley
2008

Library of Congress Cataloging-in-Publication Data

The new political geography of California / edited by Frédérick Douzet, Thad Kousser, and Kenneth P. Miller.

p. cm.

ISBN-13: 978-0-87772-426-1

1. California—Politics and government—1951- 2. Political geography. I. Douzet, Frédérick. II. Kousser, Thad, 1974- III. Miller, Kenneth P.

JK8716.N48 2007

320.9794—dc22

2007039620

To Nelson W. Polsby, who would have drawn these maps on his napkin.

Contents

Introduction

Frédérick Douzet, Thad Kousser, and Kenneth P. Miller

California is often viewed as a trendsetter state where change happens sooner, faster and more radically than anywhere else in the United States. This is as true in the state's demographics as it is in its politics and popular culture.

For decades, California has attracted migrants from across the country, including displaced residents of the Dust Bowl, blacks escaping the Jim Crow South, economic refugees from the Rust Belt, high-skilled workers from the Northeast, and various other seekers of good climate and high quality of life. California has now also become the primary destination for foreign immigrants to the U.S. and the first state with no ethnic majority. As recent immigrants move in, white middle-class residents as well as second- and third-generation immigrants are moving out of the state or changing locations within the state.

With a population constantly on the move, the answers to questions about who lives in California and where they live change dramatically every decade. So do the political consequences of these questions. The formal rules of politics in California, and the United States as a whole, make geography crucial to the political process. With district-based elections and an Electoral College that creates a presidential winner out of a jigsaw of red and blue states, where voters live becomes as important as how they behave. And because California's demographics change so quickly, they constantly redraw the state's political map.

These two principles lead to one lesson for political observers in the Golden State: understanding California's ever-changing political geography is paramount.

This volume aims to contribute to the understanding of California's political geography through macrolevel studies of the state's broad patterns, focused microlevel portraits of specific regions, and essays on the interaction between geography and the state's political institutions. Our collaborative research agenda emerged from a colloquium bringing together French and American scholars of Californian politics, generously supported by the Borchard Foundation. After meeting in a June 2006 conference, we worked together to produce studies of California's political geography that fit into three categories.

The chapters in Part I explore the state's Emerging Political Divides, beginning with Frédérick Douzet and Kenneth P. Miller's analysis of "California's East-West Divide." While California has always had well-known North-South regional differences, recent population shifts and related factors have reduced the partisan division between northern and southern California while increasing the divide between the state's inland and coastal regions. This chapter presents census and voting data to show how the state is segregating and realigning along east-west lines, and analyzes the implications of this new political geography for the state's partisan balance.

In "Residential Segregation and Political Balkanization," Frédérick Douzet shows how the increasing diversity of California's population has led to the emergence of areas of great residential diversity but also pockets of social, racial, and political homogeneity at different levels of analysis. By using the "H index," a measure developed by demographers, and applying it to demographic and political data, she measured the evolution of segregation patterns in California over the past decade and demonstrated that overall, residential segregation has increased in California, particularly along place boundaries. Because of the highly decentralized, fractionalized, and localized nature of power in the state, residential segregation has generated a territorial fragmentation of the state politically autonomous and competing entities.

Ariane Zambiras' exploration of "Shifts in the Religious Divide" uses surveys and church attendance figures to describe the changing distribution of religious groups in California over the past three decades. The chapter focuses in particular on the state's largest religious groups—Roman Catholics, Mainline Protestants, and Evangelical Christians—and also describes the changing religious characteristics of the state's Latino population. By analyzing the political behavior of religious groups at the regional level, the chapter shows how religious differences have contributed to changes in the state's political geography.

All of the chapters in Part II, Local and Regional Developments, look closely at individual cities and regions to answer broader questions about political geography. The first is "Urban Coalitions in the Age of Immigration: The Geography of Mayoral Politics on Los Angeles," by Raphael Sonenshein and Mark Drayse. It asks how demographic shifts caused by immigration and residential mobility have affected political coalitions and voting patterns in L.A. mayoral politics. Combining census tract with precinct-level data, the authors examine how the coalition that Jimmy Hahn assembled in the 2001 contest fragmented, paving the way for the election of L.A.'s first Latino mayor of the modern era. ***

Gérald Billard and Emmanuelle Le Texier provide a comparative analysis of political participation in "Urban Change and Neighborhood Politics in San Diego: A Comparative Perspective." Since the 1960s, California's demographic changes have affected the urban landscape not only of ethnic enclaves such as Barrio Logan but also white middle-class neighborhoods such as Ocean Beach. In both neighborhoods, residents became involved in the planning process, trying to defend their interests and the identity of their community. Despite mixed results, their involvement has stimulated political activism but also shown the limits of the power of residents in these two San Diego communities. Based on their extensive field work in both areas, the authors examine how differences in ethnicity, class, and race shape local politics.

Traditionally considered a black city since the end of the 1970s, Oakland has undergone major demographic changes over the past three decades due to strong Latino and Asian-American immigration, Frédérick Douzet's argues in "The Geopolitical Transition of Oakland." The push for political participation among these minorities has led to new multicultural alliances and seriously challenged the old black leadership. Douzet reviews the historical factors and recent demographic, political and economic developments that have undermined the black electoral base and old leadership, calling for new forms of coalitions in the city.

In " The San Joaquin Valley: Republican Realignment and its Limits," Kenneth P. Miller and Justin Levitt show that while California as a whole has become more Democratic, the fast-growing San Joaquin Valley has shifted to the GOP and contributed to the state's East-West partisan divide. This chapter notes, however, that the Valley's partisan realignment is complicated by another trend—the rapid increase in the region's Latino population. Latino communities now form the core of the Democratic Party's strength in the region, especially at the district level. The chapter concludes that if Republicans want to increase their gains in the San Joaquin Valley, they will have to find a way to win the region's relatively conservative Latino districts.

Dan Walters connects local demographic trends to statewide political changes in "Demographic Change and Political Transition: How the New Los Angeles has Reshaped Sacramento Politics." With approximately 10 million residents, Los Angeles County accounts for more than one-quarter of California's population. Over the past generation the county has experienced wrenching economic, cultural, and demographic changes which, in turn, have transformed it from a battleground to Democratic stronghold. This chapter describes this transformation and explains why it is the leading contributor to recent political changes in the state.

Part III of the book explores The Political Implications of Geography, beginning with William M. Chandler and Thad Kousser's "Governors, Geography, and Direct Democracy: The Case of Arnold Schwarzenegger." This chapter examines the rise, fall, and resurrection of Schwarzenegger through the lens of political geography. How did he win the 2003 recall, and to what extent did his victory reshape the regional patterns of California politics? What political choices explain the dramatic drop in his approval ratings during 2005, and in what areas of the state did he lose the most support? How did his dramatic turn to the left that assured his reelection in 2006 play in different parts of the state?

In "Sorting or Self-Sorting: Competition and Redistricting in California?", Bruce Cain, Iris Hui, and Karin Mac Donald explore a current debate about redistricting by redrawing the state's district in hypothetical maps. In academia and in the popular press, many have debated whether the recent increase in polarization in government is the result of voter ideologies or the way that district lines are drawn. After describing polarization and addressing this debate, the chapter provides a novel explanation: Legislators are becoming more extreme because more and more Democrats are deciding to live near other Democrats, while Republicans also cluster together.

Beginning with an overview of the laws and court decisions that govern the role of race in redistricting, J. Morgan Kousser's "Has California Gone Colorblind?" then focuses on the specific question of what sort of district lines need to be drawn in order to give Latino voters in a community the opportunity to elect a representative of their own choosing. This micro- analysis provides answers to macro-questions about the levels of ethnic group residential concentration in California, differences in voter eligibility and voter registration rates across ethnic and racial groups, and the rate of cross-over voting. The final conclusion is that California voters are not yet colorblind.

In "Is California Really a Blue State?", Morris P. Fiorina and Samuel J. Abrams investigate California's spot on the nation's political map, taking on two pieces of conventional wisdom. First, they show that Democratic dominance is a recent phenomenon, and that the state turns purple when viewed through a longer lens of history. Second, they use a geographic analysis to show that

Pete Wilson's endorsement of Proposition 187 is not what doomed the Republican Party's electoral fortunes. Although the GOP lost some of its already-tepid support among Latinos in areas such as East Los Angeles, it lost control of the state when it social conservatism alienated white voters in the Silicon Valley and wine country.

Finally, François Vergniolle de Chantal's "The Antifederalist Moment in California Politics" shows how Californians have taken up the anti- centralization Republican rhetoric of the past forty years. At the national level, Republicans have promoted a powerful political critique of the federal government that emphasizes views similar to the antifederalist ideas back in the late 18th century.

At the state level, benefiting from a long tradition of autonomy, local governments in California are currently characterized by a wave of resentment and lack of trust versus state authorities. The author underlines the key part played by tools of direct democracy to account for this crisis. These two elements – decentralization and direct democracy – combine up to support the idea of an "anti-federalist moment" in California politics that mirrors the national criticisms against big government and raise the question of the governability of the state.

Several overall themes connect these individual chapters. Since the 1950s, California's dynamic economy, booming high-tech and defense industry and outstanding infrastructures have attracted workers from all over the country. At the same time, the permeability of our borders and society has opened the way to massive and continuing demographic shifts. Over the past four decades, the state as a whole has become more Democratic, more ethnically diverse but also more segregated along racial, socio-economic and political lines. These changes happen at different geographic levels and affect politics at different levels of government. Douzet and Miller's work on the East-West divide and Zamibiras' chapter on the religious divide address it at the state level. Sonenshein and Drayse's chapter study how such changes in Los Angeles have affected local politics, while Walters connects them to Sacramento. Douzet's chapter on Oakland and Billard and Le Texier's on San Diego trace their implications in neighborhoods.

In California, the high level of decentralization and the strong political autonomy of local governments makes particularly relevant the level of homogeneity or diversity of different cities belonging to the same region or metropolitan area. Douzet's chapter on residential segregation addresses this theme broadly, while Miller and Levitt's study of the San Joaquin Valley and both chapters on Los Angeles politics consider its implications in specific areas. Placing decentralization in a broader historical context, de Chantal's chapter discusses the philosophical origins and current controversy over local autonomy.

According the social, racial or political composition of their constituency, elected officials are likely to promote very different interests and have conflicting political agendas. In addition, popular initiative measures are increasingly used to challenge or bypass the legislative process, because of the persisting gap between on the one hand, a majority white moderate electorate and on the other hand, an overwhelmingly Democratic legislature that is comprised of many minority group representatives. Chandler and Kousser address the theme of competing constituencies in their chapter on gubernatorial politics, while Fiorina and Adams demonstrate its implications for partisan trends. Both of the redistricting chapters touch on the role of race in determining legislative district lines, the geographic boundaries that shape constituencies.

A final question about this work as a whole is whether it is a purely parochial endeavor or something relevant to other nations. Since California is indeed a trendsetter in many ways, we argue that this volume contains some broader lessons.

Similar immigration trends and segregation dynamics can be observed in many democratic countries, with comparable political consequences. The French riots of November 2005 just like the urban riots of the 1960s or the 1990s in the United States are only the tip of the iceberg, the most visible and spectacular aspect of segregation. Indeed, segregation processes are at work at all levels of the socio-economic ladder and are mainly driven by the desire of those in middle and upper classes to move away from an environment they perceive as being unfavorable if not dangerous, in order to move into areas where they are likely to find good schools and favorable social interactions. These choices are also driven by the desire to maximize their investments and preserve their property value. Although many enjoy the diversity, others are motivated by more or less overt and conscious racial prejudices that often translate into residential choices. This dynamic is at work both in California and in Europe.

In California just like in France, Spain, The Netherlands, Germany and many other wealthy countries, immigration generates fears, unease and rejection. These trends are also observed among second- or third-generation immigrants who move away from the latest comers or the poorest neighborhoods cumulating disadvantage, including high crime rates. The lessons learned from California might therefore be of use to other democracies confronted with high immigration rates and population mobility.

I. Emerging Political Divides

Chapter 1

California's East-West Divide

Frédérick Douzet
Kenneth P. Miller[1]

California looks far different than it did just a generation ago. In recent decades, the state's political map has undergone a major transformation, becoming more Democratic overall and realigning along a new east vs. west regional divide. For most of its history, California's dominant political divide has been between north and south (Wolfinger and Greenstein, 1969), but the dramatic changes of the last generation have blurred distinctions between northern and southern California while accentuating differences between the coastal and inland regions. In this chapter, we describe some of the demographic forces that have contributed to the state's partisan realignment and discuss the dimensions and significance of the state's emerging east-west divide.

---

[1] We wish to thank Anita Lee, Nicole Boyle, Justin Levitt, and Ian Johnson for their assistance with data and maps presented in this chapter.

Statewide Demographic Change

In demographic terms, California is one of the most complex and dynamic places on earth. With a total population fast approaching 40 million, California is by far the most populous state in the U.S., and its growth shows no signs of slowing. In the quarter century after 1980, the state's population increased by more than half (from 23.7 million to 36.5 million in 2006), and demographers project it will expand to approximately 60 million by 2050 (California Department Finance, 2007), rivaling the population of countries such as Italy (currently 58 million) and France (63 million). See Figure 1.1.

Moreover, in the past generation the state's population has become much more diverse. As late as 1980, whites made up two-thirds of the population, but by 2006 over 57% of Californians were "minority"—either Latino, Asian, or African American.

Signs of these changes can be seen in every corner of the state. Places like Orange County and the San Gabriel Valley that used to be white suburbs of Los Angeles are now home to large numbers of Latino and Asian immigrants, and many other areas that were almost exclusively white have become more mixed. Nearly all the old black neighborhoods are now at least partially Latino, while some neighborhoods that used to have a substantial Latino community have become highly segregated in the sense that they are now almost exclusively Latino.

Many white Californians have welcomed this diversity and have moved to the state's major urban centers to enjoy a dynamic cultural mix, great ethnic foods, and colorful neighborhoods. But others have either left the state or found refuge in pockets of homogeneity in segregated if not gated communities within metropolitan areas or at the far periphery, in places urbanists have named "exurbs." Many of the new developments are therefore being built inland, where people seek more affordable space, lower crime rates, better schools, and greater socio-economic, racial, cultural, and political homogeneity.

Immigration has been the primary force driving the state's demographic changes. After the liberalization of U.S. immigration laws in 1965, immigration levels progressively increased, considerably accelerating in the 1980s and the following decades. In part because of its geographic location, California became the leading destination of new immigrants from Latin America (40%) and Asia (35%). Legal immigration, strongly reinforced by undocumented immigration mostly (over two-thirds) from Mexico, has quickly diversified the population so that the state now has no majority racial or ethnic group. Non-Hispanic whites have rapidly receded in percentage terms, and demographers project they will decline to approximately one-quarter of the population by 2050.

By contrast, Latinos are the state's fastest growing demographic group. The Latino population will continue to grow even independently of future immigration because its increase is more strongly correlated to natural growth than to

Figure 1.1. California Population 1850–2000 and Projected to 2050

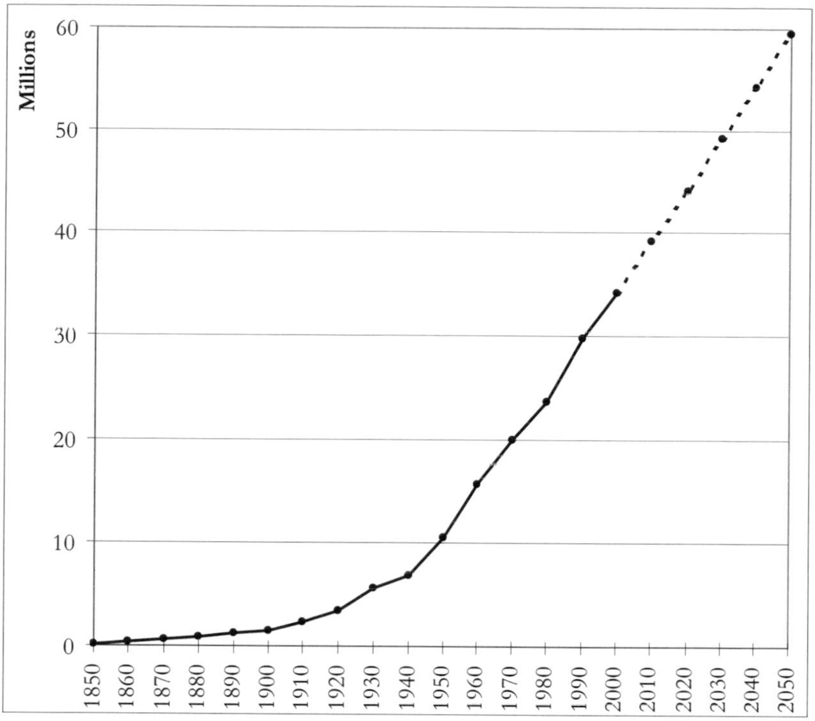

Sources: U.S. Census Bureau (2002); California Department of Finance (2007).

immigration. In 2004, the birth rate for Latino women was 40% higher than for African-American and Asian women and 60% higher than for white women (Child Trends Databank, 2006). In 1980, Latinos constituted 19% of the state's population; by 2000 they had increased to approximately one-third, and recent projections indicate they will become a majority of the state's population by 2042 (Department of Finance, 2007). Meanwhile, California's diverse Asian population has also increased sharply, constituting over one-tenth of the state's total population by 2000, while the African American share of the population is slowly declining in percentage terms. See Table 1.1.

These figures indicate that as California continues its fast growth, Latinos are emerging as the state's dominant population group in a highly diverse mix.

However, the short-term electoral impact of these demographic changes is diminished because most recent immigrants are ineligible to vote due to age and citizenship barriers. Census data demonstrate the size of these obstacles: Over one-fourth (26.2%) of California's population was born abroad and only 39% of

Table 1.1. California Population Percentages by Race/Ethnicity, 1980 and 2000 (with 2050 Projected)

	1980	2000	2050
White	66.6	47.3	26.4
Hispanic/Latino	19.2	32.4	52.1
Black/African American	7.7	6.5	4.5
Asian/Pacific Islander	5.3	11.0	14.0
American Indian	0.9	0.6	0.6
Multirace	*	1.9	2.4

Sources: U.S. Census Bureau (2002); California Department of Finance (2007).
*No data available.

the foreign-born are American citizens—figures that do not take into account California's estimated 2.5 million undocumented immigrants, approximately 9% of the state's population.

National data show that the Latino population is much younger than non-Hispanic whites. As of 2004, the median age of Latinos in the U.S. was 27.4 compared to 40.5 for whites, and of the estimated 40 million Latinos living in the United States, only 27 million were of voting age. Only 9.3 million Latinos were registered to vote in 2004 and 7.6 million voted—a number equal to 28% of the total U.S. Latino voting age population. By comparison, only 2% of non-Hispanic whites were noncitizen, 75.1% of the white voting age population was registered to vote, and 67.2% actually voted (U.S. Census Bureau, 2006). Latino voting power is certain to grow in the long term because the political participation rates of immigrant groups rise in the second and third generations. But as they move up the social ladder, Latinos tend to adopt the voting behavior of their socio-economic group, so the electoral impact of an expanding Latino middle class is difficult to predict.

Meanwhile, in the past generation California also attracted many white-collar workers from other parts of the U.S. who seized opportunities in the state's expanding high-technology, service, and research industries. A range of amenities—including a wonderful climate, dynamic economy, and world-class public university system—made the state extremely attractive for both workers and companies. Many highly educated young people came to California eager to work in an innovative economic sector and enjoy a more relaxed lifestyle. They tended to be fiscally conservative but liberal on social and environmental issues.

These and other demographic trends have placed California at the heart of the national debate over immigration and multiculturalism. Yet the diversification of the state's population has not happened uniformly. The mobility of many Californians has allowed for internal population shifts, which, among other things, has accentuated differences between the state's coastal and interior regions.

Definition of Regions and Methodology

California extends approximately 770 miles from its northern to southern borders, encompassing about 158,400 square miles—a total area larger than Great Britain, Germany, or Japan. It is internally divided not only by physical features such as mountain ranges, but also by distinct racial and ethnic concentrations, regional economies, media markets, and local political cultures. More than three-quarters of Californians live in the state's coastal counties, mostly in the densely populated San Francisco Bay Area and in the sprawling communities from Los Angeles to San Diego. More recently, however, the fastest population growth has shifted to the state's inland region.

As Baldassare (2000) notes, there is no general agreement on the definition of California's regions. Traditionally, the state's most prominent regional divide has been between north and south, with the transverse range of mountains north of Los Angeles, or county boundaries slightly farther north, often serving as an unofficial dividing line. See Figure 1.2.

Recent analyses have suggested other regional divides. Walters (1992) identified 14 distinct regions within the state; Gimpel and Schuknecht (2003) divided the state into five regions (Bay Area, North, South, Central Valley/Mountains, Coast), while Baldassare (2000) focused on four regions (the Bay Area, the Central Valley, Los Angeles County, and Orange County/Inland Empire). To analyze regional distinctions along east-west lines, we separate the state's 58 counties into the 20 counties that approximately border the Pacific Ocean or the San Francisco Bay (the "west" or the "coast") from the 38 interior counties (the "east" or "inland.").[2] See Figure 1.3.

In addition, for some purposes we divide these two regions into sub-regions (see Figure 1.4):
Coastal:
    1. Bay Area
    2. North/Central Coast
    3. Los Angeles County
    4. South Coast

---

[2] Although Napa County does not physically touch the San Francisco Bay, we include it in the "coastal" region because it is generally considered part of the nine-county San Francisco Bay area. Because San Benito County does not touch the Pacific Coast we designate it as an "inland" county for purposes of East-West analysis, but because it is more closely related to Monterey County than to the Central Valley, we treat it as a "Central Coast" country for purposes of regional analysis.

Figure 1.2. Traditional North-South Regional Divide

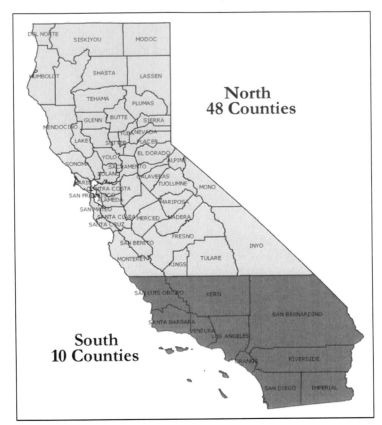

Inland:
   1. Central Valley
   2. Mountain
   3. Inland Empire

The maps presented in this chapter use county-level demographic and political data to analyze the evolution of the state's political geography over time.
Comparing California's 58 counties requires caution because their geography
and population vary greatly. For example, Los Angeles County with over 10
million inhabitants is the most populous county in the U.S. and accounts for
over one-fourth of California's total population, while tiny Alpine County in the
Sierra Nevadas has only 1,241 inhabitants. On the other hand, as Eugene Lee
(1963) noted, county-level analysis is valuable because counties have long been
the basic reporting units for population, registration, and voting data, and county

Figure 1.3. East-West (Inland-Coastal) Regional Divide

boundaries have remained stable over time, while census tracts and blocks regularly change. In addition, some data such as religious affiliation are available at the county but not at the census tract level. Counties are therefore the most convenient unit of analysis for comparing demographic and political changes over several decades.

In analyzing trends among demographic groups, we have sometimes analyzed the difference between the group's proportion of a county or region and its proportion of the total population of the state. The result is expressed in percentage points. For example, in 1990 whites accounted for 84.7% of the population of Marin County compared to 57.3% of the statewide population—a difference of 27.4%. A decade later, the population of Marin County was 80.8% white while California was 47.7% white—a difference of 33.1 percent. Analyzing data from Marin County in isolation would show that the white share of its

Figure 1.4. Subregions

population decreased, but would hide the fact that it actually declined more slowly than the rest of the state.

Demographic East-West Divide

The White Migration

At the level of the county, race/ethnicity and socio-economic group are the main factors determining demographic change. A notable trend is the migration of non-Hispanic whites from coastal to inland counties. Regional racial and socio-economic segregation has been driven primarily by the self-segregation of whites who have moved inland or out of California in search of higher standards of living at lower cost. As the state's coastal region has become more urbanized and diverse, new and highly homogeneous white residential developments have appeared in inland counties that until recently were almost exclusively rural. (See Figures 1.5 to 1.9.)

One example is the area around Modesto, a town located in the Central Valley, an hour and a half drive from Sacramento and two hours from San Fran-

Figure 1.5. White Population by County in California, 1980–1990

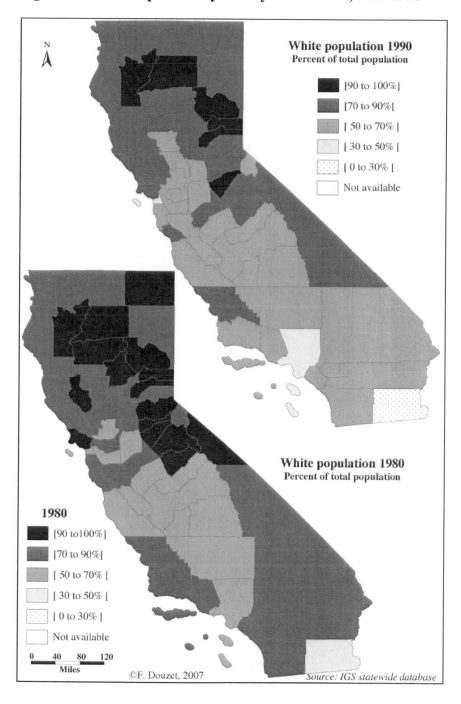

White population 1990
Percent of total population

[90 to 100%]
[70 to 90%[
[50 to 70% [
[30 to 50% [
[0 to 30% [
Not available

White population 1980
Percent of total population

1980

[90 to100%]
[70 to 90%[
[50 to 70% [
[30 to 50% [
[0 to 30% [
Not available

0   40   80   120
Miles

©F. Douzet, 2007

Source: IGS statewide database

Figure 1.6. White Population by County in California, 2000

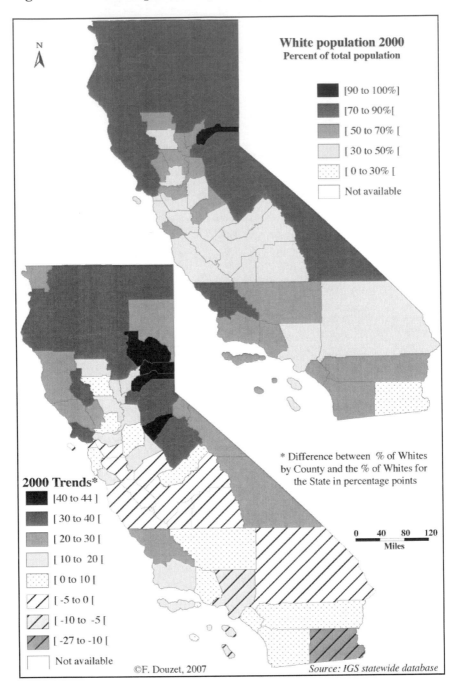

Figure 1.7. Black Population by County in California

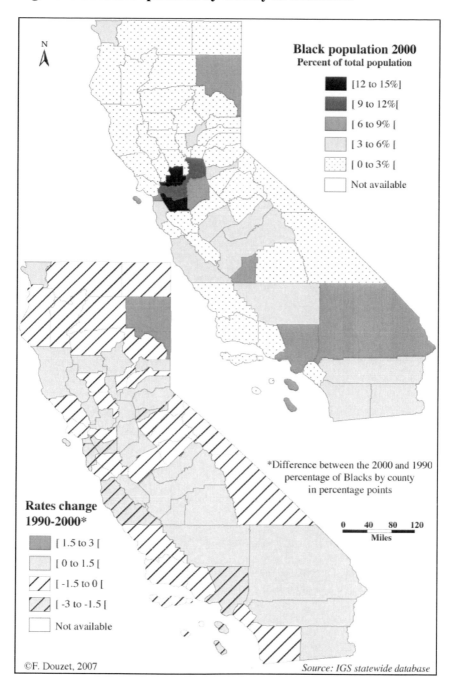

N

Black population 2000
Percent of total population

[12 to 15%]
[9 to 12%[
[6 to 9% [
[3 to 6% [
[0 to 3% [
Not available

*Difference between the 2000 and 1990
percentage of Blacks by county
in percentage points

0   40   80   120
Miles

Rates change
1990-2000*

[1.5 to 3 [
[0 to 1.5 [
[-1.5 to 0 [
[-3 to -1.5 [
Not available

©F. Douzet, 2007

Source: IGS statewide database

Figure 1.8. Hispanic Population by County in California

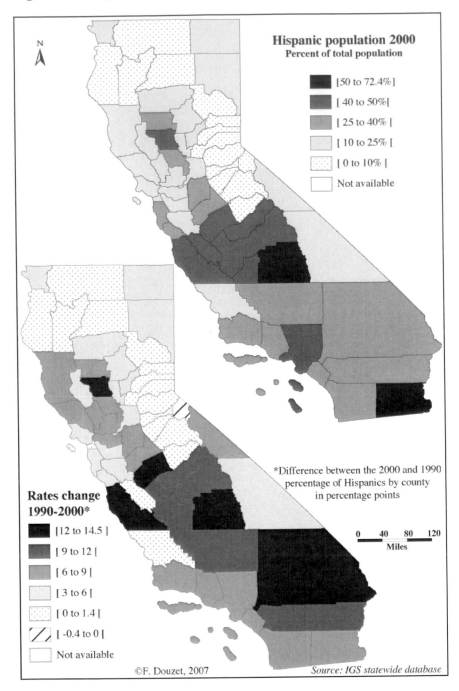

N

Hispanic population 2000
Percent of total population

[50 to 72.4%]
[40 to 50%[
[25 to 40% [
[10 to 25% [
[0 to 10% [
Not available

Rates change 1990-2000*

[12 to 14.5]
[9 to 12 [
[6 to 9 [
[3 to 6 [
[0 to 1.4 [
[-0.4 to 0 [
Not available

*Difference between the 2000 and 1990 percentage of Hispanics by county in percentage points

0   40   80   120
Miles

©F. Douzet, 2007

Source: IGS statewide database

Figure 1.9. Asian Population by County in California

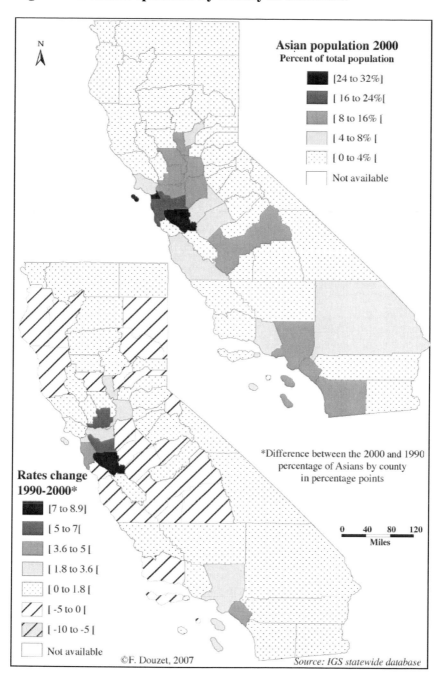

Asian population 2000
Percent of total population

- [24 to 32%]
- [16 to 24%[
- [8 to 16% [
- [4 to 8% [
- [0 to 4% [
- Not available

*Difference between the 2000 and 1990 percentage of Asians by county in percentage points

Rates change 1990-2000*

- [7 to 8.9]
- [5 to 7[
- [3.6 to 5 [
- [1.8 to 3.6 [
- [0 to 1.8 [
- [-5 to 0 [
- [-10 to -5 [
- Not available

0   40   80   120
Miles

©F. Douzet, 2007

Source: IGS statewide database

cisco. Modesto used to be a rural community but has recently become a high-growth exurb with over 20% of its population commuting to work outside the county. Since 1980, Modesto's population has more than doubled, and although an increase in Latinos has made it more diverse, the migration of whites to the area has caused the city and surrounding Stanislaus County to maintain a comparatively high percentage of whites (10% higher than the rest of the state).

Farther north and east, most of the counties in the mountain region are 80 to 90% white. Seven of California's 13 whitest counties are located in this region. The proportion of whites has slightly decreased in these counties over the past decade but at a much slower rate than in the rest of the state. As a result, the gap between the proportion of whites in these counties and the state average has strongly increased: up 13% in Alpine, nine percent in Amador, Tuolumne, and Plumas, and over 5% in Calaveras, El Dorado, Mariposa, Nevada, Placer, Shasta, Sierra, Siskiyou, and Trinity.

In the San Francisco Bay Area during the 1970s and 1980s, many whites settled in surrounding counties such as Napa or Sonoma, where the white share of the population was higher than the state average. While the white percentage in these outlying Bay Area counties has decreased slightly over the past decade, in Marin County the proportion of whites is now 34% above state average, an increase from 27.4 points a decade earlier. Marin County therefore appears to be the most attractive county in the Bay Area for wealthy whites in search of racial homogeneity. In Alameda, San Mateo, Solano, and Contra Costa, the proportion of whites has declined faster than the state average, implying that white departure from these counties is higher than for other places. In San Francisco, the proportion of whites is growing as more whites move into the city.

In southern California, many middle-class whites departed the coastal counties, with Los Angeles County experiencing the largest exodus. Although many whites who left L.A. County headed out of state, others resettled inland in the fast-growing communities of the Central Valley and Riverside and San Bernardino Counties.

Education and Income Segregation

Overall, the levels of education and income are higher in the coastal region than inland, but the coastal region has become more stratified and parts of the inland region have seen increases based on migration from the coast. See Figures 1.10 to 1.13.

Education
The Bay Area and the coastal counties in general have a much larger share of college educated population and a lower proportion of people without a high

Figure 1.10. College Educated Population in California

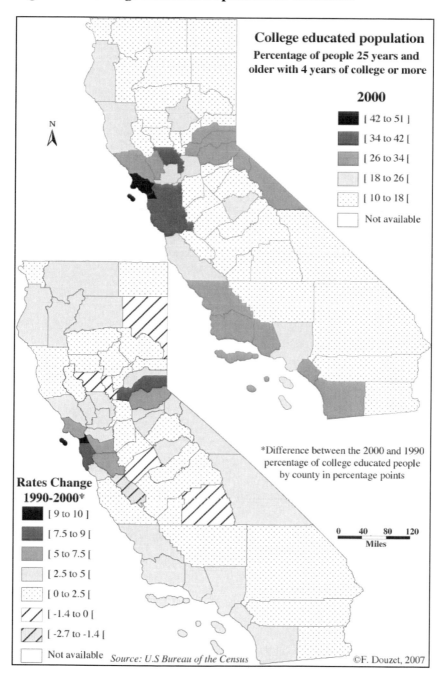

Frédérick Douzet and Kenneth P. Miller

Figure 1.11. Population with No High School Degree in California

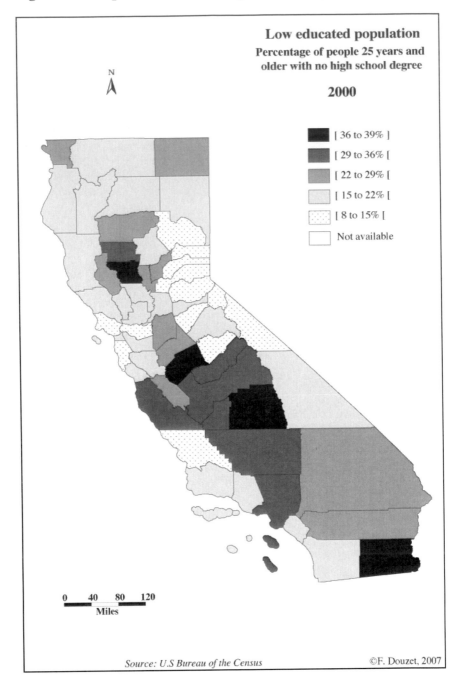

Low educated population
Percentage of people 25 years and
older with no high school degree

2000

[36 to 39%]
[29 to 36% [
[22 to 29% [
[15 to 22% [
[8 to 15% [
Not available

N

0   40   80   120
Miles

Source: U.S Bureau of the Census   ©F. Douzet, 2007

Figure 1.12. Median Household Income by County in California

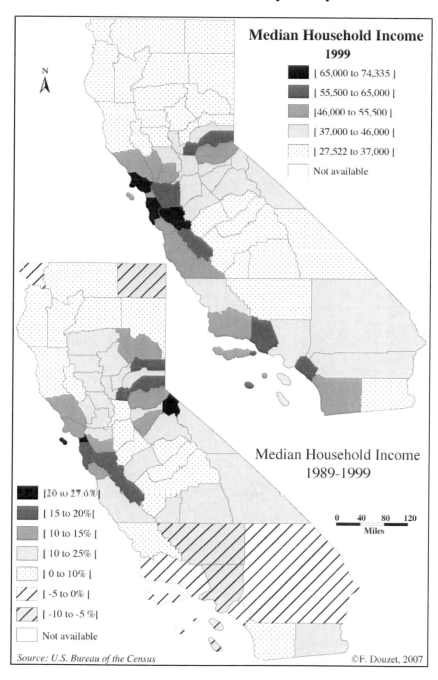

Median Household Income
1999

■ [65,000 to 74,335]
■ [55,500 to 65,000 [
▨ [46,000 to 55,500 [
▨ [37,000 to 46,000 [
▨ [27,522 to 37,000 [
☐ Not available

Median Household Income
1989-1999

■ [20 to 27.6%]
■ [15 to 20%[
▨ [10 to 15% [
▨ [10 to 25% [
▨ [0 to 10% [
▨ [-5 to 0% [
▨ [-10 to -5 %[
☐ Not available

0   40   80   120
Miles

Source: U.S. Bureau of the Census   ©F. Douzet, 2007

Figure 1.13. Homeownership by County in California

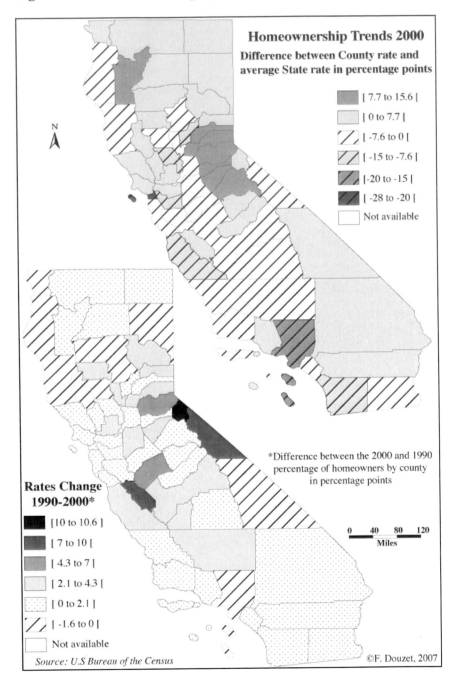

Homeownership Trends 2000

Difference between County rate and average State rate in percentage points

- [7.7 to 15.6 [
- [0 to 7.7 [
- [-7.6 to 0 [
- [-15 to -7.6 [
- [-20 to -15 [
- [-28 to -20 [
- Not available

N

*Difference between the 2000 and 1990 percentage of homeowners by county in percentage points

Rates Change 1990-2000*

- [10 to 10.6]
- [7 to 10 [
- [4.3 to 7 [
- [2.1 to 4.3 [
- [0 to 2.1 [
- [-1.6 to 0 [
- Not available

0　40　80　120
Miles

Source: U.S Bureau of the Census

©F. Douzet, 2007

school diploma. All the Bay Area counties except Solano have higher rates of college education than the state average. Marin has the region's highest rate at 51.3%, perhaps not surprising for a county that is also second wealthiest in the state. The proportion of people with a high school diploma is also much higher in the Bay Area than in the state as a whole. Meanwhile, only three coastal counties—Del Norte, Monterey, Los Angeles—have a lower percentage of high school graduates than the state average. Del Norte's score can be explained mostly by the county's rural character. This factor is also important in Monterey but the score there, as in Los Angeles, is tied to massive immigration of Latinos with low levels of formal education.

Compared to the coastal counties, inland areas have lower rates of college education. Only three of the inland counties—Alpine, Mono, and Yolo—have higher percentages of college educated residents than the state average. However, most inland counties have higher-than-average percentages of high school graduates, in particular in the mountain region. These rates are lower in the Central Valley, where all but three counties have below-average percentages of those with a high school degree.

Recent trends show that levels of education are mostly increasing in places with already highly educated populations. But some high-growth inland areas also saw their proportion of highly educated population increase, in part as a result of migration from the urban coastal counties. All but two counties in the mountain region (Colusa and Lassen) experienced rising rates of education, with particularly high growth in Placer (7.6% in 10 years), Mono (7%), and El Dorado (5.7%). Meanwhile, the percentage of residents without a high school diploma increased mostly in areas of high immigration (Monterey, Los Angeles, Orange, and San Bernardino) and remained stagnant in most of the Central Valley counties.

Income

The level of income, just as the level of education, has increased even more strongly in the regions where it was already high—essentially in the coastal counties. In general, the coastal region's concentration of high skilled, high paying jobs in technology, research, finance, insurance, information, and entertainment, as well as the boom of the region's real estate market and the influx of white collars from other parts of the U.S., has contributed to a persistent education and income gap between the west and the east of the state.

However, there are significant internal variations. For example, median income in Los Angeles actually dropped in the 1990s as the population growth in low-income, immigrant communities outpaced high-income neighborhoods. Over the past decade, poverty in Los Angeles has deconcentrated from the urban core to outlying areas. Minority suburbanization has substantially increased the poverty level of many older southern California suburbs, because many recent immigrants have settled directly into the suburbs where they are surrounded by supportive immigrant networks and are more likely to find jobs (Jargowsky, 2001, 2003; Berube and Frey, 2002; McConville and Ong, 2003). In the past 30 years, the proportion of poor in Los Angeles suburbs has quadrupled and Asian and Hispanic population growth in the city of Los Angeles has progressively spread to the suburbs. The Hispanic population has increased by 71% in the suburbs over the past 10 years and now accounts for 54% of the total Hispanic population (Suro and Singer, 2002). As a result, many inhabitants of these suburbs have moved further out toward the interior of the state or to neighboring states.

Inland exurbs that have attracted many of the middle-class families leaving the coastal region have benefited from hot housing markets, new home construction, and retail development. As well-educated whites have gravitated to these communities, the inland region's median incomes and rates of home ownership have increased. Many of the high-growth exurban communities are located in the mountain region counties of Alpine, Calaveras, El Dorado, Placer, Plumas, and Sierra, as well as parts of the Central Valley and Inland Empire.

Despite subregional variations, demographic trends clearly appear at the regional level. The eastern population of California tends to be more white, less highly educated, and less wealthy than the coastal population which is overall more diverse, more educated, and wealthier. This demographic sorting has had additional dimensions, some of which will be discussed later in this book. For example, as Chapter 3 discusses in detail, the state's coastal and inland regions are differentiating on the basis of religion, with the population of the inland region more highly religious (as measured by surveys and reports of religious institutions) than the more secular coast.

In combination, these changes have had important political consequences.

The Partisan East-West Divide

California's demographic and cultural shifts of the past generation have produced a partisan realignment along regional lines. Whereas in 1980 the primary partisan divide was between northern and southern California and there was a rough partisan balance between east and west, today the north-south distinctions are diminishing while a prominent east-west divide has emerged. To be specific, Democrats have now become dominant in almost every coastal county from the Oregon border in the north to the "Orange Curtain" in the south. Figures 1.14 to 1.16 show the magnitude of the changes in partisan registration at the county level over the past several decades. These shifts can also be seen in Figures 1.17 and 1.18, which show that especially in the past decade the state's partisan divide has become greater between east and west than between north and south, with the east-west gap widening as the north-south divide narrows.

Figure 1.14. Democratic Registration in California by County, 1970–1980

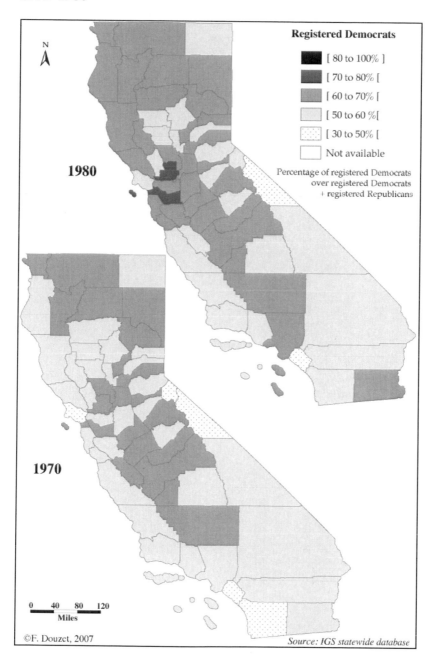

Registered Democrats

[80 to 100%]
[70 to 80% [
[60 to 70% [
[50 to 60 %[
[30 to 50% [
Not available

Percentage of registered Democrats
over registered Democrats
+ registered Republicans

1980

1970

0   40   80   120
Miles

©F. Douzet, 2007

Source: IGS statewide database

Figure 1.15. Democratic Registration in California by County, 1990–2000

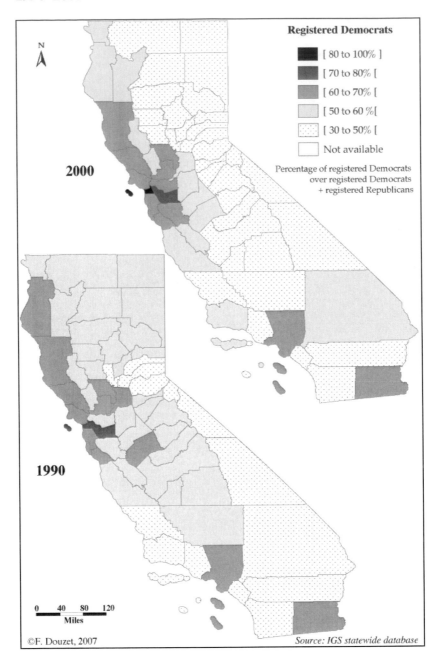

Figure 1.16. Republican Registration in California by County

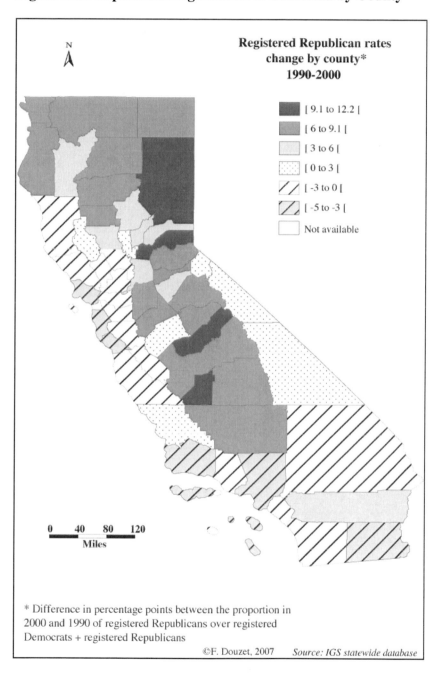

N

**Registered Republican rates
change by county*
1990-2000**

[9.1 to 12.2 [

[6 to 9.1 [

[3 to 6 [

[0 to 3 [

[-3 to 0 [

[-5 to -3 [

Not available

0   40   80   120
Miles

* Difference in percentage points between the proportion in
2000 and 1990 of registered Republicans over registered
Democrats + registered Republicans

©F. Douzet, 2007   *Source: IGS statewide database*

Figure 1.17. Democratic Share of Two-Party Registration, Inland vs. Coastal Regions, 1930–2000

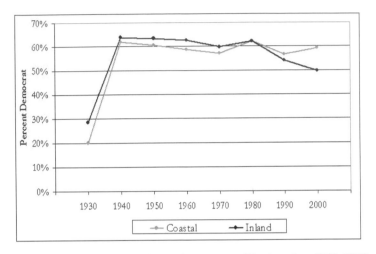

Source: California Secretary of State Statements of Registration, 1930–2000.

Figure 1.18. Democratic Share of Two-Party Registration, Northern vs. Southern California, 1930–2000

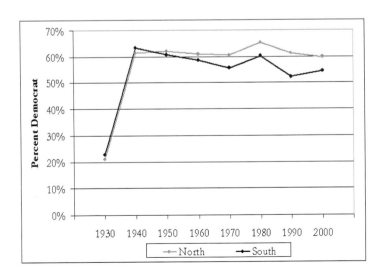

Source: California Secretary of State Statements of Registration, 1930–2000.

The electoral impact of these changes can be observed by placing the state's political map of 1980 next to a map from the 2000s.

California's Political Map in 1980

In 1980, California was a highly competitive two-party state. To the extent the state had a regional partisan divide, it was largely between north and south. Democratic strength was concentrated mainly in the Bay Area and northern California, with an important pocket of support in Los Angeles, while Republicans dominated the rest of southern California. The lightly populated inland region remained a battlefield between the two parties. Overall, the state leaned Democratic in legislative elections, but Republican in top-of-the-ticket races for president and governor. It was thus possible in November 1980 for Ronald Reagan, viewed as one of the most conservative presidential candidates in American history, to outpoll the Democratic incumbent Jimmy Carter in California by 52.7 to 35.9%.[3] Moreover, that year Reagan captured nearly every corner of the state, including almost the entire coastal region. Carter managed to win only three counties—San Francisco, Alameda, and Yolo.

Even more notably from today's perspective, Republicans in 1980 were competitive in congressional districts across the state, including many coastal areas. California elected 43 members of the 97th Congress, with Democrats winning a narrow majority (22 vs. 21 seats). Republicans won 14 of their 21 seats in coastal counties. Coastal Republican districts included:

- District 2 (Eureka/North Coast): Don Clausen
- District 12 (Palo Alto/Peninsula): Pete McCloskey
- District 19 (Santa Barbara): Bob Lagomarsino
- District 20 (North L.A. County/Ventura): Barry Goldwater, Jr.
- District 21 (San Fernando Valley): Bobbi Fiedler
- District 22 (Burbank, Glendale, Pasadena): Carlos Moorhead
- District 26 (San Gabriel Valley): John Rousselot
- District 27 (Malibu to Palos Verdes): Bob Dornan
- District 33 (Whittier): Wayne Grisham
- District 34 (Long Beach): Dan Lungren

Republicans David Dreier and Clair Burgener won two southern California districts that straddled the coast and inland regions and Republicans controlled four districts in Orange and San Diego Counties. By contrast, only five Republicans elected in 1980 represented districts exclusively in the inland region. Most significantly, in 1980 Republicans were highly competitive in the Los Angeles region. Republican candidates won nine of L.A. County's 19 congressional seats that year—which meant that Republicans won almost twice as many seats in Los Angeles County than they did in the state's entire inland region. See Figures 1.19 and 1.20.

---

[3] Independent presidential candidate John Anderson won 8.6% of California's popular vote in 1980.

Figure 1.19. California Congressional Districts in the 97th Congress (1981–1982)

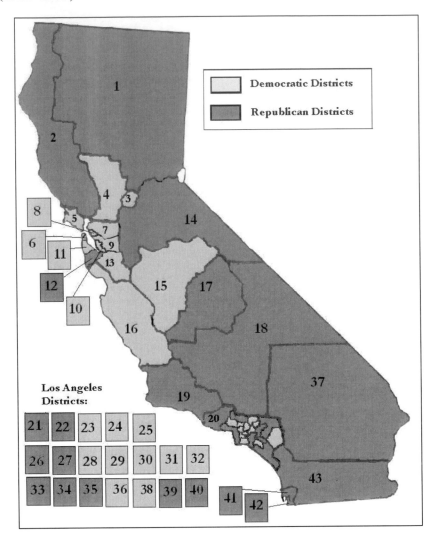

California's Political Map in the 2000s

Just one generation later, the state's political map had significantly changed. Most notably, by the early 2000s the state as a whole became solidly Democratic. Starting with Bill Clinton's first election in 1992, Democratic candidates

Figure 1.20. Los Angeles County Congressional Districts in the 97th Congress (1981–1982)

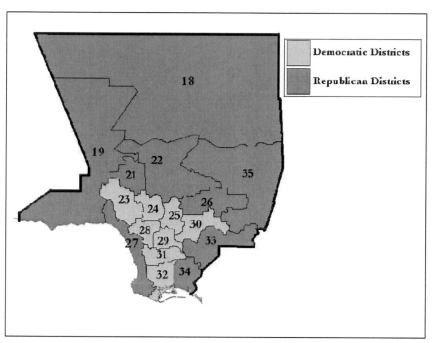

decisively won California's vote for president; after 1994, they won almost all other statewide elections (for U.S. Senate, and state constitutional offices—with Arnold Schwarzenegger the most important exception); and after the mid-1990s they progressively tightened their grip on the state legislature and the California congressional delegation. In contrast to the evenly divided congressional delegation of 1980 (22 Democrats, 21 Republicans), the delegation elected in 2006 (53 members) had a wide 34–19 Democratic advantage.

This shift can be readily explained in geographic terms: *Democrats gained dominance over the state's coastal region*. Almost all of the Democratic gains in the past generation have come in the coastal counties—most importantly, but not exclusively, in Los Angeles. Comparing the results of congressional elections in 1980 and 2006 shows that Democrats took control of formerly Republican districts on the North Coast, the mid-San Francisco Peninsula, and Santa Barbara, and now represent all coastal congressional districts north of Ventura County. But the shift in Los Angeles was even more consequential, with large swaths of the county—including the San Fernando Valley, Malibu, Santa Monica, Long Beach, Glendale, Pasadena, Whittier, and much of the San Gabriel Valley and southeastern parts of the county—switching from Republican to Democratic control. By the 2000s Democrats represented almost the entire county, with Republicans relegated to its outer edges, in districts that straddled the inland region or Orange County.

Moreover, although Ventura and Orange Counties remained solidly Republican in the 2000s, Democrats made important inroads in San Diego. In 1980 Democrats won no congressional districts in San Diego County but by the 2000s they held two (represented by Bob Filner and Susan Davis) and, to make way, some San Diego Republican districts such as Duncan Hunter's were forced to move farther inland.

The geographic shifts in party strength can thus be summarized as follows: Democrats have locked up the remaining territory in the Bay Area and the North Coast, turning the area into a virtual one-party region; they have gained control of almost all of Los Angeles County, by far the largest and most politically important county in the state; and they have made key inroads in parts of San Diego County. As a consequence, the Republican presence has receded in the coastal region, leaving only a remnant in Ventura, Orange, and San Diego counties, and the outer fringes of Los Angeles. Republican strength has moved east. Of the 19 congressional districts Republicans controlled after the 2006 election, 13 were either completely or partially in the inland region. See Figures 1.21 and 1.22.

The shifts have created within California an increasingly prominent east-west partisan divide that in many ways replicates the recent national division of liberal "blue" states on the coasts and the upper Midwest from conservative "red" states in much of the interior West, lower Midwest, and South. Indeed, one might say that California has internally realigned such that its coastal region politically resembles New York state while the interior looks like Texas.

To be sure, just like the national red vs. blue divide, California's east-west alignment has important exceptions. For example, Democrats retain pockets of strength in the inland region—including areas of the Central Valley, Inland Empire, and Imperial County that have higher concentrations of Latinos—and Republicans remain strong in parts of the southern coastal region outside of Los Angeles. But while these variations are important, the larger trends are redrawing the state's political map along east-west lines.

The past generation has also witnessed important demographic changes in the state's congressional delegation and legislative membership. The 43 Californians elected to the House of Representatives in 1980 included three African Americans (Ron Dellums, Julian Dixon, and Mervyn Dymally); two Asian Americans (Bob Matsui and Norman Mineta); but only one Latino (Ed Roybal from Los Angeles), demonstrating that in 1980 the state's Latino population in particular had yet to achieve significant political power. But by the 2000s, the number of California Latinos in Congress had increased several fold with many southern California districts now represented by Latinos.

Notably, the demographic changes in the congressional delegation have lagged behind those in the legislature, a difference that can be attributed in part

Figure 1.21. California Congressional Districts in the 110th Congress (2007–2008)

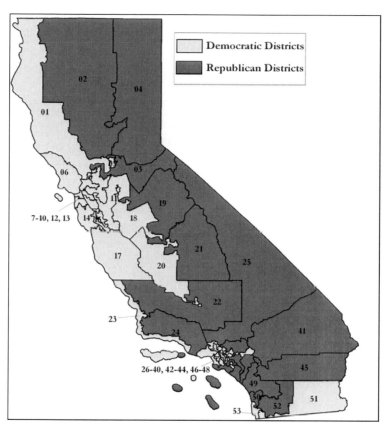

to term limits. Members of Congress, with unlimited terms, can often use incumbency advantages to remain in office long after the demographics of their districts have changed. By contrast, in the state legislature term limits have broken the power of incumbency, created regular open-seat elections, and facilitated the election of more Latino members. As a consequence, the membership of the legislature now better reflects the state's changing demographics than does the congressional delegation.

In both the congressional delegation and the legislature, nearly all Latino and Asian members are Democrats, demonstrating the Democratic party's superior connection to the state's emerging majority. Republicans have had limited success appealing to the state's increasingly diverse population and have largely retreated to mostly white districts in the state's south coast and inland regions. If

Figure 1.22. Los Angeles County Congressional Districts in the 110th Congress (2007–2008)

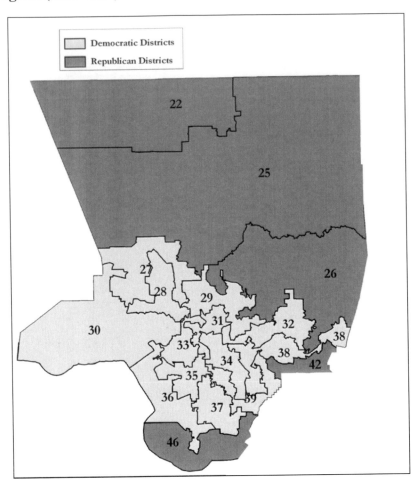

these trends continue, Democrats will control the legislature and the state's congressional delegation for the foreseeable future.

But while Republicans face the prospect of permanent minority status in the legislature, they have retained a share of power in the state, in large part because of the dynamics of "at-large" statewide elections and the availability of direct democracy. More specifically, although Democrats currently win many legislative districts with large minority populations and low voting rates, their advantage is diminished in statewide contests where success is tied more closely to voter turnout. Because the California electorate is presently older, whiter, wealthier, more suburban, and more conservative (at least on some issues) than the state's population, Republicans have found more success appealing to this electorate than competing at the district level in the state's increasingly diverse urban settings.

In the eight gubernatorial elections since 1980 (including the 2003 recall), California voters elected Republicans six times—George Deukmejian (1982, 1986), Pete Wilson (1990, 1994) and Arnold Schwarzenegger (2003, 2006). The voters elected Democrat Gray Davis governor in 1998 and 2002—but Davis was more centrist than legislative Democrats and even then was recalled and replaced by the Republican Schwarzenegger in 2003.

Moreover, in the past three decades, Republicans have used direct democracy to override the legislature and establish conservative policies in a number of areas. Citizen initiatives limited taxes; established tough criminal sentencing laws; imposed term limits on elected officials; prohibited race- and gender-based affirmative action in state contracting, hiring, and university admissions; banned same-sex marriage; and sought to deny public benefits to illegal immigrants.[4] Although California's Democratic-controlled legislature refused to enact most of these policies, the state's voters adopted them all. These outcomes help explain why California Republicans distrust and seek to weaken the legislature but are devoted to a strong executive and to direct democracy.

The gap between the electorate and the general population varies by region. It is most pronounced in parts of Los Angeles and other mostly coastal urban areas with high concentrations of recent immigrants. These areas are well-represented in the legislature but because of their low voting rates have less clout in statewide elections. By contrast, voting rates are higher in the inland region than in the rest of the state. In 2006, for example, inland residents made up 23.92% of the state's population, but cast 28.49% of the vote in the November general election, a difference that magnifies the region's strength in statewide contests.

Figure 1.23 demonstrates that over the past generation the inland region provided strong support for conservative ballot initiatives such as Propositions 140, 187, 209, and 22, with inland voters favoring these measures at higher rates than coastal voters. Comparing Figure 1.23 with Figure 1.24 shows that the east-west divide on these ideologically polarizing ballot measures exceeded the north-south divide.

A map of the vote on Proposition 66 of 2004 further illustrates how geography influences direct democracy on certain issues. Proposition 66 sought to soften California's tough "three-strikes" criminal sentencing law by, among other

---

[4] Some of these measures were later invalidated by the courts, including Proposition 164 in *U.S. Term Limits v. Thornton*, 514 U.S. 779 (1996), and most of Proposition 187 in *League of United Latin American Citizens v. Wilson*, 1998 U.S. District LEXIS 3372 (USDC C.D. Cal. 1998).

Frédérick Douzet and Kenneth P. Miller

Figure 1.23. Coastal vs. Inland Divide on Selected "Conservative" Initiatives, 1990-2000

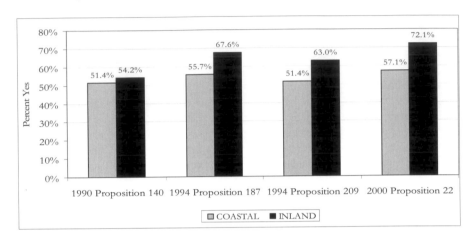

Source: California Secretary of State Statements of the Vote, 1990, 1994, 2000.

Figure 1.24. North vs. South Divide on Selected "Conservative" Initiatives, 1990–2000

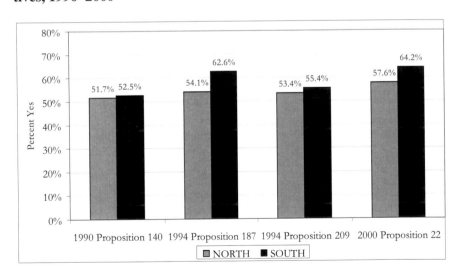

Source: California Secretary of State Statements of the Vote, 1990, 1994, 2000.

Figure 1.25. Vote on Proposition 66 (2004), by County

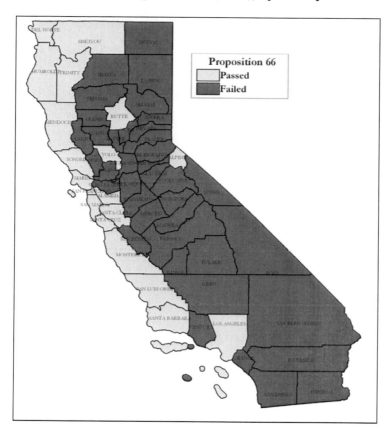

things, reducing the list of crimes that qualified as "strikes" and further narrowing the definition of crimes that can count as a third strike. Although most coastal voters from Los Angeles north supported the proposal, inland voters decisively rejected it, and it went down to defeat. See Figure 1.25.

"Inland values" have thus fared better in the initiative process than in the legislative arena, and the availability of the initiative process has given conservative inland voters a stronger voice in state policy than if the legislature had a monopoly on lawmaking power.

Conclusion

Demographic changes of the past generation have altered California in many ways. The state has become much more densely populated and diverse, and has increasingly segregated demographically both within and between regions. This sorting has had political consequences. Most importantly, Democrats have gained greater control of the coastal region while Republicans have largely retreated and consolidated their strength inland. The Democrats' success in district elections in the more heavily populated coastal region has ensured their control of the state legislature and congressional delegation. But the persistent gap between the state's population and its electorate has at least temporarily preserved for Republicans and the inland region a measure of strength in the direct democracy arena and occasionally in statewide candidate elections.

References

Baldassare, Mark. 2000. *California in the New Millennium: The Changing Social and Political Landscape.* Berkeley: University of California Press.

Berube, Alan, and William Frey. 2002. "A Decade of Mixed Blessings: Urban and Suburban Poverty in Census 2000." The Brookings Institution, Center on Urban and Metropolitan Policy.

California Department of Finance. 2007. *Population Projections for California and Its Counties 2000-2050,* Sacramento, California (July 2007). http://www. dof.ca.gov/HTML/DEMOGRAP/ReportsPapers/Projections/P1/P1.asp

Child Trends Databank. 2006. Report. http://www.childtrendsdatabank.org.

Cook, Sherburne F. 1976. *The Population of the California Indians, 1769–1970.* Berkeley: University of California Press.

Gimpel, James G., and Jason E. Schuknecht. 2003. *Patchwork Nation: Sectionalism and Political Change in American Politics.* Ann Arbor: University of Michigan Press.

Jargowsky, Paul A. 2001. *Job Sprawl: Employment Location in U.S. Metropolitan Areas.* The Brookings Institution, May.

———. 2003. *Stunning Progress, Hidden Problems: the Dramatic Decline of Concentrated Poverty in the 1990s.* The Brookings Institution, May.

Lee, Eugene C. 1963. *California Votes: 1928–1960* (with 1962 Supplement): *A Review and Analysis of Registration and Voting.* Berkeley: Institute of Governmental Studies.

McConville, Shannon, and Paul Ong. 2003. *The Trajectory of Poor Neighborhoods in Southern California, 1970–2000.* The Brookings Institution, November.

Starr, Kevin. 2005. *California: A History.* New York: Modern Library.

Suro, Robert, and Audrey Singer. 2002. *Latino Population Growth in Metropolitan America: Changing Patterns, New Locations.* The Brookings Institution.

U.S. Census Bureau. 2002. "Historical Census Statistics on Population Totals By Race, 1790 to 1990, and By Hispanic Origin, 1970 to 1990, for the United States, Regions, Divisions, and States Table 19. California—Race and Hispanic Origin: 1850-1990," available through http://www.census.gov/population/www/documentation/twps0056.html.

U.S. Census Bureau. 2000. Summary File 1 (SF1).

———. 2006. Current Population Survey, *Voting and Registration in the election of November 1994.* March.

———. 2007. Historical Census Statistics. Table 17-Resident Population—States: 1980 to 2005 http://www.census.gov/compendia/statab/

Walters, Dan. 1992. *California: Facing the 21st Century.* Sacramento: California Journal Press.

Wolfinger, Raymond E., and Fred I. Greenstein. 1969. "Comparing Political Regions: The Case of California." *The American Political Science Review*, Vol. 63, No. 1 (March): 74–85.

Chapter 2

Residential Segregation and Political Balkanization

Frédérick Douzet[1]

Over the past three decades, California has undergone tremendous demographic changes linked to massive immigration and internal migration. As the state's population has risen rapidly and visibly become more ethnically diverse, the impact on California's underlying political geography and governance capacity has been equally dramatic. California is often perceived from outside as an overwhelmingly "blue" state, with numerous racial and ethnic minorities and with Democrats holding control of the legislature, five of seven statewide elected executive offices, and both seats in the U.S. Senate. Yet diversification can follow many different patterns, and in California, it has not been uniform.

The first chapter in this volume showed two major trends. At the state level, the most obvious consequence of these demographic evolutions is the change of political majority: California switched from a light red to a light blue state, as a result of an influx of democratic voters in the state. The second trend is the

[1] Acknowledgements to John Hanley, Shiro Sakaiya, and Iris Hui for their assistance with data analysis. This research project was supported by a Fulbright scholarship.

emergence of an east-west divide challenging the traditional north-south divide over time.

This chapter asks several related questions: is California's diversity only found at the regional level? What pattern, if any, does it follow at the sub-regional level? And finally, what implications does California's population distribution have for the state's governance?

The central thesis is that California has become a patchwork state. Along with pockets of diversity, high mobility rates and urban segregation have created islands of strong social and ethnic homogeneity that have in turn encouraged political homogeneity both at the regional, county, and neighborhood level. In other words, as the population grows and gets more diverse, voters are sorting themselves along socio-economic, racial, cultural, and political lines. These demographic spatial dynamics redraw the political map of the state and create real challenges in terms of governance. Considering the highly decentralized, fractionalized, and localized nature of power in the state, these dynamics lead to increasing balkanization.

The term balkanization refers to the situation of Central Europe at the end of the 19th century and is increasingly used, in other regions of the world, to characterize the fragmentation of a country or an empire into autonomous geographic and political entities, formed to the detriment of the preexisting political territory. In California, the high level of autonomy of the different local governments, the commitment of the elected officials to preserve it as well as the increasing defiance of part of the voters against representative democracy and state power create the conditions of a form of balkanization. In other words, residential segregation has generated a territorial fragmentation of the state into politically autonomous entities. In the most affluent areas, voters and well-organized community organizations put pressure on elected officials to increase the resources of their territories, which often preserves the level of homogeneity of its population (Miller, 1981). Conflicts and power rivalries between these geographic and political entities are both the result and a cause of the demographic trends, reinforcing the tendency of many Californians to move out of the most diverse areas, if not out of the state, or gate themselves in neighborhoods and municipalities in search of greater homogeneity as well as social and economic opportunities. These territories therefore end up competing among themselves and with the state government, the power of which they often try to undermine. In that sense, we can talk about the political balkanization of the state.

This chapter examines the evolution of California's population distribution and its political consequences. In the previous chapter, using maps created with a geographic information system, we identified regional trends and documented the emergence of an east-west divide. To refine this analysis down to the subregional level, in this chapter we will apply statistical tools traditionally used by demographers to measure the evolution of not only racial and socio-economic segregation, but also political segregation. This will allow us to identify segregation patterns at different geographic levels and to understand the extent to which California is a patchwork state. This then raises the question of how to govern a patchwork state in a context of increased territorial competition and political balkanization.

Methodology

Recent studies by demographers have shown that segregation has been decreasing for the first time in the United States over the last decade (Iceland, 2002). It has particularly been the case for black segregation in California over the previous decade (Frey and Farley, 1996; Sandoval, Johnson, and Tafoya, 2002). Our central question is therefore to understand whether more population diversity meant more or less segregation in California. The correlated question is whether demographic segregation led to political segregation.

Measuring Segregation

The term "segregation" is probably not the most appropriate one to describe the trends in which we are interested. In many people's minds, segregation refers to the involuntary—mostly unwanted—clustering of disadvantaged populations, such as in a black ghetto. It is therefore not necessarily the best choice to describe a phenomenon largely driven by the desire of well-off populations for greater homogeneity. While there is certainly a case to be made for analytically separating voluntary and involuntary segregation, statistical tools do not distinguish them. Residential segregation therefore refers to the degree to which groups of people (defined along racial, socio-economic or political lines) live separately from one other, meaning the unequal distribution of groups across space.

Measuring the evolution of segregation over time is challenging, since for some minorities the census terminology has evolved over time, particularly for Native Americans. Also, data on Asian populations are available at the census tract level only back to 1980. But the main challenge, as far as California is concerned, is the "reference group" to which minority residential patterns should be compared.

Up to the resumption of massive immigration in the 1980s, the main color line was black and white, and most studies until the 1990s were based on the distinction between the dominant group and a minority group, usually blacks (Iceland, 2004; Massey and Denton, 1988). Although segregation remained more severe for blacks than any other group, similar studies have shown that Hispanic and Asian segregation have increased over the past two decades (Logan, Stults, and Farley, 2004). Yet in a state where there is no longer a clearly dominant group, it has become difficult to establish a single reference group. In southern California, for example, the dividing color line has become Latinos vs. non-Latinos. Because of the tremendous degree of population diversity in California, we had to use a tool that would take into consideration several groups as opposed to the traditional minority population versus majority population measure of segregation.

The other challenge we encountered was to factor in the spatial dimension of this segregation to understand whether people were mostly segregating along regional, municipal, or neighborhood boundaries. The most commonly used indexes to measure segregation ("dissimilarity" and "isolation") are aspatial (Douzet and Iceland, 2006). For example, the dissimilarity index calculates what proportion of a population should move from each tract in order to achieve complete integration. But it doesn't take into consideration whether the most segregated tracts are close to each other or scattered across the area.

The methodology responding the best to our concerns was Theil's "H index" (Reardon and Firebaugh, 2002; Fischer et al., 2004), which allowed us to establish a diversity index (or entropy score) for the state of California and then measure the level of diversity of each of its spatial units according to the state's diversity. It is therefore the most comprehensive measure of segregation when trying to look at multiple groups, multiple variables, and multiple geographic levels. It allows us to address the spatial dimension of segregation. Finally, it has the specific advantage of being a perfectly additive measure. We can therefore measure segregation at the state level and calculate the contribution of segregation at each geographical sublevel to the total level of segregation.

The H index

The H index calculates the segregation level of a spatial unit by measuring how much each of its constituent parts deviate from its diversity (or entropy) score. We first need to calculate "E," the state diversity (or entropy) score. This is not a measure of segregation. It measures to what extent each group is present but not their distribution across space. Therefore a high level of diversity for a county or a city does not mean there are more minorities but *a better mix of all groups*. A city can therefore have a high diversity score if all groups are present but also a high segregation score if these groups live in separate neighborhoods.

For example, imagine a state that is 50% white, 20% Hispanic, 20% black, and 10% Asian. In order to achieve complete integration, each census tract of this state should be 50% white, 20% Hispanic, 20% black, and 10% Asian. In that case, segregation would be zero and diversity ("E") would be the same as the state's. However, if a city or a neighborhood were 10% white, 80% Hispanic, 5% black, and 5% Asian, the city's score on the "E" index would be lower. Even though there are more minorities in this hypothetical city, they are not equally represented.

The H score is the average deviation of each unit's diversity score from the statewide diversity, expressed as a fraction of the state's total diversity. Therefore, as opposed to E, H is not influenced by the size of the groups. It is a measure of evenness for a given diversity level. H varies between 0 and 1. We calculated H for the state (how the census tracts deviate from the state's diversity score), H for regions (either inland vs. coastal or the eight regions defined in the first chapter), H for counties, H for place (that is a city, town, or village, including unincorporated areas) and H for tracts within places (this is the remainder when subtracting all other H levels from the state level). The results can be expressed in percentages of the state's H level.

We constructed five mutually exclusive and exhaustive categories: non-Hispanic whites, non-Hispanic African Americans, non-Hispanic Asians and Pacific Islanders, non-Hispanic American Indians and Alaska Natives, and Hispanics.[2] Most prior studies were based on metropolitan areas' population data, which is considered the best approximation of a housing market and is therefore a good reflection of residential choices in a given area. Yet the new demographic trends at work in California make this choice rather arbitrary since it leaves out many counties that formerly had small populations but have attracted suburbanites moving out of urban areas to avoid inner-city issues. In addition, considering the rural character of most of the inland counties, it would have proved impossible to measure any regional demographic or political trends.

We therefore ran the H index on two datasets, one based on all census tracts in California comprising demographic and political data, and one based on metropolitan area population data, using the data and methodology elaborated at the national level (Fischer et al., 2004).[3]

In addition, we introduced party registration data in order to measure partisan segregation, compare its evolution to demographic segregation and observe geographical trends that are of significance in the context of California's dual democracy system (representative democracy and direct democracy). We used two party registration as our measure, ignoring independent voters for several reasons. Independent registration often expresses Californians' rejection of partisan politics and is difficult to categorize. Yet, independent voters are often found to be leaning toward the majority party of their region. In an overwhelmingly conservative region, independent voters are more likely to vote Republican than in a liberal region, where they might vote for the green party. Our measure therefore allows us to identify trends more clearly.

---

[2] We had to make some adjustments to account for people selecting two racial identifications, an option introduced in the 2000 census, following Allen and Turner (2001.)

[3] We would like to thank the authors, most particularly Jon Stiles, for sharing their data and expertise.

Results

California's demographic changes have an impact at all levels of government. In the first chapter of this volume, we have seen how, with the massive arrival of white-collar workers from the Northeast and immigrants from Latin America and Asia, California has switched from a light red to a light blue state, up to the point that it is seldom considered a swing state in presidential elections. Yet Californians recalled their Democratic governor to elect a Republican one in 2003. We have also discussed how diverse the state has become. California no longer has a racial majority, the number of Hispanic elected officials strongly increased over the past decades, and in 2005 Los Angeles elected its first Latino mayor of the modern era. The Latino Caucus of the state legislature now comprises 27 legislators, up from five when the Chicano Legislative Caucus was formed in 1973. Yet California was the first state to dismantle affirmative action policies and bilingual education and to enact a "three strikes" sentencing law, which has primarily affected the sentences of young blacks and Latinos. The answer to these apparent contradictions lies in the fact that these demographic changes went along with segregation dynamics at the regional and local level that have major political implications. Computing the H score for the counties and the metropolitan areas, along with the maps presented in this volume's first chapter, allows us to better understand these trends.

The first major finding is that the increased diversity of California's population does not translate into an increased diversity of all its regions or neighborhoods. Changes do not occur at the same rate or speed in every geographic area. Some regions underwent dramatic changes while others have been essentially unaltered. Increased diversity has not ended segregation dynamics. The opposite seems to be happening as California trends differ notably from national ones.

The second finding is that residential segregation is mostly driven by the self-segregation of the white and high-income populations, taking the form of a white flight or increased "gating" along municipal boundaries.

The third finding is a consequence of the previous two. Residential segregation is a source of competition for resources between territories, which in turn encourages more residential segregation. Place matters. Understanding demographic spatial dynamics and the political trends associated with them requires a sound understanding of the underlying geography. See Table 2.1.

Increased Racial Segregation at the State Level

While many areas in California now include more minorities, segregation has increased overall by 6.9% over the past decade, according to an analysis of all census tracts. Interestingly, black segregation has decreased substantially

Table 2.1. Amount of Segregation Contributed at Different Levels, California

Partisianship— Dems., Reps., All Others

	1990		2000		90-00
	Seg.	%	Seg.	%	
Total	.06235		.05744		-7.87
Region	.01339	21	.01609	28	20.16
County	.00481	8	.00543	9	12.89
Place	.02304	37	.02032	35	-11.81
Tracts in places	.02111	34	.01560	27	-26.10

Partisianship—Dems., Reps. Only

	1990		2000		90-00
	Seg.	%	Seg.	%	
Total	.09053		.09477		4.68
Regions	.01912	21	.02718	29	42.15
County	.00645	7	.00757	30	17.36
Place	.03464	38	.03568	38	3.00
Tracts in places	.03032	33	.02434	26	-19.72

Blacks

	1990		2000		90-00
	Seg.	%	Seg.	%	
Total	.31121		.25692		-17.44
Region	.02956	9	.02981	12	0.85
County	.02793	9	.02973	12	6.44
Place	.11133	36	.09336	36	-16.14
Tracts in places	.14240	46	.10402	40	-26.95

Latinos

	1990		2000		90-00
	Seg.	%	Seg.	%	
Total	.24014		.25135		4.67
Region	.03773	16	.03741	15	-0.85
County	.01467	6	.01664	7	13.43
Place	.09012	38	.09830	39	9.08
Tracts in places	.09672	40	.9900	39	2.36

Frédérick Douzet

Whites

	1990 Seg.	%	2000 Seg.	%	90-00
Total	.26442		.30908		16.89
Region	.04223	16	.04745	15	12.36
County	.01565	6	.01629	5	4.09
Place	.09220	35	.11860	38	28.63
Tracts in places	.11434	43	.12674	41	10.84

Asians

	1990 Seg.	%	2000 Seg.	%	90-00
Total	.16870		.14081		-16.53
Region	.03030	18	.03076	22	1.53
County	.01720	10	.01386	10	-19.41
Place	.05680	34	.05232	37	-7.90
Tracts in places	.06440	38	.04387	31	-31.88

All Races

	1990 Seg.	%	2000 Seg.	%	90-00
Total	.26607		.28448		6.92
Region	.04070	15	.04242	15	4.23
County	.01959	7	.02162	8	10.36
Place	.09388	35	.10632	37	13.25
Tracts in places	.11189	42	.11412	40	1.99

Highest Income Quintile

	1990 Seg.	%	2000 Seg.	%	90-00
Total	.13618		.14283		4.88
Region	.01560	11	.02507	18	60.71
County	.00928	7	.00863	6	-7.00
Place	.03901	29	.04000	28	2.54
Tracts in places	.07229	53	.06913	48	-4.37

Lowest Income Quintile

	1990		2000		90-00
	Seg.	%	Seg.	%	
Total	.09313		.09484		1.84
Region	.01044	11	.01344	14	28.74
County	.02314	25	.02255	24	-2.55
Place	.00707	8	.00584	6	-17.40
Tracts in places	.05247	56	.05300	56	1.01

(-17.44%), which is faster than in the rest of the nation (-13%). Asian segregation has strongly decreased (-16.5%) while Latino segregation has increased by 4.7%. It is very clear, according to these results, that white segregation is driving the rest of segregation, with an increase of 16.9% in a decade. In 1990, blacks had by far the highest segregation score (0.31 compared with 0.26 for whites, 0.24 for Latinos, and 0.17 for Asians). In 2000, the whites became the most segregated group with a score of 0.31 before the blacks (0.26), the Latinos (0.25), and the Asians (0.14).

Analysis of the metropolitan area dataset, which only measures trends in urban areas, gives a less contrasted picture, closer to the national trend. Segregation is slightly decreasing overall (-3%) and more strongly for blacks (-21%). Hispanic segregation, however, is increasing (4.6%). In both datasets, there is an increase in racial segregation at the place level for all races except blacks, with this being particularly true for whites. In other words, more of California's segregation occurs between different cities, towns, or villages and unincorporated areas than was previously the case. Census places are used here to designate cities. They consist in cities and unincorporated areas. While looking at all tracts, white segregation between places increased by 28.6% and accounts for 38% of all white segregation in the state. Both datasets also show that white segregation is the highest of all groups, which was not true in 1990 when black segregation was much higher.

Similar studies at the national level have shown a decrease in black segregation. From 1950 to 1990, the residential segregation of African Americans has progressively increased in the United States. Yet for the past decade, the trends have for the first time reversed, and black segregation has slightly decreased according to most of the studies conducted on the basis of the 2000 census, whatever the index used by demographers (Iceland and Wilkes, 2004; Frey and Farley, 1996; Clark and Blue, 2004). This reverse trend has started even earlier in California. African Americans, however, remained the most segregated group across all dimensions, and it is clear that desegregation is not even across the state (Douzet, 2006). Hispanic and Asian segregation levels are either stable or increasing, depending on the dimensions measured. Segregation strongly increases in areas of high immigration with growing ethnic enclaves and the constant influx of new immigrants, who primarily settle in places where they are likely to find a support network, affordable housing, and a familiar cultural environment. Segregation therefore increases despite the spatial assimilation of second- and third-generation immigrants. For the first time in 2000, Hispanics were in a situation of hypersegregation in two cities, Los Angeles and New York, meaning a situation of very high segregation across several dimensions (Iceland and Wilkes, 2004). A national study using the multirace H index found that the decline in segregation was mostly due to desegregation for blacks and whites, with little change or a slight increase for Asians and Hispanics, but that growing diversity was associated with increases in overall segregation, as well as white, Asian, and Hispanic segregation (Iceland, 2004). The study conducted by Fischer, Stockmayer, Stiles, and Hout using the H index supports these findings and adds a particularly interesting geographic dimension, showing that overall, class segregation increased, at least among the most affluent. They also show that white segregation decreases but at a much slower rate than black segregation, which seems to indicate that white residential areas do not welcome diversity at the same rate as the rest of the country.

They also emphasize the importance of place differences within metropolitan areas, overriding the old city versus suburbs division and suggesting that "by inference, advantaged groups are increasingly using municipal lines to sequester themselves" (Fischer et al., 2004).

These results are likely to be magnified in California, considering the rate of population growth and immigration. Previous studies of California have measured the evolution of diversity at the neighborhood level and found that the number of diverse neighborhoods had dramatically increased over the past decade while the percentage of California's residents living in segregated neighborhoods significantly declined (Sandoval, Johnson, and Tafoya, 2002). Segregated neighborhoods were defined according to the overwhelming racial or ethnic majorities of households. However, diversity was not weighted against the diversity of the city or state they were located in, therefore missing metropolitan area or regional trends. Their paper only briefly examined the benefits of studying racial sorting at a regional level, acknowledging that large swaths of less populated regions remained extremely homogeneous and that despite the diversity, many cities showed high levels of segregation.

By contrast, our study shows the significance of place and regions in the segregation processes that happen partly—though not exclusively—in reaction to increased diversity. Breaking down these results by spatial levels and looking at geographic differences is therefore likely to give a more complete picture of the demographic trends and look into the apparent contradiction of a double trend: an increase in overall population diversity and in segregation.

Racial Segregation, Geographic Breakdown

National and regional trends often mask strong differences within some regions. The Bay Area is home to the most diverse counties but also the most homogeneous neighborhoods. Many of California's coastal counties that show high diversity levels also show high segregation levels. More generally, all the counties with a segregation level above 0.2, except for Imperial and Kern, are located in coastal areas: Los Angeles stands out as the most segregated, well above others, followed by Monterey. Alameda is the most diverse (1.11, the maximum "E" score being 1.61) and presents a high segregation rate, like Santa Cruz, Orange, San Francisco, Fresno, Santa Clara, and Ventura. Fourteen out of the 20 coastal counties have rates of segregation above 0.2. All the coastal counties south of Sonoma, except for Solano in the Bay Area have particularly high segregation rates. This shows that segregation is much higher on the coast and in the southern areas of the state, where most of the immigrants are located and where the diversity rates are high. See Figures 2.1 and 2.2.

The increase in segregation in many inland and northern counties is primarily due to the fact that they previously had little diversity. The most homogeneous counties are located in the interior mountain area. Except for Alpine, Colusa, Glenn, and Lassen, these counties have the lowest levels of diversity in the state (under 0.6), led by homogeneous Nevada County (0.3). In many of the less populated regions inland, diversity can largely be attributed to American Indian tribes (i.e., Alpine), the presence of military bases, or prison facilities. All three counties of the north coast have seen their segregation level increase as their racial diversity went up, as in 70% of the counties where diversity increased.

Immigration has clearly transformed the southern part of the state and California's coastal population, contributing to higher diversity in many areas. Yet other areas where immigrants are moving in are getting more segregated and less diverse, which suggests that their share of one immigrant population is getting higher and/or their share of white population is decreasing. This is the case of many coastal counties such as Orange, Los Angeles, San Francisco, San Diego, and increasingly the Central Valley. A typical example is the city of Monterey Park, which is now 62% Asian, up from 15% in 1970 and now nicknamed the "Chinese Beverly Hills." As Asians keep moving in and whites keep moving out, the county is becoming less diverse and more segregated. Hispanic immigration has affected the entire state, but some regions have undergone more rapid changes as more immigrants move to places already inhabited by Hispanics. The Hispanic population increased from 25 to 48% in 20 years in the city of San Bernardino and from 27% to 60% in Ontario. In Santa Ana (Orange County) it reached 76%. San Francisco has experienced the largest decrease in racial diversity, down from 1.25 in 1990 to 0.96 in 2000.

Figure 2.1.

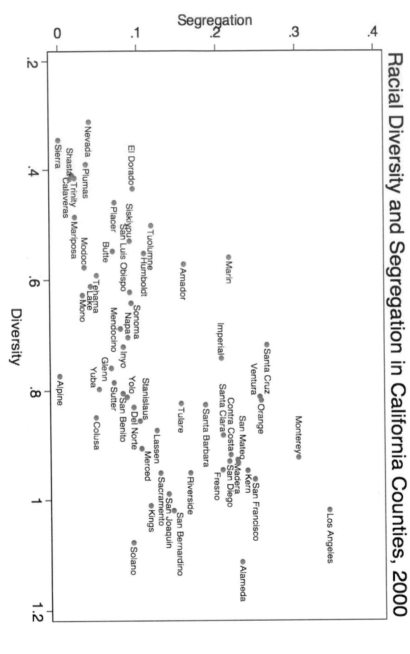

Racial Diversity and Segregation in California Counties, 2000

Figure 2.2

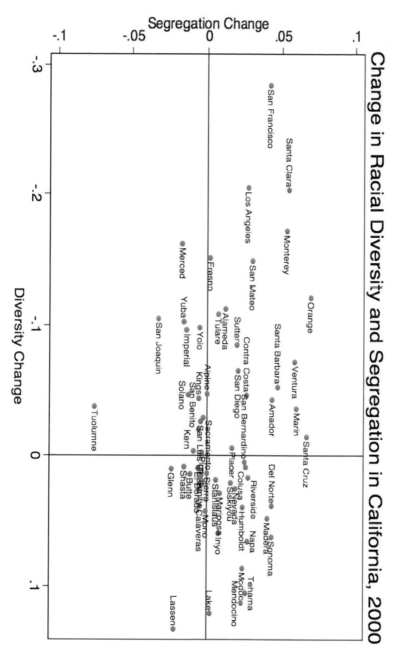

Change in Racial Diversity and Segregation in California, 2000

White Segregation

A major trend we can draw from the results is that the self-segregation of whites and those earning the highest incomes greatly contributed to overall segregation and the emergence of new regional trends in California. As neighborhoods and cities became more mixed, part of the white population sought to isolate itself in pockets of social and racial homogeneity. The phenomenon can be observed at all geographical levels: whites are increasingly moving out of the state, moving inland and segregating themselves along municipal boundaries in pockets of homogeneity. This is also true of middle- and upper-class minorities, who are often second- or third-generation immigrants.

White Flight

Since the 1990s, domestic migration to and from California radically changed. More people move out to other states—about two million more during the 1990s—than move into California, and the number of white inhabitants has greatly decreased. California lost over a million white residents, more than half of the net outflow of the state population. Many of them settled in Arizona, Nevada, and Colorado (Perry, 2003; Johnson, 2000). The net outflow of Latinos and Asians is also high, with over 430,000 Latinos and 110,000 Asians moving out in the 1990s, the vast majority of whom were third-generation immigrants. Yet unlike whites and blacks, California's Asian and Latino populations continued to grow. The maps in Chapter 1 of this volume show that the departure of whites has been much greater in the western part of the state and much slower inland, where some areas have seen their white population actually increasing.

Whites have also moved to new areas inland that were once nearly empty. Some inland California counties that were very homogeneous and had small populations have substantially grown. Although they did not escape the growing diversity trend, they offer enclaves of strong homogeneity. Nevada County has seen its population increase by 78% in 20 years and the proportion of whites is 27 percentage points higher than that of the state, growing from only 16 points higher in 1980. In Calaveras County, the Hispanic population has grown slowly while the population has nearly doubled in 20 years. The proportion of whites is now 24 percentage points above that of the state average, up from 10 points above 20 years ago. While the white population decreased by 7% in the state overall during the 1990s, it increased by 13% and 21% in these particular counties.

Many whites therefore seem to be leaving the diverse coastal parts of California either to move out of the state or east, into areas too far from major cities to be considered suburbs. Urban scholars have named these areas exurbs. Temecula, in Riverside County, is a good example of the dramatic population growth inland. With the completion of Interstate 15 linking Los Angeles to San

Diego, many middle- and upper-class families were able to settle in racially and economically homogeneous areas, such as Temecula. In 1970, the city's population was 2,770 inhabitants. It rose to 8,300 in 1980 and then to 81,400 in early 2005. The number of minority residents in the city grew but at a much slower rate than in other parts of the state. Despite the high level of diversity in Riverside County, Temecula is 70% white. White segregation, as a result, increased by 12.4% across regions.

Affluent white families and second- and third-generation immigrants who have succeeded economically have moved inland in substantial numbers in search of affordable housing space, better schools, lower crime rates, and more generally, a family friendly environment where they can enjoy a better quality of life. Priced out of major urban centers and discouraged by the poor performances of public schools, they often commute long hours to settle their families in new exurbs or former rural areas turned into exurbs.

The H index shows a decline in white segregation along the water-inland dividing line, which can probably be explained by the much higher and growing significance of white segregation within counties and places. It can also be explained by the fact that the white flight to the exurbs has been followed by blacks and economically successful immigrants. Yet the white share of population clearly increased inland, as the first chapter in this volume showed. Although the white population has decreased across California in the last decade, the gap between the proportion of whites leaving in the interior counties and the state average has strongly increased, particularly in the mountain area where all the counties followed the same patter. In Alpine, the proportion of whites was 12.1 percentage points higher than the state average in 1990. It went up to 25.3. In Calaveras, it grew from 34.3 to 40.9, in Amador, from 26.4 to 35.7, in Plumas from 33.9 to 42.1.

The Gating of White Californians

As they moved inland, whites clearly segregated themselves in their new environment. The places where the highest increases of white segregation were recorded are mostly up north and inland: Colusa, Mono, Modoc, Mariposa, Sutter, Tehama, Placer, Humbolt, Napa, Nevada, Mendocino, Sonoma, and Yolo. Yet, in the highly diverse coastal counties, the level of white segregation is higher than anywhere else and still increasing: 0.38 in Los Angeles (+17.3%), 0.32 in Monterey (+38.2%), 0.29 in Orange (+53.8%) and Ventura (+34.8%), 0.27 in Alameda (+22.6%) and Kern (+1.8%), 0.26 in Contra Costa (+34.5%) and San Francisco (+67.5%), 0.25 in San Diego (+19.1%) and 0.22 in Marin (+41.1%). Whites tend to increasingly segregate themselves in areas where there are many minority residents—areas where diversity is high but not necessarily increasing and where immigrants keep moving in, creating a more homogeneous environment—and in the inland counties where they are moving and where diversity is low but somewhat increasing.

Along with regional segregation, white populations increasingly sort themselves along municipal boundaries, which now account for 38% of white segregation. It would be interesting to study the significance of school district
boundaries to explain this phenomenon as quality education ranks high in residential choices among middle- and upper-class families. Areas of great diversity
also attract white and wealthy people who enjoy the ethnic mix of the neighborhoods, are bored with the homogeneity of suburban life, and welcome cultural
experience and exchange. Yet they tend to be disproportionately young and
highly educated with no children (Fischer et al., 2004). Families looking for
larger houses and better schools tend to move to more protected areas, where
school population and neighbors are selected by their income. Houses in Palo
Alto have become extremely expensive and largely unaffordable for the children
who grew up there, unless they earn two salaries in the dot-com industry. Income segregation, in that sense, tends to drive racial segregation as minorities
still cannot afford such highly expensive housing in the same proportions as
whites. Gated communities or municipalities therefore use this tool to select the
population they target in order to ensure good housing values and social homogeneity. Through zoning laws, for example, they impose minimum requirements
in housing size and other constraining local regulations.

Social and racial sorting through municipalities leads to fascinating contrasts. Marin County, in the north of the Bay Area, has a growing Hispanic
population. Yet some of its neighborhoods and cities are more and more white.
At 7am on Andersen Drive, in San Rafael, dozens of immigrants wait along the
road to get picked up for day labor, only a few miles from Sausalito, a 90%
white city. The same contrast can be found in San Francisco where whites live
in neighborhoods that are 90% white on average while only 44% of the city's
population is white (Phu et al., 2005).

The voluntary segregation of the wealthiest reinforces involuntary segregation of the most recent immigrants and disadvantaged populations. The residential segregation of those making incomes in the lowest 20% of the income ladder
has increased by 7.6% in San Francisco. Yet this did not prevent black segregation from decreasing in the same proportions. Latino segregation decreased
slightly (-5.2%) and Asian segregation decreased strongly (-53.4%). White segregation, however, increased by 67.5%, suggesting that black desegregation is
primarily due to other minorities moving into black neighborhoods and less so to
whites mixing with blacks.

Black Segregation

In addition to the consequences of the civil rights movement and the rise of
a middle class encouraged by affirmative action measures, African Americans
have certainly benefited from a greater tolerance to diversity as second- and

third-generation immigrants have helped break the homogeneity of previously white places. Thanks to strong immigration rates, young white professionals moving back into major cities, and a hot housing market, a number of middle-class blacks have sold their houses and moved to outer suburbs or inland areas, leaving highly segregated neighborhoods for more diverse suburbs. The black populations in cities like Oakland, in the Bay Area, have substantially decreased over the past two decades as the old ghetto of West Oakland became partially gentrified and black owners were able to cash in their property. Many of these families settled in suburbs like Antioch and Pittsburg, moved further inland, or even out of the state.

Still, African Americans remain, in California as in the rest of the nation, the minority group that is by far the most segregated. African Americans remain highly segregated in all the major urban counties despite a substantial decrease over the past decade: 0.30 in Los Angeles (-20%), 0.27 in San Francisco (-.6%), 0.17 in San Diego (-15.7%) and Fresno (-26.1%), 0.27 in Alameda (-23%), 0.26 in Contra Costa (-26%). In some highly segregated counties, black segregation has increased over the past decade, especially in counties that used to have a large majority of whites and have either undergone a white flight or an increase in their white segregation score: Imperial (+80%), Madera (+60.9%), San Benito (54.6%), Solano (+14.6%), Napa (+10.1%), and Santa Barbara (+9.9%). Some inland counties have also seen their black segregation increase (Amador, Placer, Del Norte, Glenn, Madera), but the black population is too small to be really significant.

A second barrier to further integration is that spatial assimilation is not happening as fast for African Americans as it is for Asians or Latinos. (National Urban League, 2005; Iceland and Wilkes, 2004). Finally, black desegregation in California can be widely attributed to an overall decline in the size of the black population in the state, down to 6.4% of the population, as well as to an increase in the number of Latinos moving into formerly black ghettos. To verify this hypothesis, we have used the H index, comparing black versus Hispanic segregation (non-Hispanic blacks plus Hispanics serving as the reference group, ignoring whites and others) and black versus white segregation overtime (non-Hispanic blacks plus whites serving as the reference group, ignoring Hispanics and others), following Reardon, Yun and McNulty Eitle (2000). The results for blacks versus Hispanics shows H scores of .59 (1970), .45 (1980), .33 (1990), and .26 (2000). For blacks versus whites segregation, the H scores were .67 (1970), .55 (1980), .45 (1990), and .41 (2000). These results suggest that blacks and Latinos are becoming more mixed than blacks and whites. Therefore a greater part of black desegregation can be attributed to blacks living in areas with Latinos than areas with whites.

Hispanic and Asian Segregation

Latino segregation is particularly high in areas that already had a substantial Latino or Asian population and where their numbers have kept growing: 0.32 in Monterey (+6.6%), 0.30 in Santa Cruz (+16.3%), 0.28 in Los Angeles (+3.45%), 0.27 in Ventura (+14.2%), 0.27 in Orange (+11.9%), 0.20 in Marin (+47.5%), San Diego (+20.1%) and Santa Clara (+13.1%), 0.19 in Santa Barbara (+19.7%) and San Mateo (+39.4%), 0.18 in San Francisco (-5.2%), 0.16 in Riverside (+13.26%), 0.14 in San Bernardino (+22.8%) and Contra Costa (+57.9%). In many other northern and inland areas, the Latino population is much smaller but its segregation scores went strongly up as diversity increased in these highly homogeneous counties: Modoc, Mariposa, Humboldt, Colusa, Mendocino, Inyo, Siskiyou, Napa, Nevada, Shasta, Sonoma, Tehama, and Yuba have seen their segregation levels rise by 55 to 260%, with a record increase of 7,400% for Modoc and its 9,500 inhabitants.

As opposed to the Latino population, the Asian population has faced a strong decrease in segregation (-16.5%) over the past decade and is much lower than any other group. Yet there are a few places where segregation has increased, mostly high immigration areas already highly segregated: 0.09 in Imperial (+51.65%) and Orange (+4.2%), 0.1 in San Bernardino (+40%), 0.03 in Sonoma (+17.2%), 0.02 in San Benito (+53.5%). Asian segregation went up inland and in northern counties where homogeneity has recently declined with an influx of migrant farm workers: Amador (+334%), Trinity (+198%), Tehama (+167%), Mono (+150%), Plumas (+130%), Madera (+119%), Tuolumne (15%), and Sutter (+9%). Everywhere else, it seems that Asians have benefited from a good spatial assimilation, integrating more easily into white and wealthy neighborhoods than Latinos or blacks have.

The low levels of Asian segregation and their strong desegregation trends can be interpreted in different ways. High levels of segregation are found mostly in areas containing many recent immigrants, who tend to settle in neighborhoods where they are likely to find a support network and a familiar cultural environment. The Chinatowns, Koreatowns, and Japantowns in many cities draw new immigrants who need specific services the ethnic neighborhoods offer: language assistance, housing search, banks, or food products. They often serve as transition places. The strong solidarity within the Asian community, particularly the large Chinese community in California, and the emphasis on education help immigrant families move up the socio-economic ladder faster and afford housing outside the community neighborhood, in less segregated places. Asian immigrants are generally less poor than Hispanic immigrants, with many families coming with either financial assets or at least a good education background. Finally, Asians have a much higher rate of intermarriage than any other group—except for American Indians—(Zhenchao and Lichter, 2007) and face less discrimination while settling in white suburban or exurban neighborhoods. Their population is only half of the Latino population, which makes assimilation a little less challenging. Even though differences are likely to be found between subgroups, Asians therefore benefit from a good spatial assimilation.

Social and Political Segregation

Both data sets (all population and metropolitan population) show a clear increase in segregation by income, especially among regions or metropolitan areas. The residential segregation of households making incomes in the top 20% has increased by 60%. Yet over half of the high and low income segregation happens at the neighborhood level, suggesting that while regional sorting is on the rise, neighborhood segregation by income greatly prevails.

High income segregation (of those in the top 20% of household incomes) increased along regional lines and was particularly high and on the rise in fast-growing neighborhoods with a substantial minority population: 0.58 in Orange (+9.55) and Ventura (+5.19%), 0.52 in Napa (+8.8%), 0.48 in San Diego (+3.64%), 0.46 in Los Angeles (+1.8%), 0.42 in Riverside (+31.6%), 0.40 in San Bernardino (+6%), and 0.33 in Kern (+2%). It remains high though slightly declining in Contra Costa, Fresno, San Joaquin, and San Francisco counties. The strongest increase in high income segregation was recorded in northern inland counties: Lassen, Mariposa, Mendocino, Merced, Placer, Plumas, Tulare, Tuolumne, Yolo, Shasta, Calaveras, Del Norte, and Colusa. All these counties saw their segregation levels increase by 10 to 210%.

The Bay Area is one the most segregated places in California according to education level. When measuring people with high school degrees or less versus people with a college education or more, the counties with the highest levels of segregation are Fresno (0.12), Marin (0.10), Contra Costa (0.09), Santa Clara (0.09), San Francisco (0.09), and San Mateo (0.08), along with major urban centers and immigration places: Monterey (0.15), Los Angeles (0.14), Orange (0.14), Santa Cruz (0.12), San Diego (0.10), and Santa Barbara (0.09).

Yet the steepest rises in educational segregation were found in less populated inland and northern counties such as Amador, Del Norte, Lassen, Modoc, Placer, Plumas, Sutter, Tehama, and Trinity. Interestingly, high increases were also found in fast-growing counties such as Marin (+70%), Napa, Sonoma, Riverside, San Bernardino, and Orange.

Political Segregation

The segregation of voters went up by 4.7% between 1990 and 2000, with a spectacular increase along the water-inland divide. The share of the state's segregation in party affiliation that could be explained by the water-inland divide was a mere 0.4% in 1990. This share skyrocketed to 6% in 2000. The H index therefore clearly indicates the emergence of a noticeable political east-west divide and confirms the trends observed in this volume's first chapter. This trend can be explained by several factors. First, counties experiencing an increase in the white population have simultaneously experienced an increase in Republican registration. This is particularly true of the interior mountain area and of the north coast. In the most diverse counties of the Bay Area or the Central Valley, the picture is more complex as highly educated liberals moved into exurbs, bringing more political diversity to the counties. The migrants and immigrants moving in these regions seem to be either conservative or, when Democratic, less politically active. In addition, many recent immigrants do not have citizenship or do not vote.

There is certainly a cultural dimension to the phenomenon of the east-west divide, as low-income and less educated populations from inland could have an economic interest in supporting the Democrats, but are at odds with the party on social issues such as gay marriage, minority rights, and abortion. In California as much as anywhere else, Democratic officials tend to be very liberal on these issues. The share of Republican voters in inland areas has increased by seven percentage points between 1980 and 2000, despite the fact that the inland counties are much less populated than the coastal counties. In 2000, 32.7% of Republican voters lived inland compared to 25.6% in 1980. Chapter 8 in this volume explores the political transformation of the Central Valley in greater depth.

Geographic Breakdown

Despite the emergence of the east-west divide, most of the segregation remains due to people sorting themselves along place and county lines. Here again, the highest levels of political segregation were found in the most diverse and racially segregated places: 0.11 in Alameda (+3.9%) and Los Angeles (-10.3%), 0.09 in Contra Costa (-18.7%), 0.08 in Imperial (-2%), 0.07 in Kern (+6.5%) and San Francisco (+0.7%), 0.06 in Monterey (-4.8%), 0.05 in Fresno (-41%), San Mateo (-16.7%) and Sacramento (+1.7%).Yet the level of political segregation has decreased in many of these areas and remains overall much lower than racial or social segregation. It has increased in four counties along the coast in the south: San Louis Obispo (0.02; +54.7%), Santa Barbara (0.05; +32.5%), Orange (0.04; +21.8%) and Ventura (0.05; +11.4%).

The largest increases over the decade occurred in the less segregated inland and northern counties: Del Norte (+96.2%), Modoc (+56.7%), Tuolumne (+54.3%), Glenn (+51.9%), Lassen (50.2%), Placer (+45.4%), Mariposa (44.3%), Butte (+35.8%), Shasta (+35.8%), Sutter (+33.8%), Yuba (+29.6%), Yolo (+29%), Merced (26.7%), Lake (26.2%), El Dorado (+25.5%), Mendocino (25.1%), and Inyo (+24.3%).

There are therefore good reasons to think that Republican voters have substantially different views depending upon where they live, how recently the place was developed, and the level of homogeneity, income, or education of the population. Just as inland Democratic voters are more likely to be socially conservative, Republican voters who choose to remain in highly diverse areas are more likely to be moderate than Republican voters who move inland seeking greater homogeneity. The political homogeneity essentially results from the racial and social sorting of the population and is likely to evolve as diversity increases. But in the meantime, it contributes to the increasing gap between California's electorate and the state's population. Many counties that are becoming increasingly Latino leave most of the voting power to white conservatives, especially in the context of a dual democracy system. This topic is explored further in Chapter 10 of this volume.

The Great Competition for Resources between Political Territories

These new trends have several implications in terms of urban policies. Increasing place segregation challenges the traditional opposition between cities and suburbs since we found high levels of segregation among municipalities even within suburban rings. These territories have conflicting political interests since they differ so widely in their population, geography, public concerns, and politics. The lack of political consensus among—if not the fierce competition between—elected officials representing these municipalities impedes the public debate and decision process on general interest issues like infrastructure, land use, public transit systems, environment, economic development, and social issues. It encourages the defense of specific interests, the political survival of many elected officials depending on their ability to push the agenda of their constituents.

The mayor of Murrieta in Riverside County was recalled in 2005 for bad growth management. The most vocal opponents were angry at the mayor for letting developers build condominiums next to single-family houses. To some extent, the secession movement of San Fernando Valley also expressed a concern for controlling development and resources for a community that underwent substantial demographic changes and worried about not getting their tax dollars back in services (Hogen-Esch, 2001). Although it failed to gather a majority of Los Angeles city voters, the secession measure was approved by San Fernando Valley voters and attested to the lack of financial solidarity between urban territories and the desire of the most affluent communities not to support the cost of a massive immigration of poor residents.

These trends reinforce the fragmentation of the urban space. Exurbs, ghettos, barrios, and gated communities, coexist within a metropolitan area and compete for resources. Conflicts arise between citizens in areas that used to be exclusively rural and whose residents feel invaded by exurbanites. Elected officials and community organizations fight to attract favorable investments (retail, high tech industries, entertainment) and to protect their areas against developments detrimental to their quality of life or housing values, a phenomenon largely described by urbanists as Nimbyism (Not in my backyard). This helps to explain the Smart Growth or Slow Growth movements that aim to control new developments and perhaps prevent the influx of "undesirable" populations, primarily minorities and recent immigrants (Fong, 1994).

This increased competition between territories trying to protect their assets and maximize their resources, is usually won by areas that have the greatest political power. Their power, originated by large populations of voters who have the wealth to generate political contributions, could be efficiently balanced by a legislature that closely reflects the state population. But the direct democracy system has clearly reinforced the political power of the most advantaged territories. Very often, the representatives of the most disadvantaged territories lack the financial resources or political clout to compete with their rivals.

At the regional level, there are clearly strong disparities. Places of high immigration and high diversity do not have great voting power, because many of their inhabitants are not citizens or do not participate in politics at high rates. This is likely to change over time but for the moment, the gap between the active electorate and the population remains great. The east-west divide leads to the concentration on the inland territories of populations that are whiter, older, and wealthier and have higher citizenship rates that combine to guarantee higher voting power. The electorate of these territories often resorts to popular initiative measures to promote their specific interests (see Chapter 1).

Yet the most anti-immigrant measure was most strongly supported in an area that underwent the most radical demographic transformation. Proposition 187, "Save Our State," which would have denied public services to undocumented immigrants, was a classic case of political backlash. Approved by 59% of all Californians, it was strongly supported by Orange County voters in 1994. New "Minutemen" branches are emerging throughout the Bay Area. However, the support for other measures perceived as unfavorable to minorities mostly came from white and Republican regions during the 1990s. The division between whites and minorities was particularly striking over Proposition 209: 37% of whites, 74% of blacks, 76% of Hispanics, and 61% of Asians voted against (Preston, Cain 1998; Douzet, 2000). The division between white and minority voters was equally important over bilingual education (Proposition 227). On the contrary, counties with a greater racial diversity usually support measures in favor of minorities and liberal policies in general.

This shows all the contradictions of a dual democracy system, as we have seen in Chapter 1 of this volume. Representative democracy, through an Assembly and a Senate with legislative power, reflects quite closely the interests of the residents of the state. But its legislative action is subject to multiple constraints. The multiplication of popular initiatives creates a great number of budgetary constraints that directly affects the ability of the state to govern. As the perform-ance of the state gets undermined, the level of distrust for state government among local elected officials keeps rising and the recourse to popular initiative increases. This form of democracy favors the territories with the most voters (rather than residents), and those that have the social and financial resources to raise money, lobby administrations and the legislature, and mobilize voters on initiatives. This helps explain how such a Democratic state has passed many conservative initiatives. It can also explain how Governor Gray Davis was re-called and Governor Arnold Schwarzenegger elected among a jungle of 135 candidates.

Conclusion

California has clearly become a patchwork state, and the question this trend raises is whether governing a patchwork state is different from governing a less segregated state, whatever the diversity level. This patchwork state creates more diversity in Republican views, depending upon whether they are located in highly diverse urban places or remote rural areas. It also encourages competition for resources, particularly when race is correlated with class. The spatial distri-bution of the population and its political affiliations are even more of a chal-lenge in California because of the highly decentralized, fractionalized, and local-ized nature of the power structure and the existence of a the dual democracy system.

California government is often confronted by a vicious circle of distrust and competition for power between territories, impeding its ability to elaborate and finance public policies. Local elected officials are caught between a strong defi-ance toward state government and great electoral pressure to promote the spe-cific interests of their constituency, which often creates an incentive for them in Republican areas to resort to popular initiatives to push their agenda. These in turn create great constraints on the state budget and set legal precedents likely to conflict with state legislation.

The state has limited resources and flexibility to pass and implement effi-cient public policies and to perform state services people associate with a good quality of life: good schools, roads, transportations, and public services. The poor performance of the state government feeds the incentive for Californians to gate themselves in homogeneous enclaves and for their representatives to use direct democracy to protect their own interests. This tends to reinforce the clout of high voting power territories and the unequal spatial distribution of resources, hurting the most disadvantaged areas that are the most in need of state policies and whose interests are better represented by the legislature. It can also poten-tially damage the quality of life for all when levels of traffic congestion, air pollution, or crime rise, ignoring political boundaries Californians have set for themselves.

The challenge for California is working through the contradictions of the dual democracy system, navigating between two electorates both highly diversified and territorialized while absorbing the rapid changes produced by strong mobility and migration trends.

References

Allen, James P., and Eugene Turner. 2001. "Bridging 1990 and 2000 Census Race Data: Fractional Assignment of Multiracial Populations." *Population Research and Policy Review* 20: 513–33.

Baldassare, Mark, Bruce E. Cain, D. E. Apollonio, and Jonathan Cohen. 2004. *The Season of Our Discontent: Voters' Views on California Elections.* PPIC, October.

Berube, Alan, and William Frey. 2002. "A Decade of Mixed Blessings: Urban and Suburban Poverty in Census 2000. The Brookings Institution, Center on Urban and Metropolitan Policy, August.

Cain, Bruce E., Karin Mac Donald, and Iris Hui. 2006. *Competition and Redistricting in California: Lessons for Reform.* Berkeley: Institute of Governmental Studies, University of California, February.

Cain, Brucc E., and Thad Kousscr. 2004. "Adapting to Tcrm Limits: Rcccnt Experiences and New Direction." PPIC, November.

Chandler, William, and Thad Kousser. 2006. "Arnold Schwarzenegger's Leadership Style and Policy Agenda." International Studies Association, San Diego, California, March.

Child Trend Databank Report. 2006. http://www.childtrendsdatabank.org.

Clark, William A. V., and Sarah A. Blue. 2004. "Race, Class, and Segregation Patterns in U.S. Immigrant Gateway Cities." *Urban Affairs Review* 39:6 (July): 667–88.

Douzet, Frédérick. 2006. "Les Évolutions Récentes de la Ségrégation aux Etats-Unis." *L'information Géographique.* January-February, 20–31.

———. 2006. "Ségrégation et Balkanisation Politique de la Californie." *Hérodote,* no. 122, 3d tr.

Fischer, Claude S., Gretchen Stockmayer, Jon Stiles, and Michael Hout. 2004. "Distinguishing the Geographic Levels and Social Dimensions of U.S. Metropolitan Segregation." *Demography* 41:1 (Feb.): 37–59.

Fischer, Mary. 2003. "The Relative Importance of Income and Race in Determining Residential Outcomes in U.S. Urban Areas, 1970–2000." *Urban Affairs Review* 38: 5 (May).

Fong, Timothy P. 1994. *The First Suburban Chinatown.* Temple University Press, Philadelphia.

Frank, Thomas. 2004. What's The Matter With Kansas? How Conservatives Won The Heart of America. New York: Metropolitan Books.

Frey, Wiulliam H., Reynolds Farley. 1996. "Latino, Asian and Black Segregation in U.S. Metropolitan Areas: Are Multiethnic Metros Different ?" *Demography* 33:1 (February).

Hogen-Esch, Tom. 2001. "Urban Secession and the Politics of Growth. The Case of Los Angeles." *Urban Affairs Review* 36: 6 (July): 783–809.

Iceland, John. 2004. "Beyond Black and White. Metropolitan Residential Segregation in Multi-Ethnic America." *Social Science Research* 33: 248–71.

Iceland, John, and Frédérick Douzet. 2006. "Mesurer la ségrégation raciale et eth-
    nique dans les milieux résidentiels." *Hérodote*, no. 122, 3d tr.
Iccland, John, and Rima Wilkes. 2004. "Hypersegregation in the Twenty-First
    Century." *Demography* 41:1 (February): 23–36.
Iceland, John, and Daniel H. Weinberg. 2002. *Racial and Ethnic Residential Seg-
    regation in the U.S.: 1980–2000.* Census 2000 Special Reports, U.S. Census,
    August.
Logan, John R., Brian J. Stults, and Reynolds Farley. 2004. "Segregation of Mi-
    norities in the Metropolis: Two Decades of Change." *Demography* 41:1 (Feb-
    ruary): 1–22.
National Urban League. 2005. *The State of Black America, 2005.* New York: Na-
    tional Urban League.
Massey, Douglas S. and Nancy A. Denton. 1988. "The Dimensions of Racial Seg-
    regation." *Social Forces* 67: 281–315.
Miller, Gary J. 1981. Cities by Contract: The Politics of Municipal Incorporation.
    Cambridge, Mass.: MIT Press.
Perry, Marc J. 2003. *State-to-State Migration Flows, 1995–2000.* Census Special
    Report 2000. U.S. Bureau of the Census, August.
Phu, Mey, Anita Lee, Kathryn Londenberg, Athena Whitmore, and Carey
    O'Sullivan. 2005. "Racial Sorting in California." Working paper, IGS, UC
    Berkeley, May.
Preston, Michael B., Bruce E.Cain, and Sandra Bass (eds.). 1998. *Racial and Eth-
    nic Politics in California*, vol. 2. Berkeley: Institute of Governmental Studies
    Press, University of California.
Reardon, Sean F., and Glenn Firebaugh. 1988. "Measures of Multigroup Segrega-
    tion." *Sociological Methodology* 32:1: 33–67.
Reardon, Sean F., John T. Yun, and Tamela McNulty Eitle. 2002. "Segregation
    and Inequality—The Changing Structure of School Segregation: Measure-
    ment and Evidence of Multiracial Metropolitan-Area School Segregation,
    1989–1995." *Demography* 37:3.
Sandoval, Juan Onésimo, Hans R. Johnson, and Sonya M. Tafoya. 2002. "Who's
    Your Neighbor? Residential Segregation and Diversity in California." *Cali-
    fornia Counts*, PPIC 4:1 (August).
Suro, Robert, and Audrey Singer. 2002. "Latino Growth in Metropolitan America:
    Changing Patterns, New Locations." The Brookings Institution, July.
Zhenchao, Qian, and Daniel T. Lichter. 2007. "Social Boundaries and Marital
    Assimilation: Interpreting Trends in Racial and Ethnic Intermarriage." *Ameri-
    can Sociological Review*, February.

Chapter 3

Shifts in the Religious Divide

Ariane Zambiras

A question repeatedly asked of Americans has received the same answer for the last 30 years. When asked whether they would vote for an atheist, only 45% of Americans say they would. However, more than 88% of Americans say they would vote for a woman, and 94% for an African-American candidate. These results illustrate the extent to which religion structures political trust in America today (*USA Today*/Gallup 2007).[1]

The interaction between religion and politics has received much attention at the national level, and the religious constituencies of the main political parties and candidates are the object of renewed political scrutiny. But how do religious dynamics play out at the state level? How does the spatial distribution of religion impact the political landscape of California? This chapter explores these questions by analyzing how religious trends are helping reshape California politics.

After providing an overview of California's largest religious groups and their changing geographic distribution throughout the state, the chapter presents

---

[1] Gallup Poll 2/09/2007–2/11/2007 shows that 45% of Americans would vote for a candidate who is an atheist. The rate has remained constant since the 07/18/1987–07/18/1987 Gallup Poll.

three brief case studies. The first continues the theme of Chapter 1 by examining the religious dimension of the state's growing east-west divide. The second concentrates on an increasingly important religious group: evangelical Christians. While much media and scholarly attention has focused on Evangelical influence in the Republican party, this section documents the diversity of Evangelicals in California, a diversity that translates into contrasting political preferences along ethnic and geographical lines. The final case study focuses on the state's fast-growing Latino population. Although Latinos are often thought to be uniformly Catholic and Democrat, the section sheds light on important variations among Latinos, including the emergence of a new category: evangelical Latinos. Throughout the chapter, the line of analysis is to assess the role played by geography on the interaction between religion and politics.

Data and Methods

California is "at the cutting edge of the 'new religious pluralism' emerging within the United States" (Roof 2007). Many religious groups are represented in the state (Eastern Orthodox Christians, Mormons, Jews, Muslims, Hindus, Buddhists, Sikhs, etc.) but three groups constitute the largest share (63%) of the population: Roman Catholics (27.7%), evangelical Christians (22.8%), and mainline Protestants (13%). This research focuses primarily on these three groups.

Two main sources of data are used throughout the chapter. Given the absence of questions on religion in the U.S. Census, it is difficult to find reliable data to study religion over long periods of time at the state or county level. However, the Glenmary Research Center's Religious Congregations and Membership Survey (RCMS) makes it possible to present the numerical and geographical distribution of religious groups in California as reported by religious institutions that participated in the survey.[2] For this dataset, denominational groups participating in the survey were recoded into five major categories: Catholics, Evangelicals, mainline Protestants, Jews, and Muslims.[3]

---

[2] For Jews, data is available beginning in 1990, and for Muslims beginning in 2000.

[3] The ARDA list of denominations was used to classify denominational groups into larger categories (see, e.g., http://www.thearda.com/mapsReports/reports/catholic.asp.) Additional sources included Mead, Frank Spencer, and Samuel S. Hill, 1995. *Handbook of Denominations in the United States*. Nashville, Tenn.: Abingdon Press; Melton, J. Gordon. 1998. *Encyclopedia of American Religions*. Detroit, Mich.: Gale Research; Brian Steensland, Jerry Park, Mark Regnerus, Lynn Robinson, Bradford Wilcox, and Robert Woodberry (2000), "The Measure of American Religion: Toward Improving the State of the Art," Social Forces 79:291–318.

The RCMS project has been repeated every 10 years since 1971 and is the only source of county-level data submitted by religious groups.[4] RCMS is the source for the data presented in the first section of this chapter.

The data used in the rest of the chapter come from the Public Policy Institute of California Statewide Surveys. Three datasets were merged (July 2005, N = 2502; August 2005, N = 2004; December 2005, N = 2504). They are the most recent databases containing questions on religion at the county level in California (the most recent RCMS study was conducted in 2000). For clarity, results are presented aggregated at the regional level and the classification used for regions is in keeping with that presented in Chapter 1.[5] The original datasets were recoded because the question "Would you describe yourself as a 'born again' or evangelical Christian, or not?" was asked separately from the question "What is your religious preference?" In this analysis, the category "evangelical Christian" was isolated from other religious groups so that it could be studied independently. This category cuts across denominational lines—22% of this group is Catholic; others belong to a range of Protestant traditions.

The defining characteristics of Evangelicalism are the belief in the authority of the Bible, activism based on this belief, and reverence of the figure of Christ as a personal Savior. In the media, "evangelical Christian" has often been used as a synonym for "conservative Christian." One should be careful about this association since for many Christians being "evangelical" is to put the emphasis on the sharing of one's beliefs, regardless of the ideological content of those beliefs. Of course, with survey data, there is no way of checking what people think about when they declare themselves "Evangelical." It should be kept in mind that 19% of evangelical Christians consider themselves to be "somewhat or very liberal" (PPIC survey 2005).

---

[4] The data were downloaded from the Association of Religion Data Archives, www.TheARDA.com, and were collected by the Association of Statisticians of American Religious Bodies. For the detailed methodology of data collection, please refer to http://www.glenmary.org/grc/default.htm. For a detailed description of the limitations of the 2000 dataset, see Roger Finke and Christopher Scheitle (2005), "Accounting for the Uncounted: Computing Correctives for the 2000 RCMS Data," *Review of Religious Research* 47:1.

This research used the corrected dataset for 2000, available at http://www.religion atlas.org/.

[5] Regional definitions: the Bay Area (Alameda, Contra Costa, Marin, Napa, San Francisco, San Mateo, Santa Clara, Solano, Sonoma); the Central Coast (Monterey, San Luis Obispo, Santa Barbara, Santa Cruz, Ventura, San Benito); the Central Valley (Butte, Fresno, Kern, Kings, Merced, Sacramento, San Joaquin, Stanislaus, Sutter, Tulare, Yolo, Yuba); the mountain region (Alpine, Amador, Calaveras, Colusa, El Dorado, Glenn, Inyo, Lake, Lassen, Madera, Mariposa, Modoc, Mono, Nevada, Placer, Plumas, Shasta, Sierra, Siskiyou, Tehama, Trinity, Tuolumne); the Inland Empire (Imperial, Riverside, San Bernardino); Los Angeles (L.A. County); the North Coast (Del Norte, Humboldt, Mendocino), and the South Coast (Orange, San Diego).

In the three case studies of this chapter, the category "Catholic" is thus limited to Roman Catholics who do not identify as Evangelicals, and "mainline Protestant" is defined as Protestant Christians who do not identify as Evangelicals. Statistics for the category "no religion" are presented, and this category is defined as people identifying themselves as "not a believer, not religious, atheist, or agnostic."

It must be noted that data on religion collected using surveys generally differs from data reported by religious organizations. It is usually observed that more people declare themselves religious than are counted by religious institutions. The difference between self-identification and numbers reported by institutions is particularly high in California, a sign of Californians' weak institutional loyalty when it comes to religion (Roof and Silk, 2005), and of the fluidity of their religious identity.

The Geography of Religious Groups in California

Distribution of Religious Affiliations in California
(as Reported by Religious Institutions), 1971–2000

This section traces the geographical distribution of the five most numerous religious groups in California (Roman Catholics, mainline Protestants, evangelical Christians, Jews, and Muslims) from 1971 to 2000. Statistics reported by religious institutions participating in the RCMS study show three main trends. The first is the rapid increase of the state's Catholic population, from 20% in 1971 to almost 30% in 2000, and their concentration in the southern regions of the state. Second, mainline Protestants have suffered the greatest losses, both in absolute value and in their relative share of the state population, which has been divided by two over the past 30 years. Finally, during this period Evangelicals have increased their share of total population by almost tripling their constituency to about 2.6 million. See Figure 3.1.

Catholics
The first striking observation is the increase of the Catholic share of the total population of California, from 20% in 1971 to nearly 30% in 2000.[6] This represented a net gain of 6.3 million people in 30 years. In terms of ethnic distribution, by 2000 Latinos made up the greatest share (57%) of the Catholic

---

[6] In comparison, Catholics represent 22% of the total population in the country as a whole.

Figure 3.1. Catholic, Evangelical, and Mainline Protestant Share of California Population, 1971–2000

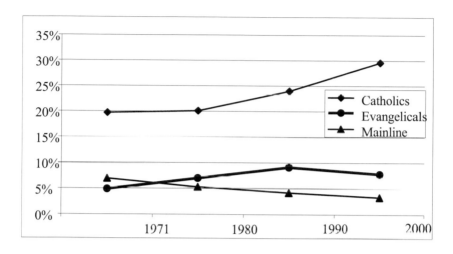

California	1971	1980	1990	2000
Catholics	19.7%	20.1%	24.0%	29.6%
Evangelicals	4.9%	7.0%	9.1%	7.8%
Mainline	6.9%	5.3%	4.2%	3.3%

Source: Religious Congregations and Membership Surveys (1971–2000).

population. Their higher birthrate—3.3 children per woman (Reyes, 2001: 17) —contributed to this increase.

The spatial distribution of Catholics in 1971 reflected the historically strong diocese of San Francisco. At that time, 22% of the Bay Area's population was Roman Catholic, making it the state's most Catholic region. But by 1980, the proportion of Catholics in L.A. County had increased to 25%, surpassing the Bay Area. In 1990 and 2000, the Catholic share in coastal regions was reinforced and reached a maximum of 40% in L.A. See Figure 3.2. This trend paralleled the strongly positive Hispanic migration during the 1970s and 1980s in those regions, and the high birth rate of Latinos. Hispanics accounted for almost half (48%) of all births in California in 1996 compared to only 20% in 1970 (Reyes, 2001: 27–28). This strong Hispanic presence has helped modify the rites of Catholicism in the state, especially after Vatican II, in order to accommodate the multicultural profile of parishioners.

Data on the north/south and coastal/inland divides indicate that most of the Catholic presence in California is located and reinforcing in the south and

Ariane Zambiras

Figure 3.2. Catholic Share of California's Population 1971–2000, by Region

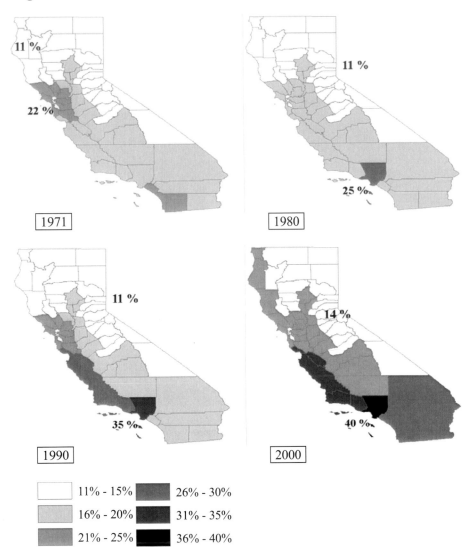

Source: RCMS 1971–2000 Maps © A. Zambiras.

western parts of the state, with a widening divide between north and south. Overall, California now ranks 12th in the country in terms of Catholic presence.

Mainline Protestants

Mainline Protestants have been declining in California, and their share in the total state population is half its 1971 level (7% versus 3.5% in 2000). The reduction in mainline adherents mirrors a national trend (Stump, 1984: 289) and is likely to continue given the group's advancing age, which is now the highest of all religious groups (56 years old). This decline is occurring at a similar pace in all parts of California, and the mainline Protestant share of the state's population now ranks third-to-last in the country. See Figure 3.3.

Evangelical Christians

By contrast, the proportion of Evangelicals in the state has been increasing, from 5% to 7% of the total population. Evangelicals have replaced mainline Protestants as the second largest religious group in California. This may seem odd in a state widely perceived as a bastion for secular culture and liberalism.[7] However, many of the prominent figures and institutions of Evangelicalism today have been based in California, and in particular in southern California: three of the most prominent New Evangelical Movements originated in southern California (the Vineyard Christian Fellowship, Calvary Chapel, and Hope Chapel); Charles E. Fuller of Los Angeles founded the Fuller Theological Seminary, an institution that helped promote "reform fundamentalism," in 1947 in Pasadena; the Institute of Creation Research (ICR) was founded in San Diego in 1972; Tim LaHaye (bestseller author of the *Left Behind* series) spent the first two decades of his activism in southern California; Beverly LaHaye founded Concerned Women for America in 1978 and organized its first meeting that year in San Diego; and James Dobson created Focus on the Family in southern California after working in the children's hospital in Los Angeles.[8] See Figure 3.4.

The geographical distribution of Evangelicals in the last 30 years shows the clear emergence of the Central Valley (extending from Redding to Bakersfield) as a key region. Evangelicals comprise 10.5% of the Central Valley population, twice as high as their share of the Bay Area population (5.2%). See Figure 3.5.

In the last 40 years, Evangelicals have started to relocate in the southeastern regions of the state. Absolute numbers show a net loss in the total num-

---

[7] California was the first state in the country to permanently overthrow Sabbath laws in 1883, one of the first historical decisions that helped establish the state's liberal reputation.

[8] For more on the historical growth of evangelicalism in California, and in particular in southern California, see Douglas Firth Anderson (2005), "Toward an Established Mysticism: Judeo-Christian Traditions in Post-World War II California and Nevada," in *Religion and Public Life in the Pacific Region: Fluid Identities*, edited by Wade Clark Roof and Mark Silk: AltaMira Press.

Figure 3.3. Mainline Protestant Share of California's Population 1971-2000, by Region

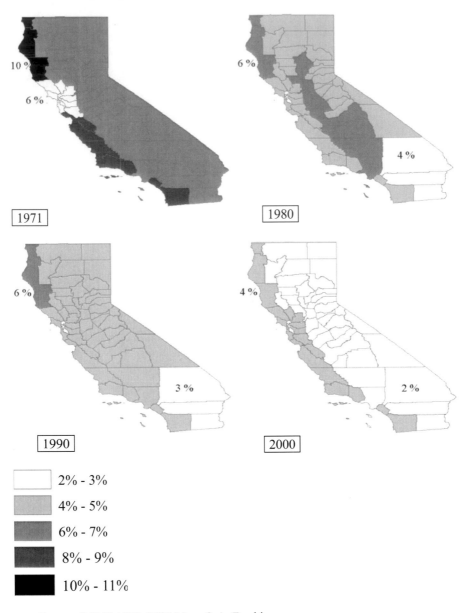

Source: RCMS 1971–2000 Maps © A. Zambiras.

Figure 3.4. Evangelical Share of California's Population 1971–2000, by Region

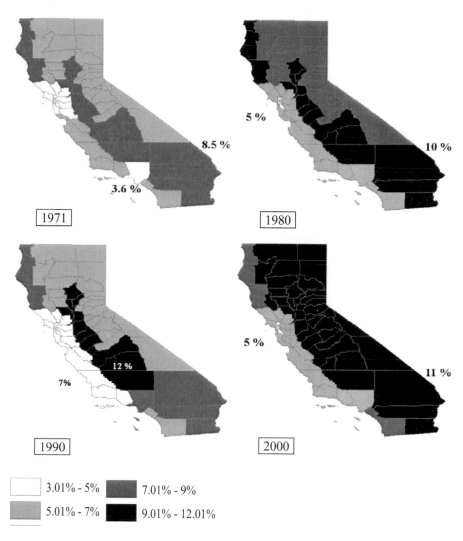

3.01% - 5%

5.01% - 7%

7.01% - 9%

9.01% - 12.01%

Source: RCMS 1971-2000 Maps © A. Zambiras.

Fig 3.5. Inland/Coastal Distribution of Evangelicals in California, 1971–2000

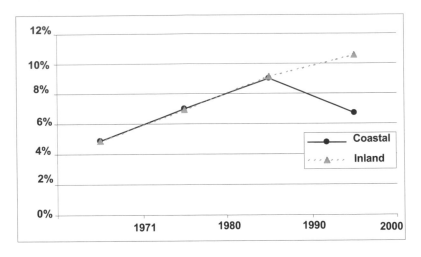

Evangelicals	1971	1980	1990	2000
Coastal	4.9%	7.0%	9.0%	6.7%
Inland	4.9%	7.0%	9.1%	10.5%

Source of the data: Religious Congregations and Membership Survey.

ber of Evangelicals in the Los Angeles region, the Bay Area, and the north Coast between 1990 and 2000, and a net increase in the Central Valley in spite of the small decrease in their share of the total population in that region (from 12% to 11%). California ranks 39th in the country for Evangelical presence, ahead of most northeastern states. Again, regional differences are important here. If the Central Valley region were a state in itself, it would rank 8th in the country, with 27.8% of Evangelicals in its total population.

Jews

The RCMS estimates for 1990 and 2000 indicate a roughly constant Jewish presence in California (around 3% of the state population). In 2000, 57% of the Jewish population in California was located in Los Angeles County, which is twice as much as the county's percentage of the total state population.

Muslims

The 2000 RCMS edition was the first to collect data on adherents of Islam; it showed that Muslims represented less than 1% (0.77%) of the state's population. Most Muslims in California live in Los Angeles County and surrounding areas (36% of the total Muslim population lives in L.A. County, 15% in Orange County). Muslim presence is also strong in and around the Bay Area (9% in Alameda and in San Francisco, 7% in Santa Clara).

The Geography of Religion in California (Self-Reported Results), 2005

The previous section presented the geographical distribution of religious groups in California based on data collected by religious institutions. In order to complement those numbers and present a more up-to-date profile of religion in California, this section uses survey data. See Table 3.1.

The first noticeable difference between the survey data presented here and the data collected by religious institutions is that a higher proportion of Californians claim to be Evangelicals (23% in the surveys) than are reported by institutions (7.2%). Similarly, a higher percentage of Californians identify themselves as mainline Protestants (13%) than are reported by religious institutions (3.5%).

Only Catholics do not follow this rule: there are more Catholics counted by parishes than people who claim to be Catholic. Thus, in spite of their numeric preponderance, Catholics are not as prominent a public religious presence as their numbers might suggest, because of the large number of "nominal Catholics" or "low-commitment Catholics" (Roof and Silk, 2005: 42). Only 37% of Catholics attend church weekly, compared to 62% of Evangelicals and 25% of mainline Protestants.

The proportion of Californians who say they have no religion (17%) stands in sharp contrast with the proportion of atheists in the country as a whole, since fewer than one-in-ten Americans (9%) say they have no religion (Pew Research Center, 2003). Regional differences are strong since 32% of California's atheists live in the Bay Area. See Table 3.2.

The Politics of Religious Groups in California

This section analyzes briefly the political behavior of religious groups in California. Results are broken down by ethnicity and region to understand how religion and geography impact partisanship among ethnic groups. See Figure 3.6.

Catholics and Party Registration

Catholics in California lean Democratic more than the other largest religious groups, with 42% of registered Catholics aligning Democrat. Indeed, Catholics predominately identify with the Democratic Party in all regions of the state except the south coast (Orange and San Diego counties).

Ariane Zambiras

Table 3.1. Religious Presence in California Regions, 2005

	Roman Catholics	Mainline Protestants	Evangelical Christians	Jews	Muslims	No religion
Bay Area	24.3%	14.5%	13.9%	2.1%	.4%	26.5%
CV	28.0%	13.1%	27.8%	1.2%	.2%	12.2%
Mountain	12.8%	15.9%	31.7%	1.0%		21.7%
Central Coast	29.1%	10.3%	19.1%	2.1%	.3%	20.6%
Inland Empire	27.8%	11.7%	32.3%	1.3%		10.3%
Los Angeles	31.4%	11.9%	22.2%	3.9%	.2%	14.8%
North Coast	15.7%	14.6%	18.0%			29.2%
South Coast	29.5%	13.7%	23.7%	2.5%	.5%	13.4%
California	27.7%	13.0%	22.8%	2.4%	.2%	16.9%

Source: PPIC Statewide Surveys, 2005.

Table 3.2. Religious Presence in California Regions, 2005

	Roman Catholics	Mainline Protestants	Evangelical Christians	Jews	Muslims	No religion
Bay Area	24.3%	14.5%	13.9%	2.1%	.4%	26.5%
CV	28.0%	13.1%	27.8%	1.2%	.2%	12.2%
Mountain	12.8%	15.9%	31.7%	1.0%		21.7%
Central Coast	29.1%	10.3%	19.1%	2.1%	.3%	20.6%
Inland Empire	27.8%	11.7%	32.3%	1.3%		10.3%
Los Angeles	31.4%	11.9%	22.2%	3.9%	.2%	14.8%
North Coast	15.7%	14.6%	18.0%			29.2%
South Coast	29.5%	13.7%	23.7%	2.5%	.5%	13.4%
California	27.7%	13.0%	22.8%	2.4%	.2%	16.9%

Source: PPIC Statewide Surveys, 2005.

Figure 3.6. The Political Preferences of Religious Groups in California

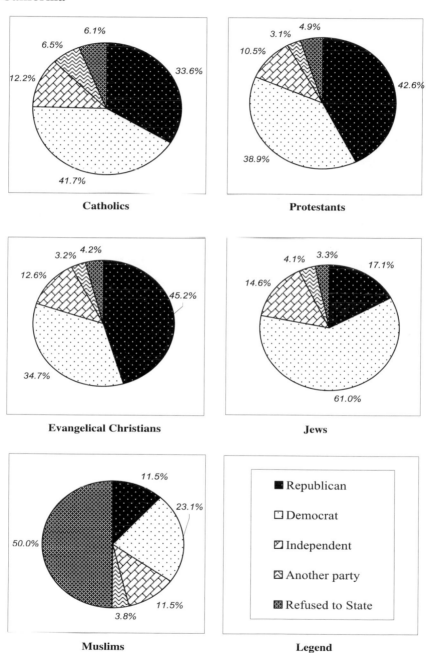

Catholics

Protestants

Evangelical Christians

Jews

Muslims

Legend

- ■ Republican
- ☐ Democrat
- ▨ Independent
- ▧ Another party
- ▦ Refused to State

Source: PPCI Statewide Surveys, 2005.

Catholics form one of the most ethnically diverse religious groups in the state. The Caucasian/Hispanic ratio varies greatly from region to region: for example, in Los Angeles County, 70% of Catholics are Latino and 21% are Caucasian, but the ratio is reversed in the mountain region (counties in the northeastern half of the state) where 68% of Catholics are Caucasian, and 30% are Latino. Overall in California, 57% of Catholics are Latino, 33% Caucasian.

Mainline Protestants and Party Registration

California's mainline Protestants have on balance supported the Republican Party, with 43% of those registered aligning with the GOP. The percentage reaches 64% in the mountain, region and 54% in the Inland Empire (San Bernardino and Riverside counties).

As seen in the previous section, the demographic strength of mainline Protestants is declining, which might push the Republican Party to work harder to mobilize Evangelicals as the latter are growing numerically.
Mainline Protestants are by far the more ethnically homogeneous of the three largest religious groups in California (80% of mainline Protestants are Caucasian). This homogeneity is reinforced by the ethnic segmentation of congregations, which often organize services in different languages at specific hours or cater to specific ethnicities such as Korean or Chinese congregations. The recent trend, however, is to promote ethnic diversity in mainline congregations by exploring styles of worship that appeal to a more diverse audience. For Caucasians, being mainline Protestant reinforces ties with the Republican Party (47% of Caucasian Protestants are Republican against an average of 40% for all religions).

Evangelical Christians and Party Registration

While a large share (45%) of California's evangelical Christians are registered Republican, the group has important internal political divisions. For example, 64% of Evangelicals in the mountain region are registered Republican, compared to only 35% in the Bay Area. Race also divides Evangelicals politically. For Caucasians, being Evangelical reinforces Republican Party affiliation, while for African Americans, being Evangelical reinforces Democratic affiliation. Fifty-eight percent of Caucasian Evangelicals in California are registered Republican (compared with 29% of all Caucasians). By contrast, 68% of African-American Evangelicals are registered Democrat (compared to 64% for all African Americans).

Jews and Party Registration

Of all religious groups, Jews have the highest rate of support (61%) for the Democratic Party. Jews have long been noted for holding liberal attitudes at variance with their increasing economic status (Sonenshein, 1991). In spite of their relatively small demographic presence in California (less than 3% of the state's total population in 2000), Jews have long interested scholars because of their high rate of political participation and their impact in the large metropolitan areas where they tend to live (Sonenshein and Valentino, 2000).

Muslims and Party Registration

Muslims are overrepresented in California compared with the rest of the country, with 16.7% of the United States Muslim population living in the state. Muslims are one of the most ethnically diverse religious groups; in California, 35% identify as Asian, 23% identify as Caucasian, 18% as African American, and 12% as Hispanic. The Muslim presence in California grew after the 1965 liberalization of immigration policy, a time when Muslims also forged an anti-establishment image (Machacek, 2005). In California, the proportion of Muslim support for the Democratic Party is twice as high as support for the Republican Party (23% and 11.5% respectively).

Which Divide is Significant?

As Chapter 1 indicates, California's political fault-line is shifting from a north/south to an inland/coastal divide. How does the state divide along religious lines? The compilation of survey data collected by the Public Policy Institute of California (PPIC) (2005) shows that the most significant split is the inland/coastal divide for Evangelicals, with 10 points more Evangelicals living in the eastern regions of California (Evangelicals represent 30% of the population in the East, and 20% in the West). The second most significant divide is the north/south divide for Catholics, with a 5.4 point difference (Catholics represent 30% of the population in the South, and 25% in the North), because of the high proportion of Catholic Latinos in southern regions (in L.A., 70% of Catholics are Hispanic).

Religious attendance is an often-used and yet imperfect indicator of how religion influences politics. Research has shown that politics in church is less a top-down process (from the clergy to the members) than a more organic movement (Zambiras, 2007). Church attendance also varies greatly according to the particular requirements of different religions: for instance, 76% of Catholics believe that church attendance is not required to be "a good Catholic" (D'Antonio et al., 2001; in Tamney, 2007).

With those limitations in mind, the map of weekly church attendees reinforces the idea of a split between a more religious Inland California and a more secular coast. See Figure 3.7.

In spite of the numeric strength of coastal California—coastal voters represent 71% of all voters and contribute to the overall reputation of California as a liberal state—pockets of conservatism are emerging inland. The Central Valley in particular has one of the highest growth rates in California (Johnson and Hayes, 2004). From 5 million in 2000, the population in the region is predicted to more than double by 2040 and reach 10.7 million.[9] This growth is likely to give the region more political clout and shift statewide politics in a more conservative direction, in particular with the increasing Evangelical presence in the region.

Evangelical Christians

At the national level, much attention has been devoted to one religious category: evangelical Christians. Evangelicals are the second-largest religious group in California, with 23% of the state's population, after Catholics (28%). This section presents a sociological profile of Evangelicals in California to add to the current understanding of their political behavior.

Evangelicals: A Sociological Profile

The ethic composition of the evangelical group is fairly similar to California's overall population: 48% are Caucasian, 31% are Latino, and 5% are Asian. The only noticeable difference is the proportion of African Americans, since 11.6% of Evangelicals are African Americans, which is almost twice as high as the proportion of African Americans in the state as a whole.

Evangelical Christianity is the preferred religion of the state's African Americans: 46% of African Americans identify with an evangelical Christian faith, which is well above the state average of 23% of all people in California declaring to be Evangelicals.

Compared to a statistically average Californian, an Evangelical is roughly the same age (45 years old), a little less likely to be a homeowner (56% of Evangelicals own their current residence, two points less than the average in California), and less likely to have some college education (49% against 54%). Evangelicals are a little more likely to be unemployed (32% compared to an average

---

[9] Projections from the State Department of Finance, July 2007.

Figure 3.7. Regional Patterns of Church Attendance (Percentage of "Weekly" or "Almost Weekly" Church Attendees in Region's Population)

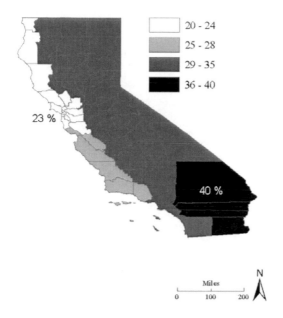

Source: PPIC Statewide survey, 2005. Map © A. Zambiras.

of 30%); a little more likely to be married (33% against an average of 30%), and more likely to be a woman (54% of Evangelicals are women). A sharp difference between Evangelicals and the rest of Californians is their assiduity in church, since 62% of Evangelicals attend church weekly or almost weekly, when only 32% of Californians do.

Where are Evangelicals in California?

Evangelicals are unequally distributed in California's regions. The three regions where they represent the highest share of the total population are the Inland Empire (32%), the mountain region (32%), and the Central Valley (28%)—all well above the state average of 23%. Those regions are among the fastest-growing in California—with, for instance, a 26% growth in the Inland Empire from 1990 to 2000 (Johnson, 2002). The lowest proportion of Evangelicals is found in the Bay Area, which at 14% is nine points below the state average. These numbers confirm what we have seen at the beginning of this chapter in Figure 3.2, Evangelicals have been relocating from the coastal regions to inland ones since the 1990s.

Evangelicals: A Political Profile

Ideology is a variable that clearly separates Evangelicals from other religious groups. Notably, Evangelicals have by far the highest rate of people declaring to be "very conservative"—at 20%, twice the state's average, and the lowest rate of "very liberal"—5.5%.

In the 2005 surveys, evangelical Christians strongly supported Arnold Schwarzenegger. At that point, Evangelicals formed 26% of the governor's support base, exceeding all other religious groups. In addition, Evangelicals identified with the Republican Party at high rates. Forty-five percent of Evangelicals in California were registered Republican, exceeding the state's overall 34% Republican registration rate. However, a substantial share (35%) of Evangelicals were registered Democrats, not far below the state's overall 38% Democratic registration rate. Thus, although Evangelicals as a whole were more likely to be Republican (and conservative) than the statewide electorate, the group had significant internal differences in political views and voting behavior (Yamane, 1999: 547).

To clarify the interaction between Evangelicals and party identification, the following table breaks down party registration numbers by region. See Table 3.3.

These results testify to the great regional variation in evangelical party registration. In the Bay Area and Los Angeles, the proportion of Evangelicals registered as Democrats is higher than the proportion of Evangelicals registered as Republicans. Outside those singular geographical contexts, however, Evangelicals more frequently register Republican. The relationship between evangelicalism and Republican registration is the highest in the mountain region (64.5% of Evangelicals in the mountain region are Republicans, compared to 54% in the south coast and 51% in the Inland Empire. If we look at Caucasian Evangelicals specifically, the rate of Republican registration increases even more: 58% of Caucasian Evangelical Christians are registered Republicans, compared to only 22% registered as Democrats. This is the highest rate of support for the Republican Party of all Caucasian religious groups. We can see that the Republican Party has an incentive to mobilize this constituency, and increase its turnout rate (64% of Caucasian Evangelicals say they always vote, which is less than Caucasian mainline Protestants or Catholics). The rate of Republican registration is comparatively lower for non-Caucasian Evangelicals: 39% of Asian-American Evangelicals, 35% of Latino Evangelicals, and only 19% of African-American Evangelicals are registered Republican.

It is essential to consider emerging conservative pockets in California. If in statewide elections, it might be more difficult to push a conservative agenda

Table 3.3. Party Registration of Evangelicals in California Regions, 2005

	Party Registration of Evangelicals			
	Democrat	**Republican**	**Another Party**	**Independent**
Bay Area	40.6%	34.8%	4.3%	14.5%
CV	32.0%	44.8%	2.3%	16.9%
Mountain	22.6%	64.5%	1.6%	9.7%
Central Coast	36.4%	47.7%		13.6%
Inland Empire	27.0%	51.1%	7.1%	13.5%
Los Angeles	46.7%	35.4%	1.7%	10.8%
North Coast	25.0%	50.0%		
South Coast	26.6%	54.3%	3.8%	10.3%
California	34.5%	45.2%	3.2%	12.6%

Source: PPIC Statewide survey, 2005.

given the overall moderate atmosphere of the statewide constituency, the "protection" offered by district elections can allow for the expression of more radical ideas at the district level. Indeed, the legislative constituency reflects redistricting efforts to follow ethnic and neighborhood lines, and thus enables minority views to be represented in the legislature. This divide between a moderate statewide electorate that elects (among others) the governor and decides on initiatives, and a more diverse legislative electorate, directly feeds the concerns about the effectiveness of California's institutions (Cain, 1997).

Evangelicals are the primary religious constituency for Republicans. Twenty-nine percent of California Republicans are Evangelical (compared with 24.5% Catholic and 18% mainline Protestant). The proportion stays about the same when only Caucasian Evangelicals are considered (29.5% of Caucasian Republicans in California are Evangelicals).

As a whole, Evangelicals' turnout rate (49% say they always vote) is slightly lower than the state's average (52%), and much lower than mainline Protestants' turnout (68%). This has to be balanced against the declining demographic strength of mainline Protestants discussed above.

Soper and Fetzer (2000) argue that because conservative Christians are the most loyal constituency within the GOP in California, and because they would have no voice without the Republican Party, the two are "necessarily yoked." This is however an imperfect association for both parties concerned. Because of the overall moderate leaning of the state, the politically active Christian Right groups have had very little policy influence in California politics. This lack of influence is also a consequence of the highly candidate-centered elections in California that prevent the Christian Right from setting the political agenda.

Conservative Christian groups find themselves more in a position of consolidating candidates and responding to issues rather than imposing either.

In spite of this strong support, the Republican Party in California has to be cautious about associating too closely with Evangelicals for fear of being portrayed as social-issue conservatives and alienating more moderate Republicans.[10] Support from the Christian Right can be helpful to win a nomination in Republican primary elections, but it becomes a potential liability in the general election.

The relationship between the Republican Party and the Christian Right in California has been described as one of "consolidation" (Green, Rozell, and Wilcox, 2000) where conservative Christians can provide support to the GOP around issues that are moderately socially conservative, such as opposition to late-term abortion or homosexual adoption of children. The question that arises is whether mobilization around "soft" political issues will generate enough interest among conservative Christians to boost their turnout rate (Soper and Fetzer, 2000: 109).

Latinos

The religious diversity of Latinos has only been recently emphasized, and Latinos are too often perceived as a monolithic (Catholic) group. As their share of the state's registered voters is increasing—from 10% in 1990 to 19% in 2005 (DiCamillo, 2006)—the need arises to analyze their voting behavior and how religion impacts it.

Latinos and Religious Affiliation

As expected, the majority of the Latino population in California is Catholic (55%). However, one-fourth of Latinos are Evangelical, which is three points higher than the state average.

The proportion of evangelical Latinos in the total Latino population varies greatly in California regions. In the mountain region, the proportion of evangelical Latinos is higher than the proportion of Catholic Latinos. At the other end of

---

[10] For example, in the 1998 U.S. Senate Election, Republican candidate Matt Fong paid a high political price for a $50,000 contribution he made to the Traditional Values Coalition. If the support from this Christian Right group was helpful to the Republican candidate during the primaries, it became a heavy political weight to carry during the general election. Fong eventually lost to his Democratic opponent Barbara Boxer. See J. Christopher Soper, and Joel Fetzer (2000), "The Christian Right and the Republican Party in California: Necessarily Yoked." in *Prayers in the Precincts: The Christian Right in the 1998 Elections*, ed. Luther A. Green, Kenneth N. Rozell, and Kevin D. Wilcox, Washington, D.C.: Georgetown University Press, 93–111.

the spectrum, the Latino population is predominantly Catholic in the Central Coast and in the L.A. region.

Another variable important when considering Latinos is the length of time spent in the U.S. For those who have lived all their life in the U.S., there is a declining attachment to Catholicism. Sixty percent of Latinos born abroad and currently living in California are Catholic, but only 48% of those born in the United States maintain their attachment to the Catholic faith.[11] This could be related to the role played by the Catholic Church as a social resource for newcomers. Recent immigrants can find community support through the church (with housing, job-searching, social integration), but this need is likely to decrease as integration is successful.

Latinos and Party Identification

Latinos of all religious traditions support the Democratic Party more than they do the Republican Party (44% of Latinos in California are registered Democrats, 26% are registered Republicans). See Tabe 3.4. This preference has many causes, but it can be traced in part to Latino backlash against Republican support for Proposition 187 in 1994 (Soper and Fetzer, 2000: 98). This controversial measure, which was championed by Republican Governor Pete Wilson, sought to deny public services to immigrants entered illegally in the state. Although the initiative's restrictions applied only to illegal immigrants, many saw it as anti-Latino, not just anti-illegal immigrant. After voters adopted the measure, it was largely invalidated by the federal courts—but memories of the divisive campaign lingered and led many Latinos to mobilize and register as Democrats.

Evangelical Latinos have the smallest rate of "Independent" or "other party" registration. They also have the highest proportion of Democratic registration (47% of evangelical Latinos are registered Democrats), followed by Catholics (45% registered Democrats). The highest level of Republican registration is also found among evangelical Latinos (35%). Overall, those numbers confirm the general expectation of Latinos' support for the Democratic Party, but this support never exceeds 50% in California. Evangelical Latinos are one of the most polarized subgroups with high level of support for both major parties.

Once again, we observe significant differences for Latinos born in the United States and those born abroad. For Latinos born in the U.S., being Catholic reinforces support for the Democratic Party, but being mainline or Evangelical significantly increases the support for the Republican Party. For foreign-born

---

[11] This move away from Catholicism is not particular to Californian Latinos. See Kelly and Kelly (2005) for a national analysis of Latinos based on NES data.

Table 3.4. Party Registration of California Latinos According to Religious Tradition, 2005

	Party Registration			
	Democrat	**Republican**	**Independent**	**Other**
Catholic	45%	26%	12%	8%
Evangelical Christian	47%	35%	10%	3%
Protestant	38%	34%	14%	3%
No Religion	45%	9%	22%	13%
All Latinos	45%	26%	13%	7%

Source: PPIC Statewide Surveys, 2005.

Latinos, however, being Evangelical reinforces support for the Democratic Party.

The duration of residence in the United States influences the relationship between religious tradition and partisanship: the connection between Catholicism and the Democratic Party is much stronger for Latinos who have spent longer in the U.S. The effect is reversed for evangelical Latinos: the longer they have lived in the United States, the more they lean Republican. However, we must keep in mind that with time, attachment to the Catholic faith decreases among Latinos. Two trends are thus identifiable: a growth in Latino immigration is likely to favor Democratic registration rates, but a growth in the birth rate of Latinos who are already living in California is likely to favor allegiance to the Republican Party.

However, the political behavior of Latinos is often more complex than a direct allegiance to one party. Latino voters tend to lean left on economic issues, and support the conservative side on moral issues, following the recommendations of the Catholic Church. As their voting base expands, the Latino vote could add support to conservative initiatives (Baldassare, 2000).

When asked in 2005 PPIC statewide surveys to identify the most important issues facing people in California today, Latinos replied "crime, gangs, drugs" in the first position, "unemployment" second, and finally "the economy." The results varied, however, according to religious preference. Evangelical Latinos showed a heightened concern for "crime" (number one issue), "immigration," "moral and family values," and "race relations." For Catholic Latinos, concern for "the economy" and "health care" were higher than for Latinos in general. These results indicate that the priorities of Latino voters are impacted by their religious belief. This is notably the case for "crime" (number one concern for evangelical Latinos) and "the economy" (number one concern for Catholics). See Table 3.5.

Table 3.5. The Most Important Issue Facing People in California Today According to Latinos, 2005

	Catholic	Evangelical	Total
Abortion	.8%		.5%
Crime, gangs, drugs	12.4%	18.6%	14.3%
Economy	12.9%	9.3%	11.2%
Education, schools, teachers	9.3%	6.2%	9.0%
Gasoline prices	4.1%	3.1%	3.5%
Health care, health insurance	4.7%	1.2%	3.5%
Housing costs, housing	2.6%	2.5%	3.0%
Immigration	3.4%	6.2%	4.3%
Illegal immigration	1.3%	3.1%	2.0%
Jobs, unemployment	13.4%	15.5%	14.0%
Moral and family values		2.5%	.7%
Poverty, the poor	.8%	2.5%	1.3%
Race relations, racial and	3.6%	5.0%	3.6%
Terrorism, security issues	.8%	1.2%	1.2%

Source: PPIC Statewide Surveys, 2005.

Conclusion

The religious landscape of California has undergone tremendous changes in the past four decades, and those changes are crucial to understanding the make-up of California today. Focusing on intrastate dynamics is a great way to refine the analysis of the interaction between religion and politics and takes into account not only how religion as a broad indicator might influence political dynamics, but rather how religion as it develops in a particular geographical context influences politics.

One of the first findings of this chapter is that geographical mobility in California does not bring homogenization. In spite of the great mobility of Californians within their state, and of the high attractiveness of the state to national and international migrants, the contrast between distinct religious and ideological areas is reinforced rather than leveled off.

Catholics, the most numerous religious group in the state, are increasing their presence in the southern regions of the state. This change is crucial for the political equilibrium of southern California since Catholics tend to cross party lines to support the Democratic Party on social issues, and the Republican Party on so-called "moral" issues. Even if in the state as a whole Catholics primarily support the Democratic Party, Catholics in the south coast are an exception and register Republican at a higher rate.

Mainline Protestants suffer from declining demographics. As mainline congregations have aged and have had limited success attracting younger, nonwhite members, their share of the state population has steadily dropped. This erosion is spread equally in all regions of the state and brings California to a very low rank nationally in terms of mainline Protestant presence.

Evangelicals are reinforcing their presence in the state. Although their share of the population (7%, according to the report of religious institutions) is still relatively small, Evangelicals are now the second largest religious group in California. Ethnicity and location are crucial when examining the political behavior of Evangelicals. White Evangelicals living in inland California support the Republican Party to a much greater extent than nonwhite Evangelicals living in coastal regions. These variations should be kept in mind when talking about "Evangelicals," too-often perceived as a monolithic conservative block. With those remarks in mind, the data presented in the chapter clearly point to a strengthening of Evangelical presence in the south and eastern regions of California, and this trend is likely to reinforce conservative strength in those regions.

The heightening of regional contrasts in California will have repercussions for the overall political equilibrium of the state: If regions on opposite ends of the ideological spectrum achieve population parity, statewide politics runs a higher risk of policy gridlock and increased polarization.

References

Anderson, Douglas Firth. 2005. "Toward an Established Mysticism: Judeo-Christian Traditions in Post-World War II California and Nevada." In *Religion & Public Life in the Pacific Region: Fluid Identities*, ed. Wade Clark Roof and Mark Silk. Walnut Creek, Calif.: AltaMira Press.

Baldassare, Mark. 2000. "Balance of Power Shifting in State." Public Policy Institute of California.

Cain, Bruce E. 1997. "Epilogue: Seeking Consensus among Conflicting Electorates." In *Governing California: Politics, Government, and Public Policy in the Golden State*, ed. Gerald C. Lubenow and Bruce E. Cain. Berkeley: Institute of Governmental Studies Press, University of California, 331–43.

D'Antonio, William V., James D. Davidson, Dean R. Hoge, and Katherine Meyer. 2001. *American Catholics*. Walnut Creek, Calif.: AltaMira Press.

DiCamillo, Mark. 2006. "Three California Election Megatrends and Their Implications in the 2006 Gubernatorial Election." The Field Poll.

Green, John C., Mark J. Rozell, and Clyde Wilcox (eds.). 2000. *Prayers in the Precincts: The Christian Right in the 1998 Elections*. Washington, D.C.: Georgetown University Press.

Johnson, Hans P. 2002. "A State of Diversity: Demographic Trends in California's Regions." In *California Counts. Population Trends and Profiles*. Public Policy Institute of California.

Johnson, Hans P., and Joseph M. Hayes. 2004. "The Central Valley at a Crossroads: Migration and Its Implications." San Francisco, Calif.: Public Policy Institute of California.

Machacek, David W. 2005. "New Players and New Patterns." In *Religion & Public Life in the Pacific Region: Fluid Identities*, ed. Wade Clark Roof and Mark Silk. Walnut Creek, Calif.: AltaMira Press, 89–107.

Mead, Frank Spencer, and Samuel S. Hill. 1995. *Handbook of Denominations in the United States*. Nashville, Tenn.: Abingdon Press.

Melton, J. Gordon. 1998. *Encyclopedia of American Religions*. Detroit, Mich.: Gale Research.

Pew Research Center. 2003. "Evenly Divided and Increasingly Polarized: 2004 Political Landscape." The Pew Research Center for the People and the Press.

Reyes, Belinda I. 2001. "A Portrait of Race and Ethnicity in California: An Assessment of Social and Economic Well-Being." San Francisco, Calif.: Public Policy Institute of California.

Roof, Wade Clark. 2007. "Pluralism as a Culture: Religion and Civility in Southern California." *The Annals of the American Academy of Political and Social Science* 612:82–99.

Roof, Wade Clark, and Mark Silk (eds.). 2005. *Religion & Public Life in the Pacific Region: Fluid Identities*. Walnut Creek, Calif.: AltaMira Press.

Sonenshein, Raphael J. 1991. "Jewish Participation in California Politics." In *Racial and Ethnic Politics in California*, ed. Byran O. Jackson and Michael B.

Preston. Berkeley: Institute of Governmental Studies Press, University of California.

Sonenshein, Raphael J., and Nicholas A. Valentino. 2000. "The Distinctiveness of Jewish Voting: A Thing of the Past?" *Urban Affairs Review* 35: 358–89.

Soper, J. Christopher, and Joel Fetzer. 2000. "The Christian Right and the Republican Party in California: Necessarily Yoked." In *Prayers in the Precincts: The Christian Right in the 1998 Elections*, ed. Luther A. Green, Kenneth N. Rozell, and Kevin D. Wilcox. Washington, D.C.: Georgetown University Press, 93–111.

Steensland, Brian, Jerry Park, Mark Regnerus, Lynn Robinson, Bradford Wilcox, and Robert Woodberry. 2000. "The Measure of American Religion: Toward Improving the State of the Art." *Social Forces* 79: 291–318.

Stump, Roger W. 1984. "Regional Divergence in Religious Affiliation in the United States." *Sociological Analysis* 45: 283–99.

Tamney, Joseph B. 2007. "Methodological Biases in the Study of Religion and Politics." *ASA Sociology of Religion Section Newsletter*.

Yamane, David. 1999. "Faith and Access: Personal Religiosity and Religious Group Advocacy in a State Legislature." *Journal for the Scientific Study of Religion* 38: 543–50.

Zambiras, Ariane. 2007. "Reversing the Causality: Considering the Impact of Politics on Religion." *MPSA annual meeting*. Chicago.

II. Local and Regional Developments

The Political Geography of Coalitions in an Age of Immigration: The Case of Los Angeles

Raphael J. Sonenshein and Mark H. Drayse[1]

1. Introduction

As immigration transforms the ethnic structure of American cities, support and opposition to immigration will create new kinds of urban coalitions. Like the racially tinged coalitions that preceded them, these new coalition lines may well affect the course of state and national politics. And California, with its growing diversity, will undoubtedly mark the leading edge of these developments.

Who will be likely to join pro- and anti-immigrant coalitions and on what basis will such coalitions be built? Will Latinos, who represent the largest and most visible immigrant group, forge coalitions based on color and class with African Americans, create alliances based on ideology with either liberal or conservative whites, or go it alone? How will Asian Americans, growing in numbers but of uncertain political influence, find their way? What do these changes mean for white voters? And African Americans, the pivot of the previous era of urban politics, will be searching for their direction.

[1] The authors thank the Russell Sage Foundation for a research grant that supported the preparation of this chapter.

Like African Americans before them (Holloway, 1968), political activists in today's immigrant communities will be forced to make difficult decisions about whether to go it alone, to forge temporary alliances of mutual interest, or to seek longer-term relationships with other groups.

There is a growing body of research on the relationship among Latinos, whites, African Americans, and Asian Americans. Much of the research has been based on surveys of attitudes among groups (e.g., Uhlaner, 1991; Kauffman, 2003b). One of the most ambitious set of studies has explored whether there is competition between blacks and Latinos for jobs in city government and in schools (McClain and Karnig, 1990; McClain and Tauber, 1998).

In this study we measure explicit coalition behavior that results from action rather than a stated belief. Therefore, we are most interested in such political behavior as voting (Kauffman, 2003a, 2004). Increasing interest is being devoted to the political participation of immigrant communities (Lien, 1994; Ramakrishnan and Espenshade, 2001; Ramirez, Segura, and Pantoja, 2001; Wong 2005; Wong, Lien, and Conway 2005). We consider such research to be essential to any understanding of new urban coalitions. Our own approach adds to this work by exploring the connections *between and among* groups in an age of immigration. Thus, we are as interested in how whites and blacks behave politically in an environment shaped by immigration as we are by the participation of immigrant communities themselves.

The experience of decades of black-and-white politics offers some perspectives that may help guide us through this new era. A prominent theory of *minority political incorporation* established that, for African Americans, winning political power required a major mobilization of their group combined with the backing of white liberals (Browning, Marshall, and Tabb, 2001; Sonenshein, 1993).

An elaboration of this theory by Sonenshein (1993) argued that coalitions between racial groups were not only guided by ideology, but by a mixture of interest and leadership. *Ideology* refers to a set of beliefs that structure positions on individual issues that often persist even when they do not advance, and in some cases conflict with, self-interest. *Interest* refers to perceptions of concrete, often material gains or losses that result from specific political decisions. Political interest may change as circumstances change. The balance between interest and ideology is not fixed in politics, but can be shaped by *leadership*. Leaders can widen or narrow interest conflicts.

Sonenshein contended that interracial coalitions must be understood over time, rather than as isolated phenomena. Drawing on the work of Barbara Hinckley, this view found that while some coalitions are highly stable and persistent, others are temporary and changeable. Rather than a set of individual transactions between self-interested political actors (as game theorists sometimes portrayed coalitions), Hinckley saw real-life coalitions as built over time between and among trusting partners. Hinckley complained that much of the study of coalitions involved single games played one time.

[I]n sharp contrast, real political games occur in time. They occur as one of an experienced or expected series, where players know each other and expect to meet and play again. . . . Bargaining is shaped by historical alliances. Deception is constrained by the risk of retaliation. . . . The single-game situation, then, deliberately excludes the temporal context within which political activity occurs. (66)

In this study, we include and move beyond these coalition theories by noting that coalitions occur in time *and* place. Cities are territorial entities situated in national and global contexts. For example, the city of Los Angeles, and its entire metropolitan region, has become one of the major immigrant gateways in the world, transforming the ethnic composition of its population. As a result, a neighborhood that had once been homogeneous becomes diverse. A neighborhood once dominated by one minority group is taken over by another. Established residents may react positively or negatively to ethnic neighborhood change.

Two identical voters are less likely to make the same voting decisions if they live in different neighborhoods, because of spatial differences in context and information. These differences can be due to the diffusion of information horizontally, through formal and informal social interaction, and vertically, through dissemination by mass media or activities of political campaigns and other organizations. Whom individuals talk to, what media they read and listen to, and how they perceive their locale affect how they think and how they vote (Agnew, 2002; Books and Prysby, 1991; Cox, 1969; Johnston et al., 2001; Burbank, 1995).

As Oliver and Wong note (2003), most of the work on interracial contact considers white reactions to African Americans. In a multiethnic urban setting, the reactions of African Americans and whites to new immigrant communities may be quite different. Their multicity analysis of opinion surveys indicated that "interethnic propinquity corresponds with lower levels of out-group prejudice and competition." This finding challenges the assumption among many observers that mixed neighborhoods, especially of blacks and Latinos, will be hotbeds of conflict, and it is testable as an electoral phenomenon.

With these dimensions in mind, we have explored evolving coalition politics in Los Angeles, the nation's second largest city, looking at group voting behavior over time and in place.

We analyzed four elections that took place in the city of Los Angeles: the mayoral primaries and general elections of 2001 and 2005. In those four mayoral elections, a leading candidate was Antonio Villaraigosa, a Latino. We analyze the voting behavior of four key groups across these elections—Latinos, blacks, whites, and Asians. In this chapter, we look most specifically at the political behavior of whites and African Americans.

The 2001 and 2005 mayoral elections developed as one of those relatively rare pairs of urban contests in which the same candidates get another shot at each other in a manner that helps illuminate emerging coalition patterns. These elections are already generating research (Sonenshein and Pinkus, 2002, 2005; Austin and Middleton, 2004).

Our data may shed light on the debate over interracial contact in a new multiethnic environment. Does coalition thrive or starve in the presence of actual contact among groups in neighborhoods? By analyzing the relative contribution of class, partisanship/ideology, ethnicity, and proximity to immigrants, we hope to reach conclusions about these questions.

2. Immigration and Ethnic Change in Los Angeles

Shaping the scene is the vast immigration that has transformed Los Angeles. Recent immigration has altered the possibilities for electoral coalitions in the city of Los Angeles. The new diversity in Los Angeles is part of a broader restructuring of the region's economy and created a sprawling global city-region (Soja, 2000). It has also shaken up existing political coalitions and provided the basis for new coalitions to confront urgent social and economic problems.

The city of Los Angeles is the largest municipality in the metropolitan Los Angeles region, with a population now approaching four million. Built territorially through a series of annexations in the early 1900s, the city encompasses the dense urban core of the region now populated mostly by Latinos and other immigrants, the vast suburban neighborhoods of the San Fernando Valley, wealthy communities in the Westside and Pacific Palisades, and stretches south to capture the harbor it built a century ago (see Figure 4.1).

Table 4.1 shows the ethnic composition of the city of Los Angeles in 1940, 1970, and 2005. In 1940, almost *nine in ten* residents were white, and Latinos made up only 7% of the population. By 1970, African Americans had made their presence felt. Initially drawn to Los Angeles by wartime jobs, blacks continued to migrate from the segregation-era South to Los Angeles after the Second World War. The African American population grew from 64,000 in 1940 to 504,000 in 1970, increasing their share of the city's population from 4% to 18%. Suburban out-migration of whites, a result of the postwar housing boom as well as a desire to escape the diverse urban core, resulted in their share of the city's population falling to 61%.

This era was the zenith of black demographic strength in Los Angeles, soon to be parlayed into political clout with the election of Tom Bradley as mayor in 1973. Since then, the white and black population shares have plummeted as a result of international migration, as well as intraregional and interstate out-migration by both blacks and whites. Between 1970 and 2005, the white population fell from 1.7 to 1.1 million, while the black population declined from 504,000 to 369,000. By 2005, the city of Los Angeles was 49% Latino (including 34% Mexican), 29% white, 11% Asian American, and 10% African American. Though more than a third of Latinos are ineligible to vote because they are

Figure 4.1. City of Los Angeles Areas and Surrounding Cities

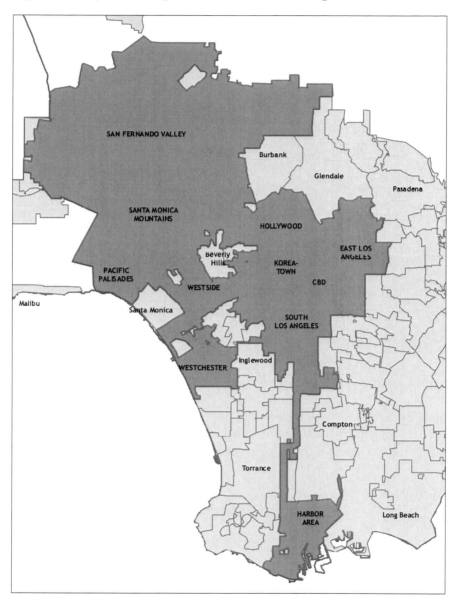

Table 4.1. Ethnic Change in the City of Los Angeles, 1940–2005

Year	Total	White		African American		Latino		Asian American	
		Number	%	Number	%	Number	%	Number	%
2005	3,731,437	1,063,362	28.5	368,711	9.9	1,824,378	48.9	415,652	11.1
1970	2,816,061	1,720,108	61.1	503,606	17.9	481,668	17.1	101,615	3.6
1940	1,504,277	1,298,917	86.3	63,774	4.2	107,513	7.1	33,211	2.2

Source: U.S. Census Bureau.

not American citizens, their political strength is catching up with their demographic presence, as the recent mayoral elections show.

The balkanized geography of ethnic groups in Los Angeles is shown in Figure 4.2. Whites are mostly found in the middle-to-high income, more affluent coastal and foothill neighborhoods. By 2005, whites had vacated much of the central core and eastern San Fernando Valley. Spatially, whites now dominate the western half of the city, in four distinct areas: the western San Fernando Valley, the Santa Monica Mountains, West Los Angeles (including communities such as Palms, Mar Vista, and Rancho Park), and Westchester. In the central core, the remaining white majority communities are found in the Hollywood Hills, the Hancock Park-Fairfax areas, and Silver Lake.

Latinos are concentrated in densely populated neighborhoods surrounding Downtown Los Angeles, and in the industrial corridor of the eastern San Fernando Valley. Eastside neighborhoods such as Boyle Heights and Lincoln Heights were the traditional hearts of the city's Latino population. Immediately west of downtown, Latinos settled in the Pico-Union and Westlake areas, neighborhoods with some of the highest population densities in the country. South of downtown, Latinos have moved into neighborhoods once dominated by African Americans, especially east of the Harbor Freeway. The Latino community in the Wilmington harbor area has grown considerably. Latinos have also increased their presence in the San Fernando Valley, where they are the majority in much of the eastern half of the valley.

African Americans, while highly concentrated in the South Los Angeles region, straddle the boundaries between Los Angeles and surrounding cities. In the mid-1900s African Americans moved into Watts and other neighborhoods in South Los Angeles, in close proximity to the main industrial districts of central and southeastern Los Angeles County (Laslett, 1996). By 1960, the only significant African-American presence outside of their major concentrations was in the industrial communities of Pacoima and Wilmington.

Since the 1970s, African Americans have moved west into the Crenshaw and West Adams districts that had been dominated by whites. In the eastern neighborhoods of South Central Los Angeles, Latinos moved into traditional black neighborhoods. In the process, the black population in the city of Los Angeles has declined, and is increasingly fragmented across municipal boundaries. In smaller cities bordered by the city of Los Angeles such as Inglewood and Compton that once had black majorities, their demographic role is threatened by large and growing Latino populations. The westward shift of the black community has created black majorities in unincorporated county districts such as View Park-Windsor Hills, West Compton, and West Adams, but weakened their political power in the city of Los Angeles.

As a result of new migration, the Asian community in the city of Los Angeles increased fourfold between 1970 and 2005. Most new Asian immigrants are Korean, Chinese (mainly from Taiwan and Hong Kong), and Southeast Asian. While the largest Asian communities in the region are outside of the city of Los

Figure 4.2. Balkanized Metropolis: City of Los Angeles and Environs, 2000

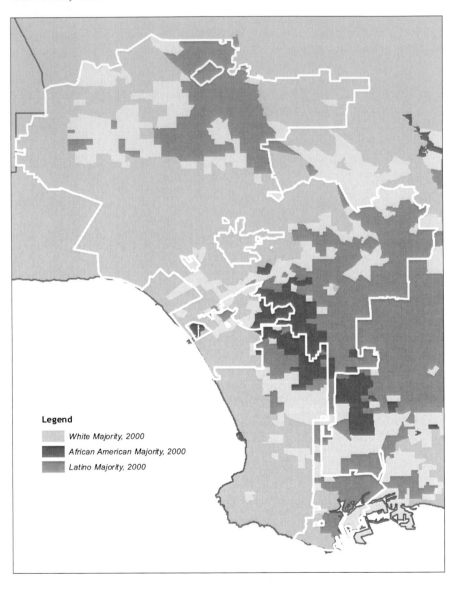

Legend

White Majority, 2000

African American Majority, 2000

Latino Majority, 2000

Angeles (e.g., the Chinese ethnoburbs of the San Gabriel Valley, or Little Saigon in Orange County), many Asians—especially Koreans and Filipinos—have moved into neighborhoods west of downtown and in the San Fernando Valley (Cheng and Yang, 1996; Li, 1998).

The newly diverse and changing ethnic geography of Los Angeles has reconfigured the map of urban politics (see Figure 4.3). Three characteristics of the city's political demography stand out: (1) the decline of a black population struggling to hold on to political gains made during the civil rights era and the Tom Bradley administration (1973–1993); (2) a Latino community whose political clout is catching up to its rapidly growing population; and (3) the consolidation of a politically diverse white electorate in the western half of the city.

Recent immigrants are less likely to register to vote and participate in elections than established residents. As a result, the number of precincts in which Latinos are a majority of registered voters is significantly smaller than the number of precincts in which Latinos are a majority of the total population. The electoral strength of Latinos is lagging behind their demographic presence, a situation that will change in the near future with continuing mobilization of the Latino community. By the 2001 Los Angeles mayoral election, Latinos cast 22% of all votes (*Los Angeles Times*, exit poll, 2001).

There is considerable ethnic and ideological diversity within the white population. For example, the western San Fernando Valley is predominantly conservative white Republican territory, as are portions of Westchester. In between, the Santa Monica Mountains and West Los Angeles areas are home to a high concentration of politically mobilized, liberal whites, many of whom are Jewish. In 1993, Jews in Los Angeles were nearly twice as likely as non-Jewish whites to call themselves Democrats and to hold racially liberal views (Sonenshein and Valentino, 2000).

The economic and ethnic restructuring of Los Angeles has created major challenges for urban governance, while at the same time undermining and reconfiguring political constituencies and ethnic coalitions. Rocco (1996) identifies three political challenges facing the Plural Metropolis: (1) coping with economic inequality and the growth of an increasingly Latino working poor population; (2) confronting racial and ethnic hostility; and (3) creating a new sense of community linking the city's diverse ethnic groups for a common purpose.

3. The Political Context

In the 1950s and early 1960s the study of urban politics focused on power: who governed the city? Was it a plurality of interest groups indirectly representing the people (Dahl, 1956) or was it a self-interested alliance of economic elites? The rise of race as a social and political issue profoundly altered that discussion. Then as now, Los Angeles was at the center of the dramatic shift. When the Watts riot shocked Americans in 1965, Los Angeles became the first case study of the impact of racial fault lines in a new urban politics.

Figure 4.3. Ethnic Blocs: City of Los Angeles

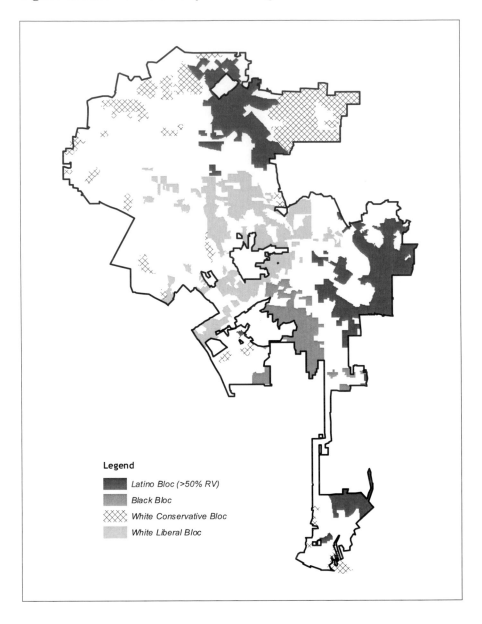

Legend
- Latino Bloc (>50% RV)
- Black Bloc
- White Conservative Bloc
- White Liberal Bloc

For several decades, Los Angeles played out the politics of race. In the 1969 mayoral election, incumbent mayor Sam Yorty ran one of the most explicitly racist campaigns ever in a city election in order to hold off a strong challenge from African-American City Councilman Tom Bradley and his alliance of African Americans and mostly Jewish white liberals. Four years later, Bradley defeated Yorty and a new, interracial liberal alliance began an historic 20 year run at city hall.

Between 1973 and 1993, Los Angeles politics was dominated by a biracial coalition of African Americans and Jewish liberals. Built around Mayor Bradley, this coalition featured strong interracial leadership ties and a high degree of coherence and coordination (Sonenshein, 1993).

The lines of Los Angeles politics remained firm for two decades, with the Los Angeles Police Department (LAPD) and race as the pivots. White conservatives and some Latino voters favored the LAPD's autonomy. African Americans and white liberals supported Bradley's efforts to bring LAPD under civilian oversight (Sonenshein, 1993).

With Bradley's retirement in 1993, a transitional era emerged under Republican businessman Richard Riordan, and the role of African Americans declined in city politics. Whites had made an unlikely comeback behind Riordan, as part of a pattern of African-American mayors being succeeded by whites in the three largest cities: New York City, Los Angeles, and Chicago (Sleeper, 1993).

Throughout these epic political battles, there was little mention of Latinos or Asian Americans despite their increasing population. Latinos were often called the "sleeping giant." Despite their great numbers, they cast only 8% of all votes in Riordan's 1993 election. Asian Americans cast an even smaller percentage, even though an Asian-American candidate, Michael Woo, made it into a spirited runoff against Riordan in 1993.

Under the surface, though, emerging forces were gathering that would not only change who won and lost elections, but the very framework and structure of Los Angeles politics. It began not with a rise of Latino participation, but with white conservatives' efforts to capitalize on resentment against Latino immigrants.

At the height of an economic recession that began in the early 1990s, and with racial tensions high as a result of the Los Angeles civil disorder of 1992, anti-immigrant forces placed a measure on the California ballot to prevent undocumented residents from receiving most public services. Beleaguered Republican governor Pete Wilson grabbed the political lifeline of Prop. 187 to revive his flagging 1994 re-election campaign, running a memorable TV commercial showing shadowy running figures with the tag line, "They keep coming." The measure passed with 60% of the vote (although it was soon invalidated by the federal courts), Wilson was re-elected and California politics was profoundly changed. Now immigration was at the head table.

We believe that Proposition 187 created a framework for the struggle over Latino empowerment in Los Angeles, and laid the groundwork for the new ethnic coalitions that would emerge in the 2001 and 2005 elections.

We consider Proposition 187 to be comparable to another ballot measure that shaped the rise of urban *racial* politics, the measure known as Proposition 14 that in 1964 overruled a state fair housing act (Wolfinger and Greenstein, 1968). Proposition 14 was later recognized as a landmark in the evolution of racialized politics, moving constituencies that had been considered progressive into a more conservative posture while also mobilizing minority groups threatened by the measure (Sonenshein, 1993).

There have been a number of analyses of the statewide vote on Proposition 187 (Alvarez and Butterfield, 2000; Ramirez, 2002; Tolbert and Hero, 1996). There are indications that the African-American ambivalence to Latino power that was evident in the 2001 mayoral election was foreshadowed by the split vote on Proposition 187 among blacks (Meyerson, 2001), although some have questioned how strong this black counter-surge was in the 187 vote (Morris 2000).

Among the effects of Proposition 187 was a major boost to Latino political mobilization statewide. In the 1990s, more than a million Latinos registered as new voters (Field Poll, 2000). What began as a method for white conservatives to exploit anti-immigrant sentiment backfired into a massive anti-Republican surge among Latino voters and an assertive push to elect Latino candidates.

In 2001, the campaign for an open mayoral seat generated new types of competing coalitions in this demographically, politically, and geographically transformed city. In 1993, Latinos cast 8% of all votes in the mayoral primary election; by 2005, Latinos represented 25% of all votes cast in the runoff election (Sonenshein and Pinkus, 2005).

The rise of Latinos in Los Angeles politics was dramatized by Antonio Villaraigosa's campaigns to become the first Latino mayor of Los Angeles in over 130 years. His main opponent in both elections was fellow Democrat and City Attorney James K. Hahn, son of Kenneth Hahn, who had been a white politician with tremendous appeal to African Americans because of his long service representing South Los Angeles on the city council and the county board of supervisors.

In 2001, Villaraigosa finished first in the nonpartisan primary. But in the runoff election, Hahn came back and defeated him for the mayoralty. The candidates also faced each other in the 2005 primary. Villaraigosa again finished first, with 33% of the vote, to Hahn's second place finish of 24%. A runoff election between the two top finishers was set for May 17, 2005, which Villaraigosa won handily with a landslide 58% of the vote.

We ask what coalition patterns emerged in these races, and what do these results say about the ideological and interest lines of electoral coalitions in an age of immigration?

4. Data and Methods

Our study builds on a precinct-level database for the city of Los Angeles, combined with individual-level data from the *Los Angeles Times* exit polls. The precinct-level data includes votes for mayor in the 2001 and 2005 general elections, and data from the Statewide Database (California's redistricting database maintained by the Institute for Governmental Studies at the University of California, Berkeley), which includes the ethnicity and political party of registered voters aggregated by precinct. Contextual data from the 2000 Census by census tract were linked with the precinct-level data. Census variables include race, ethnicity, income, and educational attainment.

We also acquired individual voter data. The *Los Angeles Times* conducted an election-day exit poll of 3,191 voters in 2005. Voters were asked their candidate preferences, personal characteristics (e.g., ethnicity, ideology, education, income), and precinct of residence, among other questions.

To describe and analyze the results of the 2001 and 2005 mayoral elections, we first tabulated votes by groups of precincts based on ethnicity and ideology, and identified characteristics of voters preferring Villaraigosa and Hahn. We calculated votes by four groups of precincts that represent different ethnic blocs. The city of Los Angeles has more than 1,700 precincts, with an average population of 2,087. The precinct groups were identified based on the combined census and voting data, and represent combinations of ethnicity and partisanship. These include: Latino, white Liberal, white Conservative, and African-American blocs.[2]

The election results were mapped, allowing us to visually identify shifts in voting patterns between the two elections. Tests for spatial autocorrelation were used to specify the spatial structure of the mayoral vote. Spatial autocorrelation is based on the relationship between the vote for a candidate in a precinct, and the average of the vote for that candidate in neighboring precincts. This analysis computes Moran's I statistic, which indicates spatial autocorrelation (a clustering of values). High Moran's I values (near 1.0) denote a high degree of spatial

---

[2] Latino precincts are those in which at least 50% of the registered voters are Latino. The actual Latino population is higher, especially in areas with high concentrations of Latinos without U.S. citizenship. White Democratic precincts are at least 70% white, with at least 52% of registered voters Democratic. This equals the share of all registered voters in the city of Los Angeles stating a Democratic Party preference. White Republican precincts are at least 70% white and 40% Republican. This is 1.5 times the concentration of Republicans in the city. African-American precincts have a population at least 50% African American. African-American areas accounted for 125 precincts, while by contrast there were only *eight* precincts in which Asian Americans represented at least 50% of the population—despite the fact that each group represents one-tenth of the city's population. This clearly shows the much higher degree of residential segregation of African Americans in Los Angeles compared to Asian Americans (Sonenshein, 2004).

autocorrelation, confirming evidence of bloc voting obtained by mapping the voting results. We also generated results for serial correlation, which tests the relationship between the votes for a candidate in the same precinct in two elections.

We then constructed spatial regression models based on precinct-level data and logistic regressions based on individual data, to evaluate the influence of ethnicity, ideology, class, and place on the mayoral election. Using the *GeoDa* program developed by Luc Anselin (2005), we began with ordinary least squares regression to identify the expected spatial autocorrelation in the values or the dependent variables. Regression diagnostics suggested that both the spatial lag and spatial error models were appropriate alternatives to OLS regression. We show the results for the spatial lag models, which include a spatial weight based on the value of the dependent variable in surrounding areas. A significant spatial lag coefficient indicates that a candidate's vote in a precinct is partly explained by his or her vote in surrounding precincts, suggesting that place-based factors are influencing voting behavior.

Given aggregate voting data reported at the precinct level, what inferences can we make regarding voting behavior? The standard solution is ecological inference, in which independent variables (e.g., percent foreign born, percent Latino) are regressed against a dependent variable (e.g., vote for Candidate A). However, this method is vulnerable to the inherent ecological fallacy: inferring individual behavior from spatially aggregated data. Spatial autocorrelation is another unavoidable limitation in ecological analysis, since most variables of interest are not randomly distributed across space.

Nonetheless, in recent years there has been a renewed interest in ecological analysis in the social sciences (King, 1997; Sui et al., 2000; Palmquist, 2001; Tam Cho, 2001). When available, as in our research, individual voter surveys can be used to strengthen ecological analysis (Johnston and Pattie, 2003). The problem of spatial autocorrelation can be reduced by using geographically weighted regressions, as we do here with the spatial regression models. This method assigns higher weights to data in neighboring areas, and lower weights to areas further away (Fotheringham, 2000).

To further our analysis of the vote for Villaraigosa, we linked the 2005 *Times* Poll data with the precinct data. First, we ran a set of logistic regression models to evaluate the relationship between ethnicity, ideology, education, and income and preference for Villaraigosa. As a result, we are able to directly examine voting behavior in a spatial context. This complements the ecological analysis that is based on the universe of votes cast, and allows us to analyze aggregate voter preferences in each precinct. In this chapter, we use the individual voter data to better understand the behavior of African-American voters in the two elections.

5. Stability and Change in Los Angeles Coalitions Between 2001 and 2005

Antonio Villaraigosa, a Latino Democrat, received the most votes in the 2001 mayoral primary in the city of Los Angeles. Villaraigosa gained 30.4% of the vote, followed by fellow Democrat James Hahn with 25.1%. Running a close third was a Jewish Republican, Steve Soboroff, who came away with 21.3% of the vote. Independent city councilperson Joel Wachs was fourth with 11.0% of the vote. The top two candidates, Villaraigosa and Hahn, faced off in the 2001 general election. Hahn reversed the candidates' showing in the primary, defeating Villaraigosa by 53.5% to 46.5%.

The 2005 primary involved a rematch between Villaraigosa and Mayor Hahn. Another similarity to the 2001 primary was the candidacy of a moderate Jewish candidate, San Fernando Valley Democrat Robert Hertzberg. The results were parallel to those four years earlier. Villaraigosa again won the primary, receiving 33.1% of the vote to Hahn's 23.6%. This time, though, Villaraigosa almost doubled his margin over Hahn, no small feat versus an incumbent mayor. Hertzberg finished third with 22.0%, narrowly missing a chance to go up against Villaraigosa in the runoff election. Former police chief Bernard Parks, an African-American Democrat recently fired by Hahn, received 13.6% of the vote.

In the general election Villaraigosa defeated Hahn in a landslide, with 58.6% of the vote to Hahn's 41.4%. What happened between the two elections, resulting in a historic victory giving Los Angeles its first Latino mayor in 150 years?

The Consolidation of Villaraigosa's Latino-based Coalition

In 2005, Villaraigosa mobilized his core Latino supporters while increasing his support among other constituencies in the city. The Latino community represented a record 25% of all votes cast, according to the *Los Angeles Times* exit poll. Latino neighborhoods supported Villaraigosa with 83% of their vote in 2005, compared to 81% in 2001. Villaraigosa's core precincts were Latino neighborhoods in the eastern half of Los Angeles, including the traditional Mexican neighborhoods of East Los Angeles, and newer immigrant neighborhoods in South Los Angeles, west of downtown Los Angeles and in the eastern San Fernando Valley.

However, something fundamental changed between the 2001 and 2005 mayoral elections. Villaraigosa extended his support in white liberal neighborhoods, mostly in Westside Los Angeles. Voters in these neighborhoods were evenly split between Villaraigosa and Hahn in 2001, but Villaraigosa won 58% of their vote in 2005. Also, Villaraigosa received 40% of the vote in white conservative neighborhoods in 2005, versus 29% in 2001. Although these neighborhoods supported Hahn in both elections, Villaraigosa made important gains. More dramatically, though, Villaraigosa received 59% of the vote in African American precincts in 2005, compared to 22% in 2001.

The maps of preference for Villaraigosa in 2001 and 2005 show a clear spatial pattern in his electoral support (Figures 4.4 and 4.5). The spatial autocorrelation of the vote for Villaraigosa was a very high 0.762 in 2001, and 0.713 in 2005. In both elections, Villaraigosa's strongest support came from Latino neighborhoods in the eastern half of Los Angeles, including the traditional Mexican neighborhoods of East Los Angeles, and newer immigrant neighborhoods in South Los Angeles, west of Downtown Los Angeles, and the San Fernando Valley. A careful comparison of the maps reveals stronger support for Villaraigosa in many neighborhoods in 2005, especially African-American areas of South Los Angeles.

We ran spatial regression models to evaluate the significance of ethnicity, ideology, education, income, and place in the elections. (See Table 4.2.) The dependent variable was the percentage of voters who selected Villaraigosa. Models were constructed for all precincts in the 2001 and 2005 elections. Independent variables included two indicators of ideology, Percent Liberal and Percent Conservative. These were based on registered voters in each precinct affiliated with the Democratic Party and small left-of-center parties (e.g., the Green Party) on the one hand, and the Republican Party and small right-of-center parties (e.g., the American Independent Party) on the other hand.

Four variables measured ethnic composition, including Percent White, Percent Black, Percent Latino, and Percent Asian. The white and black percents are based on the voting age population, and the Latino and Asian percents are based on registered voters. Variables for education and income were Percent with College Degree (four-year), and Median Household Income (in thousands). These models include a spatial lag coefficient, which is a weighted average of the dependent variable based on proximity to a given neighborhood. If votes for and against Villaraigosa are clustered spatially, this coefficient will be significant.

The results show that all independent variables were highly significant in each election. The spatial lag coefficient was more strongly associated with support for Villaraigosa in 2005 than in 2001. This means that the vote for Villaraigosa can be explained in part by his level of support in surrounding neighborhoods. This confirms the hypothesis that place-based factors, including local social interaction, the development of neighborhood identity, and spatial differences in the diffusion of information, influenced the vote for mayor.

Spatial differences in ideology were reflected in the vote for Villaraigosa. More liberal neighborhoods supported Villaraigosa, and more conservative neighborhoods opposed him. The coefficient for Percent Liberal was greater in 2005, while the coefficient for Percent Conservative was smaller, although still highly significant and negatively signed. This suggests that Villaraigosa rein

Figure 4.4. Vote for Villaraigosa in 2001

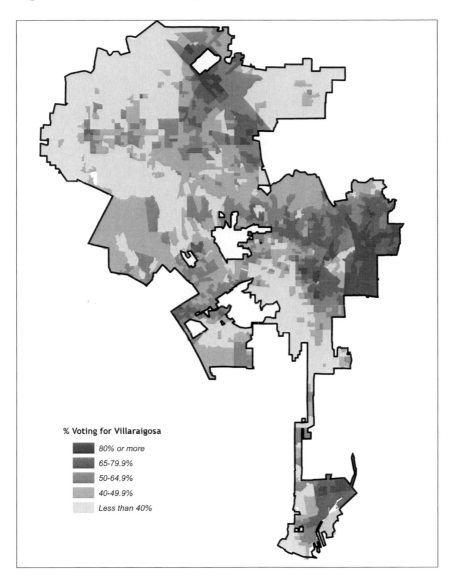

Figure 4.5. Vote for Villaraigosa in 2005

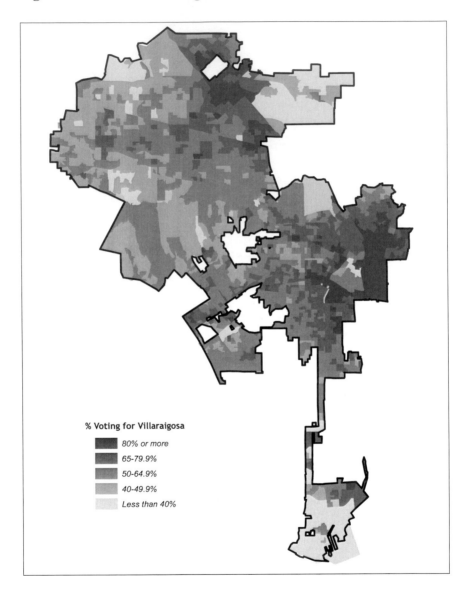

% Voting for Villaraigosa

■ 80% or more
■ 65-79.9%
■ 50-64.9%
■ 40-49.9%
□ Less than 40%

**Table 4.2. Spatial Regression Models, Vote for Villaraigosa
City of Los Angeles Mayoral General Elections, 2001 and 2005**

Dependent Variable: Preference for Villaraigosa

Variable	All Precincts	
	2001	**2005**
	(n=1,417)	(n=1,417)
Constant	49.111***	59.018***
Spatial Lag*	0.127***	0.157***
Percent Liberal	0.138***	0.173***
Percent Conservative	-0.429***	-0.322***
Percent White (VAP)	-0.182***	-0.253***
Percent Black (VAP)	-0.631***	-0.345***
Percent Latino (RV)	0.283***	0.090**
Percent Asian (RV)	-0.792***	-1.254***
Percent College Degree (4yr)	0.380***	0.214***
Median Household Income (thousands)	-0.110***	-0.044***
Log likelihood	-4719.54	-4909.68

Significance levels: ***p<0.001, **p<0.01, *p<0.05
*spatially-weighted dependent variable

forced his hold on liberal constituents, while making some inroads into conservative neighborhoods.

Interestingly, Percent Latino was the weakest of the four ethnic variables in 2005, though still positive and highly significant. This is indicative of inroads made by Villaraigosa in other neighborhoods. Higher concentrations of whites, blacks, and Asians were negatively associated with support for Villaraigosa. The magnitude of the Percent White coefficient was greater in 2005, while the Percent Black coefficient was smaller. This can be explained by the growing support for Villaraigosa in black precincts in 2005.

Variables for education and income were also highly significant. Neighborhoods with higher percentages of adults holding a four-year college degree were more likely to vote for Villaraigosa in both elections. On the other hand, median household income was negatively associated with support for Villaraigosa. Although education and income are positively associated with each other, in controlling for other variables in these models, their respective signs are opposite. This can be explained primarily by the ideological split among higher income white voters.

The results of the spatial regressions are broadly consistent with the individual-level survey conducted by the *Los Angeles Times* on election day (Sonenshein and Pinkus, 2005). The *Times* poll also found a large difference in voting between white liberals and white conservatives, and a relatively high degree of mobilization of Latinos.

Villaraigosa consolidated his Latino base while forging a Latino-white Liberal coalition between 2001 and 2005. But he also made significant gains among white Conservatives, and trounced Hahn in the African-American neighborhoods. Why did Hahn's support evaporate? We now turn to the collapse of Hahn's coalition, which opened the door for Villaraigosa.

The Collapse of Hahn's Coalition

Hahn's victorious coalition in 2001 was comprised of two unlikely partners: African Americans and white Conservatives. Political decisions made by Hahn within his first year of office alienated both parts, effectively crippling his chances to win a second term.

In the 2001 primary, Hahn's core strength was in African-American neighborhoods. In the 2001 general election, Hahn maintained his base in African-American neighborhoods, where he received 78% of the vote, and expanded his support in conservative white neighborhoods, winning 71% of the vote. Hahn especially gained votes in San Fernando Valley neighborhoods that supported Steve Soboroff in the primary.

However, the picture was different in 2005. Former police chief Bernard Parks, an African American fired by Hahn in 2002, ran in the primary. The African-American community shifted its support behind Parks. Hahn's support in black precincts nearly disappeared, as he received only 15% of the vote in the 2005 primary, compared to 71% in the 2005 primary. In geographic terms, Hahn appeared to be a man without a base except in his own Harbor neighborhoods in the south. He was strong enough everywhere to inch into the runoff, but not strong enough anywhere to have a springboard for further growth. In the 2005 runoff election, Hahn received 41% of votes in black precincts, a far cry from the 78% support in 2001.

Hahn made certain key decisions that alienated both elements of his coalition. Both came in 2002, when he fired African-American police chief Bernard Parks, and when he led the campaign against San Fernando Valley secession. This is an unusual political phenomenon, in which a skilled, experienced politician essentially loses his entire electoral coalition within one year after taking office. Hahn's decision not to re-hire African-American police chief Bernard Parks cut deeply into his black support. African Americans have seen their political power decline in Los Angeles through a combination of immigration and declining African-American population in the city. By firing Parks, Hahn removed a major symbol of remaining black political power in the city of Los Angeles.

Hahn saw Parks' firing as necessary to reorient the Los Angeles Police Department (LAPD) towards a community policing model and to staunch an exodus of police officers. He had no choice but to oppose the Valley secession movement, which would have resulted in Los Angeles losing 40% of its population.

Interests and ideology mediated by leadership tie coalitions together (Sonenshein, 1993). In 2001, African Americans and white Republicans seemed to share a concern about the changing city and its demographics, and helped elect Hahn. But on a host of issues, they had little in common and much in conflict. On each of the controversial decisions Hahn had to make, his coalition allies were in opposite camps. Privatization of city services was most heatedly opposed by African Americans and supported by white Republicans. African Americans suspected that the police union, long a darling of white conservatives, was behind the Parks firing. No group supported secession as actively as white conservatives, and no block opposed secession as vociferously as blacks.

Thus the high stakes of the choices Hahn had to make exemplified the strangeness of his coalition. Time did not knit it together rather, it tore it apart. When Sam Yorty had a similar coalition in 1961, he simply chose white conservatives, abandoned African Americans, and rode that right-wing alliance to victory (Sonenshein, 1993). Hahn had less choice in a city with a far smaller proportion of whites or African Americans in the electorate.

The greatest attrition in support for Hahn occurred in South Los Angeles, the heart of the city's African-American community. African-American precincts supported Hahn by a four to one margin over Villaraigosa in 2001; however, the same neighborhoods gave 59% of their votes to Villaraigosa in 2005.

Hahn's active campaign against Valley secession in 2002 hurt him among the moderate and conservative white voters who favored secession. Though a majority of these voters chose Hahn in 2005, Villaraigosa made some inroads into this group. Of the voters in the *Times* poll who switched support from Hahn to Villaraigosa between 2001 and 2005, 62% were white and 51% were Conservative or Moderate. By contrast, Villaraigosa's core supporters who had backed him in both elections were 43% Latino and 65% Liberal.

The disruptive, contextual shifts that undermined Hahn's reelection can be understood as reflections of interest, rather than ideology. They are straightforward changes in political behavior as a result of actions that generated reaction from groups. In addition, these interest-based reactions are closely associated with place.

Meanwhile, the ideological underpinnings of white voting behavior that had been a feature of the era of racial politics remained consistent in an age of immigration. The minority candidate, despite changing context, did significantly better among white liberals than among white conservatives.

But what about African Americans? Did proximity to Latino neighborhoods create a "perception of threat" that would incline them to vote against the Latino candidate? Our data may shed light on the debate over interracial contact in a new multiethnic environment. As Oliver and Wong note (2003), most of the work on interracial contact considers white reactions to African Americans. In a multiethnic urban setting, the reactions of African Americans to new immigrant communities may be quite different. Their multicity analysis of opinion surveys indicated that "interethnic propinquity corresponds with lower levels of out-group prejudice and competition." This finding challenged the assumption among many observers that mixed neighborhoods, especially of blacks and Latinos, will be hotbeds of conflict, and it is testable as an electoral phenomenon using our data.

We constructed a logistic regression model using data on individual African-American voters collected in the *Los Angeles Times* exit poll sample in the 2005 election (Table 4.3). We included variables to test whether or not the ethnic composition of a black voter's neighborhood was associated with voting for or against Villaraigosa. A one-mile buffer was created around the census tract in which each voter resided. Using ArcGIS, we determined the percent of African Americans and Latinos living within the neighborhood. (The same analysis was performed for different neighborhood scales, including the census tract of residence only, and an area covered by a two-mile buffer around the census tract. The results were consistent with those for the one-mile buffer reported here.)

The results suggest that the ethnic context of black voters' neighborhoods had an influence on support for Villaraigosa. In both the 2001 and 2005 elections, there was an inverse relationship between support for Villaraigosa and the percent of African Americans living in the area. Blacks living in more homogeneous black neighborhoods were less likely to support Villaraigosa, controlling for the other variables in the model. The Latino composition of the neighborhood was weakly associated with African-American support for Villaraigosa in both elections. In 2001, a higher percentage of Latinos was associated with black support for Villaraigosa. However, the coefficient was only significant at the .16 level in 2001. There was no relationship between Latino composition of the neighborhoods and black support for Villaraigosa in 2005. This suggests that while African Americans living outside core black neighborhoods were more likely to support Villaraigosa, this was not necessarily because they had greater interaction with Latinos. More specifically, we can argue that African Americans living in homogeneous black neighborhoods were less amenable to voting for Villaraigosa.

Almost There: The Third Coalition

We also examined consistency in the third coalition, the white alliance that third-place candidates built in 2001 and 2005, in each case nearly winning a spot in the runoff. In the 2001 primary, Steve Soboroff ran strongly in white Republican precincts. In the 2005 primary, Hertzberg ran strongly in white precincts, receiving a similar share of the vote in both Democratic and Republican blocs.

Table 4.3. Logistic Regression Model, Vote for Villaraigosa, 2001 and 2005 African-American Voters in *Los Angeles Times* Poll Sample

Variable	Odds Ratio (Exp(B))	
	2001	2005
SPATIAL VARIABLES		
Percent Black in 1-mile buffer	0.981**	0.988*
Percent Latino in 1-mile buffer	1.012	1.003
AGE (reference: 65 and older)		
Under 30	6.594**	6.181***
Age 31–40	1.145	2.762*
Age 41–50	1.044	2.494*
Age 51–64	0.497	1.969
EDUCATION		
(reference: Graduate Degree)		
High School Degree or Less	0.516	0.386*
Some College	0.305**	0.514
College Degree	0.306**	0.335**
INCOME (reference: more than $100,000)		
Less than $20,000	1.229	1.872
$20,000 to $39,999	0.673	2.407*
$40,000 to $59,999	1.731	2.532*
$60,000 to $74,999	1.182	1.666
$75,000 to $99,999	1.456	2.097
UNION MEMBER	1.229	1.107
n=	255	332

***$p<0.01$, **$p<0.01$, *$p<0.05$

We compare the vote for Soboroff in 2001 with the vote for Hertzberg in 2005 (Table 4.4). The vote for both candidates is positively related to percent white, percent Republican, percent Jewish, and income. This suggests a voting

Table 4.4. Spatial Regression Models, Votes for Hertzberg and Soboroff, City of Los Angeles Mayoral Primaries, 2001 and 2005

	Hertzberg 2005	Soboroff 2001
Constant	5.489	1.745
Spatial Lag*	0.322***	0.104***
Percent Democratic	-0.110*	-0.142***
Percent Republican	0.337***	0.602***
Percent Latino	-0.021	0.001
Percent White	0.064**	0.072***
Percent Black	0.031	0.070***
Percent Asian	-0.041	-0.007
Percent Jewish	0.848***	0.471***
Percent with College Degree	-0.010***	-0.012
Median Household Income (in thousands)	0.021	0.057***
Citizens - Percent Foreign Born	0.033	-0.031
Percent Recent Immigrants	-0.037	0.149***
Valley	0.877**	0.268
Log Likelihood	-4371.870	-3985.360
N	1399	1399

*p < 0.05, **p <0.01, ***p <0.001

*spatially-weighted dependent variable

bloc united by ethnicity and class—upper income whites. The Hertzberg vote was the only one in which the Valley variable was significant. This suggests that place-based identity may have been a factor in this race, as many Valley voters coalesced behind a moderate Democrat from their side of the Hollywood Hills.

There was a definite spatial pattern in the votes for Soboroff and Hertzberg. In the 2001 primary, the spatial autocorrelation of the vote for Soboroff was 0.822, and the spatial autocorrelation of the 2005 vote for Hertzberg was 0.845. The serial correlation of the Soboroff and Hertzberg votes was an especially high 0.763, even higher than the respective value for the Villaraigosa votes in 2001 and 2005. The consistency is particularly striking because they were both losing candidates who failed to make the runoff and because they were different politicians, and even of different political parties.

6. Conclusion and Implications

The coalition patterns that emerged in these two elections show that in Los Angeles a bipolar model of black-and-white politics has been replaced by a tripolar framework for a city election system that only has room for two seats at the table of the runoff. Oddly, the rise of immigration has re-empowered whites by opening the door to a third coalition.

In terms of the coalition models presented above, each primary coalition can be seen as a potential base from which to build a citywide majority alliance in a runoff election. With three strong contending primary candidates, the two runoff candidates would seek to monopolize the vote of the third candidate and others who do not make the runoff. At the same time, any primary candidate who has broad and deep support in one community can preempt other candidates from poaching in those neighborhoods. Villaraigosa's strength in Latino neighborhoods marked those areas as off-limits to other candidates, as did Hahn's 2001 support in African-American neighborhoods. Had either failed to make the runoff, though, another candidate could then try to pick up those core neighborhoods.

Hahn's option in 2001 was to start with African-American voters and get to a majority where votes were available to him, which meant white Republicans and conservatives especially in the San Fernando Valley. Villaraigosa's chance was to expand his base among white liberals, especially on the west side of the city. While Hahn's alliance of blacks and white conservatives prevailed in 2001, it proved highly unstable and collapsed in 2005.

The surprisingly stable white base behind the third-place candidates in the two mayoral primaries could become the basis for a majority coalition but only if such candidates could greatly increase their appeal to either African-American or Latino voters as happened in New York City's recent mayoral elections. Coalitions of color would face some significant obstacles, but because of the fluctuating stance of African Americans, could be formed on a pragmatic basis. The potential for white candidates to win minority support or for minority candidates to win white support would depend heavily on the ideological identification of the candidates.

The rise of immigration as a factor in Los Angeles politics suggests that the new structure of urban coalitions has not fully replaced earlier fault lines but has been superimposed on top of them. Race created strong ideological fissures among whites in urban politics that had not been so evident before the 1960s. These racialized lines persist in an age of immigration. Those whites who supported Proposition 187 would be less likely to vote for a Latino mayoral candidate, and the opposite would be true of white liberals.

The most interesting and paradoxical role is that of African Americans. Once the center of race-based urban coalitions, blacks have a new, uncertain role as the balance wheel of victory for competing coalitions. We have found that contrary to conventional wisdom, interracial settings actually increased their likelihood of supporting the Latino candidate. While the relationship between these two minority groups is uncertain, our research suggests that greater, rather than less contact between the groups may yield the best coalition results.

References

Agnew, John. 2002. *Place and Politics in Modern Italy*. Chicago: University of Chicago Press.

Alvarez, Michael R., and Tara L. Butterfield. 2000. "The Resurgence of Nativism in California? The Case of Proposition 187 and Illegal Immigration." *Social Science Quarterly*, vol. 8, no. 1 (March): 167–79.

Austin, Sharon, D. Wright, and Richard T. Middleton, IV. 2004. "The Limitations of the Deracialization Concept in the 2001 Los Angeles Mayoral Election." *Political Research Quarterly* 57(2): 283–93.

Body-Gendrot, Sophie. 1995. "Models of Immigrant Integration in France and the United States: Signs of Convergence?" In *The Bubbling Cauldron: Race, Ethnicity, and the Urban Crisis*, ed. Smith, Michael Peter, and Joe R. Feagin. Minneapolis: University of Minnesota Press, 244–62.

Books, John W., and Charles L. Prysby. 1991. *Political Behavior and the Local Context*. New York: Praeger.

Browning, Rufus, Dale Rogers Marshall, and David Tabb (eds.). 2001. *Racial Politics in American Cities*, 3d ed. New York: Longman.

Burbank, Matthew. 1995. "The Psychological Basis of Contextual Effects." *Political Geography* 14: 621–35.

Cox, K. R. 1969. "The Voting Decision in Spatial Context." *Progress in Geography* 1(2): 81–117.

Dahl, Robert. 1961. *Who Governs? Democracy and Power in an American City*. New Haven, Conn.: Yale University Press.

Eisinger, P. 1976. *Patterns of Interracial Politics*. Madison, Wis.: Academic Press.

Field Poll. 2000. The Expanding Latino Electorate. Release no. 1960, May 1.

Fotheringham, A. Stewart. 2000. A Bluffer's Guide to a Solution to the Ecological Inference Problem. *Annals of the Association of American Geographers*, 90: 582–86.

Hinckley, Barbara. 1981. *Coalitions and Politics*. New York: Harcourt Brace Jovanovich.

Holloway, Harry. 1968. "Negro Political Strategy: Coalition or Independent Power Politics?" *Social Science Quarterly* 49: 534–47.

Johnston, R. J., and C. J. Pattie. 2003. "Evaluating an Entropy-Maximizing Solution to the Ecological Inference Problem: Split-Ticket Voting in New Zealand." 1999. *Geographical Analysis* 35: 1–23.

Johnston, R. J., C. J. Pattie, D. F. L. Dorling, I. MacAllister, H. Tunstall, and D. J. Rossiter. 2001. "Social Locations, Spatial Locations and Voting at the 1997 British General Election: Evaluating the Sources of Conservative Support." *Political Geography* 20: 85–111.

Jones-Correa, Michael. 2006. "Reshaping the American Dream: Immigrants and the Politics of the New Suburbs." In *The New Suburban History*, ed. Thomas Sugrue and Kevin Kruse. Chicago: University of Chicago Press, 183–204.

————— (ed.). 2001. *Governing American Cities: Inter-Ethnic Coalitions, Competition, and Conflict.* New York: Russell Sage Foundation.

Kaufmann, Karen M. (2004). *The Urban Voter: Group Conflict and Mayoral Voting Behavior in American Cities.* College Park, Md.: University of Maryland Press.

—————. 2003b. "Cracks in the Rainbow: Group Commonality as a Basis for Latino and African American Political Coalitions." *Political Research Quarterly* 56(2): 199–210.

—————M. 2003a. "Minority Empowerment in Denver, Colorado: How Black and Latino Voters Respond to Each Other's Political Leadership." *Political Science Quarterly* 118(1): 107–25.

King, Gary. 1997. *On a Solution to the Ecological Inference Problem: Reconstructing Individual Behavior from Aggregate Data.* Princeton, N.J.: Princeton University Press.

Lien, Pei-te. 1994. "Ethnicity and Political Participation: A Comparison Between Asian and Mexican Americans." *Political Behavior*, June 16, (2): 237–64.

McClain, Paula, and A. K. Karnig. 1990. "Black and Latino Socioeconomic and Political Competition." *American Political Science Review* 84(2): 535–45.

McClain, Paula, and S. Tauber. 1998. Black and Latino Socioeconomic and Political Competition: Has a Decade Made a Difference? *American Politics Quarterly* 26(2): 237–52.

Mollenkopf, John, David Olson, and Timothy Ross. 2001. "Immigrant Political Participation in New York and Los Angeles." In *Governing American Cities,* ed. Michael Jones-Correa. New York: Russell Sage Foundation, 17–70.

Mollenkopf, John, Ana Champeny, Mark Drayse, and Raphael Sonenshein. 2006. "Race, Ethnicity, and Immigration in the 2005 Mayoral Elections in Los Angeles and New York." Paper presented at the annual meeting of the American Political Science Association.

Morris, Irwin. 2000. African American Voting on Proposition 187: Rethinking the Prevalence of Interminority Conflict. *Political Research Quarterly,* 53(1): 77–98.

Oliver, J. Eric, and Janelle Wong. 2003. "Intergroup Prejudice in Multiethnic Settings." *American Journal of Political Science* 47(4). October: 567–82.

Palmquist, Bradley. 2001. "Unlocking the Aggregate Data Past: Which Key Fits?" *Historical Methods* 34(4): 159–69.

Ramakrishnan, S. Karthick, and Thomas Espenshade. 2001. "Immigration Incorporation and Political Participation in the United States." *International Migration Review* 35: 870–909.

Ramirez, Ricardo. 2002. "Race, Social Context and Referendum Voting." *Working Paper No. 14.* Center for the Study of Law and Politics, University of Southern California.

Ramirez, Ricardo, Gary M. Segura, and Adran D. Pantoja. 2001. "Citizens by Choice, Voters by Necessity: Patterns in Political Mobilization by Naturalized Latinos." *Political Research Quarterly.* 54: 729–50.

Riker, William. 1962. *The Theory of Political Coalitions*. New Haven: Yale University Press.

Sonenshein, Raphael J. 1993. *Politics in Black and White: Race and Power in Los Angeles*. Princeton, N.J.: Princeton University Press.

Sonenshein, Raphael J., and Mark H. Drayse. 2006. Urban Electoral Coalitions in an Age of Immigration: "Time and Place in the 2001 and 2005 Los Angeles Mayoral Primaries." *Political Geography* 25: 570–95.

Sonenshein, Raphael J., and Susan H. Pinkus. 2005. "Latino Political Incorporation Reaches the Urban Summit: How Antonio Villaraigosa Won the 2005 Los Angeles Mayor's Race." *PS: Political Science and Politics* 38 (October): 713–21.

Sonenshein, Raphael J., and Susan Pinkus. 2002. "The Dynamics of Latino Incorporation: The 2001 Los Angeles Mayoral Election As Seen in *Los Angeles Times* Polls." *PS: Political Science and Politics*, 67–74.

Sui, Daniel, A. Stewart Fotheringham, Luc Anselin, John O'Loughlin, and Gary King. 2000. Book review forum: "On a Solution to the Ecological Problem: Reconstructing Individual Behavior from Aggregate Data," by Gary King. *Annals of the Association of American Geographers*, 90: 579–606.

Tam Cho, Wendy K. 2001. Latent Groups and Cross-Level References. *Electoral Studies* 20: 243–63.

Tolbert, Caroline J., and Rodney E. Hero. 1996. "Race/Ethnicity and Direct Democracy: An Analysis of California's Illegal Immigration Initiative." *Journal of Politics* 3: 806–18.

Uhlaner, Carole. 1991. Perceived Discrimination and Prejudice and the Coalition Prospects of Blacks, Latinos, and Asian Americans." In *Racial and Ethnic Politics in California*, ed. Byran O. Jackson and Michael Preston. Berkeley, Calif.: IGS Press.

Waldinger, Roger, and Mehdi Bozorgmehr (eds.) 1996. *Ethnic Los Angeles*. New York: Russell Sage Foundation.

Wolfinger, Raymond W., and Fred I. Greenstein. 1968. "The Repeal of Fair Housing in California: An Analysis of Referendum Voting." *American Political Science Review* 62 (September): 753–59.

Wong, Janelle S. 2005. "Mobilizing Asian American Voters: A Field Experiment." *Annals, AAPSS* 601 (September): 102–14.

Wong, Janelle S., Pei-Te Lien, and M. Margaret Conway. 2005. "Group-Based Resources and Political Participation Among Asian Americans." *American Politics Research* 33, 4 (July): 545–76.

Chapter 5

Urban Change and Neighborhood Politics in San Diego: A Comparative Perspective

Gérald Billard and Emmanuelle Le Texier

Since the 1960s, demographic changes have played a major role in shaping the politics, culture, and urban landscape of California, especially in cities of high immigration, which are facing a restructuring of their social and political organization. The transformation of neighborhoods, due to changes in urban policy-making and a growing minority population, has a pronounced effect on political participation and forms of local activism. It affects not only ethnic enclaves but white, middle-class neighborhoods. Extensive qualitative fieldwork in two San Diego neighborhoods allows us to contrast a Latino segregated enclave (the Mexican barrio) to a white, middle-class neighborhood (Ocean Beach). On the one hand, it is often stated that barrio residents are distinguished by their weak capacity for mobilization. Indeed, low voter registration and turnout, the lack of party campaigning, and a large proportion of disenfranchised individuals define a space characterized by, among other factors, a high proportion of undocumented migrants, low rates of naturalization, and low socio-economic attainment. On the other hand, white, middle-class neighborhoods are supposed to benefit from more socio-economic resources, higher political involvement, and interest from the political parties. Residents of these communities are considered well equipped to influence the design of local and urban politics. To sum it up, ethnic minorities are supposed to have less influence on urban development and are therefore less likely to benefit from change.

This study of two San Diego communities might reverse in part the conventional wisdom. We raise two questions. The first is whether contemporary urban changes differently impact activism at the neighborhood level depending on their socio-economic characteristics. The second is how radically different neighborhoods can experience similar or divergent entries into local politics, as well as varied responses from local governments. This chapter begins with a comparative presentation of Ocean Beach and Barrio Logan regarding the urban and demographic changes that occurred in San Diego in the last two decades. Then, it focuses on forms of political activism in reaction to urban restructuring in Ocean Beach and gentrification in Barrio Logan. Finally, it draws conclusions from the contrasted results obtained from the two neighborhoods.

Urban Changes and Community Participation in San Diego

San Diego has often been portrayed as a place where everything is "under the perfect sun" (Davis *et al.*, 2003). Nevertheless, urban change and gentrification have initiated new political dynamics. It has become one of the wealthiest areas in the United States. It is home to approximately 1.3 million people (three million inhabitants for the metropolitan region), composed of diverse racial and ethnic backgrounds: 27.2% Latinos, 15.3% Asian, 7.2% blacks, 46.7% white (U.S. Census 2006 estimates for the city). A quarter of the population (25.72%) is foreign-born, and 37.4% speaks a language other than English at home. However, the economic growth has not been distributed evenly. The local Latino population has not benefited as much as the population at large. For instance, racial residential segregation in San Diego has increased in the last decade, both at the city and metropolitan levels. In 1990, suburban Latinos lived in census tracts that were 58% white; in 2000, they lived in census tracts that were 45% white. Segregation rates are even higher for Latino children than for the adult population.[1]

The housing market in San Diego is a crucial issue for the lower and middle classes as well as regional economic growth. In 2006, in order to be able to afford a median-priced house ($550,000),[2] buyers needed an annual income of about $134,000. Yet, according to the San Diego Association of Governments (SANDAG), the county's median household income was a mere $64,273 (San Diego Housing Commission, March 2006). The average apartment rent in San

---

[1] "High levels of segregation for blacks in the City and increasing segregation rates for Latinos metro-wide suggest that much remains to be done to insure that these populations have equal access to all communities," in Harvard Civil Rights Project, (2002: 2) *Race, Place and Opportunity: Racial Change and Segregation in the San Diego Metropolitan Area: 1990–2000,* http://www.civilrightsproject.harvard.edu.

[2] Compare to a national median price of $211 000.

Diego was $1,254, a 100% increase from 1990. Combined with a low 4.4% rental vacancy rate, it is increasingly difficult to find an affordable home in the city. "We've dropped out of the top 20 on Forbes magazine's ranking of the best places for business and careers [. . .]. The primary factors: cost of living (we're sixth costliest out of 150) and cost of doing business (we're third costliest out of 150)."[3] In the past few years, San Diego has experienced a large job increase in leisure, hospitality, and food services. But because most of them are low-paying jobs, many workers were unable to find affordable housing in the area.

The shortage of affordable housing and more particularly its cost is not new to San Diego. It is correlated with the larger issue of urban growth management in an attractive metropolitan area. Since World War II, the "Navy Sleepy Town" has slowly transformed itself into a vibrant city with a diversified economy dominated by aerospace, electronics, military research, and tourism. In the early 1970s, the job creation rate was approximately 25,000 per year in the metropolitan area. As a result, the population of San Diego increased by 21% between 1960 and 1970 (696,769 inhabitants). In order to answer the growing demand for housing, parcels of land increasingly far from the central city were opened to construction, encouraging an increasingly incoherent urban sprawl beyond the city's boundaries (Calavita, 1992). The city of San Diego had an old tradition of city planning, as illustrated by the first two Comprehensive Plans designed by John Nolen in 1907 and in 1924. At that time, the debate over urban growth versus growth control had already become central not only to city planning but to election campaigns (Billard, 1999). Breaking with a pro-growth elite that had controlled the city for over half a century, Pete Wilson, elected mayor in 1971, put the issue of urban growth control on the agenda. He supported strong municipal government with powerful tools to control the location and density of new urban developments. Wilson followed two political strategies. First, he used state legislative opportunities to pass environmental protection measures and quality of life improvements. In 1974, Kevin Lynch and Donald Appleyard were appointed to prepare a study advocating a strict protection of the environment in accord with the California Environmental Quality Act (1970) and the California Coastal Act (1974). Second, Wilson used the population itself as a strategic tool. In 1974 for example, the city council adopted a thirty-foot height limit supported by the inhabitants of the coastal communities to limit constructions density. The mayor also relied on the support of community planning groups (CPG), the city council created in 1966. These groups of residents, gathered in nonprofit and nonpartisan organizations and still operating on about 50 planning areas today, often seek to preserve their quality of life against urban development.

By the end of the 1970s, this joint legislative and community influence led San Diego to experience a brutal drop in building permits, and housing vacancy reached a record low (1%), causing real estate prices to soar. This was an impor-

---

[3] Tom Blair, *San Diego Magazine*, July 2005.

tant political and social turn for San Diego because the city planning process still bore the weight of this legacy in 2007. Since the appointment of Pete Wilson to the senate in 1982, successive mayors (P. Wilson, R. Hedgecock, M. O' Connor, S. Golding, D. Murphy, and J. Sanders) have had to balance the interests of the private sector—some who were crucial in campaign founding—who favored deregulation, and homeowners who generally favor growth control and the limitation of new multifamily housing. The compromise was the adoption of a smart growth policy that does not limit growth but directs it towards urban areas (Billard, 2003). The Downtown Community Plan initiated by the Center City Development Corporation (CCDC) is a typical example of this process: today, downtown San Diego is "home to 30,000 residents and the population is anticipated to grow to almost 90,000 residents by 2030" (CCDC, 2007: 2). However, this urban renewal policy is inequitable: it often preserves stable and socially organized districts from urban change at the expense of more vulnerable minority and lower-middle class neighborhoods. This gentrification movement is best illustrated in the communities of Ocean Beach and Barrio Logan.

These two residential communities obviously have little in common except for being under the jurisdiction of the San Deigo city council and planning department. Ocean Beach had an 80% white population and a household median income of $49,082 in 2006. It is a typical peaceful, residential middle-class community by the Pacific Ocean. Barrio Logan, however, has a 90% Hispanic population. Its median household income is $30,375. Yet over the past three decades, both areas have undergone major urban and social change with little control by the residents, despite their involvement in the planning process and the actions of various community organizations. Officially introduced in San Diego in 1966, resident participation in the city planning process could have been able to influence the morphological and, by indirect impact, the social evolution of neighborhoods. The neighborhood planning process, which defines the urban morphology of an area, has the potential to ensure the sustained development of a community and to define the nature of community relations.

The importance of urban morphology has been emphasized in many studies conducted in the second half of the twentieth century in the United States, as cities ceased to be perceived as a global organism, and the individual became the center of the analysis (Williams, 1985). Influenced by the works of Lewis Mumford, Yates (1973) argued that the concept of neighborhood seemed to be the only practical response to the gigantism and inefficiency of the hyperconcentration of metropolis. At the beginning of the 1980s, Gates and Rohe (1985) mentioned that more than a third of U.S. cities over 500,000 inhabitants had already integrated residents into the process of city planning, by conducting development at the neighborhood scale. This systemization of the concept of community urban development in American cities raises two series of questions. First, what is the place given today to the concept of community in the United States? The community of interest seems to have supplanted the community of place (the neighborhood), the idealized urban variation of the pastoral community. Second, what place do the American people occupy today in the daily exercise of democracy and in the neighborhood planning process? Tocqueville praised citizen participation through community-based organizations. Nevertheless, there is a danger in confusing the values defended by the elite (including local) speaking in the name of the people and the values really conveyed by the average citizen (Billard, 1999). This study conducted in the communities of Ocean Beach and Barrio Logan highlights the concept of community in its spatial, social and political dimension. See Table 5.1 and Figure 5.1

Ocean Beach: White Resistance against White Gentrification

The community of Ocean Beach is located eight miles northwest of downtown San Diego, along the Pacific coast. It is a small, mainly residential area of 742 acres with 13,752 inhabitants in 2006. This community has been under pressure from two sources. The first is tourism: during the summer, up to 250,000 people daily go to the beach, famous for its fishing pier and surf spots. Beyond the problem of road congestion, this attraction has impacted the residential area.

At the beginning of the 20th century, Ocean Beach was a resort area composed of little summer cottages. After World War II, the morphology of the resort community started changing quickly as the arrival of a massive influx of workers put pressure on the housing stock. A rezoning process authorized the construction of small buildings (four or five stories) that made Ocean Beach the densest community of the coastal area. In the 1960s, a young, white and often student population moved to Ocean Beach, attracted by the beach lifestyle and affordable housing. The Bohemian way of life and a sometimes "contentious environment" gave the community a specific identity distinct from the conformism of the other coastal communities (e.g., La Jolla), and from the conservative political context of San Diego. However, the land pressure was so intense that the intrinsic qualities of the place (access to the beach, proximity of the downtown area, housing opportunities) quickly turned the community into a prime target for gentrification. This change in the housing structure of Ocean Beach and its social profile was accompanied by a form of community resistance that revealed the limits of resident involvement in urban planning.

Residents' Involvement in Community Planning

In 1968, the inhabitants of Ocean Beach had the opportunity to take part in the development of their first community plan. Unfortunately, organizational problems delayed the recognition of the area as a community planning area. In

Table 5.1. Barrio Logan and Ocean Beach General Profile, 2006

Community Planning Area	Pop. 2000	Pop. 2006	Pop. Change 2000-2006	White 2006	Hispanic 2006	Median Age 2006	Median House-hold Income 2006
Barrio Logan	3,636	3,896	7.2%	7.7%	89.9%	27.7%	$30,365
Ocean Beach	13,656	13,752	0.7%	80.6%	10.2%	36.3%	$49,082
City of San Diego	1,223,400	1,311,162	7.2%	46.6%	27%	26.9%	$61,043

Source: U.S. Census 2006.

1972, the creation of the Ocean Beach Implementation Planning Group[4] made (OBIPG) the urban planning partnership between the community and the municipality official. However, the institutionalization of a partnership does not guarantee efficiency. The social make-up of Ocean Beach quickly proved to be a barrier to the implementation of effective community participation. At the time, a strong concentration of hippies hostile to any kind of government control lived in the neighborhood. The slogan "U.S. out of Ocean Beach"—the rallying sign of some of the residents—illustrated this rebellion. This rejection of any public authority limited, in a contagious manner, the process of vertical integration inherent to the community planning process.

Community participation radicalized the residents and led to more spectacular and tough actions. They responded to housing rehabilitation projects or the opening of franchised stores with sit-ins, mass demonstrations, vandalism, and illegal occupation of building sites. After 1975, the movement faded and a plan was adopted.[5] The 1975 plan, San Diego's oldest planning document, underlined the lack of community control of beach use. Moreover, in accord with the California Coastal Act, measures were taken to limit erosion of the beach, fix the parking congestion, and reduce building densities. Even if this last policy guaranteed the control of demographic growth in the community, it did nothing to regulate rent increases.

Some sort of fatalism can be detected in the speeches of community leaders in the early 1980s, contrasting with their spectacular actions over the previous decade. Urban change in Ocean Beach was bound to happen in the future no matter what, and it would be better to model these changes rather than start a never-ending struggle (Casing, 1993). For example, after a 10-year battle, a 7-Eleven store and a Kentucky Fried Chicken restaurant were finally built. But public mobilization started again in 1983 when the city council agreed to allow

---

[4] Today: Ocean Beach Board Planning.

[5] In 1975, Ocean Beach was part of the Peninsula Community Planning Area and under the control of the Peninsula Inc. (Community Planning Group).

Figure 5.1. Map of the Study Area

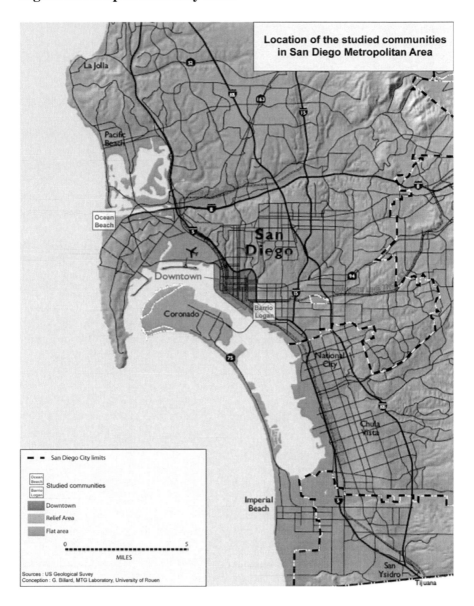

higher density buildings in several areas. At first, the OBIBG board of directors supported this rezoning but, during the public hearing, 49 residents (out of the 55 who spoke) firmly opposed the project and won. This victory for the preservation of the existing quality of life in the community further encouraged the gentrification process by compressing the housing market. Moreover, at urging of the California Coastal Commission, Ocean Beach prepared its own local coastal land use plan in 1985 with no input from the neighbors. According to the recommendations of the California Coastal Act, the preservation of the community landscape led to a reduction in building densities, which inevitably induced a rise in the price of real estate because the area was increasingly attractive. Without any external regulation, the private market was unlikely to serve the interests of the community. By acting to protect their quality of life, some residents thus indirectly accelerated gentrification. On the contrary, the Ocean Beach Merchants Association obtained some funds to revitalize Newport Beach, the main commercial street, and succeeded in maintaining the maximum number of community stores (nonfranchise), which is generally a central element to strengthening social links within a community. This strategy was difficult to apply because another nonprofit organization (Ocean Beach Front Improvement Committee) wanted to develop beach-oriented business activities instead.

At a time when the new policy of city planning was based on the principle of a "city of villages,"[6] Ocean Beach seemed to represent the archetype of a community with a strong spatial and social identity: a relatively restricted and enclosed territory, some community-oriented retails, iconographic public spaces (a main street—Newport Avenue, the pier, the beach) and an important activist legacy. If we consider that the presence of 10 associations testifies to the intensity of social life within a community, the case of Ocean Beach illustrates, just like the Barrio, the existing gap between strong community participation and its real capacities to control its destiny.

Lessons from Ocean Beach

Affordable housing has been the main concern for the inhabitants of Ocean Beach. The stability of the real estate market is often a determining element in the maintenance of a community identity. But the OBIPG cannot really fight global urban change. In 2006, the median income per capita and per annum of the inhabitants of Ocean Beach amounted to $49,082, far from the average for the city of San Diego ($61,043). But for 10 years, this median income had experienced an estimated 29.1% increase. The median contract rent grew by 30% between 1990 and 2000,[7] a revealing sign of the social evolution of the commu-

---

[6] City of San Diego, *General Plan: The City of Villages*, Final Public Review Draft, October 2006, 452.

[7] Median contract rent in 2000 = $ 711.

nity. This increase was four points higher than the growth of median contract rent in the city of San Diego. Far from the cheap real estate opportunities of the 1970s, the average contract rent in Ocean Beach is now similar to that in San Diego. Besides, the median housing value is around $269,753 (census 2000) that is to say approximately $30,000 above the median housing value in the entire city of San Diego. More precisely, it is difficult today to find a detached house for sale at less than $460,000, and prices can climb up to more than $3 million.[8]

Community leaders have always been aware that Ocean Beach needed a more sustainable collective mobilization: "if you snooze, you lose!"[9] But the community hardly believes in a vertical integration in the city planning process. The rate of multiple family housing (61% in 2000) and renters (83%) does not facilitate residents long-range involvement. Moreover, the nonconformist legacy of the community as well as some victories registered through mass demonstrations [10] reinforce the idea that collective actions in the streets better match the profile of the residents. For 20 years, the community movement in Ocean Beach has remained active despite a continued turnover among the residents: it proves the deeply rooted sense of collective identity (Pryde, 1993). A slogan on some license plates reads: "Ocean Beach is not an address, it's an attitude."

The few victories obtained through specific demonstrations by community organizations do not compensate for their difficulty anticipating urban changes on the long term. Residents massively mobilized during periods of crises when the community was directly threatened. It is obviously a positive point that shows that the defense of the community interest is a reality in Ocean Beach. However, the relative failures of the first community plan (1975) and its updated versions to preserve more particularly the diversity of housing, shows the complexity for the leaders of developing a real culture in urban planning. Indeed, this exercise does not live on collective enthusiasm only. As the study of another community of San Diego (La Jolla) shows, a high level of education and high financial resources are often good assets when confronting the long technical process of city planning.[11] The case of La Jolla also proves the importance of individual and professional networks. Contrary to La Jolla, Ocean Beach does not have the capacity to negotiate back stage at City Hall. It is essential to differentiate between the theory of community planning and its daily political practice.

---

[8] 140 listed homes for sale, *zipreality.com*

[9] Caldwell Orb, Community leader, *The Obecian*, April-May 1997.

[10] In 1996, after a demonstration of 800 people, the creation of Saratoga Park on the sea front is accepted by the municipality of San Diego after 14 years of fight!

[11] G. Billard (1999), *Citoyenneté, planification et gouvernement urbains aux Etats-Unis*, Paris, L'Harmattan.

The Mexican Barrio:
Latino Activism against White Gentrification

As it faces rapid gentrification, the Mexican barrio of San Diego has become a symbolic place to study how minority communities can challenge, protest, or resist power relations in a global and dual city (Sassen, 1991; Mollenkopf and Castells, 1991). Although Chicano residential patterns have spread far beyond the original barrio and have expanded to suburban areas such as San Ysidro, Chula Vista, and National City, Barrio Logan remains a focal point to study minority politics (Griswold del Castillo, 2007). In fact, the significant demographic shift experienced in San Diego, now a majority-minority city with Latinos and Asians being the two main groups, has paradoxically provoked both a decline in the traditional barrio, as well as a revival of its social, political, and cultural significance.[12] Chicanos constitute now the largest ethnic group in San Diego. This translates into increased demands for political representation and for resources to resolve community issues, focusing in particular on the reconstruction of the barrio (affordable housing, environmental hazards, recreation places, economic development, transportation systems, and social infrastructure).

San Diego's inner-city barrio, located southeast of downtown, is composed of three specific spatial zones: Barrio Logan, Logan Heights, and Sherman Heights. They are home to approximately 40,000 inhabitants, with about 70% of the population made up of Latinos (primarily of Mexican origin, up to 90% for Barrio Logan only) and about 40% living below the poverty level, following the trend of an increase in Latino poverty in the U.S.[13] (Iceland, 2006). Unemployment rates in San Diego's barrio are more than threefold those for the entire city, and the median household income is less than half the median income for the city ($30,375 versus $61,043). Education levels are extremely low, which also adversely affects involvement in politics. Census data report a set of negative predicaments accounting for much of the political disenfranchisement. Two-thirds of the residents are native born, whereas one-third are foreign born. Among the foreign-born population, only 22% are naturalized citizens. Access to the electoral process is thus limited to a fraction of the residents. Both at the local and state levels, voter registration and turnout are extremely low. For instance, voter turnout for city council elections in District 8, which encompasses

---

[12] "Barrios in these and other cities are still a convenient distance from the civic center and suburban areas. The demographic transition has not been completed. Extended family members maintain residence in these barrios, thus continuing a historic lineage with the middle class in suburbs," in D. Diaz (2005), *Barrio Urbanism. Chicanos, Planning and American Cities*. New York, Routledge, 247.

[13] "As of 2000, 11.3% of the population was poor, according to the official measure. Poverty rates are higher when using either the NAS (13.8%) or relative measure (17%). While 7.5% of the non-Hispanic white population was poor, according to official measure, a little over a fifth of both African Americans and Hispanics were poor," in J. Iceland (2006), *Poverty in America*, Berkeley, University of California Press, 41.

the barrio, ranged from 7% to 36% of the registered voters over the past 20 years. In addition, a significant segment of the barrio population does not have legal immigration status.

San Diego is also peculiar because of its location on the border, its stability, and limited openness to minority politics. General absenteeism and Republican Party dominance have been unchallenged (Davis, 2003). Mayor Pete Wilson, former governor of California known for his anti-immigrant stances, and Mayors Hedgecock, Murphy, and Sanders have favored little diversity at the city level. Until the 1990s, power relations had been clearly set up on to exclude formally and then indirectly minorities from politics. Since then, however, in addition to the demographic changes, a reform of the electoral charter took place in 1992 in order to create a redistricting commission after each decennial census. The redistricting has led to a better representation of minorities at the municipal district level. In fact, District 8 is now owned by candidates of Mexican origin, who often refer to the barrio, specifically to Chicano Park, as the source of their commitment to the Latino community. Chicano Park was founded in 1971 by a community "take over" of the land during the Chicano Movement peak in San Diego. See Table 5.2

But conversely to what appears to be increasing minority political participation, the system actually offers only a symbolic visibility to minorities. The fact that no substantial redistricting occurred after the 2000 Census shows the local reluctance to open the political opportunity structures to ethnic groups. The districts remain "ghost districts," meaning statistically majority-minority districts, but in reality mainly Anglo voter districts. As a consequence, ethnic candidates compete with each other for the single reachable position. There is an institutionalization of minority exclusion and of power rotation among the Latino elite: Ralph Inzunza was replaced by Benjamin Hueso (District 8, municipal); Juan Vargas (District 79, state assembly) and Denise Moreno-Ducheny (District 40, state senate) "represent" the Latino constituency. So the barrio is not really at the core of conventional politics, but Mexicans and Mexican-origin residents use symbolic resources such as territorial identity and solidarity to help politicize a socially isolated and changing urban space.

Political deficiency is certainly a complex phenomenon, but excluded groups get involved in different ways. Gentrification has become a mobilizing agenda for Mexican and Mexican-origin residents. The constitution of new forms of activism, such as social networks based on gender solidarity and territorial identity, extend the definition of social capital in determining participation at the neighborhood level. Nevertheless, the traditional tools of evaluation of political participation (such as electoral behavior, political parties, unions, formal organizations, etc.), miss some forms of participation chosen by excluded people. It is thus necessary to explore the day-to-day political experiences (de

Table 2. Elected Officials and Candidates in District 8 (1991-2006)

Date	Name	Votes	%
10/01/2006	**Ben Hueso****	6 408	70.60
	Luis Acle	2 600	28.65
08/11/2005***	**Ben Hueso**	7 439	38.38
	Luis Acle	3 619	18.67
	Remigia Bermudez	3 001	15.48
	Dan Coffey	1 587	8.19
05/03/2002	**Ralph Inzunza***	6 103	69.90
	Yolanda Escamilla	2 620	30.00
27/02/2001	**Ralph Inzunza***	4 759	62.10
	Richard Babcok	714	9.32
	Rafael Ramirez	606	7.91
	David Gomez	325	4.24
	Christian Ramirez	238	3.11
02/09/1998	**Juan Vargas***	8 666	76.51
	David Gomez	2 660	23.49
19/09/1995	**Juan Vargas***	2 596	100
21/09/1993	**Juan Vargas****	2 778	100
16/02/1993	Juan Vargas	2 534	28.62
	Mike Aguirre	2 033	22.96
	Francisco Estrada	1 361	15.37
17/09/1991	**Bob Filner***	5 507	70.28
	Andrea Palacios	2 055	26.23

Sources: San Diego City Clerk Archives.
* Elected first round.
**Elected second round.
***Special elections after City Counselor Ralph Inzunza's renunciation.

Certeau, 1990; Scott, 1990[14]), as they define or defend a certain type of social organization (the barrio) and a collective identity (*la comunidad*). This leads to an analysis of less visible forms of political participation and to a refining of what is active citizenship in ethnic neighborhoods. That's why as far as method-

---

[14] "For a social science attuned to the relatively open politics of liberal democracies, and to loud, headline-grabbing protests, demonstrations, and rebellions, the circumspect struggle waged daily by subordinate groups is, like infrared rays, beyond the visible end of the spectrum. That it should be invisible, as we have seen, is in large part by design—a tactical choice born of a prudent awareness of the balance of power,", in J. Scott (1990), *Domination and the Arts of Resistance. Hidden Transcripts*, New Haven: Yale University Press, 183.

ology is concerned, an ethnographic study[15] was conducted in the barrio from August 2002 to February 2004: observation of community meetings, cultural events, political demonstrations, and marches; participation in daily community life at different stages and levels (voluntary work, citizenship classes). In addition to participatory observation, 98 semistructured interviews were completed with community leaders, members of organizations, elected officials, and governmental agencies' representatives involved in the barrio and 18 life-story interviews with nonmobilized residents. More than a hundred informal discussions took place during the fieldwork. Local newspapers and archives from the San Diego City Redevelopment Agency for a 12-year period, from 1991 to 2003, were examined. Finally, phone interviews were conducted on an occasional basis from 2005 to 2007.

Gentrification and Activism in Barrio Logan

Urban planning for the barrio has been framed without taking into account the opinion of the residents. During the 1960s and 1970s, residents engaged in opposition movements to protest land use, freeway construction, and community dismantling, especially with the creation of Chicano Park in the Barrio Logan. It is only since the late 1980s and early 1990s that planners and elected officials have started seeking consensus and asking for community input (Le Texier, 2005). Nevertheless, residents are still not seen as important stakeholders in discussions concerning the revitalization of their neighborhood. As stated by Diaz: "Planners defined the urban cartel and real estate industry as their main clients rather than the lower-income communities. Lower-income communities were stigmatized as an underclass with limited comprehension of technical aspects of revitalization" (Diaz, 2005: 194). Today, new forms of activism are emerging in the neighborhood because of conflicting views on social space, gentrification,[16] and land-use control.

These new forms of activism are a way to resist power relations and claim equality of treatment (Valle and Torres, 2000). San Diego's local government initiated the process of urban renewal in the late 1960s. The "redevelopment," "revitalization," and "beautification" programs started with major investments in the downtown area. These programs transformed the downtown area into an entertainment and commercial area (cafés, restaurants, shopping malls, movie theatres). The construction of the Padres Ball Park accelerated the gentrification.

---

[15] E. Le Texier (2006), *Quand les exclus font de la politique. Le barrio mexicain de San Diego*, Californie, Paris, Presses de Sciences Po.

[16] Gentrification is the process "by which poor and working-class neighborhoods in the inner city [neighborhoods that have previously experienced disinvestment and a middle class exodus] are refurbished via an influx of private capital and middle-class homebuyers and renters," in N. Smith and P. Williams (1986), *Gentrification of the City*, Boston: Allen and Unwin, 32.

The city adopted the so-called City of Villages urban plan to promote a "smart growth" approach that focuses on redeveloping "historically or culturally distinct communities" (Gale, 1984; Smith and Williams, 1996). The complexity of gentrification is reflected in the changing discourse of media (*San Diego Union Tribune*) and public officials about the San Diego "poor inner-city area." The metaphors have shifted from the barrio as a "gang-plagued neighborhood" to a "vibrant residential community." An optimistic vision stresses the revitalization of neighborhoods through ethnic mixing and private investments. But a pessimistic approach would rather link beautification projects with a form of "cleaning up" (also labeled "strategy of containment") that evicts minorities from a historically Mexican-origin space. In fact, part of the barrio was turned into a redevelopment project area. In 1998, residents started suffering from a sharp increase in rents, eviction, and displacement. In fact, the data show that 80% of San Diego's inner-city barrio residents are renters. More than half of the barrio population spends over a third of their household income in gross rent; with over a quarter of the population paying for housing with more than half of their income. Because recent urban changes threaten residents both individually by displacement and collectively by the disappearance of the community, gentrification constitutes a mobilizing agenda.

The example of some community organizations' activities illustrates the forms of activism that emerge. For example, in 2000, barrio residents created DURO, Developing Unity through Resident Organizing (in Spanish, *Desarrollando Unidad a Través de Residentes Organizados*) an almost exclusively female grassroot group. A loose voluntary association of first and second-generation women and students of Mexican origin composed DURO. Among other things, the organization is dedicated to the defense of barrio renters against forced and unlawful evictions. The association asks for low-income and affordable housing units, and promotes community input for the use of vacant lots in the barrio. As one flyer states, members "who work or were born and raised in the communities of Logan Heights and Sherman Heights (gathered) to dialogue about signs of gentrification that seemed to have gained momentum with the Ballpark development and the downtown redevelopment efforts."

Community meetings were held either in private homes or in the local Sherman Community Center. The first "victory" of the movement happened when a DURO member won an eviction court hearing in May 2001. Different activities started, such as door-to-door contacts, bilingual flyer distribution on tenant's rights and responsibilities, petitions for rent stabilization, and community meetings and marches. For instance, on June 30, 2001, over a hundred residents participated in a march to protest displacement.[17] Another march entitled a

---

[17] Yvette Tenberge, "Ballpark Dream Leaves Residents Homeless," in *La Prensa San Diego*, July 13, 2001; "Renters Crying Foul Ball Over Proposed Ballpark," in *La Prensa San Diego*, July 6, 2001; Leonel Sanchez, "March to put focus on rising rents, displacement," in *San Diego Union Tribune*, June 30, 2001.

Trail of Tears March (*Caminata de Lágrimas*) took place, and bilingual slogans stated: "We are organizing to claim our human right to housing. Our inherent dignity is being violated"; "Make your Voices heard"; "Here we are, and we will not move"; "Uniting is strength"; "Unite to our community effort." The association attempted to raise consciousness about the housing problem during city council meetings but received only limited media coverage, mostly from local Spanish-language or bilingual media (*La Prensa San Diego, Frontera*). In 2002, the organization tried to build up coalitions and networks with other groups, but the mobilization began to decrease due to the lack of results and organizational skills. In 2003, DURO started to meet on a regular basis, addressing the specific issue of the use of vacant lots in the barrio, as well as low-income/affordable housing projects. The results were limited but set a new political agenda in local politics.

Another example is the Chicano Park Steering Committee, Unión del Barrio and Raza Rights Coalition, which are intimately related organizations led by former Chicano activists involved in the Chicano movement and a new generation of educated first- and second-generation youth of Mexican origin, who inherited from the discourse of emancipation. All organizations have limited but extremely politicized and organized activists advocating for identity recognition and equality of rights at the national and local level, as mentioned in their statement: "We invite all honest people who will no longer live their lives being ashamed of being Mexicano or Mexicana but are willing to plug into concrete struggle to better our community for ourselves and by ourselves, today."[18] They have helped to the politicize the issue of housing and gentrification, as well as other issues (such as regularization for undocumented immigrants, police racial profiling, border control, etc.). Several marches were organized, one of them during children's day with parents and children. Although poorly covered by the local English-speaking media but better by bilingual or Spanish-speaking media, the marches are moments of territorial and ethnic identity formation—and political socialization. They allow residents to voice their concern using the public space and marking it by their presence. Another symbolic event was the pressure put on the local government to call a barrio street "César Chávez Avenue," from the name of the former Chicano leader of the United Farm Workers union. This struggle gave residents a sense of pride and community. The last example is the community preservation of Chicano Park, created in 1970 by community take over (*la tierra mía*, my land). Every year, the Chicano Park Steering Committee[19] celebrates this "victory" by gathering activists, local artists, and hundreds of residents to create a sense of common belonging around a common cultural heritage (Chicano murals and history). The last celebration on April 21, 2007 voiced concerns about gentrification in the presence of media and elected offi-

---

[18] http://uniondelbarrio.org
[19] http://chicano-park.org

cials: Sal Barajas, a muralist and activist noted that: "in the past, the committee has addressed bilingual education, police brutality and pollution of San Diego Bay. Gentrification and unattractive development are issues that might be taken up in the future."[20] The new elected official of District 8, Benjamin Hueso, has family roots in the barrio and refers to it constantly, indicating the importance of territorial and ethnic identity.

Lessons from the Mexican Barrio

Latino activism is essentially linked to gentrification for two main reasons: the neighborhood is highly invested with social meanings of the community; and domestic and community space are intertwined in Latinos' actions. By questioning the traditional dichotomy established between private and public spheres, civic involvement in grassroots associations provide more benefits than the limited entry into conventional politics.

First, residents' narratives constantly illustrate two conflicting visions of space that is social versus abstract representations (Lefebvre, 1974). In fact, elected officials, developers, institutional representatives, and media discourses present the barrio as a material space, a product of costs and benefits. The terms revitalization, beautification, revival, clean up, and redevelopment are metaphors of the reification of the barrio territory. A district representative expresses her perception in these terms: "In terms of issues, I think housing is what my constituents are worried about, the first issue they are concerned about, to beautify the areas, such as Barrio Logan and Sherman Heights." Redevelopment projects are conceived as a privatization of the space, carried out through rhetoric of progress and security, the stigmatization of the homeless population, and claims for ethnic and economic diversity. On the contrary, representations of barrio activists recall that the neighborhood is a product of common history whose memory has to be passed on to next generations. Living in the neighborhood means a need to preserve the community's cultural specificity.

Second, residents feel attachment to this territory, because—simply stated—living in a Mexican barrio means something important to them (Hardy-Fanta, 1993; Hondagneu-Sotelo, 1994). One activist stated: "The rent is increasing a lot. Then there is no home anymore for low-income people [. . .]. This is not fair. This is a very old community, a Latino community, for Latino people, and it is not good that Americans come here. Because every community has its own thing, right?" Opposite types of representations show how some individuals seek to maximize the exchange value of the space whereas others emphasize its intrinsic value. This is why the struggle against gentrification is not only a

---

[20] Jennifer Vigil, "Celebration Honors Chicano Park," *San Diego Union Tribune*, April 22, 2007.

struggle for the defense of a physical space but for a definition of symbolic boundaries (Barth, 1969) and collective identity. Resistance to gentrification is a defense of private homes against eviction and rent increase, but also a defense of the overall community. Not only are homes being destroyed and renters being evicted, but vacant lots, public parks, community centers, and the character of the streets are being redefined by gentrification. In this respect housing and living conditions affected by increasing household costs are a key issue for collective participation and politicization. As a consequence, activists link the private and the public spheres. By doing so, they reinvent forms of participation, dialogue, and political activism that extend beyond the family space. If gentrification threatens the public space, it also overlaps with the domestic place, and vice versa.

Contemporary changes deeply affect the political organization of California cities, and urban change imposed in a top-down approach does create a space for ethnic and political mobilization. Although it remains more informal, Latinos do struggle at the neighborhood level to protest unequal changes, and claim rights in a political structure that limits minority electoral representation and foster territorial identity.

The Mexican Barrio and Oceanside:
A Surprising Comparison

Extensive qualitative fieldwork in the two San Diego neighborhoods shows that urban restructuring and gentrification are being fought, although in two radically different communities, with different and similar implications.

Both communities create a strong territorial and community identity. Community residents tend to construct similar views of the world and of the situation in which they are embedded. The social ties built in the mobilization against urban change increase the likelihood for common ideas, values, interests, and identities, which are the basis for collective action (Putnam, 2001). As a consequence, informal sociability builds up relations of trust and reciprocity. The concept of social capital is useful to understand how participation emerges in these neighborhoods. In a white, middle-class community, as well as in an ethnic enclave, where social networks are supposedly truncated because of distrust and lack of contacts with external social networks (Fernández-Kelly, 1995; Body-Gendrot and Gitell, 2003), solidarity establishes bonding forms of social capital.[21]

---

[21] "Social capital is all about the value of social networks, bonding similar people and bridging between diverse people, with norms of reciprocity. Social capital is fundamentally about how people interact with each other," in P. Dekker and E. Uslaner (2001), *Social Capital and Participation in Everyday Life*, New York: Routledge, 3.

The difference relies on the fact that in Ocean Beach, activists have a way to create forms of bridging social capital, which allow them to build coalitions with other groups and to enter into formal politics, whereas entry into formal politics is strictly limited for Latinos. That is due to the lack of political opportunity structure in San Diego. Both communities share experiences, cultural practices, and memory of past history and collective identities, and they both transmit the repertoires of collective action inherited from past struggles or mobilization. In the Mexican barrio, for instance, the constant reference to the establishment of Chicano Park (*la tierra mía*) by community control of the public land during the Chicano Movement, socializes residents into specific references of successful community demands. Even if idealized, romanticized, or reconstructed, the collective memory is passed on to generations: "Ocean Beach is not an address, it's an attitude.

Shared concerns about housing and community boundaries similarly serve to mobilize residents. They reinforce the politicization of residents and reduce the costs of participation. On the one hand, though the Mexican barrio is not at the core of conventional politics, unorthodox forms of participation are present. In fact, Mexican-origin residents use symbolic resources such as territorial identity and ethnic solidarity to politicize their neighborhood. This is not an idealized vision of segregated spaces where collective action can easily emerge, but an argument for the existence and transformation of ethnic resources into political ones. These informal politics might also turn to more formal although limited political representation. Residents of white, middle-class Ocean Beach are inclined to use territorial resources as well, but rely also on class identification, as they can explore an entry into formal politics to voice their claims. For instance, they participated in the Ocean Beach Board Planning and other institutionalized forums.

But actually, coming from different strategies and resources, the concrete results and power of these two communities might be quite surprising. Neighborhood activism in the Mexican barrio shows that active citizenship can result from "noncitizens or denizens" (undocumented individuals) and "second-class citizens" (excluded individuals), as well as "full citizens." Minority politics encounters obstacles, and concrete changes are still awaited. Vertical networks are missing, but resistance is present and might spill over the formal politics. A strong collective identity is built on and ensures a more common political discourse against gentrification. Ocean beach residents' activism might be less cohesive in their approach to urban change, since conflicting interests appeared between the merchants and the inhabitants. Although more able to voice their concerns in the San Diego political structure, divisions might hamper their demands.

The comparison is thus surprising, because low-income communities can try to resist urban change as well as white, middle-class communities, although based on different tactics and resources. Nevertheless, both neighborhoods show little power in front of developers, gentrifiers, and local political interests that have been developed since the 1980s in San Diego. Could solidarity between the two communities possibly emerge? And could neighborhood-based activism build vertical networks and bridge a common front to urban changes? The San Diego, *nihil novo sub soli*, is probably coming to an end.

References

Ackelsberg, Martha. 2003. "Broadening the Study of Women's Participation." In *Women and American Politics*, ed. Susan Carroll. New York: Oxford University Press.

Alba, Richard, John Logan, and Brian Stults. 2000. "The Changing Neighborhood Contexts of the Immigrant Metropolis." *Social Forces* 79: 587–621.

Barth, Freferik. 1969. Ethnic Groups and Boundaries: The Social Organization of Cultural Differences. London: Allen & Unwin.

Becker, Howard. 1986. *Doing Things Together*. Evanston: Northwestern University Press.

Billard, Gérald. 2003, "Les grandes villes-centres des Etats-Unis face au défi actuel de la métropolisation." *Espace Population et Sociétés*, No. thématique: diversité des populations d'Amérique du Nord, no. 1: 51–63.

———. 1999. "Citoyenneté, planification et gouvernement urbains aux Etats-Unis: des communautés dans la ville. " Paris: L'Harmattan.

Body-Gendrot, Sophie, and Marylin Gittell. 2003. *Social Capital and Social Citizenship*. Lanham: Lexington Books.

Bourdieu, Pierre, and James Coleman. 1991. *Social Theory for a Changing Society*. Boulder: Westview Press.

Burns, Nancy, Kathy Lehman, and Sidney Verba. 2001. *The Private Roots of Public Action. Gender, Equality, and Political Participation*. Cambridge: Harvard University Press.

Calavita, Nico. 1992. "Growth Machines and Ballot Box Planning: The San Diego Case." *Journal of Urban Affairs*, Jai Press Inc., vol. 0 14, no. 1: 1–24.

Centre City Development Corporation. 2007. *Downtown Living Guide*.

U.S. Census Bureau. 2006.

Certeau, Michel (de). 1990. *L'invention du quotidien*. Paris: Gallimard.

City of San Diego. 2003. 2002–2004 Community and Economic Development Strategy. http://www.sannet.gov.

———. 2006. *General Plan: The City of Villages*. Final Public Review Draft, October.

Davis, Mike, Kelly Mayhew, and Jim Miller. 2003. *Under the Perfect Sun. The San Diego Tourists Never See*. New York: New Press.

Dekker, Paul, and Erik Uslaner. 2001. *Social Capital and Participation in Everyday Life*. New York: Routledge.

Diaz, David. 2005. Barrio Urbanism. Chicanos, Planning, and American Cities. New York: Routledge.

Edwards, Bob, and Michael Fowley. 1998. "Beyond Tocqueville: Civil Society and Social Capital in Comparative Perspective." *American Behavioral Scientist* 42(1).

Frazier, John, et al. 2003. *Race and Place*. Boulder: Westview.

Gale, Dennis. 1984. *Neighborhood Revitalization and the Postindustrial City: A Multinational Perspective*. Lexington: Lexington Books.

Gans, Herbert. 1962. *The Urban Villagers*. New York: The Free Press.

Garcia, John. 2003. *Latino Politics in America.* New York: Rowman and Littlefield.

Garcia Bedolla, Lisa. 2005. *Fluid Borders. Latino Power, Identity, and Politics in Los Angeles.* Berkeley, University of California Press.

Gates, L., and W. Rohe. 1985. *Planning with Neighborhoods*, Chapel Hill: The University of North Carolina Press, 149–67.

Gotham, Kevin. 2001. *Critical Perspectives on Urban Redevelopment.* Amsterdam: JAI.

Grebler, Leo, and Joan Moore. 1970. The Mexican American People. The Nation's Second Largest Minority. New York: The Free Press.

Griswold del Castillo (ed.). 2007. *Chicano San Diego.* Austin: University of Arizona Press.

Grix, Jonathan. 2001. "Social Capital as a Concept in the Social Sciences: The Current State of the Debate." *Democratization* 8(3): 189–210.

Gurr, Ted. 1970. *Why Men Rebel.* Princeton: Princeton University Press.

Hardy-Fanta, Carol. 1993. Latina Politics, Latino Politics: Gender, Culture, and Political Participation in Boston. Philadelphia: Temple University Press.

Hondagneu-Sotelo, Pierrette. 1994. *Gendered Transitions: Mexican Experiences of Immigration.* Berkeley: University of California Press.

Hondagneu-Sotelo, Pierrette (ed.). 2003. *Gender and U.S. Immigration: Contemporary Trends.* Berkeley: University of California Press.

Iceland, John. 2006. *Poverty in America.* Berkeley: University of California Press.

Jargowsky, Paul. 1997. *Poverty and Place. Ghettos, Barrios and the American City.* New York: Russell Sage Foundation.

Jones-Correa, Michael. 1998. "Different Paths: Gender, Immigration and Political Participation." *International Migration Review* 32(2): 326–49.

Katz, Michael. 1993. *The Underclass Debate: Views from History.* Princeton: Princeton University Press.

Klandermans, Bert, and Dirk Oegema. 1987. "Potentials, Networks, Motivations, and Barriers: Steps Toward Participation in Social Movements." *American Sociological Review* 52: 519–31.

Lamphere, Louise, Helena Ragoné, and Patricia Zavella. 1997. *Situated Lives: Gender and Culture in Everyday Life.* New York: Routledge.

Lefebvre, Henri. 1974. *La production de l'espace.* Paris: Anthropos.

Le Texier, Emmanuelle. 2005. "Minorités et espace public dans la ville. Le 'Chicano Park' à San Diego (Californie)," in *Espaces et Sociétés* 123(3): 10–28.

Le Texier, Emmanuelle. 2006. "Quand les exclus font de la politique. Le barrio mexicain de San Diego, Californie. " Paris: Presses de Sciences Po.

Lewis, Oscar. 1968. "The Culture of Poverty." In *On Understanding Poverty*, ed. Daniel Moynihan. New York: Basic Books.

Logan, John, Richard Alba, and Wenquan Zhang. 2002. "Immigrant enclaves and ethnic communities in New York and Los Angeles." *American Sociological Review* 67: 299–322.

Massey, Douglas, and Nancy Denton. 1993. *American Apartheid: Segregation and the Making of the Underclass.* Cambridge: Harvard University Press.

Melville, Margarita. 1980. *Twice a Minority. Mexican American Women.* St Louis: Mosby.

Meyer, David, Nancy Whittier, and Belinda Robnett. 2002. *Social Movements: Identity, Culture, and the State.* Oxford: Oxford University Press.

Mollenkopf, John, and Manuel Castells. 1991. *Dual City. Restructuring New York.* New York: Russell Sage Foundation.

Moore, Joan, and Raquel Pinderhughes. 1993. *In the Barrios. Latinos and the Underclass Debate.* New York: Russel Sage Foundation.

Oboler, Suzanne. 1995. Ethnic Labels, Latino Lives. Identity and the Politics of Re(Presentation) in the United States. Minneapolis: University of Minnesota Press.

Ochoa, Gilda. 2004. Becoming Neighbors in a Mexican American Community: Power, Conflict, and Solidarity. Austin: University of Texas Press.

Pardo, Mary. 1998. Mexican American Women Activists: Identity and Resistance in Two Los Angeles Communities. Philadelphia: Temple University Press.

Piven, Frances, and Richard Cloward. 1979. *Poor People's Movements: Why They Succeed, How They Fail.* New York: Vintage Books.

Press, Daniel. 2002. *Saving Open Space.* Berkeley: University of California Press.

Pryde, Philip. 1992. *San Diego: An Introduction to the Region*, 3d ed. Dubuque: Kendall/Hunt Publishing Company.

Putnam, Robert. 2000. Bowling Alone: The Collapse and Revival of American Community. New York: Simon and Schuster.

Rocco, Raymond. 1999. "The Formation of Latino Citizenship in Southeast Los Angeles." *Citizenship Studies* 3(2): 253–66.

Ruiz, Vicki. 1998. From the Shadows: Mexican Women in Twentieth Century America. New York: Oxford University Press.

Scott, James. 1990. Domination and the Arts of Resistance: Hidden Transcripts. New Haven: Yale University Press.

Smith, Neil, and Peter Williams. 1986. *Gentrification of the City.* Boston: Allen and Unwin.

Smith, Neil. 1996. The New Urban Frontier: Gentrification and the Revanchist City. New York: Routledge.

Squires, Gregory (ed.). 2002. *Urban Sprawl.* Washington, Urban Institute Press.

Stokes, Atiya. 2003. "Latino Group Consciousness and Political Participation." *American Politics Research* 31: 361–78.

Tarrow, Sidney. 1994. *Power in Movement: Social Movements and Contentious Politics.* Cambridge: Cambridge University Press.

Tocqueville, A. 1835–40. *De la démocratie en Amérique (1835–1840): les grands thèmes*, ed. J. P. Mayer (1968). Paris: Gallimard.

Valle, Victor, and Rodolfo Torres. 2000. *Latino Metropolis.* Minneapolis: University of Minnesota Press.

Verba, Sidney, and Kay Lehman. 1993. "Race, Ethnicity, and Political Resources: Participation in the United States." *British Journal of Political Science* 23: 453–99.

Wilson, Julius. 1987. The Truly Disadvantaged: The Inner City, the Underclass, and Public Policy. Chicago: University of Chicago Press.

Sassen, Saskia. 1991. *The Global City*. Princeton: Princeton University Press.

———. 2005. "The Repositioning of Citizenship and Alienage: Emergent Subjects and Spaces for Politics." *Globalizations* 2(1): 79–94.

Williams, Michael. 1985. Neighborhood Organizations: Seed of a New Urban Life. Westport: Greenwood Press.

Yates, D. 1973. Neighborhood Democracy: The Politic and Impact of Decentralisation. Mass.: Lexington Books.

Chapter 6

The Geopolitical Transition of Oakland

Frédérick Douzet

After a very tight race, in June 2006 Ron Dellums, a retired black congressman in his 70s, was elected mayor of Oakland against Ignacio De La Fuente, a long-time Latino union leader and city council member. Coming a few months after Antonio Villaraigosa became the first Latino mayor of Los Angeles, Dellums' victory brought sighs of relief in the African-American community. Not another major Californian city would go to the Latinos.

Despite the election of Ron Dellums, the balance of power has dramatically changed over the past decade in Oakland. The city once governed by a black mayor with a majority black city council based on a biracial white progressive-black coalition has now become multicultural, forcing the black leadership to adapt to a much more flexible coalition building strategy where the options are multiple and the competition fierce. In this context, relying on a formerly retired political star as a strategy for survival is a sign that Oakland has yet to make the transition to the next generation of black leaders.

Oakland's Transition to a Multicultural City

In just over 10 years, Oakland moved from a government where the mayor and five of nine city council members were African American to a government where, up to Ron Dellums' election in 2006, the mayor was white and only two city council members were African American. The transition was largely driven by major demographic changes, although that alone does not explain this political evolution. The conflict over redistricting in the early 1990s clearly empowered Asian and Latino minorities and weakened the hold of the African-American community over the city council. The persistence of high crime, low public education performance, and economic depression has plagued black administrations since they came to power at the end of the 1970s.

Demographic Changes: from a White to a Black to a Multicultural City

During the second half of the twentieth century, Oakland went through the same process as many industrial cities both economically and demographically. The Second World War brought thousands of industrial workers and African Americans from the South to the city to work in the war industries. Federal money poured into the state: $35 billion between 1940 and 1946, $8 billion in 1945 alone. "The Second Gold Rush hits the West," announced the *San Francisco Chronicle* on April 25, 1943. At the time, Oakland was a strong industrial city, home to canneries and mills that provided parachutes for the troops. With one of the largest ports of the Pacific, Oakland benefited from a unique location. Engineer Henry J. Kaiser chose to settle in Oakland to build ships, generating thousands of jobs in naval factories that were running 24 hours a day. Between 1940 and 1945, Oakland's population increased from 302,163 to 400,935 inhabitants.[1]

The desegregation of war industries by President Roosevelt opened new opportunities for minority workers who could afford the trip. Between 1942 and 1945, more than 50,000 blacks moved to the East Bay. The Oakland black population was 8,462 in 1940. It reached 37,327 in 1945, more than 65% of them coming from the southern states: Louisiana, Texas, Oklahoma, and Arkansas. They made up 85% of the naval industry workers.[2] Yet separation remained the rule both within the work place and housing. The new minorities packed into overcrowded ghettos. The proportion of overcrowded households in West Oakland increased from 15.2% to 30.7% between 1940 and 1950, while the proportion of black people in the neighborhood rose from 16% to 62%. A wave of violence hit Oakland while other cities, like Detroit, were undergoing severe racial

---

[1] U.S. Bureau of the Census.
[2] Johnson, *The Second Gold Rush*, 53.

riots. A riot broke out in Oakland, following a fight in public transportation, involving 2,000 black and white people.[3]

Although there had always been a substantial minority population in Oakland, the Second World War changed the demographic dynamics and the perception of the city. Up to then, Asians were the largest minority group in the East Bay, with a substantial Chinese settlement partly linked to the construction of the railroad. A number of blacks working for the Pullman Company had established their residence in Oakland, the terminus of the first transcontinental railroad completed in 1869. After the Second World War, the number of blacks tripled, and they became the largest minority group. Despite urban renewal programs launched by the white administration that demolished thousands of housing units and disrupted black neighborhoods and the construction of the Nimitz highway in 1958 and the BART (Bay Area Rapid Transit), the black population kept increasing in Oakland, mostly from natural growth and the migration of more black families to the East Bay.

Many white families took advantage of federal loan programs to move to the suburbs in search of a greater quality of life or retreated to the hills of the city to escape racial tensions, crime, poverty, and black residents. As a result, the city started losing population, which engendered serious economic consequences I will discuss later. This created an increasing gap between the hills and the flatlands, with the MacArthur Freeway (I-580) appearing as an urban frontier. The flatlands became the land of the poor and the minorities while the hills largely remained the land of the whites and the wealthy. See Figure 6.1.

The departure of white residents and the sustained increase in the black population progressively made it essentially a "black city," although African Americans never were a majority. In 1970, Oakland's population was 33.8% black, compared to 2.8% in 1940. In 1980, the peak year, blacks were 46.4% of the total population.

Yet it took all the efforts of the federal administration to force the political desegregation of the city, mostly by involving the black community leaders in the decision process of urban federal programs. The emergence of a black political leadership during the 1960s along with the creation of the Black Panther Party in 1966 in Oakland eventually led to the election of the first black mayor, Lionel Wilson, in 1977, thanks to a coalition between black leaders and white liberals. Up to then, whites had remained the dominant racial group in the city. They were still 85% of the population in 1950 and 50.5% in 1970. Their decrease in population accelerated thereafter, dropping to 28.3% in 1990, and 23.5% in 2000. See Table 6.1.

---

[3] *Ibid.*, 93. "Seminar Report: What Tensions Exist between Groups in the Local Community," Oakland Institute on Human Relations, 1946, 2. Wilson Record, *Minority Groups and Intergroup Relations in the San Francisco Bay Area,* University of California, Berkeley, 1963, 11. "That Riot on Twelfth Street . . . ," *The Observer,* March 11, 1944, 1.

Figure 6.1. The Geography of Oakland's Transition

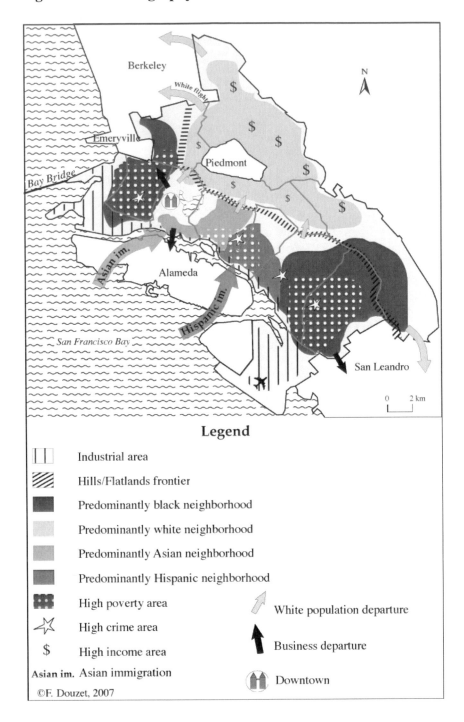

Legend

||| Industrial area

Hills/Flatlands frontier

Predominantly black neighborhood

Predominantly white neighborhood

Predominantly Asian neighborhood

Predominantly Hispanic neighborhood

High poverty area

High crime area

$ High income area

Asian im. Asian immigration

©F. Douzet, 2007

White population departure

Business departure

Downtown

Table 6.1. Racial Composition of Oakland, 1940–2000 (by percentage)

	1940	1950	1960	1970	1980	1990	2000
Whites	95.3	85.5	73.6	50.5	34.8	28.3	23.5
Blacks	2.8	12.4	22.8	33.8	46.4	42.8	35.1
Hispanics				9.8	9.6	13.9	21.9
Asians				5.9	7.4	14.2	15.1
Others	1.9	2.1	3.6	0.0	1.8	0.8	4.4

As blacks were gaining political power, massive Hispanic and Asian immigration started. Between 1980 and 1990, the Hispanic population increased by half while the Asian population doubled. Many moved into the Chinatown area, expanding its boundaries. The Chinese primarily located in the old Chinatown, while South-East Asians settled further east, in a neighborhood nicknamed "New Chinatown." In the meantime, second generation immigrants had moved further up in the lower hills, renamed by local residents "China Hill." In the following decade, Hispanic immigration increased even more strongly, reaching almost 22% of the total population in 2000. While at first concentrated in the Fruitvale area, Hispanics increasingly spread out in the flatlands and settled in black ghettos where affordable housing was available. As a result, the proportion of blacks started decreasing slightly in the 1980s and, in the following decade, Oakland actually started losing black residents. Many of the middle-class African Americans who had benefited from the economic opportunities offered by affirmative action policies and a black administration in Oakland moved to the suburbs. See Figures 6.2, 6.3, 6.4, and 6.5.

Soon after gaining power, the black political elite was challenged by demographic changes. Yet numbers do not automatically translate into political power. The conflict over redistricting offered a unique opportunity for the emergence of an Asian and Hispanic leadership in the city, and for a new type of coalition building.

Redistricting

Since the Voting Rights Act of 1965, and particularly the 1982 amendment, cities are required to redraw electoral district boundaries after each decennial census in order to ensure fair political representation of all racial and ethnic groups. The massive Asian and Hispanic immigration of the 1980s had primarily settled in high immigration areas of the city, namely Chinatown, parts of West Oakland, San Antonio, and the Fruitvale district, substantially increasing both the population size and the racial and ethnic minorities in these areas. The demo-

Figure 6.2. Evolution of the Non-Hispanic Black Population

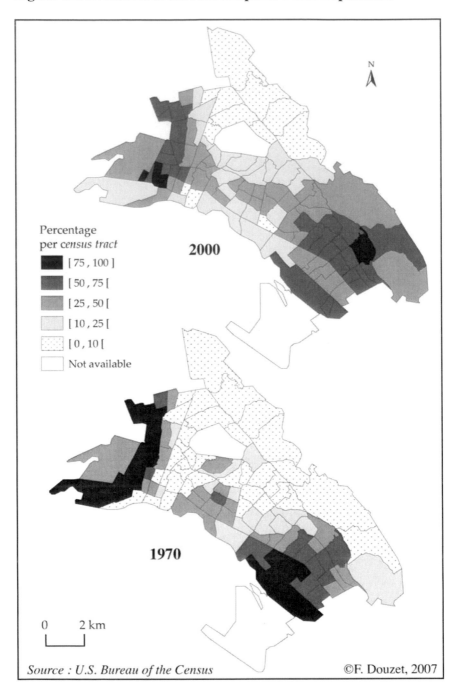

Source : U.S. Bureau of the Census   ©F. Douzet, 2007

Figure 6.3. Evolution of Non-Hispanic White Population

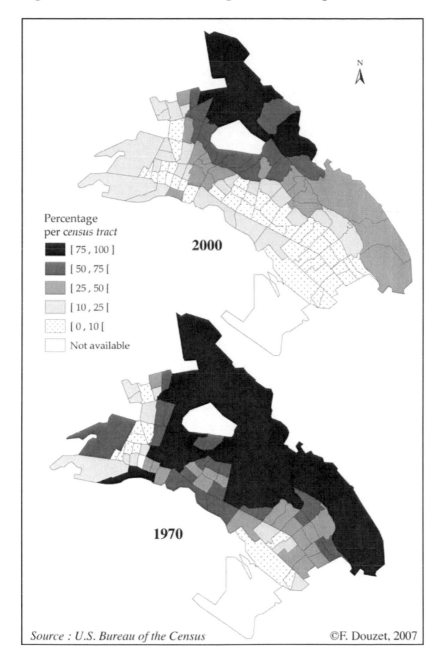

Figure 6.4. Evolution of the Hispanic Population

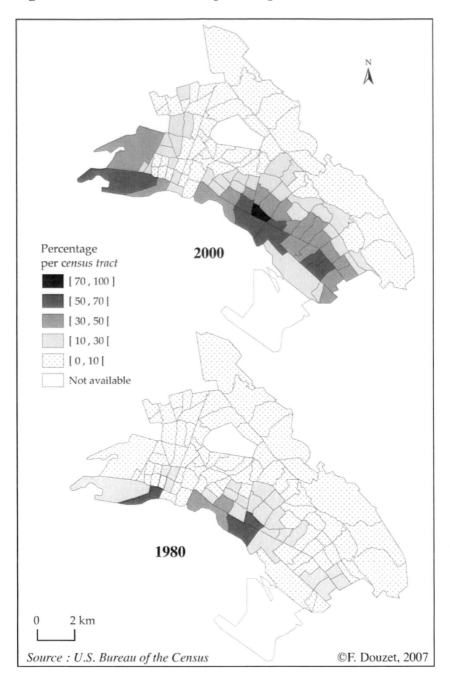

Figure 6.5. Evolution of the Non-Hispanic Asian Population

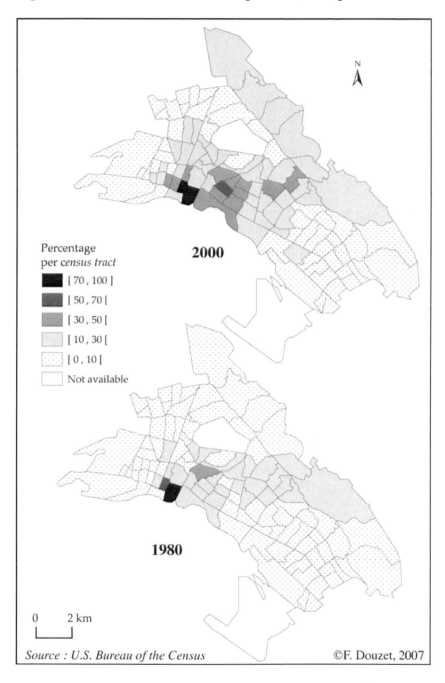

Percentage
per *census tract*

[70 , 100]
[50 , 70 [
[30 , 50 [
[10 , 30 [
[0 , 10 [
Not available

2000

1980

0   2 km

Source : *U.S. Bureau of the Census*   ©F. Douzet, 2007

graphic changes made obsolete the district boundaries established a decade earlier. Instead of appointing a city commission to do the redistricting, Mayor Elihu Harris, in the early 1990s, chose to involve the citizens. Guided by the vision of a truly multicultural city where all groups should get their share of power and work together for the common good, Mayor Harris and the city council hired an expert, Bruce E. Cain, professor of political science at the University of California, Berkeley, to give basic training to the population and supervise the process. He distributed maps, demographic data, and the list of criteria to respect such as equal population size, contiguity, cohesion, and fair representation of minority populations (nondilution). These criteria are detailed in Chapter 10 of this volume.

In 1992 the districts were still based on the 1980 census data. In three districts, African Americans were a majority of voting age citizens. Neither the Asians nor the Hispanics were able to get a majority or even a plurality of the potential voters in any district, because they were spread across several districts. There was therefore a clear incentive for Asian-American and Hispanic leaders to get involved. A Hispano-Asian coalition had sued the city in 1992 to accelerate the redistricting process, which had been postponed by referendum until 1993. In their view, the delay was the result of a conspiracy by white and black leaders to maintain their seats. The judge dismissed the complaint since a readjustment of the minority count had been claimed by the city and was taking time. The undercount of new immigrants was another good reason for the Hispanic and Asian leaders to get involved. At the beginning of the 1990s, there was no Hispanic council member or school board member. The at-large council member[4] was Asian as well as two of the school board members.

After a few weeks, the Asians and Hispanics came to agree on a common map, granting both communities a plurality in their district and clearly encroaching on the black West Oakland District 3 and white District 2. The Chinese leaders Yui Hay Lee and Allan Yee had so far been playing politics from back stage, with what they called a "guest mentality," giving out money and delivering votes to other candidates. After struggling to get a few projects through, such as the Asian Cultural Center, they started feeling the frustration of limited access to city government. Their involvement was also boosted by a more vocal community leader, Shirley Gee, who did not belong to the Chinatown establishment but had been involved in a fight against the creation of a drug rehabilitation center in her "China Hills" neighborhood The Hispanics, led by Ignacio de la Fuente and Linda Olvera, were eager to gain political representation as they struggled to obtain redevelopment projects in their neighborhoods and complained about a glass ceiling in city jobs. When in 1992, the Port commission vice president, Celso Ortiz, failed to be elected president, it was received as a

---

[4] The city council was composed of seven district representatives, an at-large council member, and the mayor, also elected at-large.

"major slap in the face of the Hispanics."[5] A black friend of the mayor ended up being elected by a majority black commission. The perception of limited access for Hispanic and Asian minorities was reinforced by the fact that so many of the city government entry jobs were held by African Americans, partly as a result of affirmative action policies. Any encounter with the administration therefore reinforced the feeling that African Americans controlled the city and that the other minorities were not receiving equal treatment. The perceptions were highly different among some of the African-American leaders who had struggled to bring a black administration to power and had not yet seen the results they had hoped for for the black community. It seemed clear to Fernando Cheung, executive director of the Oakland Chinese Community Council in 1993: "There is a clear consciousness among the blacks that they have struggled so much throughout these years, they have fought so hard for the civil rights movement. And all of the sudden, the Asians and Hispanics are jumping on the bandwagon. A few years ago, when we were talking about affirmative action, we were essentially essentially talking about blacks. All of the sudden, they are no longer the only minority. It's a real challenge for them"[interview, 1993]

Of the three map projects eventually retained for discussion by the expert and the city services, two were African American. The African-American Urban Crisis Center, a group of middle-class African Americans, offered an alternative that essentially preserved the existing boundaries while the Niagara Movement and African-American Caucus proposition sought to maximize black representation, offering plurality only to the Hispanics in District 5 but not to the Asians in District 2. The public hearings and city council debates that followed were particularly passionate, with "strange bedfellows" fighting along to preserve their seats. Mary Moore, white representative of District 2 and Natalie Bayton, black representative of District 3, both affected by the creation of an Asian and a Hispanic district, ended up voting against the final proposal. In the middle of a council meeting,[6] Mary Moore pulled out the *Washington Post* and read aloud the *Shaw v. Reno* decision of the Supreme Court (June 28, 1993). She accused the city of gerrymandering, of pursuing a racial goal that was no longer legal, and argued that the whites had become a minority in Oakland whose community of interest had been violated. Meanwhile, the radical black leaders felt betrayed by the African-American middle class.

The compromise ended up being very close to the map drawn by the Asian and Hispanic coalition, with a strengthening of the black population in District 3 and of the white population in District 2. The final map was eventually adopted

---

[5] Martin Malstuk, "Oakland Latino Struggle for Clout. Leaders Say Victories are Scarce," *San Francisco Chronicle*, August 31, 1992.

[6] June 29, 1993.

on July 20, 1993, inspiring this comment to the *San Francisco Chronicle*: "In the end, it was politics at its most brutal."[7]

This apparent victory for the Hispano-Asian coalition was limited by the low rates of citizens of voting age among the population and by the low turnout in these districts. Ignacio de la Fuente and Noel Gallo were elected respectively to the city council and the school board just before the redistricting was passed, showing that the candidate's ability to reach beyond its community was at least as important. Yet, shortly after the redistricting, Natalie Bayton lost District 3 to a white candidate but Asian candidate Lily Hu lost against John Russo in District 2. In 1994, Mayor Elihu Harris was challenged by an Asian candidate, Ted Dang, who played the racial card by running a very aggressive campaign against the mayor. His candidacy raised concerns among the black population, reportedly prompting comments from former Mayor Lionel Wilson suggesting that if Dang was elected, the whites were going to wait in line to take power in Oakland. Despite their previous criticisms, all the black leaders rallied around Harris in the runoff.

The redistricting process turned out to be a multicultural conflict, which was successfully and peacefully—yet passionately—resolved through democratic debate. Most of the leaders turned out to be proud of this achievement, even though a few remained bitter. In the long run, it probably accelerated the weakening of the black leadership by empowering the Asian and Hispanic leaders—just as the involvement in federal programs did for the African Americans in the 1960s—and by reflecting politically the ongoing demographic changes. Yet the misfortunes of black candidates in the late 1990s can also be attributed to the frustration of voters with an administration that failed to fulfill the promises of a better social and economic situation for Oakland.

Bad Timing, Bad Luck

The timing of their ascension to power was particularly unlucky for Oakland's black mayors. When Lionel Wilson was elected in 1977, Oakland was going through the same hardship as most industrial cities in the United States. The deindustrialization led to massive unemployment and accelerated the departure of financially stable populations to the suburbs, precipitating central cities into inextricable financial crises. Between 1980 and 1990, Oakland lost 30% of its industrial jobs and another 16.7% in the following decade. Traditional sectors such as chemistry, glass, refinery, metal, and concrete each lost between half and three quarters of their jobs, a total of 6,250 (67.7%) between 1981 and 1991.

---

[7] Rick Delvecchio, "Oakland Voting Ds Okd," *San Francisco Chronicle*, July 21, 1993.

The food manufacturing industry remained the primary employer in Oakland, despite a 40% job loss between 1981 and 1990. Many of the major companies left the city—including five with over 250 employees—but the number of small businesses increased. Food manufacturing used to be the leading sector in Oakland and remained active thanks to good transportation infrastructures allowing rapid and convenient transportation of food products. In addition, the region produces raw material in abundance thanks to a dynamic agricultural sector.

As residents and their tax revenues were moving out of the city, so were businesses. The financial needs of the city kept growing as did unemployment, crime, and other social issues, while revenues kept decreasing as factories were closing and businesses were leaving.

At the same time, the entire state was going through a major budget crisis following Proposition 13 in 1978, known as the "tax-payer revolt." This popular initiative measure severely limited property tax and drastically reduced local revenues, leading to major cuts in public expenses. The most severely impacted cities turned out to be those with the lowest revenues.

Finally, the economic recession of the late 1980s and early 1990s hit California particularly strongly because of major cuts in defense contracts and the closure of military bases. Oakland was yet again strongly affected as the closure of the naval base led to major job losses and about $30 million in related contracts.

The Bay Area resisted rather well this last recession, thanks to the dynamism of its high technology and research industry. But Oakland lost half of its high-technology jobs between 1981 and 1991 even as they doubled for Alameda County as a whole. The city was clearly not benefiting from the expansion of Silicon Valley. The growth of the service sector was also much slower in Oakland than in the rest of the Bay Area or the county (90% compared with 165% for Alameda County). Overall, the job growth in the private sector in that decade was over 30% for Alameda County compared to only 1.5% for Oakland.

In addition, Oakland was struck by two natural disasters: the Loma Prieta earthquake in 1989, which destroyed the Cypress freeway, and a major fire in October 1991 that destroyed 3,000 houses in the north hills. Elihu Harris admitted leaving office when many of these problems were eventually easing up: "I think I achieved a lot of the things that I wanted to achieve. But the times dictate a lot of what you're able to achieve. There were earthquakes and fires, recessions and base closures; having to finish strategic plans, having to install structural changes in government, took a lot more time than I had imagined. We had to get a general plan, new public works projects, lighting projects, we had to replace the freeway that was lost in the earthquake; all those things took time, and when I left office most of those things had been done: structural changes were made, we got out of the recession, we rebuilt from the fire and earthquake, we had a structured program with the base closing" [interview, 2001].

Beyond the bad timing and bad luck issues, Oakland was clearly having difficulties attracting or even retaining businesses. The obvious image deficit of the city, which remained plagued by crime, certainly did not help. Despite excellent transportation infrastructures, an active container port, an international airport, and an enviable location, Oakland was facing tough competition from fast developing areas eager to attract resources and tax money. With higher revenues, cities located in the I-580/I-680 corridor (Hayward, Fremont, Pleasanton, Dublin, Union City, San Ramon) were able to offer better tax incentives and commercial opportunities for businesses attracted by their high-skilled population. Between 1980 and 1995, the population of Dublin grew by 75%, Pleasanton 66%, and Fremont 40%, compared with only 14% in Oakland. In the following decade, the population of Dublin increased by another 52%.

Aside from this regional competition, a reputation of poor management contributed to undermine the economic development of the city and feed the frustration of voters who were still waiting to see Oakland benefit from the economic boom of the mid-1990s in the Bay Area. A number of development fiascos tarnished the image of the administration, such as a costly ice rink construction and the renovation of the Coliseum in order to keep the football and basketball teams, the Raiders and the Golden State Warriors in Oakland. The deals negotiated with the teams turned out to be very expensive for the city. The Raiders deal ended up losing money and the litigation between the team and the Coliseum was settled only in 2003. In the meantime, in the early 1990s, a number of redevelopment projects and investments had not yet paid off, such as the Jack London Square commercial area.

Up to 1992, poverty and crime continued to increase in Oakland, affecting particularly poor black communities. This raised sensitivities about racial issues in the city, as almost every single conflict potentially bore a racial aspect, which was often brought up by one of the protagonists. Whether it was the relationship between community and police, the teachers' strike, school achievement, neighborhood development, or city contracts, a number of issues pitted racial and ethnic groups against one another and impeded the performances of city government.

When Elihu Harris left office in 1998, many of the voters were disillusioned by the administration and did not trust the established black leadership to turn the situation in Oakland around. When Jerry Brown came with the promise of a change, he was welcomed as a messiah.

Reinventing Minority Coalitions

Jerry Brown, the Messiah

Coming into the race just eight months before the election, against 10 other candidates, most of them African American, Jerry Brown won the election in the primary with over 59% of the vote. He gained the support not only of the white, middle- and upper-class voters, who live in the hills, but of a majority of voters throughout the flatlands. He won all the precincts of the hills, North Oakland, West Oakland, San Antonio, and Central/Chinatown and scored at least 40% of the votes in almost all the other precincts. Ed Blakely, a prominent black scholar and an Oakland resident for over 22 years, reached 30% of the votes only in a few precincts. Brown was elected in June 1998 and managed to pass a strong mayor measure in November, approved by 74% of the voters. Harris had tried unsuccessfully to pass a similar measure two years before.

It is likely that Brown's personality and aura more than his project for the city won over the voters. Brown had been the governor of the state from 1974 to 1982, and like his father Pat Brown, also governor from 1959 to 1967. He was highly appreciated by minorities, as he promoted equal opportunity and re-cruited women and minorities in his administration. His nonconventional, highly creative style and sometimes loony ideas—he was nicknamed "governor moon-beam" by editorialist Mike Royko for proposing that California launch its own satellite—prompted sarcastic comments in the media but fostered great enthusi-asm among voters. Oakland Ecopolis, his rather utopian project for Oakland, was characterized by editorialist Peter Schrag as a mix in equal parts of "rose-water, moralization, and moon dust."[8]

Yet Jerry Brown was bringing unprecedented media attention to Oakland. While his opponents were spending loads of money on TV ads to gain name recognition, Jerry Brown was invited to the largest national networks, speaking on talk shows, and answering interviews with the national press. The last week of May 1998, just before the election, Jerry Brown was interviewed by Associ-ated Press, Reuters, The Today Show, and the *New York Times*, which wrote about the mayoral race in Oakland three times during the month. Less than 12 hours after his victory, Brown received a phone call from Vice President Al Gore, congratulating him. Aside from the media, Brown had the power to cap-ture the attention of investors and as opposed to Lionel Wilson and Elihu Harris, he got elected at a better economic time.

In Oakland as in the rest of the country—Brown's key plan to turn the city around was gentrification. He planned to build 10,000 housing units downtown, most of which he ended up achieving, in order to bring the white middle-class

---

[8] Peter Schrag, "Jerry Brown, born again, and again, and again, and . . . ," Nando.net.

back to the city, boost the downtown economy, and change the image of the city. The timing could hardly have been better as the Bay Area was facing an economic boom, partly linked to the dot-com industry (up to the early 2000s), and a major housing shortage. People started turning to Oakland and its out-standing transportation facilities for a place to live. West Oakland, right off the Bay Bridge, was the first neighborhood to welcome gentrifiers who rediscovered the once beautiful Victorian houses in desperate need for renovation. This had more to do with the situation of the real estate market than the mayor's plan. The fact that the number of homicides had dropped—in Oakland like in the rest of the countr—probably helped, even if West Oakland remained one of the high crime-high poverty areas of the city.

The mayor then launched a massive construction plan downtown and, unlike his predecessor, was very successful in attracting developers. His popu-larity, his connections, and his know-how are precisely the reasons why voters had trusted him in the first place. Ted Dang, the real estate business man who ran against Elihu Harris in 1994, was enthusiastic: "In terms of what Jerry Brown has done for business, we have no complaints. My business has just been terrific. And it's a coincidence, but he does bring this image that really helps business. The economy started to really shoot up just when he took office; and the fact that we had new leadership in Oakland and it was open for business, and he had advisors that came within the business community, and he was very pro-development. All of a sudden we did have new money, new capital, rushing into Oakland. He gave tours, brought busloads of developers from SF who were hav-ing trouble developing there, and that resulted in a handful of deals for Oakland. And the property values in Oakland doubled over a couple of years, just like that."

Yet a question we can legitimately raise is to what extent the fact that he is white contributed to reassure the investors and convince them that the place was safe enough for them. And some black leaders like lawyer Clinton Killan raised the question: "Investors never got rid of their image of Oakland, the image of a ghetto filled with drugs and black revolutionaries bearing a weapon. That's why they never got close. Then Jerry Brown was elected and they figured: 'if it's safe enough for a white guy like Jerry to be the mayor, then it's safe enough for me to come back" [interview, 2001].

The multifamily housing built downtown did attract a new white population downtown, although mostly composed of small families, dinkies (couples with double incomes, no children) or single people. Overall, so far, the census esti-mates have not shown an increase in white population. Crime and public schools remain a major drawback for the city in its capacity to attract or retain middle-class families with children. Aside from creating a controversial military acad-emy and a failed attempt to take control of the school board, the Brown adminis-tration did little to improve education in the city. High concentrations of poverty and a permanent influx of non-English speakers added to the challenge of improving a school system that has been struggling for years.

The changing housing patterns of the city raised fears of displacement. The skyrocketing housing prices led some unscrupulous landlords to evict people in order to raise rents. In July 2001, a landlord was found guilty of discrimination against African-American tenants. He had acquired 150 housing units in the city and was bypassing rent control laws by replacing the tenants with recently arrived Mexican-American families who were willing to crowd into an apartment to afford a rent that had doubled in the meantime. Most of them spoke little English and knew nothing about their civil rights. In November 2002, a group of citizens brought to the ballot a "just-cause eviction" measure, opposed by the mayor, to forbid such tactics.

Yet for a number of reasons, the people who ended up being displaced by the changes are not necessarily the poorest, as many had expected. Most of the newcomers moved into either new housing or vacant houses, as many were available in West Oakland. The city maintained the same level of social housing and systematically rebuilt as many units as were demolished. With the just-cause eviction measure, people who were renters were able to stay in the neighborhood where they lived, no matter how high the housing prices were climbing around their house. The city housing services were in fact less worried about the potential displacement of poor people than about protecting from developers older single people sitting on half-million dollar houses without knowing it.

Most of those who actually left the city were middle-class families who owned their house and took the opportunity to cash in their property and move to the suburbs of Contra Costa County. As a result, the black populations of Antioch or Pittsburg have rapidly increased. In Antioch, for example, there were 1,626 black residents in 1990[9] (2.6%), 8,824 in 2000 (9.7%) and an estimated 16,981 in 2005 (16.4%).

The result is a spatial dilution of the black population into the Bay Area. This is a sign of better integration, even if the new settlements remain limited to a few suburbs and are not necessarily as widespread as complete integration would show. Yet it has implications in terms of electoral power. As the black middle class gets geographically dispersed, so does its ability to vote as a block since the voting power gets even more diluted because middle and upper classes tend to register and participate more than lower classes. As a result, in Oakland, as in the suburbs, black candidates are increasingly going to need to reach out of their community in order to be elected, and advocacy groups and communities will need to build coalitions to get their issues on the political agenda of elected officials. A better residential integration requires a better political integration in order to get fair political representation. But in Oakland, black political leaders have felt literally shut out from power by the new administration.

---

[9] Including blacks of Hispanic origin.

Black Leaders Shut Out by the Brown Administration

Both the attitude of Jerry Brown and the way he has conducted politics have given many black leaders the feeling that they had lost not only council members but political access. During his two terms, Jerry Brown relied mostly on the support of Senator Don Perata and council member Ignacio De La Fuente, whom he endorsed for the mayoral election in 2006. With only two black elected officials on city council, Ignacio De La Fuente did not need to reach out to the black leaders to deliver a majority to the mayor on the city council, even though District 7 council member Larry Reid was among his allies.

Brown shocked many by firing Police Chief Joseph Samuels, who was particularly popular with the African-American elite. As the first black police chief in Oakland, he had worked hard at easing the long-standing tensions between police officers and communities and succeeded in winning their confidence. He had also recruited many minority officers. After six years in service, he was forced to resign and was replaced by another African-American police chief, perceived as the mayor's henchman. Brown sought to import the "zero tolerance" methods that had made the reputation of the mayor of New York. He dismantled community policing, following a long fight with the police union led by the police chief and city attorney John Russo, who was then a council member. In 2007, the police chief considered reinstalling the system, as crime and more specifically homicides were on the rise again. In 2006, Oakland registered 148 homicides, back to the level of the early 1990s.

Many black leaders were also upset by Brown's attempt to take over the school district by directly appointing all the members. The level of racial susceptibility about schools could be measured through a series of conflicts in Oakland: the choice of the textbooks in 1995, the debate over ebonics in 1997, or the schoolteachers' strike (Douzet, 2007). The chronic failure of a proportion of black children in Oakland public schools encourages the perpetuation of poverty and the resentment of leaders who feel that children are not getting enough resources and lack attention from predominantly white teachers. The high rate of black employees in the school administration can also potentially turn any attack against the staff or the administration into a racial conflict. Brown managed to get an extra three appointees in addition to the seven elected members. Upset by this result, he appointed a highly vocal West Oakland activist, Paul Cobb, who ended up trading insults with the Board President Dan Siegel. The board members, who all opposed the addition of appointed members, engaged in heated debates with them. Brown was accused of sabotage through his appointees. It took the financial collapse of the schools to have them rally against a takeover of the school district by the state in 2003.

Development was the area that black leaders felt most excluded from, and they publicly voiced their complaints in March 2005. They clearly felt like mere spectators to business deals and lucrative contracts negotiated by the mayor and his allies, Ignacio De La Fuente and Don Perata, which they claimed went to friends and campaign donors. Rumors of corruption spread throughout the city. The city council commissioned a minority contracting study led by an influential black business woman, Eleanor Mason Ramsey, scheduled to be released in the heat of the 2006 mayoral campaign. It was delivered in May 2007, 15 months late and cost the city over half a million dollars. The controversial results point to racial disparities in contracting and discrimination against black contractors. Although the methodology could be debated, black leaders were quick to explain that the results came as no surprise to them.

It is precisely because they felt shut out by the administration that black political and business leaders formed a coalition with union leaders and progressives to draft the retired congressman Ron Dellums into the mayoral race. Is Ron Dellums' election going to be enough to restore black political power in the city or have demographics and political evolutions opened a new political era for Oakland?

A New Distribution of Power?

The hyperactivity of Jerry Brown in his first years in office contrasts with little action by Ron Dellums in the first year of his election. Dellums' budgetary discretion is very limited as most future tax resources have been set aside by the previous administration for redevelopment projects. After bitterly losing the battle against Dellums, De La Fuente still controls six of the eight city council votes, which makes it difficult for the mayor to implement his vision to transform Oakland into a model city. Despite opportunities, Dellums hasn't really tried to take over the city council, and his vision still has to be transformed into action. Criticisms emerged even among his supporters as Dellums developed a reputation of not working very hard and not being present. Unlike Brown who strived to attract private capital to the city, Dellums seems to bet on his political connections to attract state and federal money to the city, which, aside from being insufficient to answer the needs of the city, can potentially backfire, as editorialist Chris Thompson pointed out: "As long as Dellums calls on Sacramento and D.C. to help with Oakland's terrible problems, he's calling attention to—you guessed it—Oakland's terrible problems. He's telling entrepreneurs and developers that the city is once again desperate and broke, and they should think about starting their businesses somewhere else."[10]

But aside from the personal capacities of Dellums, the structural demographic and political evolution of the city have clearly redistributed the power cards in Oakland, while a number of issues remain salient. The black administrations definitely helped the emergence of a thriving black middle and upper class

---

[10] "Anybody Seen Hizzoner ?", *East Bay Express*, June 6, 2007.

in Oakland—even though minority businesses have not yet risen to the level of development they had hoped for—and promoted the residential and political desegregration of the city. But for all the reasons we have seen, these administrations were unsuccessful in turning the city's economy around and improving the situation of the black underclass. Despite its economic assets and a clear improvement of its economic situation, the city still faces major issues impeding its development, such as high crime, underperforming public schools, high poverty rates, and high financial vulnerability. Among all groups, the African Americans in Oakland remain the most disadvantaged by all standards.

The per capita income for 2000 reflects the presence of a substantial black middle-class in Oakland, as the revenue for African Americans ($17,619) was superior to that of the Asians ($16,527) and Hispanics ($11,813), yet largely inferior to the whites ($42,171). But the lower class is clearly struggling, with an unemployment rate of 12.7% (compared with 11% for the Hispanics, 6.0% for the Asians, and 3% for the whites) and a poverty rate of 24.9% (compared with 21.7% for the Hispanics, 22% for the Asians, and 7.7% for the whites). In the case of African Americans, as opposed to other minorities, this high poverty rate cannot be attributed to an influx of recent poor immigrants. The situation of the youth is equally troublesome. Because of high rates of teenage pregnancy and drug addiction, 14.7% of black babies are born with a low birth-weight. African-American teenagers tend to leave school early: 27% of the 16- to 19-year-old black teenagers have left school, among whom 57% left without their high-school diploma and 79% are considered idle (meaning not in school nor on the job market). Only 10% of the Asian teenagers have left school at that age. Yet the rate is even higher among Latinos, with 37% of the age class out of school, among whom 57% are considered idle.

Geography helps explain the perpetuation of poverty. Although Latinos are increasingly moving in, formerly black ghettos remain primarily inhabited by African Americans and disproportionately accumulate social and economic disadvantage: high unemployment, high dropout rates from high school, low-birth-weight babies, high percentage of renters, urban decay. Black-on-black crime remains a reality and primarily affects these neighborhoods. Convicts are usually released in the area where they were arrested and in the case of West Oakland, it contributes to feeding the neighborhood with drug-traffic and violent crime, no matter what the city may do to keep the streets safe.

Conclusion

Oakland has a new black mayor but a return to the heyday of black power in Oakland is unlikely to come any time soon. The demographic transition of the city, reinforced by redistricting and inclusive politics led to a multicultural power structure made of flexible and temporary alliances. The old coalition between black leaders and white liberals can no longer ensure political leadership for a black political elite who struggles to form the next generation of leaders. The massive influx of immigrant minorities and the empowerment of their political leaders has led to unusual forms of coalition building between Asians and Latinos. Meanwhile, gentrification has brought white residents back into the city while driving part of the black middle class to the suburbs. The 2005 Census estimates show that whites—including whites of Hispanic origin—make up 32.4% of Oakland's population and blacks—including blacks of Hispanic origin only 31.0%, compared with respectively 31.3% and 35.7% according to the 2000 Census. The process of coalition building has therefore become more complex, as white liberals and minorities can choose to ally with one or another group depending on the issues at stake.

Short of being able to produce a new charismatic leader, the black leadership has turned to a former congressman who comes from the old tradition of coalition building between middle- and upper-class blacks and middle-class white liberals. There is now definitely a necessity to build on the common ground between lower-class immigrants and poor blacks, who have comparable demands, without neglecting the aspirations of the emerging minority middle-classes. Latino Mayor Antonio Villaraigosa is struggling with the very same necessity in Los Angeles.

The black community in Oakland is heterogeneous, and the leadership divided but there is a common history, a set of perceptions, a sense of identity clearly shared by the community that tends to be reinforced by the competition with other ethnic groups. The challenge for the black leadership is to improve the situation of the long-time struggling black underclass while providing the opportunities and quality of life their middle and upper classes aspire to. It will take political power, if not political representation, to defend those interests, which are likely to clash with those of other groups eager to get their fair share of resources. A recent conflict embodies the challenge, adding to allegations of racism and discrimination that have spread throughout City Hall since Ron Dellums' inauguration. In June 2007, Latino City Council President Ignacio De La Fuente, who had been booed and hissed at the mayor's inauguration, accused City Administrator Deborah Edgerly of openly defying a law to protect city jobs for African Americans.[11] A 2001 city ordinance, rather controversial at the time, required the city to hire bilingual candidates for city jobs in order to better serve non-English speakers. Although she denied the accusations, the black city administrator admitted not having made a priority of hiring bilingual speakers. Meanwhile, a new study found that blacks were overrepresented in most city job categories while Asians and Hispanics were underrepresented.

The real challenge for the black leadership is therefore to build enough political strength to be in a position to address the needs of the black population.

---

[11] Robert Gammon, "Job Security. Oakland Councilman accuses city administrator of defying the law in order to safeguard black jobs," June 20, 2007.

And clearly, considering their dwindling numbers, confrontation will not likely work. There is, therefore, a need to frame the political debate in a way that can appeal to other minority groups, and a need to increase resources for the city without displacing the poor or scaring away the middle class and potential investors. Black leaders have to find a way to target the black underclass without shutting out other minorities but instead, winning their crucial support. The black leadership is facing the same challenge in many cities in demographic transition. Considering the persistence of racial disparities and discrimination, the loss of political clout of black leaders should be a real concern.

References

Bagwell, Beth. 1982. *Oakland, the Story of a City*. Novato, Calif.: Presidio Press.

Bradford, Armory. 1968. *Oakland's Not for Burning*? New York: McKay.

Browning, Rufus P., Dale Rogers Marshall, and David H Tabb. 1990. *Racial Politics in American Cities*. New York: Longman.

———. 1984. *Protest Is Not Enough, The Struggle of Blacks and Hispanics for Equality in Urban Politics*. Berkeley: UC Press.

Dahl, Robert A. 1961. *Who Governs?* New Haven: Yale University Press.

Douzet, Frédérick. 2007. *La couleur du pouvoir. Immigration et ségrégation à Oakland, Californie*. Paris: Belin.

———. 2003. "Immigration et géopolitique urbaine: la question du logement à Oakland, Californie." *Espace, populations, sociétés* 1: 103–15.

Dreier, Peter, John Mollenkopf, and Todd Swanstrom. 2001. *Place Matters. Metropolitics for the Twenty-First Century*. Lawrence: University Press of Kansas.

Fong, Timothy P. 1994. *The First Suburban Chinatown*. Philadelphia: Temple University Press.

Foucrier, Annick, and Antoine Coppolani. 2004. *La Californie*. Paris: L'Harmattan.

Frazier, John, Florence Margai, and Eugene Tettey-Fio. 2003. *Race and Place: Equity Issues in Urban America*. Boulder, Colo.: Westview Press.

Johnson, Marilynn S. 1993. *The Second Gold Rush*. Berkeley: University of California Press.

Lubenow, Gerald C., and Bruce E. Cain. 1997. *Governing California*. Berkeley: Institute of Governmental Studies Press, University of California.

Massey, Douglas, and Nancy Denton. 1995. *American Apartheid*. Paris: Descartes et Cie.

Portes, Alejandro, and Alex Stepick. 1993. *City of the Edge: The Transformation of Miami*. Berkeley: University of California Press.

Pressman, Jeffrey L., and Aaron Wildavsky. 1979. *Implementation*, 2d ed. Oakland Project. Berkeley: University of California Press.

Preston, Michæl B., Brucc E. Cain, and Sandra Bass (eds.). 1998. *Racial and Eth nic Politics in California*, vol. 2. Berkeley: Institute of Governmental Studies Press, University of California.

Sonenshein, Rapahel I. 1993. *Politics in Black and White: Race and Power in Los Angeles*. Princeton: Princeton University Press.

Wilson, William Julius. 1987. *The Truly Disadvantaged*. Chicago: The University of Chicago Press.

Chapter 7

The San Joaquin Valley:
Republican Realignment and Its Limits

Kenneth P. Miller and Justin Levitt[1]

This chapter analyzes demographic and political change in California's San Joaquin Valley, the heart of the state's fast-developing interior.[2] The region is naturally bounded by the San Joaquin River Delta to the north, the transverse range of the Tehachapis to the south, the Coastal Range to the west, and the Sierra Nevadas to the east. Its eight counties—San Joaquin, Stanislaus, Merced, Madera, Fresno, Kings, Tulare, and Kern—share a strong agricultural tradition,

---

[1] The authors wish to thank Doug Johnson, Tony Quinn, Ian Johnson, Tammy Nguyen, Andrew Lee, Florence Adams, and Ralph Rossum at the Rose Institute of State and Local Government at Claremont McKenna College for their assistance.

[2] We use the terms "San Joaquin Valley" and "valley" interchangeably. We limit our analysis to the eight-county region south of the San Joaquin River Delta and, except where legislative districts cross regional boundaries, exclude from our discussion the adjoining Sacramento Valley, which extends above the delta to include the city of Sacramento and the agricultural counties to the north. The Sacramento and San Joaquin valleys are often considered together as the "Central Valley" and some political analysts also treat them as a single region (see, e.g., Baldassare, 2000). However, we join Walters (1986) and others who, for purposes of political analysis, distinguish the San Joaquin region from metropolitan Sacramento and the sparsely populated northern counties.

similar economies, and a physical connection along Highway 99. The valley's venerable artery connects its main cities, including, from north to south, Stockton, Modesto, Merced, Fresno, Visalia, and Bakersfield. Driving along 99, one sees much rich agricultural land, but also many new commercial buildings and burgeoning housing developments. See Figure 7.1.

In most other states, the San Joaquin Valley would command much attention. Its largest city, Fresno, now has 450,000 residents, more than Miami or Minneapolis, and its eight-county population of over 3.2 million is greater than 21 states. But the valley exists in relative obscurity, in the shadows of larger and more glamorous places like Los Angeles, San Francisco, San Diego, and even Sacramento. Political scientists, like many others, have too often overlooked the region, its rapid growth, and its changing political dynamics.

In this chapter we begin by describing how in recent years the San Joaquin Valley has moved in a direction contrary to much of the rest of the state. While California as a whole has become solidly Democratic, the once-Democratic valley has become increasingly Republican. These opposite movements have contributed to California's increasing east-west partisan divide, where, with few exceptions, the state's coastal region has become more uniformly Democratic and its inland areas more closely aligned with the GOP. However, we also observe that the San Joaquin Valley's Republican realignment is complicated by a concurrent, dramatic increase in the region's Latino population.[3] Over the past quarter century, Latinos have accounted for approximately two-thirds of the valley's new residents and now constitute the majority of the population in Tulare County and a plurality in another three counties. Thus, after describing the broad scope of Republican realignment in the San Joaquin Valley, we analyze the ways in which the Latino population has limited the GOP's political strength in the region.

Data and Methods

To study political change in the San Joaquin Valley, we have drawn on a number of primary data sources. We obtained demographic information on the region from the U.S. Census Bureau and the University of Michigan's Social Science Data Analysis Network (SSDAN). For partisan registration and voting data, we used the California secretary of state's Statements of the Vote and Statements of Registration. For Latino voter registration and turnout, we used data from the Statewide Database (SWDB) at the University of California, Berkeley.

Most of our data are aggregated at the county level. There are advantages to using the county as our primary unit of analysis. Demographic, registration, and voting data are organized at the county level, and county boundaries are fixed,

---

[3] In this chapter we use the terms "Latino" and "Hispanic" interchangeably.

Figure 7.1: The San Joaquin Valley

offering a convenient way to analyze trends in demographics, registration, and voting over long periods of time. On the other hand, counties are large units that often contain considerable internal variation, and we recognize that one must be cautious in drawing broad conclusions about their demographic or political characteristics. In a county-level analysis we can say, for example, that Tulare County is trending Republican, but miss internal variations such as the increasing Democratic orientation of the city of Porterville. More importantly, we recognize the hazard of attempting to draw inferences about the behavior or tendencies of individuals or groups from aggregate, county-level data (Gimpel and Schuknecht, 2003; King, 1997).

Accordingly, while this chapter argues that Latinos have placed a limit on the Republican realignment in the San Joaquin Valley, we do not make specific conclusions regarding San Joaquin Valley Latinos' partisan voting patterns based on aggregate demographic, registration, and voting data. Instead, we approach the question of the Latino limit on Republican realignment in a somewhat different way, by analyzing the characteristics of the San Joaquin Valley's state legislative districts that are either majority Latino, or covered by Section 5 of the federal Voting Rights Act, or both. We believe that by analyzing these districts, we can draw tentative conclusions about the political characteristics of geographically defined core areas of Democratic strength, the most likely barriers to increased Republican dominance in the region.

For district-level data, we have used reports produced by the California Assembly Elections and Redistricting Committee and the Statewide Database at the University of California, Berkeley. These sources provide geographic and political profiles for all districts approved by the California Legislature in the 2001 redistricting. The Statewide Database includes estimated data on Latino registration, including Latino registration by party, at the district level. This information is developed by merging Spanish surname lists published by the U.S. Census Bureau with voter registration data. Although surname-based estimates of the ethnicity of registered voters are less than precise, they are usually considered the best available data, because unlike in southern states where voters self-identify by race when they register, the California voter registration process does not include self-identification by race or ethnicity (Lockyer, 2001a, 2001b).

The Dimensions of Republican Realignment

As shown in Table 7.1, the San Joaquin Valley was for many decades one of the strongest regions in California for Democrats, as measured by party registration. Prior to the New Deal realignment, California as a whole was overwhelmingly Republican. In 1930, Republicans claimed 78.2% of the state's two-party registration, and no less than a 60% share in every one of the state's 58 counties. Indeed, the Republican share of the two-party registration in the San Francisco Bay Area was then 82.9%—surely remarkable from today's perspective! During this period, the San Joaquin Valley region was also majority Republican (70.2%), but less so than the state as a whole.

The Great Depression and the New Deal caused a dramatic shift in the partisan loyalties of California voters. By 1940, the Republican share of two-party registration plummeted to 37.6% statewide, and even lower, to 33.8%, in the San Joaquin Valley. During this period, the valley's demographic and political characteristics were reshaped by a massive domestic migration, primarily from the states of Oklahoma, Arkansas, Texas, and Missouri. This great internal migration continued well into the 1940s. Many of the newcomers brought with them the conservative, southern Democratic political orientation of their home states that would long define the region's political character—relatively conservative, but solidly Democrat (Gregory, 1989; Quinn, 1981).

Table 7.1. Republican Percentage of Two-Party Registration, by Region, 1930–2000

Region	1930	1940	1950	1960	1970	1980	1990	2000
Bay Area*	82.9	40.0	39.0	40.2	39.8	33.7	36.0	33.5
Los Angeles	78.4	35.7	38.7	40.1	41.1	34.8	39.0	34.3
Other S. Calif.**	76.1	41.2	42.7	45.4	50.4	46.2	56.0	55.0
San Joaquin Valley	70.2	33.8	33.7	34.5	37.6	36.8	42.9	50.6
Statewide	78.2	37.6	38.9	40.5	42.5	37.9	44.0	43.5

Source: California Secretary of State, Reports of Registration, 1930-2000

* Bay Area includes Alameda, Contra Costa, Marin, Napa, San Francisco, San Mateo, Santa Clara, Solano, and Sonoma Counties

** Other Southern California includes Orange, Riverside, San Bernardino, San Diego, and Ventura Counties

Prior to the 1980s the voting patterns of San Joaquin Valley residents began to trend Republican, at least on some statewide and national races, but the valley's registration remained steadily and solidly Democratic. During the 1980s, however, the region's registration figures noticeably began to shift. Between 1980 and 1990, the Republican share of the region's two-party registration increased from 36.8% (about the same level as it had been for several decades) to 42.9%.

In the 1990s, the partisan realignment of the San Joaquin Valley gathered strength. The last year that voter registration was more Democratic in the region than in the state as a whole was 1992. In 1994, Republicans out-registered Democrats in Kern County, the first time Republicans had gained a registration edge in a San Joaquin Valley county since the Great Depression. Figure 7.2 illustrates the registration trends in each county. Republicans went on to achieve registration advantages in the counties of Madera and Tulare (1996) Kings and Fresno (2000), San Joaquin (2002), and Stanislaus (2004). Merced is now the only San Joaquin Valley County with a continuous Democratic registration advantage, and it likely will not last long. The Democrats' share of Merced's two-party registration started from a higher base but fell from 59.3% in 1994 to 51.7% in 2004, a comparable decline to the other counties in the region.

As of 2007, despite the state as a whole trending Democratic since 2004, Republicans maintained or improved their position in seven of the eight counties, only declining in San Joaquin County, where Democrats narrowly retook the two-party advantage in 2006. This aberration is probably related to a highly

Figure 7.2. Republican Percentage of San Joaquin Valley Two-Party Registration, by County, 1960–2004

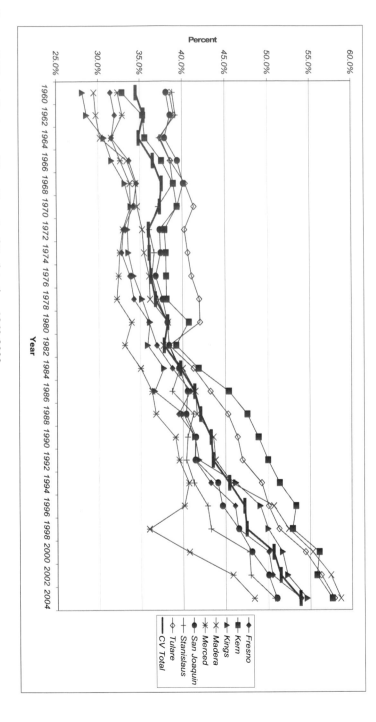

Source: California Secretary of State, Reports of Registration, 1960–2000

contested congressional race, where the state and national Democratic Party invested significant amounts of time and money in San Joaquin County to defeat incumbent Republican Congressman Richard Pombo. It seems highly likely that during the next election in which registration trends favor Republican candidates, every county in the San Joaquin Valley will have a Republican advantage.

In 2000, Republicans achieved a valley-wide majority, with 50.6% of the region's two-party registration. The party's gains did not slow thereafter. At mid-decade, the Republican percentage of two-party registration continued to increase in all eight San Joaquin Valley counties, and approached 60% in Tulare, Madera, and Kern. Partisan registration in the San Joaquin Valley was now decisively more Republican than in the rest of the state. As of 2004, Republicans enjoyed a 53.8 share of the region's two-party registration, compared to only 44.7 statewide, and San Joaquin Valley residents represented 11% of all California Republicans, compared to 5% in 1960.

The impact of these Republican registration gains could be seen in individual San Joaquin Valley districts. In addition to shoring up safe Republican districts, the registration trends made several Democratic and marginal districts more competitive for the GOP. As Table 7.2 indicates, between 2001 and 2004, Republicans gained strength in all San Joaquin Valley districts with Democratic registration advantages, and in one district, Assembly District 26, flipped the registration advantage from Democratic to Republican. AD 26, which includes the eastern parts of San Joaquin and Stanislaus counties, elected moderate Democrat Dennis Cardoza from 1996–2002, but elected Republican Greg Aghazarian in 2002. Meanwhile, Assembly Districts 17 and 30, drawn to be safe Democratic seats, became far more competitive than at the beginning of the decade. AD 17, which includes Merced County and the city of Modesto, was drawn 52.5% Democrat but had fallen to 47.2% by 2004. These registration figures include all minor parties and decline-to-state (DTS) voters, so the -5.3% drop in AD 17's Democratic registration translated into a positive 5.2% increase in the Republican share. These registration figures demonstrate increasing Republican strength, not merely Democratic decline.

Changes in partisan registration, of course, tell only part of the realignment story. As noted above, for many years a large number of San Joaquin Valley voters who registered Democrat crossed party lines to vote for Republican candidates, especially for statewide or national office. At least some San Joaquin Valley Democrats voted in this way because they were more conservative than their party's candidates for governor or president and more closely identified with the Republican nominees for these offices (Gimpel and Schuknecht, 2003; Quinn 1981). Republican Assemblyman Greg Aghazarian of Stockton notes that many of the individuals he meets in the local Chamber of Commerce and professional communities are registered Democrats because "their families were always Democrats" but have not voted for a Democrat in decades (Aghazarian, 2007).

Table 7.3 shows the gap in the San Joaquin Valley between the Republican percentage of two-party registration and the Republican percentage of the two-

Table 7.2: Republican Registration Gains in San Joaquin Valley State Legislative Districts with Democratic Registration Advantages, 2001–2004

Party	Year	AD17 D	AD26 D to R	AD30 D	AD31 D	SD12 D	SD16 D
Dem	2001	52.54	45.37	49.21	51.96	49.06	52.26
	2004	47.20	41.79	47.73	49.61	46.61	50.44
	Change	-5.34	-3.58	-1.48	-2.35	-2.45	-1.82
Rep	2001	34.71	42.02	36.46	34.14	35.77	33.58
	2004	39.89	43.81	39.49	38.14	38.36	36.94
	Change	+5.18	+1.79	+3.03	+4.00	+2.59	+3.36

Source: California Secretary of State, Reports of Registration, 2001–2004.

Table 7.3: San Joaquin Valley Republican Registration vs. Vote Cast for "Top-of-Ticket" Republican Candidates 1960–2000

	1960s	1970s	1980s	1990s*	2000s
% Republican Registration	35.78	36.48	39.84	45.38	52.30
% Vote for Republican Candidate	47.90	50.82	60.48	54.22	61.23
Difference	12.12	14.34	20.64	8.84	8.92

Source: California Secretary of State, Reports of Registration, 1960–2006; Statements of Vote, 1960–2006.

*Two-party vote in 1990s reduced by Perot vote.

party vote for the offices of president and governor between 1960 and 2006, averaged by decade. As this table indicates, there has long been a drop-off from the region's percentage Democratic registration to its percentage supporting top-of-the-ticket Democratic candidates; the Valley as a whole supported Republican candidates at a much higher rate than the partisan registration figures would suggest. Clearly, the San Joaquin region voted Republican (at least in these top-of-the-ticket races) before it registered Republican.

This gap was its widest in the 1980s, when President Reagan and Republican Governor George Deukmejian scored large victories in the still-Democratic region. Since the 1980s, the percentage of the vote going to Republican candidates has remained fairly stable, increasing only from 60.48 to 61.23%. However, the 12% increase in the Republican share of two-party registration has caused the gap between registration and voting to decline. In other words, the valley's Republican registration is catching up with its vote for top-of-the-ticket Republican candidates.

Tables 7.4 and 7.5 compare the San Joaquin Valley's vote for the Republican candidates for president and governor with the statewide vote for those candidates over the past four decades. These tables highlight two important trends: The San Joaquin Valley now consistently supports Republican candidates for top-of-the-ticket offices (even in landslide Democratic years) and the region is moving in a direction contrary to the rest of the state. Whereas in the 1960s and 1970s, San Joaquin Valley voters closely mirrored the statewide electorate, a persistent gap has now developed between valley and statewide support for Republican candidates. In the 2006 presidential election, the San Joaquin Valley vote for George W. Bush was dramatically higher than his statewide vote— 60.6% vs. 45.0%, the largest such gap on record between the valley and the state. Figure 7.3 summarizes these trends by comparing the region against the rest of California in percentage vote for Republican candidates for governor and president during this period.

Latinos as a Limiting Factor on Republican Realignment

Although San Joaquin Valley Republicans now have an edge in both top-of-the-ticket races and partisan registration, the realignment faces limits, the most important of which comes from the region's growing Latino population. In this section, we analyze ways in which Latinos, and more precisely majority-Latino legislative districts, have limited Republican electoral gains in the region.

Table 7.6 demonstrates that in recent decades Latinos have been the largest driving force behind the San Joaquin Valley's rapid population growth. The region's Latino population increased by over 825,000 between 1980 and 2000, and by nearly 500,000 in the 1990s alone. This translates into a 168.8% increase during that 20-year period. Between 1980 and 2000, Latinos accounted for nearly two-thirds (65.7 percent) of the region's overall population growth.

Moreover, although Latinos are a younger population than non-Hispanic whites, U.S. Census data indicates the Latino share of the region's voting-age population (VAP) has increased from 26.4% of the population in 1990 to 35.1% in 2000. However, for a number of reasons, including barriers of citizenship, language, and education, Latinos register and vote at far lower rates than the non-Hispanic white population (Reyes, 2003). Although Latinos constituted

Table 7.4: San Joaquin Valley vs. Statewide Vote for Republican Presidential Ticket, 1960–2004

	1960	'64	'68	'72	'76	'80	'84	'88	'92	'96	2000	'04
San Joaquin Valley	48.9	36.6	50.6	56.8	50.5	59.0	60.4	55.6	41.1	53.0	56.8	60.6
State	50.3	40.8	51.7	57.0	50.9	59.5	58.2	51.8	32.9	42.8	43.8	45.0
Difference	-1.4	-4.2	-1.1	-0.2	-0.4	-0.5	2.2	3.8	8.2	10.2	13.0	15.6

Source: California Secretary of State, Statements of Vote, 1960–2004.

Table 7.5: San Joaquin Valley vs. Statewide Vote for Republican Candidates for Governor, 1962–2006

	1962	'66	'70	'74	'78	'82	'86	'90	'94	'98	2002	'06
San Joaquin Valley	45.6	57.8	52.7	50.0	44.1	57.0	70.4	58.4	67.3	51.3	58.2	69.3
State	47.4	57.7	53.9	48.5	39.4	50.6	61.8	51.8	57.6	39.8	47.3	59.0
Difference	-1.8	0.1	-1.2	1.5	4.7	6.4	8.6	6.6	9.7	11.5	10.9	10.3

Source: California Secretary of State, Statements of Vote, 1962-2006

35.1% of the region's VAP in 2000, Table 7.7 shows that they made up only 22.0% of its registered voters. The San Joaquin Valley's 34-point gap between the percentage of non-Hispanics and Hispanics who register to vote is not as large as the 39-point gap in Los Angeles, but it is still sizeable and limits Latino political strength in the region.

Figure 7.3: Average Percent Vote for "Top-of-Ticket" Republican Candidates, 1960–2006

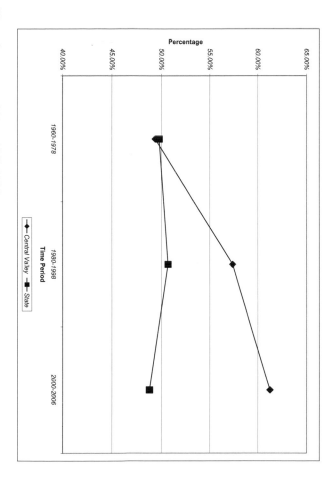

Source: California Secretary of State, Statements of Vote, 1960–2006

Table 7.6: Population Growth in the San Joaquin Valley (total population, Hispanics, and Non-Hispanic Whites), 1980–2000

	1980		1990		2000		Total Increase	% Gain	Contri-bution to Growth
	Number	%	Number	%	Number	%			
Total Pop.	2,048,104	100	2,742,000	100	3,302,792	100	1,254,688	61.3	
Total Hisp.	488,365	23.8	826,150	30.1	1,312,904	39.8	824,539	168.8	65.7
Total Non-Hisp. White	1,386,774	67.7	1,597,960	58.3	1,518,424	46.0	131,650	9.5	10.5

Source: US Census Bureau, Decennial Census of the Population, 1980–2000.

Table 7.7. Latino Registration and Turnout, San Joaquin Valley and Los Angeles County, 2000

Region	Voting age pop. (VAP) 2000	Hispanic VAP	Reg. voters	Hisp. reg. voters	Total % reg.	Hisp % reg.	Non-Hisp % reg.	Hisp % of reg. voters
San Joaquin Valley	2,250,266	788,856	1,337,308	294,724	59.4	37.4	71.34	22.0
Los Angeles County	6,851,362	2,707,234	4,064,764	964,990	59.3	35.6	74.80	23.7

Source: Statewide Database, Institute of Governmental Studies, UC Berkeley.

In important ways, however, the American political system rewards total population without regard to age, citizenship, registration, or voting. As a result of a series of U.S. Supreme Court decisions starting with *Baker v. Carr* (1962), states must draw legislative districts on an equal population basis. As a result, San Joaquin Valley Latino residents are entitled to equal legislative representation even if they do not vote in equal numbers with the rest of the region's population.

Moreover, Latinos are a protected class under the federal Voting Rights Act of 1965, as amended in 1982, and San Joaquin Valley legislative districts must be drawn in such a way as to protect Latino voting strength. More specifically, the valley includes two counties, Kings and Merced that are "covered jurisdictions" under Section 5 of the act. Under Section 5, these jurisdictions are required to show that new district boundaries "do not have the purpose and will not have the effect" of diluting minority voting strength (42 U.S.C. sec. 1973c). As a result, with each new decennial redistricting, legislative districts that include any part of Kings or Merced counties must be "precleared" to ensure they do not make minorities "worse off than they had been before the change" (28 C.F.R. sec. 5154(a)). In addition, the act's Section 2 applies to noncovered jurisdictions, and, under some circumstances, can be used to invalidate district lines that have the effect of diluting minority voting strength.

As a consequence, in creating districts that include areas such as Fresno or Bakersfield with large Latino populations, the state must take care to protect Latino voting power. These Voting Rights Act requirements have led to the creation of two majority-Latino Assembly districts (AD 30 and AD 31), a majority-Latino state Senate District (SD 16), as well as another district (AD 17) that is not majority-Latino but is covered by the provisions of Section 5.[4] In drawing these districts, the state took into consideration their percent Latino population, Latino voting age population, Latino registration, and Latino share of the Democratic registration in order to enhance Latino voting power in those districts (Lockyer, 2001a, 2001b). Compliance with the Voting Rights Act thus requires redistricters to group San Joaquin Valley Latino residents together into a few districts in order to concentrate their political strength at the district level. Table 7.8 presents these districts and their population and registration characteristics.

Majority-Latino and VRA districts in the San Joaquin Valley have the following general characteristics: a comparatively low turnout, a moderate-to-conservative voting record on statewide candidates and issues, and a solid record of electing Democrats to state legislative offices.

These districts' low turnout rates can be explained in large part by factors that presently limit Latino incorporation throughout California—barriers of age, citizenship, language, and education. Examining turnout in neighboring districts (Table 7.9) shows how large the effect can be in the San Joaquin Valley context, with the non-Latino majority Republican districts (AD 29, 32) often drawing twice as many voters (or more) than the neighboring Latino majority Democratic districts (AD 30, 31). As a result, for purposes of legislative elections (as opposed to statewide contests) the individual votes in high-turnout Republican San Joaquin Val-

---

[4] An additional VRA Section 5 state legislative district, SD 12, stretches between the San Joaquin Valley and Salinas.

Table 7.8: San Joaquin Valley Majority-Latino and VRA State Legislative Districts, 2001 Redistricting

District	VRA Sec 5	Member	% Hisp. Pop.	% Hisp. VAP	% Hisp. Reg.	% Dem Reg.	% Hisp. Dem.	% Dem. Vote 2006	Location
AD 17	Y	Gal- giani (D)	43.3	39.4	27.1	56.1	33.9	59.76	Modesto Merced
AD 30	Y	Parra (D)	61.3	55.7	40.0	55.4	52.7	51.57	Kings Bakers- field
AD 31	N	Aram- bula (D)	61.5	57.8		57.5		100*	Fresno
SD 16	Y	Florez (D)	63.2	58.6	44.0	58.8		100*	Fresno Bakers- field Kings

Sources: California Assembly Standing Committee on Elections and Redistricting, from 2001 plan reviews; Statewide Database, Institute of Governmental Studies UC Berkeley; Lockyer (2001).

*unopposed.

ley districts are effectively diminished in comparison to the votes in the neighboring, low-turnout Democratic districts.

Figures 7.4 and 7.5 show how districts in the largest San Joaquin Valley cities of Fresno and Bakersfield have been divided largely along racial lines. This is particularly evident in Bakersfield, where a claw of Assembly District 30 runs through the sparsely populated hills east of the city to grab the eastern portions of the city and avoid non-Latino neighborhoods. Although the map of Fresno only shows census tract lines, the sometimes odd lines cutting through tracts reflect the boundaries of the city's Hispanic population. Senate and congressional lines nearly overlap with these Assembly District lines. Furthermore, in all districts the eastern portions of Bakersfield and western neighborhoods of Fresno are separated from the other half of the city. Some argue that this alignment represents a community of interest in that Latinos in Bakersfield have more in common with Latinos in Fresno than with non-Latinos in Bakersfield and that to prevent dilution of the Latino community in the San Joaquin Valley it is necessary to draw districts along these lines. But these outcomes have contri-

Table 7.9: Turnout (total vote for Assembly) in San Joaquin Valley Majority-Latino Assembly Districts vs. Neighboring Districts, 2002–2006

District	Winner's party	2002 total votes cast	2004 total votes cast	2006 total votes cast
AD 31 (majority Latino)	D	41,050	86,234	45,004
AD 29	R	103,601	152,693	117,145
Difference		*-62,551*	*-66,459*	*-72,141*
AD 30 (majority Latino / VRA)	D	52,906	78,037	54,771
AD 32	R	103,141	164,640	118,649
Difference		*-50,235*	*-86,603*	*-63,878*

Source: California Secretary of State, Statements of Vote, 2002-2006

buted to the wide disparity in turnout between majority-Latino and non-Latino districts and to the concentration of Democratic strength in the region.

Despite the Democratic registration advantages in majority-Latino and VRA districts, voters in these districts display relatively conservative voting patterns. As Table 7.10 shows, in recent years in these districts voters supported the recall of Democratic governor Gray Davis, narrowly split on the 2004 Bush-Kerry race (with one majority-Latino district, AD 30, voting 56.9% for President Bush), and took the conservative position on two recent high-profile ballot measures (opposing Proposition 66, which would have weakened the state's "Three Strikes" criminal sentencing law, and supporting Proposition 73, which would have required parental notification by minors seeking abortions). These voting patterns indicate that San Joaquin Valley majority-Latino and VRA districts are more conservative than many other Democratic districts in the state.

When we compare legislative districts with a similar Hispanic percentage of the population in Los Angeles County, the voting patterns of the San Joaquin Valley's majority-Latino and VRA districts are even more striking. As further shown in Table 7.10, we have analyzed four legislative districts located in the Los Angeles suburbs—AD 40 in the south San Fernando Valley, AD 56 and 58 in the north Gateway, and AD 57, covering the central San Gabriel Valley. While these districts do not cover the historic East Los Angeles Latino community (as those districts are much more solidly Latino), these four working-class

Figure 7.4. Assembly Districts in the City of Fresno

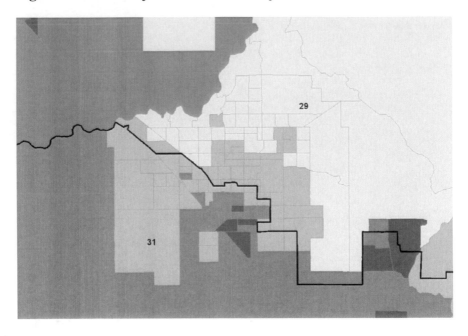

Figure 7.5: Assembly Districts in the City of Bakersfield

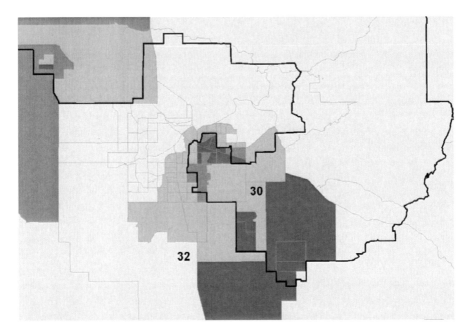

Table 7.10: San Joaquin Valley and Los Angeles Majority-Latino VRA District Votes on Selected Statewide Issues and Candidates, 2002–2006

District	Location	VRA Sec 5	Member's Party	% Hispanic VAP (2001)	% Dem Registration	% Vote Yes on 73 (2003)	% Vote Yes on Recall (2003)	% Vote Bush (2004)	% Vote Schwarzenegger (2006)	% Vote Yes on 90 (2006)
AD 17	SJV	Y	D	39.4	56.08	58.0	58.3	49.8	55.8	51.0
AD 30	SJV	Y	D	55.7	55.39	66.3	65.9	57.4	61.4	51.9
AD 31	SJV	N	D	57.8	57.54	61.0	57.4	46.6	53.6	50.7
AD 40	LA	N	D	33.98	62.54	44.3	56.1	38.9	52.6	44.5
AD 56	LA	N	D	47.75	60.86	55.5	58.8	44.2	49.5	48.0
AD 57	LA	N	D	57.87	63.34	52.7	54.5	40.6	44.4	42.8
AD 58	LA	N	D	63.13	65.74	51.0	52.0	38.5	42.9	43.9
AD 17	SJV	Y	D	39.4	56.1	54.5	58.0	58.3	49.3	55.8
AD 30	SJV	Y	D	55.7	55.4	53.8	66.3	65.9	56.9	61.4
AD 31	SJV	N	D	57.8	57.5	53.9	61.0	57.4	46.1	53.6
SD 16	SJV	Y	D	58.6	58.8	51.5	63.0	60.0	49.6	54.9
AD 45	LA	N	D	62.6	79.3	36.3	35.7	30.9	20.3	25.1
AD 46	LA	N	D	81.4	82.2	35.5	39.8	27.5	18.2	19.0
AD 50	LA	N	D	76.1	75.5	45.4	47.6	41.5	28.4	29.8

Source: California Secretary of State, Statements of Vote, 2003–2006; Report of Registration 2006.

and lower middle-class suburban districts provide an interesting comparison with the San Joaquin Valley districts. Indeed, the distinction is clear from Democrat registration alone, which runs an average of about 7% higher in the Los Angeles districts than in the San Joaquin Valley. The distinction on socially conservative issues and candidates is also clear: Proposition 73, which would have required parental notification for juvenile abortion, garnered an average of an 11% higher percentage in the San Joaquin Valley districts than in Los Angeles. President Bush received a similar 10.7% margin in 2004. While the two sets of districts are not quite as divergent on all issues, the trend of the San Joaquin Valley majority-Latino and VRA districts consistently voting more conservative than their counterparts in Los Angeles holds for all the measures analyzed.

Nevertheless, the San Joaquin Valley majority-Latino and VRA legislative districts now form the core of Democratic strength in the region. By the mid-2000s the *only* state legislative districts in the valley that Democrats controlled were majority-Latino or VRA districts; conversely, Republicans represented none of the region's Latino districts. Moreover, the concentration of Latinos into a few districts is unlikely to change in the post-2010 redistricting because to comply with to the Voting Rights Act's nonretrogression and nondilution principles (see Chapter 12 of this book) the state will continue to draw districts in the San Joaquin Valley that maximize Latino voting strength. If Republicans hope to increase their share of the region's legislative seats, they will have to find a way to win these conservative-leaning Latino districts.

Conclusion

Over the past two decades, while Democrats have solidified their hold on California, Republicans have quietly made major gains in the state's San Joaquin Valley. For the first time since the Great Depression, Republicans have gained an edge over Democrats in registration of San Joaquin Valley voters, and the Republican advantage continues to grow. Moreover, in top-of-the-ticket races, Republican candidates can now rely on strong support from the region. However, the Republican advances have stalled at the legislative district level. Notably, all the districts in the San Joaquin Valley represented by Democrats are either majority-Latino or VRA districts with large percentages of Latino constituents. San Joaquin Valley Latino districts are conservative by statewide standards, but Republicans have failed to compete effectively for them. Unless Republicans can find a way to win these seats, their otherwise impressive realignment of the San Joaquin Valley will have reached its limits.

References

Aghazarian, Greg. 2007. Interview with the author (Levitt), March 1.

Baldassare, Mark. 2000. *California in the New Millennium: The Changing Social and Political Landscape*. Berkeley: University of California Press.

Gimpel, James G., and Jason E. Schuknecht. 2003. *Patchwork Nation: Sectionalism and Change in American Politics*. Ann Arbor: University of Michigan Press.

Gregory, James N. 1989. *American Exodus: The Dust Bowl Migration and Okie Culture in California*. New York: Oxford University Press.

King, Gary. 1997. *A Solution to the Ecological Inference Problem*. Princeton: Princeton University Press.

Lockyer, Bill. 2001a. Attorney General of the State of California's Memorandum of Points and Authorities in Support of Administrative Preclearance Under 42 U.S.C. sec. 1973c for the Counties of Kings, Merced, Monterey, and Yuba. (Assembly and Board of Equalization).

———. 2001b. Attorney General of the State of California's Memorandum of Points and Authorities in Support of Administrative Preclearance Under 42 U.S.C. sec. 1973c for the Counties of Kings, Merced, Monterey, and Yuba. (Senate and Congressional Districts).

Reyes, Belinda I. 2003. "Latinos in California: Population Growth and Diversity." In *Latinos and Public Policy in California: An Agenda for Opportunity,* ed. David Lopez and Andres Jimenez. Berkeley: Berkeley Public Policy Press, University of California.

Quinn, T. Anthony. 1981. *The Political Geography of California*. Claremont, Calif.: Rose Institute of State and Local Government.

Walters, Dan. 1986. *The New California: Facing the 21st Century*. Sacramento: California Journal Press.

Chapter 8

How the New Los Angeles Has Reshaped California Politics

Dan Walters

When Vice President George Herbert Walker Bush outpolled Massachusetts Governor Michael Dukakis by 700,000 votes in California in 1988, on his way to becoming the 41st president of the United States, it was not surprising to those who chart California's politics.

Although Democratic voters had outnumbered Republicans in California for more than a half-century (Democrats first gained a majority in 1934) and Democrats usually controlled the legislature and the state's congressional delegation, the GOP was used to winning top-of-the-ticket elections in the state, especially those for the presidency, thanks to its sway among conservative Democrats and independents on such issues as crime, taxes, and resisting global communism.

As it turned out, however, the hallmark of Bush's one-term presidency, the collapse of the Soviet Union and the end of the Cold War, was also the undoing of his party's once-dominant position in California, whose economy had profited handsomely from the hundreds of billions of dollars that the nation had spent on armaments and maintaining large standing armies, navies, and air forces from the 45-year-long conflict. The end of the Cold War, coupled with a powerful surge of immigration and other factors, generated just enough political change in one county, Los Angeles, to tip the political balance away from the GOP and make Democrats as dominant in California as Republicans had been for decades.

None of that was evident in 1988, however, and to fully understand this partisan shift, one must view it in the context of California political currents over the last years of the 20th Century .

Bush's 1988 win in California was the ninth for a Republican presidential candidate in the post-World War II, post-Franklin Roosevelt period, while Democrats could claim just two presidential winners in the state during this period—Harry Truman in 1948 and Lyndon Johnson in 1964. The 1980s, in fact, were a particularly fertile period for Republicans in the state's high-profile races for president, governor, and U.S. senator. Between 1980 and 1990, the only blemishes on the GOP's record in these contests were two re-elections for Democratic U.S. Senator Alan Cranston in 1980 and 1986.

As Republicans rolled up big wins in the state during the 1980s, including several landslides, the state's Democrats were reeling. Their share of voter registration had surged during the 1970s in reaction to the Vietnam War and the Watergate scandal, topping 57% in 1976, and they had become briefly dominant in statewide and legislative offices, including the governorship with Jerry Brown, although Republican President Jerry Ford eked out a very narrow victory in California over Democrat Jimmy Carter in 1976. But the Democratic dominance began to slip in the 1980s for a variety of reasons, including the popularity of President (and former governor) Ronald Reagan and the small-government philosophy he espoused.

The harbinger of the Democratic slippage was the 1978 election cycle in which Brown won re-election but voters passed Proposition 13, the landmark property tax reduction measure, elected a flock of conservative, self-proclaimed "Proposition 13 babies" to the legislature and approved a wide-ranging death penalty ballot measure that indirectly rebuked Brown for vetoing a capital punishment bill. By the end of the 1980s, Democratic voter registration had dipped to below 50% and party leaders were openly concerned about losing traction among swing voters, both conservative Democrats and independents, who feared crime, taxes, and the prospect of slipping into minority status. Democrats debated among themselves how to staunch the hemorrhage—whether to shift to the right on those issues and try to recapture the all-important middle, or go left and organize the state's huge population of nonvoting immigrants and poor whites to counter the dominance of white, affluent voters.

Their initial efforts were concentrated along the latter approach. In 1989, Jerry Brown came out of the exile he had imposed on himself in 1982 after losing a bid for the U.S. Senate and was elected state Democratic Party chairman on his pledge to improve the party's prospects. He was a living symbol of the Democrats' left-of-center positioning, best known for his advocacy of environmental causes, his identification with Cesar Chavez and the farm worker unionization movement, and his opposition to capital punishment.

As Brown took over the party chairmanship, California's political community—elected officials, legislative and campaign staffers and lobbyists for thousands of interest groups—were fixated on the upcoming 1990 campaign for governor, not only because the powerful office was being vacated by a retiring Republican, George Deukmejian, but because whoever won it would control the all-important redrawing of legislative and congressional districts following the 1990 census, a decade after Brown and Democratic lawmakers had gerrymandered control for themselves.

The Democrats' liberal activists openly favored Attorney General John Van de Kamp as their candidate and Van de Kamp, with onetime farmworker organizer Richie Ross as his chief adviser, adopted a sweeping environmental regulation ballot measure, known as "Big Green," as his platform. Indeed, when Van de Kamp's chief primary opponent, San Francisco Mayor Dianne Feinstein, stressed her support of capital punishment during a speech to a state party convention in 1990, she was roundly booed by liberal delegates (Feinstein's advisers were delighted, knowing that a videotape of the boos could help her with moderate voters should she win the primary).

Feinstein did win the primary, thanks to the influence of conservative Democratic voters, Van de Kamp's ill-advised decision to spend most of his campaign funds on Big Green, and the failure of Brown to deliver on his promise of a massive voter organization drive. The party, in fact, lost a half-million registrants between 1988 and 1990, dipping to under 50% of the total, while the Republican candidate, U.S. Sen. Pete Wilson (who had defeated Brown for the Senate in 1982), beat Feinstein by just under 300,000 votes. Wilson later vetoed the Democrats' self-serving redistricting plans and left it to the state Supreme Court to draw new legislative and congressional districts—a plan that, ironically enough, helped Los Angeles County's surging Latino population secure political power. But that's getting ahead of the story.

Wilson's win, following on Bush's victory in the state in 1988, closed out Republicans' very strong decade. But despite Wilson's landslide re-election in 1994—defeating Brown's sister, Kathleen—the GOP's fortunes turned sharply downward in the 1990s, as a detailed comparison of Bush's win in 1988 and his son's loss 16 years later reveals.

When Reagan, the elder Bush, Wilson, and Deukmejian were winning for the Republicans in the 1980s, they relied on what Republican strategists called the "fishhook," which is what a map of the state's reliably Republican counties resembled. Rural counties in northern California, especially those in the 500-mile-long Central Valley, comprised the shank of the political fishhook, which continued through the fast-growing "Inland Empire" counties of San Bernardino and Riverside and then hooked northward into San Diego and Orange counties, the latter long considered to be the most important Republican bastion in the state.

If a Republican candidate ran up big margins in the fishhook counties, especially those in populous southern California, it would offset the big margin that any Democrat could expect in the liberal, nine-county San Francisco Bay Area and with a little push from conservative voters along the Central Coast, would be enough to win statewide. A central tenet in the fishhook strategy, however, was that Los Angeles County, with more than a quarter of the state's population, would neutralize itself—divide fairly evenly between Republican and Democratic candidates—and be, in essence, a nonfactor.

It worked like a charm for the elder Bush in 1988. Michael Dukakis won Los Angeles County, which had a 55-35% Democratic voter registration edge, but by a scant 133,000 votes out of 2.6 million cast in the county, thereby allowing the big Bush margins in the fishhook counties to carry the state.

Sixteen years later, in 2004, the macro-circumstances of the presidential contest in California were uncannily similar. An incumbent Republican named Bush, this one President George W. Bush, also was facing a Democratic challenger from Massachusetts, Sen. John Kerry. The younger Bush still won handily in the fishhook counties, but Kerry took Los Angeles County by 800,000 votes. Kerry's margin in L.A. County was six times as large as Dukakis's margin and accounted for two-thirds of Kerry's statewide edge. This outcome was similar to what had happened four years earlier, when Bush lost to Vice President Al Gore. Los Angeles, it could be said, blunted the fishhook.

Bill Clinton's two presidential wins in California in 1992 and 1996, a Democratic sweep of U.S. Senate seats in the 1990s, and Gray Davis's election in 1998 and re-election in 2002 engraved the image of California as a "blue," solidly Democratic state in the minds of national political oddsmakers, even as the party's share of voter registration continued to decline into the low 40% range.

Several factors contributed to the Democrats' success, including a shift of public consciousness away from crime and taxes into social issues such as abortion rights, as well as a decided moderation in the party's public image that attracted independents and moderate voters. Gray Davis, for instance, was a death penalty advocate who rang up several executions on his watch. But as the experiences of the two Bushes indicate, what happened in Los Angeles County during a remarkable decade of deep-seated economic, cultural, and, finally, political change was a central factor in moving California into the Democratic column, at least for the time being.

It has been said, with impressive evidentiary basis, that California is a socio-economic and political harbinger of what will happen in the rest of the nation decades ahead. If so, however, Los Angeles is an equally valid harbinger of what is likely to happen in the rest of California, for better or worse, and understanding its sociopolitical evolution is vital to understanding this often-confounding state and what it bodes for the country during the remainder of the 21st Century .

Los Angeles—the city, the county, and the surrounding region—was a hopping place in the 1980s. Having voted strongly for Californian Ronald Reagan as president in 1980 (Reagan defeated Jimmy Carter by a 53-36% margin in the county), Los Angeles's dominant aerospace industry was surging with billions of dollars in contracts from the Reagan Administration's massive military buildup, meant to confront the Soviet Union on a scale never before envisioned. Los Angeles International Airport was being remodeled and expanded in anticipation of the 1984 Olympics, which were to be financed entirely with private funds and earn a profit.

The 1980 census found that two-thirds of Angelenos were white, although the county had long-established pockets of nonwhite population and a wave of foreign immigration, primarily from Asia and Latin America, had begun in the 1970s. And while the county's overwhelmingly white, middle- and upper-class voters were mostly Democrats, many of the Democratic registrants, especially unionized aerospace workers, were conservative on such issues as crime and national defense and voted that way consistently. The communities with the highest percentages of defense industry workers, such as Long Beach with its big McDonnell-Douglas aircraft factories and its naval shipyard, elected nothing but conservative Republicans to legislative and congressional seats. Republican George Deukmejian, a former state legislator from Long Beach, had become attorney general in 1979 and was elected to the first of two terms as governor in 1982. Deukmejian's protégé, Dan Lungren, represented Long Beach in Congress.

The divide between Los Angeles's nominal dominance by Democrats and its *realpolitik* tilt toward Republicans was demonstrated starkly by Reagan's 1980 win in the county. Democratic voter registration in the county was more than 58%, five points above that in the state as a whole, while Republicans seemingly languished at 32%, a couple of points below their statewide number. But Reagan reversed the Democratic voter registration edge by running up a 53-36% win over Jimmy Carter in the county.

The county did not always vote Republican in the decade, certainly, but when Democrats did win, it was generally by a small margin that allowed the fishhook strategy to work for Republicans statewide. In the 1982 governor's race, for example, Deukmejian lost to Los Angeles Mayor Tom Bradley by just 150,000 votes in Los Angeles County, which helped him squeeze by Bradley by 93,345 votes statewide, thanks to a massive absentee voter effort by Republicans. Nor was the relatively strong GOP showing in Los Angeles merely a phenomenon of the 1980s. Reagan had won the county by 350,000 votes in 1966 as he denied Governor Pat Brown a third term, and captured the county again in 1970 while winning re-election as governor. Californian Richard Nixon won in Los Angeles County in 1968 and 1972 as he sought his first and second terms as president. The GOP's Los Angeles string in high-profile elections was broken only by Jerry Brown in 1974 and 1978 as he won two terms as governor

The county's political ambivalence in the 1980s was reflected in other ways, such as the 3–2 majority that Republicans held on the county's powerful board of supervisors and fairly strong GOP presence in the county's congressional and legislative delegation, even after the Democratic gerrymander that followed the 1980 census. Republicans tended to hold seats in the southernmost region of the county, and maintained strong enclaves along the coast and in the San Fernando Valley. Only the highly urbanized, densely populated urban core, with its large populations of nonwhite and Jewish voters, remained solidly Democratic during the decade.

If there is one constant in Los Angeles, however, it is change. The one-time outpost of the Spanish empire has undergone several economic and cultural metamorphoses during its history. It was such a small piece of California when the state was first formed that its leaders, resentful of political domination by San Francisco, sought a division of the state, but by 1960 the county contained nearly 40% of the state's population. It was once the nation's most productive agricultural county, but by the end of the 20th century had become, by far, its most populous county and the very epitome of urban sprawl with futurists painting a dark, "Blade Runner"-like picture of urban decay, environmental degradation, and random violence. As Los Angeles began to assert itself economically in the early 20th century, it had a distinctly midwestern, monochromatic feel but by century's end had become, arguably, the most complex and diverse urban mélange in the history of humankind with countless races, ethnic backgrounds, languages, religions, and lifestyles. A pivotal point in that history happened after the Cold War ended with the collapse of the Berlin Wall in 1989 and then of the Soviet Union in the early 1990s.

California's rapid expansion into an industrial power, centered in southern California, had begun with the Japanese attack on Pearl Harbor in 1941. The attack not only immersed America in an already raging global war between fascism and democracy, but by geographic default made California the launching pad for the Pacific theater of the war. Its shipyards, aircraft factories, and other arsenals of industrial war expanded rapidly, as did its military bases. Hundreds of thousands of men and women from throughout the nation came to California, and especially southern California, to undergo military training or work in war industries and they ignited a population explosion. As the Cold War (and the Korean and Vietnam wars) quickly succeeded World War II, the state's defense-centered industrial expansion continued, people kept moving to the state to work, and a postwar baby boom added to the rapid growth. California had fewer than seven million people in 1940, 5.2% of the national population, but by 1950, its population had grown by 53% to 10.6 million. It hit 15.7 million in 1960, another 48% expansion, surpassing New York to become the nation's most populous state later in that decade, and reached almost 20 million in 1970.

The state's population growth slowed a bit in the 1970s, just 19% to 23.8 million, but picked up markedly in the 1980s because of foreign immigration and a new baby boom, primarily born to immigrant mothers. California hit 30 million in 1990 and stood at 37.4 million in 2007 with 40 million just around the corner.

After 1960, Los Angeles County also grew, albeit at a somewhat slower pace than California as a whole. Its six million residents in 1960 (almost as many people as the entire state had in 1940) grew to seven-plus million in 1970, slowed to 7.5 million in 1980, then shot up again to 8.9 million in 1990 and 9.5 million in 2000. It now approaches 10.5 million, or just under 30% of the state.

The contrast between Los Angeles's 1.4 million-person growth in the 1980s and its relatively modest 600,000-person growth in the 1990s, however, was inexorably connected to the rise and fall of the county's aerospace and defense industries and what demographers believe is the flight of more than 1.5 million, people, many of them defense workers and their families, from the state during the early 1990s when the industries collapsed.

At the height of the Cold War military buildup in the 1980s, the Pentagon was spending upwards of $60 billion a year in California, roughly a fifth of its budget, and most of it was flowing into southern California. Jerry Nickelsburg, an economist with UCLA's Anderson School, has calculated that in 1990, there were 214,000 jobs in direct aerospace manufacturing in California, more than 10% of all of the state's manufacturing jobs, plus another 120,000 in dependent research and development fields, more than a quarter of all such jobs in the nation.

According to Nickelsburg (2006), "The demise of the Soviet Union and the winning of the Cold War resulted in a cutback in defense spending and a scaling back of important manufacturing programs such as the B-2 bomber. It is estimated that over 200,000 aerospace jobs were lost in California during the ensuing decade."

Aerospace jobs dropped to below 80,000 as factory after factory shut down, both big assembly lines and the countless small metal and electronics fabricating plants maintained by subcontractors. The aerospace jobs that remained were increasingly white collar and technical rather than blue collar, as Nickelsburg and others who have studied the industry conclude. And there was another heavy impact from the closure of military bases such as the Long Beach Naval Shipyard.

By happenstance, the Pentagon cutbacks occurred just as California was undergoing a mild cyclic recession and the combination of the two created the state's worst economic retreat in a half-century—one almost entirely centered on Los Angeles and environs. State employment data say that there were 887,200 manufacturing jobs of all kinds in Los Angeles County in 1987, capping several years of strong growth (although it had been as high as 924,900 in 1979), but that by 1990 the total had fallen to 834,600 and the plummet continued year after year until leveling off in the mid-1990s at about 640,000 (Southern California Association of Governments).

Aerospace was, in a sense, the last great industrial sector in California to undergo downsizing, a process that had begun in the 1970s with cutbacks in auto, steel, lumber, and other industrial sectors. But whereas the reductions in the others had been gradual, the impact on aerospace was abrupt and massive. The county's economy, like that of California as a whole, underwent a dramatic transformation in the 1980s and 1990s, from manufacturing to a "new economy" rooted in trade, services, communications, and technology. One symbol of that change: The conversion of aerospace assembly plants into movie sound stages.

As blue-collar jobs disappeared, blue-collar families fled the state in droves, reversing the state's long-standing attraction to those in other states. According to a Public Policy Institute of California (PPIC) report by Hans P. Johnson (2000), in the early 1990s, "as many as two million more people left California to live in other states." The report added that most of the migration appeared to be for economic reasons, noting "[t]he mass outflow in the early 1990s coincided with California's deepest recession since the Depression of the 1930s." Most of those who left, the report found, went to other western states where economies were more vibrant (particularly Arizona and Texas) and were largely young, married adults.

How many of those fleeing the state were leaving Los Angeles is unknown, but the sharp decline of employment in the county during the period—437,000 jobs of all kinds lost between 1990 and 1994—supports other anecdotal and statistical evidence that the recession was centered in Los Angeles and environs and much of the flight was from the county. If two million people left California during the early 1990s, as the PPIC study postulated, it is likely that around half of them were from Los Angeles, or at least Los Angeles and the immediately surrounding area. According to UCLA's Nickelsburg, "As their economic opportunities diminished in Los Angeles, they packed up and moved to Texas, Massachusetts, Georgia, or wherever their skills were in demand" (Nickelsburg, 2007).

The county's once-robust population growth flattened to just above zero, as the flight was offset by continued high flows of immigrants into the state, and into Los Angeles, from other countries, especially those in Latin America, and by a continued high birth rate.

The combination of the exodus to other states, which the PPIC study found to be overwhelmingly white, and the continuing surge in foreign immigration produced a massive cultural, economic, and political impact on Los Angeles County, especially in the communities such as Long Beach, which had been dependent on the aerospace and defense industries. Whole neighborhoods that had been occupied by industrial workers and their families were transformed, seemingly overnight, into ethnic bastions—whether Asian and Latino in Long Beach or Armenian in Glendale. And once the flight from the area ended in the late 1990s, the county's population began to grow dramatically, almost entirely driven by immigration and babies. From 8.9 million in 1990, the county's population surged to nearly 10.5 million by 2007.

By then, too, nearly half of the county's population was Latino. Non-Latino whites, more than 40% of the county's population in 1990, had shrunken by 700,000 and were now under 30%. A PPIC survey of Los Angeles conducted by Mark Baldassare (2005) reported that "[i]n 2003, L.A. County was home to 3% of the nation's population but 17% of the nation's Koreans, 14% of Mexicans (12% of all Latinos), 14% of Filipinos, 13% of Chinese and 13% of Japanese." The study also found that "[o]ver half of the county's residents (56%) speak a language other than English at home."

And the shrinkage in high-pay, high-skill, blue-collar jobs meant socioeconomic stratification in the state as a whole, but most dramatically in Los Angeles County—more rich people, more poor people, and fewer in the middle class. According to Nickelsburg (2007), "In a span of 10 years, the middle class in Los Angeles, faced with diminished economic opportunity, hollowed out."

While the phenomenon of income inequality is national in scope, Nickelsburg determined that it is much more pronounced in Los Angeles County than the rest of the nation, because it has become a destination point for poor and poorly educated immigrants seeking service industry jobs and because, as Nickelsburg noted, "Los Angeles is a magnet for the very rich." The county, with 3.4% of the nation's population, has 8% of those on the Forbes 400 list of the nation's wealthiest people. Nickelsburg observed that Los Angeles had "achieved the dubious distinction of having inequality levels similar to those found in Mexico."

Baldassare (2005) found a similar result, reporting that "[Los Angeles] County is home to 28% of California's population but 34% of California's poor." Still more confirmation was generated in statistical analyses performed by Sacramento State University professor Robert Mogull (2006a, 2006b), who calculated that 4.7 million Californians lived in poverty in 1999, a third of them in Los Angeles County, and Latinos were by far the county's largest poverty-stricken ethnic group. In fact, Mogull reported, half of Latino Californians living in poverty were in Los Angeles, and with housing costs much higher in Los Angeles than the nation as a whole, the data—which are based on federal designations of income—may understate the actual incidence of L.A. poverty.

The Cliff Notes version of Los Angeles County's history after 1990, therefore, is this: The county, home to more than a quarter of the state's population, underwent wrenching economic, cultural, and demographic change in a very brief period. And that change, which continues, albeit at a slower pace, has two distinct but interrelated political impacts that reverberate in the state as a whole.

First, and probably foremost, the rapid changes generate a cornucopia of political issues. Take, for example, the sheer impact of population growth. More human beings, regardless of their origins, create more demand for every public

and private service and commodity. They mean more cars on the road (on average a half-million more in California every year), more demand for housing
(roughly 200,000 a year), and a larger workforce (the state needs to expand employment by 20,000 jobs a month), as well as more kids in school, more enroll-
ment in college, more need for parks and recreation space, more retail shopping,
etc. Each one of those growth-driven pressures is a potential political flash-
point—witness the battles fought over freeways, residential development, and
water. The other aspects of change, such as cultural diversification and economic stratification, not only generate political issues unto themselves but combine with growth to complicate growth-related conflicts. And all of these trends
are more pronounced in Los Angeles County than anywhere else in the state. It
is well known, to cite but one example, that the county's population is growing
much faster than its housing stock and that poor immigrant families are dou-
bling, tripling, or even quadrupling up in single-family housing units and that
garages and commercial buildings are routinely converted, illegally, into housing.

Second, social and economic change alters the political atmosphere in
which those issues are addressed—or, more likely, ignored. As mentioned earlier, Los Angeles County has undergone a dramatic political transformation
since 1990, from a county that was largely neutral in the perennial struggle between the two major parties for dominance to one with a strong Democratic tilt,
thus affecting both local political power and California's overall shift into the
blue column, at least temporarily. And one of the most commonly used indices
of political orientation, voter registration, gives some indication of that change,
if viewed in relation to what has been happening in the state as a whole.

For years, the Democratic share of California voter registration has been
shrinking while Republicans have, relatively speaking, been fairly static. Democrats were near 60% of the state's registered voters in the mid-1970s but by
1980 had dropped to 53%, still substantially larger than the GOP's 34% share.
During the 1980s, the Democrats' margin shrunk further as they lost ground (to
just under 50% in 1990) while Republicans gained a bit (to 35% in 1990). The
1990s saw Democrats continue to drop (to 45% in 2000) and Republicans hold
steady (still 35% in 2000) and that trend continued into the first decade of the
21st century. Democratic losses and Republican stagnation meant that the margin between the two parties shriveled to its smallest level since the 1930s. It also
meant that an ever-larger share of California's voters were shunning identification with either party and registering as independents and, in the process, becoming the decisive factor in any close contest between nominees of the two
major parties.

Party registration in Los Angeles County has followed a somewhat similar
pattern during the same period, albeit with somewhat more decline among Republicans. Democrats enjoyed a 58-32% advantage in 1980, which shrank to 55-
35 in 1990, reflecting statewide GOP growth. But in the 1990s, which was the

county's period of economic and social upheaval, the margin widened. Democrats' share declined from 55% to 52% in the decade but GOP voter registration in L.A. dropped by 7 points to 28%. The first years of the 21st century have seen a slight narrowing of the gap, not because Republicans have recovered but because Democratic registration, reflecting the statewide expansion of independent voters, dropped to below 50%.

The changes in voter registration numbers, however, are just one, and perhaps the least important, of the indicators of what has happened in Los Angeles since 1990. The more dramatic indications are to be found in voting results, especially in high-profile contests for president and governor. During this period, a county that had long been either neutral or leaned Republican moved solidly into the Democratic column. The county's traditional neutrality was still evident in the 1990 contest for governor between Republican Pete Wilson and Democrat Dianne Feinstein. Feinstein won the county, but by a relatively small 49–47% margin. She ran six points under Democratic registration in the county while Wilson ran 11 points ahead of GOP registration, thus indicating that Republicans of the moderate variety were still doing well among conservative Democrats and independents.

The political worm began to turn in 1992 when Bill Clinton became the first Democrat to capture the state's presidential electoral votes since Lyndon Johnson in 1964. Clinton won just 46% of the statewide vote, thanks to the presence of independent Ross Perot, who clearly siphoned votes away from Republican President George H. W. Bush. With Los Angeles County feeling the full effects of the post-Cold War recession, Clinton rang up nearly 53% of its votes while Bush garnered just 29%, some 18 points lower than his 1988 showing. In 1994, Wilson won the county by just a few points in 1994, while running up a landslide re-election statewide. But in 1996 Clinton clobbered GOP challenger Bob Dole by a nearly two-to-one margin in the county. Ever since 1996, excepting races involving Arnold Schwarzenegger, the county has delivered big votes to Democrats. In the 1998 governor's race, for example Democrat Gray Davis beat Republican Dan Lungren, the one-time Long Beach congressman who later became attorney general, by a more than two-to-one margin in the county.

It was Davis's paper-thin re-election in 2002, however, that truly underscores Los Angeles's pivotal role in statewide politics. Although he had defeated Lungren handily in 1998, Davis—whose career had included stints as chief of staff to Governor Jerry Brown, state assemblyman, state controller, and lieutenant governor—was in big trouble going into his 2002 re-election campaign. His high standing with voters during the first three years of his governorship, at one time more than 60% approval, vanished as he presided over—and to critics badly mishandled—a massive energy crisis and then a state budget crisis. With his approval ratings languishing in the 20s, Davis and his advisers engaged in several high-risk maneuvers in 2002. Most importantly, Davis spent heavily on negative ads to deny Los Angeles Mayor Richard Riordan, a popular Republican moderate, the GOP's gubernatorial nomination and help William Simon, a wealthy Los Angeles businessman and civic leader, win the party's nod. The Davis camp believed that Simon, lesser known and more conservative than Riordan, would be an easier foe. Davis's strategy worked, and Simon was nominated. Davis also moved to shore up his weak standing with labor unions, Latino leaders, and other liberal elements of the Democratic Party that he had held at arm's length during the first years of his governorship while cultivating a moderate image and support from business executives. Beginning in 2002, Davis signed a number of liberal bills, including a $3 billion per year increase in worker's compensation benefits and a measure to grant driver's licenses to illegal immigrants, and negotiated generous contracts with state worker unions.

Despite having Simon—who made several injurious gaffes—as an opponent and making peace with liberal groups, Davis faced an extremely tight race and knew he needed a big turnout of Democratic voters in Los Angeles County to survive. Davis got that turnout, thanks to efforts by the county's newly ascendant union and political leaders, and scored a 358,414-vote margin in Los Angeles, while winning by a scant 5,275 votes in the rest of the state. The Davis-Simon contest, moreover, was sandwiched between two presidential elections in which Los Angeles also displayed its new blue tinge. The county voted almost two-to-one for Democratic candidates Al Gore and John Kerry, providing two-thirds of their statewide vote margins over Republican George W. Bush, who lost California to Gore by 1.3 million votes in 2000 and to Kerry by 1.2 million in 2004.

Social and economic upheaval may have set the stage for the county's political transformation into a Democratic powerhouse, but the change became a reality through the efforts of the new generation of mostly Latino labor and political leaders to organize and mobilize new voters. As manufacturing gave way to the service industries as the mainstay of the local economy, immigrants—most of them Latino—filled the new jobs. The leaders, many of them graduates of decades-long, mostly unsuccessful efforts to unionize farm workers, now focused on organizing Los Angeles's janitors, hotel maids, and other low-skill, low-wage workers. No leader was more spectacularly successful in both labor and political organization than Miguel Contreras, a one-time disciple of farm worker leader Cesar Chavez who took over the 800,000-member Los Angeles County Federation of Labor in 1996 and quickly converted it into a powerful agent of political change.

Contreras died at age 52 in 2005. Following his death, *Sacramento Bee* reporter Aurelio Rojas (2005) noted:

> The one-time farm worker—who was plucked out of a picket line by United Farm Workers union patriarch Cesar Chavez—also reversed a decline in the federation's membership by tapping into the growing Latino labor pool Unions embraced janitors and restaurant, hotel and other largely immigrant work forces and

forged a stronger coalition between labor and neighborhood groups. Until Contreras took over the 800,000-member federation, its 350 unions contributed to political candidates, hoping for political access. . . . Contreras upended that model. The federation ran its own candidates and mobilized union members to campaign for them.

Contreras and his organization not only delivered bounties of Democratic votes to top-of-the-ticket candidates such as Davis, Gore, and Kerry, but cultivated candidates and organized campaigns for city councils large and small, school boards, the legislature, and Congress. He became a kingmaker in an old-fashioned, Chicago- or New York-like sense, somewhat alien to California's experience but very effective nonetheless. Two structural evolutions that, ironically enough, Republicans had espoused and Democratic politicians had opposed—a court-ordered legislative and congressional redistricting plan after the 1990 census and legislative term limits—gave Contreras and the other new political/labor leaders an opportunity to send a whole new generation of Latino Democrats to Sacramento and Washington. They seized the opportunity, sometimes at the expense of other Democrats and sometimes taking away seats from Republicans. One Contreras protégé, Antonio Villaraigosa, became speaker of the Assembly and later the first Latino mayor of Los Angeles in more than a century. He is now arguably the leading Democratic prospect for governor in 2010. Another acolyte at the Federation of Labor, political organizer Fabian Nunez, was elected to the legislature and became speaker of the state Assembly with a clear ambition of succeeding Villaraigosa as mayor.

The Democratic—and markedly Latino—political surge in Los Angeles County during the 1990s shrank Republican members in the county's congressional and legislative delegations. Republicans held four of the county's 15 congressional seats (a third of the state delegation) in the 1980s and as the L.A. contingent expanded after the 1990 census, thanks to the state's powerful population growth in the 1980s, Republicans claimed six of 17 seats in the 1992 elections. But as the decade unfolded, the GOP ranks thinned, most dramatically in 2000 when a Democratic state legislator, Adam Schiff, successfully challenged Republican Congressman Jim Rogan in a San Fernando Valley district that long been considered to be a GOP stronghold. Rogan, a former judge, had been one of President Bill Clinton's prosecutors during his impeachment trial, making him a tempting target for Democrats as they saw his Glendale-centered district's GOP registration slip throughout the decade, thanks largely to the exodus of aerospace workers.

A similar transition was unfolding, meanwhile, in Long Beach, another one-time GOP bastion undergoing dramatic sociopolitical change from the decline in defense spending. A congressional seat held for many years by conservative Republican Dan Lungren, it remained in GOP hands for a few terms after Lungren decamped to run for attorney general in 1990, but as Republican registration shrank dramatically in the 1990s, liberal Republican Steve Horn finally threw in the towel. He ceded the seat to Democratic Latina Linda Sanchez in 2002 after its lines were redrawn to make it even less hospitable to a Republican, thus completing the Democratic sweep of politics in Long Beach, once among the most solidly Republican cities in the state. Overall, the 2001 redistricting plan dropped the county's congressional delegation back to 15 seats, but with just two held by Republicans, the Democratic ranks swelled by two members to 13 and with Sanchez's election, Latino seats rose to five.

Contreras's death created a leadership void that was eventually filled by his widow, Maria Elena Durazo, a highly regarded labor organizer in her own right. As the first decade of the 21st century unfolded, Durazo continued the successful combination of labor and political organization.

The only major blip on the otherwise overwhelming Democratic grip on the county has been Arnold Schwarzenegger. Although the county voted narrowly against the recall of Gray Davis from the governorship in 2003, former bodybuilder and action movie star Schwarzenegger garnered 45% of the county's vote to succeed Davis—with young Latinos reportedly among his strongest supporters. Republican Schwarzenegger's 2006 re-election landslide over Democratic challenger Phil Angelides saw a return of the fishhook, with Los Angles opting for Angelides by a three-percentage-point margin, just 60,000 votes, thereby allowing the strongly pro-Schwarzenegger voters in the fishhook counties, aided by his advantage among independents throughout the state, to prevail.

Schwarzenegger's re-election indicates, perhaps, that while Los Angeles remains a very blue county, its can still be competitive when a centrist Republican faces an unabashedly liberal Democrat. There are enough independents and moderates in Los Angeles to neutralize the county's statewide influence under the right circumstances. The longer-term role of the county in the state's political ambience, too, is dependent on whether the Latinos who have become the county's dominant population block will also become more politically active than they have been in the past.

The efforts of Contreras, Durazo, and others notwithstanding, the county's share of the overall state electorate has been shrinking. Its population growth, while numerically impressive, still lags behind the state as a whole and also behind that of Republican-leading inland areas, and ever-more of its residents are Latinos, whose voting participation levels are low and many of whom are noncitizens or too young to vote. Between 1990 and 2000, Los Angeles County's population grew by 7.4%, while that of southern California as a whole grew by 12.8%, paced by Riverside County's 32%. During that same period, the county's Latino population expanded by 62%, from just over 2 million to 3.4 million. Between 1990 and 2007, the county's population grew by 1.7 million, mostly due to immigration and births to immigrant mothers, but its voter registration expanded by a relatively scant 400,000 from 3.5 to 3.9 million, three-fourths of the statewide growth in voter rolls.

Los Angeles County's Latino population will continue to expand, both numerically and relatively, topping 50% by the 2010, according to projections by the southern California Association of Governments (2007). The county's continued role as a decisive factor in statewide politics, therefore, will depend largely on overcoming historic trends and raising Latino political participation to levels approximating the ethnic group's population. Although whites are now a decided minority in the state's population—and an aging group at that—they remain, overwhelmingly, the largest single ethnic bloc among voters, over 70%. Latinos, meanwhile, may be more than a third of the state's population but are a barely one-eighth of the state's voters.

According to the PPIC special survey of Los Angeles residents (Baldassare, 2005), if Los Angeles maintains the pivotal role it assumed in the 1990s, it will not only benefit the Democratic Party politically, but will drive the state's political ambience leftward on a variety of issues that the working poor consider important and wealthier liberals embrace, such as expanded health care and rights for immigrants. That said, Angelenos are, the poll found, "relatively pessimistic" about the quality of life in the county as the century wears on, with 37% expecting it to be a worse place in which to live 20 years hence and just 24% optimistic about conditions in 2025. But nearly two-thirds of those polled said they expected to continue living in the county at least five more years.

As Los Angeles goes, so goes the state? Perhaps, but with change the only constant in the huge county, who can really predict what will happen? After all, in 1990, no one expected what did happen later in the decade.

References

Baldassare, Mark. 2005. *Special Survey of Los Angeles in Collaboration with the University of Southern California.* San Francisco: Public Policy Institute of California, March.

Johnson, Hans P. 2000. "Movin' Out: Domestic Migration to and from California in the 1990s." *California Counts: Population Trends and Problems,* vol. 2, no. 1. San Francisco: Public Policy Institute of California, August.

Mogull, Robert. 2006a. "State Poverty: The Case of California." *Journal of Social Service Research,* vol. 33, no. 1 (November 29).

————. 2006b. "California Poverty without Los Angeles." *Journal of Applied Business Research* (4th quarter).

Nickelsburg, Jerry. 2006. "Where Does Southern California Aerospace Go from Here?" *UCLA Anderson Forecast* (September).

————. 2007. "Richer and Poorer: Income Inequality in Los Angeles." *UCLA Anderson Forecast* (March).

Rojas, Aurelio. 2005. "Labor leader left band of loyalists: State's Democrats were shaped by L.A.'s Miguel Contreras." *Sacramento Bee.* May 11.

Southern California Association of Governments. 2007. "Summary of Data from California Employment Development Department Labor Market Information Division."

III. The Political Implications of Geography

Chapter 9

Governors, Geography, and Direct Democracy: The Case of Arnold Schwarzenegger

William M. Chandler and Thad Kousser

Not many politicians emigrate from Austria, begin their careers in Venice Beach before rising into the Hollywood hierarchy, and then ride a surge of populist discontent fomented in San Diego all the way to the halls of power in Sacramento. To be sure, Arnold Schwarzenegger did not follow the typical road map to political success for California governors. But as anomalous as his career has been, it still holds general lessons for the role of region and of direct democracy in California politics.

This chapter examines the rise, fall, and resurrection of Arnold Schwarzenegger through the lens of political geography. We begin by describing how California's unique brand of direct democracy opened the door to Gray Davis's recall and Schwarzenegger's ascension. We then ask how this extraordinary candidate won in the 2003 special election, and whether his victory reshaped the ordinary regional patterns of California politics. Next we turn to his record as governor, seeking to explain his cycle of popularity. What political choices led to the dramatic drop in his approval ratings during 2005, and in what areas of the state did he lose the most support? How did his dramatic turn to the left that assured his reelection in 2006 play in different parts of California? We explore these questions by examining both his policy record and his political style,

215

measuring the results of his strategies through polls that group respondents by the regions in which they live. Because Governor Schwarzenegger has relied so heavily on direct democracy in his battles with the legislature, we pay close attention to how geography draws a dividing line between the constituencies represented by governors, by legislators, and in initiative contests. Overall, the successes and failures of this once-in-a-generation governor illuminate many of the geographic patterns that are ever present in California politics.

Born in Thal bei Graz, Austria in 1947, Arnold Schwarzenegger at age 18 served his one year of mandatory military service. A year later he left for England but quickly moved on to the United States in 1968. Training at Gold's Gym in Venice Beach, he developed his early career as body-building champion. In only a few years, he translated this into a monumentally successful movie career and became the world's best known action hero. Years later, his entry into California politics was made possible by his popular image, name recognition, and the special opportunities of populist direct democracy.

Institutional Opportunity: Direct Democracy in California

Bowler and Cain (2004) have noted how California's version of direct democracy consists of three essential parts: the initiative (voter initiated measures that become propositions), the citizen referendum (legislative statutes put to the voters), and the recall (removing elected officials from office without a regular election). The latter is rare but dramatic when it does occur. The recall, introduced in Los Angeles in 1903, was adopted statewide in 1911 during the Progressive Era. Governor Hiram Johnson's constitutional amendment applied to state officeholders (including judges) in an effort to combat graft and corruption (Bowler and Cain, 2004: 7; Lawrence, 2004: 1–3). Many recalls have been attempted since then but few legislators have been recalled. Recalls have been more frequent at the local level.

Although there have been gubernatorial recall attempts in other states, and half-hearted efforts before in California, in 2003 Gray Davis became the first governor to be recalled anywhere since 1921 (when North Dakota's governor was removed from office). The details of California's recall law, unique among the 18 states that allow such removals, surely contributed to this rare event. First, California's recall law is relatively easily activated. Some states, such as Minnesota, require the demonstration of malfeasance, but in California simple unpopularity is adequate (Bowler and Cain, 2004: 7). The California recall provision is purely procedural, requiring no substantive offense by the governor in order to be initiated (Institute of Governmental Studies Library, 2003: 1–4). Second, California has the lowest signature threshold, requiring the signatures of just 12% of the voters in the previous gubernatorial election (or about 900,000 signatures in 2003, with some 1.2 million needed to guarantee enough valid signatures). This hurdle was effectively reduced by low turnout in a ho-hum 2002 governor's race. Most other states require 25% or more. Third, California is more generous than most states in allowing 160 days for the circulation of a petition. Thus, as Bowler and Cain (2004: 7) note, the recall may be viewed as "an accident waiting to happen."

Entering Politics:
How to get from Graz (via Hollywood) to Sacramento

Although Schwarzenegger has been seen as the consummate outsider candidate, he was no political neophyte when he entered the recall. His first involvement in government came with his appointment by President George H. W. Bush to a three-year term (1990 to 1993) on the president's Council on Physical Fitness. By 1999, he publicly expressed interest in running for governor and in 2001 met with Karl Rove and George W. Bush on the advisability of doing so. He then made a first big splash with his highly visible sponsorship of an initiative to make state grants available for after-school programs, known as the "After School Education and Safety program Act," Proposition 49. On the November 2002 ballot, voters approved this initiative. For Schwarzenegger, this was clearly a career move that established his civic credibility and indicated his political entrepreneurship through direct democracy.

As early as 2001, he was thinking about running in 2002 but did not, deferring to the candidacy of his friend, Richard Riordan. In 2003, he again met with Rove to discuss running in 2006. Republican connections prepared the way. Aides to former governor Pete Wilson had been working for some time to prepare for his possible candidacy.

While long-term plans may have been in the works, the testimony of insiders reveals that "Arnold shock[ed] the world, including his advisors, by getting into the race" (Lubenow, 2003: 222). The recall of 2003 gave him the crucial opening, but few (beyond his wife, Maria Shriver) knew that Arnold would jump in.

He may have been tempted into the race because the unique combination of the recall and the replacement contest on the same ballot created special opportunities for challengers, especially a moderate such as Schwarzenegger (Alvarez et al., 2004: 23–26). Without a partisan primary to battle through, candidates could essentially nominate themselves with 65 signatures and $3,500. This produced a ballot comprising 135 names and meant that Schwarzenegger did not have to shift to the right to win the Republican nomination.

The dual ballot format created a double standard for victory. The incumbent could only survive by winning an absolute majority (50% +1) on the first ballot. But he was prevented from running as a candidate on the second, replacement ballot, which only took a plurality to win. It was possible that Davis would be replaced by a candidate who received fewer votes than he did. Further, the deteriorating public mood—reflected in the rapidly dropping approval ratings for both the governor and the legislature reported in Figure 9.1—set the tone for political change. By July 2003, 75% of voters thought that the state was going the wrong way, "seriously off on the wrong track." This corresponded with very low ratings on job performance for both the governor (his approval sunk to a low of 23% just before the recall) and the legislature (which was at a dismal 19% approval).

Schwarzenegger took advantage of this political opportunity on August 6, 2003 by appearing on Jay Leno's *The Tonight Show*, where he announced, apparently to the surprise of some of his closest confidants, that he would run. His communications director, Sean Walsh, claimed that "We didn't know this was going to happen" (Lubenow, 2003: 224). However, even if his campaign was unprepared in terms of infrastructure and staff, the surprise announcement created massive media coverage over the next five or six days.

Governor Davis, given his dismal approval rating, had little hope of surviving a recall vote once Schwarzenegger's popular candidacy surfaced. Faced with imminent disaster, Democrats found themselves in disarray. Senator Diane Feinstein, the only figure with a good chance of beating Schwarzenegger on the replacement ballot, refused to run and advocated that there be no Democratic candidate on the ballot. Then Democratic unity crumbled as Lieutenant Governor Cruz Bustamante announced his candidacy with a strategy based on a mixed message of "No to Recall, Yes to Bustamante." This was widely seen as suicidal by incredulous professional activists.

Schwarzenegger, with established name recognition and a positive popular image helped along by his earlier advocacy of Prop. 49, alone possessed the special recipe for political success based on personal image. A key to Schwarzenegger's support in the recall was his ability to cut across some of California's party and ideological lines, while remaining firmly in the centrist tradition of some of his Republican predecessors. Schwarzenegger has usually been described as a moderate Republican largely because of his liberal views on social issues, his support for the moderate Riordan in the 2002 primaries, and because of his ties to Pete Wilson Republicans. Early in his career, he positioned himself as a centrist and gained the confidence of pragmatists in his own party. This served him well in the 2003 recall campaign when he was able to successfully appeal to the broad middle of the political spectrum and include many disillusioned Democrats and independents who were disenchanted with Governor Davis.

A look at the geographic basis of Schwarzenegger's appeal demonstrates the benefits of his centrist strategy and its eventual limits. The Public Policy Institute of California (PPIC) reports the results of its regular *Statewide Survey* by the regions in which respondents live: the "San Francisco Bay Area" (including nine counties), the 19 counties of the "Central Valley," "Los Angeles" (L.A. County itself), and "Other Southern California" (including San Diego, Orange County, and the Inland Empire). Together, residents of these areas make up 90%

Figure 9.1. Approval Ratings of Governor Davis and Legislature

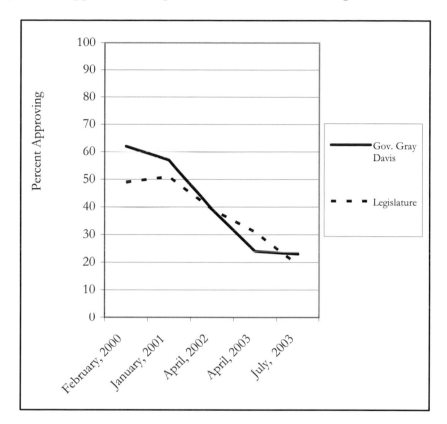

Notes: Figures taken from The Field Poll, Report #2074.

of California's population. In each of the four regions, at least 69% of residents responded that the state budget deficit was a "big problem" by June of 2003.

Geographic differences began to emerge in the August 2003 *Statewide Survey*, which asked voters whether they planned to vote to recall Governor Davis. Support for the recall ranged from 40% in the ever-liberal Bay Area to a surprisingly high 57% in Los Angeles, while those in other parts of southern California (68%) and the Central Valley (69%) strongly backed it. In this poll, Schwarzenegger's candidacy trailed Bustamante's in the Bay Area by a large margin, but he held a healthy lead in the other three main regions. What was most shocking about this poll was that Los Angeles voters responded less like their fellow Democrats in the Bay Area and more like those in the Republican-leaning portions of the state. Yet by the time of the September PPIC 2003 *Statewide Survey*,

California's political map began to look more normal again as the race polarized along party lines. Support for the recall declined to 48% in Los Angeles, dropped to 35% in the Bay Area, but remained high in the Central Valley (66%) and the rest of southern California (69%). Cruz Bustamante led Schwarzenegger by a 29% to 24% margin in Los Angeles and by 37%–16% in the Bay Area, though he trailed by large margins elsewhere.

The maps presented in Figures 9.2 and 9.3 tell the same story, showing that support for the recall (which correlated almost perfectly with support for Schwarzenegger) was low in the traditional urban Democratic strongholds but high in the suburbs and rural areas where Republicans have seen recent success. The first map reports major party registration by county, and the second shows the percentage of voters in each county who backed the recall. The resemblance between the two maps is not coincidental. Democratic strength is centered in Los Angeles County and in the Bay Area; majorities in these regions opposed the recall. The Republican heartland lies in Orange and Riverside counties and in the more mountainous parts of the Central Valley. There, the recall won over overwhelmingly.

Voters in California's "battleground" counties supplied the margin of victory for the recall campaign and for Schwarzenegger. Ventura and Santa Barbara, along with the more urbanized Central Valley counties such as Fresno and San Joaquin, are evenly split between the two parties and have seen many of the state's closest legislative contests over the past decade. A majority of voters in all four counties, and in Democratic-leaning Sacramento County, all supported the recall, contributing to its statewide total of 55.4% on the October 7, 2003 election day. On the replacement ballot, Schwarzenegger won easily. His late surge in the polls culminated in a landslide victory of 48.7% support for Schwarzenegger to just 31.7% for Democrat Cruz Bustamante. By winning just enough votes in the battleground areas, Schwarzenegger won the right to be inaugurated on November 17 to serve the remainder of Davis's term. Yet his campaign failed to make significant inroads in the regions of Democratic strength, solidifying rather than redrawing the state's geopolitical lines.

Schwarzenegger in the Role of Governor

When he was sworn into office, Governor Arnold Schwarzenegger possessed all the credentials of a political maverick. He had won office through a populist revolt, waged much of his campaign through media outlets that rarely covered politics, financed his 77-day race largely with his own money so that he could not be tied to Sacramento's interest groups, and presented himself as a figure above political parties.

Yet in his first year in office, this ultimate outsider pursued a surprisingly traditional insider strategy. Schwarzenegger used the tools of direct democracy

Figure 9.2. Major Party Registration in California, by County

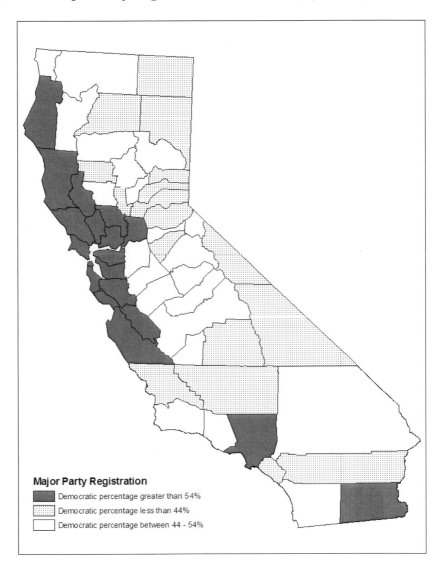

Notes: Data collected from Secretary of State (2003a).

Figure 9.3. Support for the Recall, by County

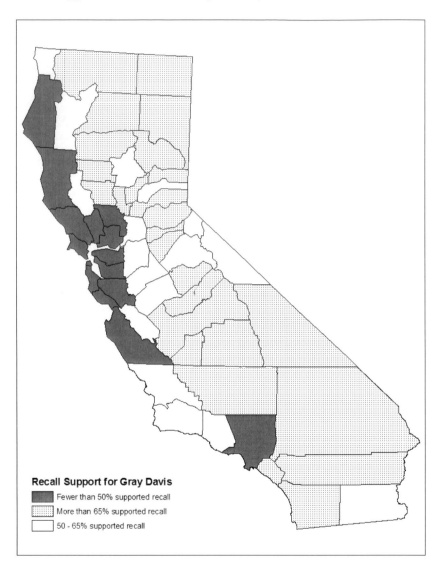

Notes: Data collected from Secretary of State (2003a).

much as his predecessors had, mixing the use of legislatively proposed ballot measures with cautious support of some initiatives authored by others. In his governing style, the actor quickly adapted to the role of charming, glad-handing politician, and engineered brilliant deals that maintained peace with the state's most powerful interests while cutting the budget allocations of their favored programs. In the November 2004 elections, Schwarzenegger tied himself closely to the Republican Party, but the policies that he pursued cast him as the same sort of moderate as his recent predecessors from both parties. As in the recall, his regional appeal came from the areas of California that have customarily supported Republicans. In short, Schwarzenegger in his first year was the most traditional of politicians.

A second surprise for political observers and California voters alike was how successful the governor was with his insider tack. Figure 9.4 shows that his approval ratings, already high at the beginning of his term, climbed to 65% throughout the summer and fall of 2004. Schwarzenegger did not suffer the political setbacks that fellow outsider Ronald Reagan had in his disastrous first hundred days as California governor (Dallek, 2001) or that Minnesota Governor (and former professional wrestler) Jesse Ventura had throughout his term. In fact, Schwarzenegger's early performance put him among the most popular chief executives in California since the Field Poll began recording gubernatorial approval. His ratings from May until October of 2004 were higher than the peak approval figures won by Gray Davis (62%), Pete Wilson (53%), Pat Brown (51%), and even Ronald Reagan (60%). Sixty-four percent of voters said that his performance exceeded their expectations, and Schwarzenegger appeared headed toward popularity levels that only George Deukmejian (72%) and Jerry Brown (69%) had reached (The Field Poll, 2004, 2).

The key puzzles of Schwarzenegger's governorship, then, are what caused the dramatic drop in his popularity in 2005, and what factors allowed him to rebound and win reelection in 2006. It is clear that Schwarzenegger's celebrity alone cannot explain these trends, because his fame remained constant while his political fortunes rose, fell, and rose again. From January through June of 2005, his approval rating fell 30 percentage points, and he remained stuck at or below 40% throughout the disastrous 2005 special election. Our explanation of this fall is that Schwarzenegger's popularity collapsed precisely when he abandoned the traditional approach that won him such success in 2004 and returned to the maverick style, policies, and institutional weapons that he used in 2003. Beginning with his January 2005 State of the State address, Schwarzenegger declared political war on the Sacramento interests with which he had made peace the previous year, became increasingly belligerent with the Democratic legislators to whom he had offered cigars early in his term, and pushed his own slate of initiatives for the first time. Abandoning his insider strategy in 2004 to reposition himself as an outsider in 2005, Schwarzenegger faced the possibility of being pushed outside of government in the November 2006 elections. Yet he survived

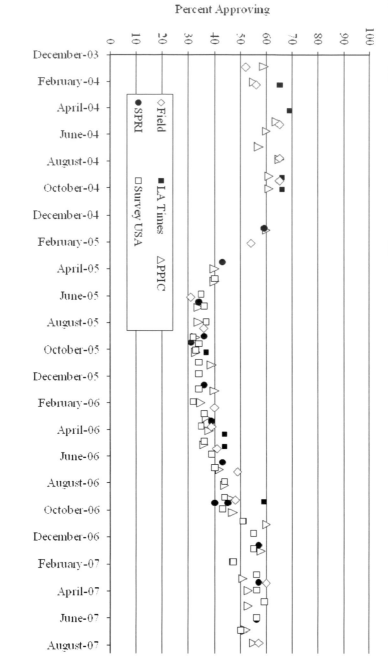

Figure 9.4. Approval of Gov. Schwarzenegger's Performance

Notes: Collected by Gary Jacobson from various polling organizations.

to win reelection—albeit over a weak opponent—when he returned to his centrist, insider path and largely abandoned direct democracy.

The First Hundred Days:
Early Victories, Early Contradictions

Six days before his victory in the recall election, Arnold Schwarzenegger laid out a list of 10 goals that he planned for the first hundred days of his governorship. By the time his honeymoon period in office was up, he had accomplished three of them (Weintraub, 2004a). All three had the following characteristics in common: They echoed major themes of his campaign, two of them could be done unilaterally, and all three put Schwarzenegger squarely in the mainstream of California politics. First, the governor engineered the repeal of a law, forced through in the final days of the Gray Davis Administration that would have allowed anyone to obtain a state driver's license without proof of legal citizenship. The issue became prime fodder for conservative talk radio, and even though SB 60 had passed the state Assembly by a 44–31 margin in September 2003, Schwarzenegger was able to use his momentum to push its repeal by a 64–9 margin in December (Legislative Counsel, 2005).

The governor's second accomplishment was equally popular. Schwarzenegger cancelled a tripling of the annual tax on car owners that Davis had initiated. Although his unilateral move to repay cities and counties the $4 billion a year that they would have collected from this tax was called a "flagrant misuse" of state law by the state's nonpartisan fiscal analyst (Talev, 2004a), few elected officials argued with it. Third, the governor ordered a freeze on administrative spending and commissioned an independent audit of state finances to look for government waste. This audit did not lead to any future savings, but was a popular move nonetheless.

A quick glance at the goals that Schwarzenegger failed to accomplish reveals them as actions that would have distanced him away from the political mainstream and set him at odds with some of Sacramento's most powerful interest groups. He did not attempt to spend his early political capital on forcing spending cuts in special session, renegotiating state employee contracts, extracting a larger share of the revenue from tribal casinos, reforming the state workers compensation system, streamlining the education bureaucracy, banning fundraising during budget negotiations, or closing the budget deficit (Weintraub, 2004a). Although Schwarzenegger would pursue some of these goals later in his first year, he began by emulating past California governors looking for the middle, where he found plenty of company from Sacramento's political establishment.

In his choice of top advisors, Governor Schwarzenegger looked for the middle ground and valued Sacramento experience. This often made for strange political bedfellows and gave rise to contradictory policy moves. According to an article listing "The People Who Have the Governor's Ear," three of his five closest advisors were Democrats. They included First Lady Maria Shriver (the niece of John F. Kennedy), environmental activist and entertainment lawyer Bonnie Reiss, and former Democratic Assembly Speaker Robert Hertzberg (Marimow, 2004). Yet while he was appointing a Democrat as the head of his Environmental Protection Agency and getting faxed jokes from Massachusetts Senator Ted Kennedy, Schwarzenegger was also filling his administration with "several dozen" advisors from former Republican Governor Pete Wilson's staff (Salladay and Nicholas, 2004).

The conservatives in his administration often led him to propose policies that when met with strong public outcry, his liberal advisors convinced him to abandon. In December of 2003, he backed off his announced plan to trim the state budget by cutting services for 200,000 people with developmental disabilities (Skelton, 2004). Later, he retreated on a budget trimming measure that would have rescinded some animal cruelty laws and allowed cities and counties to save $14 million by destroying dogs and cats at animal shelters more quickly. These strategic retreats kept Schwarzenegger in the state's political center, and even won him praise for his courage from liberal Democrat Tom Hayden, who had authored the animal cruelty law Schwarzenegger attempted to rescind (Salladay and Nicholas, 2004).

Unlike his immediate predecessor in the governor's office, Schwarzenegger proved able to get along magnificently with the capitol community and understood the importance of this insider skill. He immediately began meeting with legislators from both parties in small groups, a courtesy that Davis had rarely extended even to Democrats, and invited many of them to smoke cigars with him. Senate Appropriations Chair Dede Alpert praised him for being "willing to personally engage people. He's making a real effort to establish personal relationships, which are very important here" (Ainsworth, 2004). She did not need to explicitly contrast his style to that of Davis, who frequently fought with the legislature's Democratic leaders, nor did Assembly Speaker Fabian Nunez, who said, "I think this governor has done a very good job at extending a hand of cooperation with the legislature" (Sheppard, 2004).

Spring 2004: Playing Inside Baseball in the Primary and on the Budget

Schwarzenegger's friendly relationship with the legislature's leaders paid off, to the tune of $15 billion, when he had to close a large gap in his first budget. After the state's dot com bubble burst and its revenues (further diminished by billions of dollars of tax cuts enacted when times were good) were insufficient to pay for recently passed spending increases, a massive imbalance opened up in the state's books by the summer of 2002. Gray Davis's final two budgets had glossed over the shortfall with accounting gimmicks and short-term borrowing, leaving Schwarzenegger with a $17 billion shortfall (Legislative Analyst's Office, 2004). Budget deals in California must be approved by a two-third majority in each house of the legislature, which in recent decades has guaranteed that legislators from both parties must support it. Facing a Democratic caucus that opposed deep spending cuts and a Republican caucus that would not back any tax increases, Schwarzenegger brokered a compromise that both sides could tolerate, borrowing the money. The $15 billion bond contained in Proposition 57 would restructure and add to the debt created by Davis, lengthening the period over which the state could pay it back. It was placed on the March 2004 ballot and linked with another measure, Proposition 58, which created a rainy-day fund and strengthened the state's balanced budget requirement. Both the Democratic and Republican Parties officially backed both measures, as did prominent leaders of each party, and both passed.

This was indeed a major victory at the ballot box for Schwarzenegger, but it is important to understand the species of direct democracy that delivered it to him. There are two paths that propositions can take to the ballot in California. The first path begins in the legislature, where a "compulsory referendum" approved by a two-third vote in each house goes directly to the ballot. These measures are rarely controversial, since members of both parties must first agree to them in the legislature. Their campaigns generate relatively low levels of spending—an average of $700,000 in constant 1982 dollars —and 70% of them have passed in recent decades. By contrast, citizen initiatives that reach the ballot by obtaining voter signatures are often highly controversial, generate an average of $6 million in campaign spending, yet only pass 43% of the time (de Figueiredo, Ji, and Kousser, 2005). To pass his bond, the governor did not go around the legislature by making a direct appeal to voters with an initiative. Instead, he pushed a compulsory referendum. This required his compromising to guarantee the support of an elite consensus, which greatly increased his chances of victory. His first proposition victory resulted from his savvy use of a form of direct democracy that is deeply imbedded in the state's representative institutions.

Schwarzenegger also played an insider strategy to close the last few billions of the state's budget gap. In a stunning accomplishment, he convinced two of the state's most powerful lobbying groups—the teachers' and correctional officers' unions—to accept cuts in their program areas. His deal with the California Teachers Association even included the group's acquiescence in suspending their constitutionally guaranteed minimum level of funding in order to save $2 billion (Schrag, 2004), in exchange for a promise to return the funding when the budget became flush. This saved the governor from a major battle with a sympathetic and well-funded lobby. Schwarzenegger secured backing for $108 million in cuts to prison guard salaries from the California Correctional Peace Officers Association, a group that holds tremendous sway among moderate and conservative voters in the state's Central Valley. He also negotiated deals with the state's university system and its local governments to accept temporary cuts in exchange for future budget stability (Nicholas, 2004). All of these deals, which allowed him to finish the job of balancing his first budget, appeared more like European clientelism than the work of the Californian maverick who had railed against special interests during the recall campaign.

Perhaps this was because Schwarzenegger, who had largely self-financed his run during the recall, had begun to fundraise like a Sacramento veteran. Recognizing the vast sums of money necessary to compete in California politics—and apparently forsaking his pledge to avoid special interest donations—the governor raised $10.1 million during his first four months in office (Ainsworth, 2004). This outpaced even Gray Davis's fundraising accomplishments. Schwarzenegger collected large contributions from real estate developers, Target, Walgreens, Wal-Mart, Sempra Energy, and ChevronTexaco. To finance the campaign for his bond measure, he held an event in New York, invited Wall Street bankers, and charged up to $500,000 for a ticket (Ainsworth, 2004).

He developed close ties to the state's Chamber of Commerce, and this alliance nearly led him to his first use of the initiative process. Buoyed by the success of his propositions in March, Schwarzenegger worked closely with the state's business community to raise $5 million to back an overhaul of the state's workers compensation program. The business groups used the money to gather one million voter signatures, easily enough to qualify the measure for the November 2004 ballot (Weintraub, 2004b). Using the threat of this possible initiative, Schwarzenegger pressured Democrats in the legislature to pass the changes on their own, thus sparing him a tough fight on the ballot. Though they let his initial deadline expire, legislators ultimately passed a bill that gave the governor and his business allies some of the concessions they demanded. Splitting the difference in this face-off, Schwarzenegger used the initiative just as many governors before him had, as a threat to spur a legislative compromise.

Voters in all areas of California rewarded Schwarzenegger for his pragmatic deal-making. Figure 9.5 breaks down the governor's approval ratings by the same geographic regions used in our earlier discussion of the recall campaign. It shows that by August 2004, strong majorities approved of the governor's performance in all areas of the state. His highest ratings (77%) came in the most conservative region, the "Other Southern California" category encompassing Orange, Riverside, San Bernardino, and San Diego Counties. Yet he also won the approval of 60% of voters in the Bay Area, demonstrating that his centrism had won him support even in the state's most liberal region.

Figure 9.5. Approval of Governor Schwarzenegger, by Region

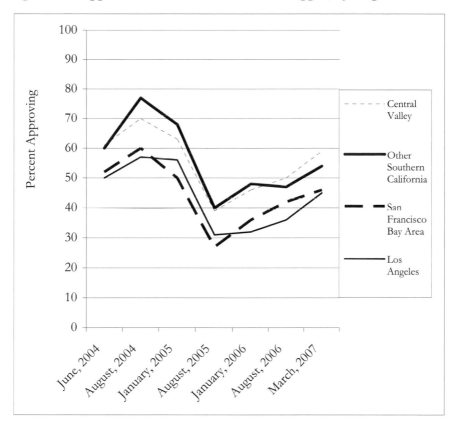

Notes: Data collected from the Public Policy Institute of California's Statewide Survey, in various months.

Fall 2004: Leading His Party,
Following the Proposition Parade

Even though he had resolved the major obstacles to balancing the budget by cutting deals with Sacramento's major interest groups, the governor still needed to secure the support of members of both parties in order to pass a budget bill. The fact that this took him most of the summer demonstrated the limits of his charm offensive. Democratic leaders who had smoked cigars with him in the capitol's atrium would not go along with significant spending cuts in the future. Republicans who scrambled to pose for pictures with the action hero governor balked at increases in fees on business and the prospect of more deficits in the coming years. Both parties got bogged down in negotiations over details such as whether or not school districts should be able to contract out to private firms to hire bus drivers (Bluth, 2004). But in June, as the constitutional deadline for passing a budget came and went, Schwarzenegger's strongest criticism came from his own party. Republican leaders publicly voiced their concerns about the absence of any deep spending cuts, and one veteran GOP lawmaker said, on condition of anonymity, "If this budget had the name Gray Davis on it, it wouldn't be supported. It walks on the wrong side of the issues relative to the Republican Party" (Halper and Nicholas, 2004).

After campaigning as a moderate and governing from the center, Schwarzenegger chose to align himself clearly with the Republican Party for the first time in his governorship. Throughout July, he targeted vulnerable Democratic legislators who represented districts that had favored the recall. He visited six of these districts, holding high-profile rallies asking constituents to pressure their representatives to sign a budget deal quickly, and famously calling legislators who opposed his budget "girlie men" and asking voters to "terminate" them (Ainsworth, 2004b; Bluth, 2004). To be sure, this was a risky strategy in a blue state, where Democratic registrants outnumbered Republicans by a 43% to 35% margin at the time (Secretary of State, 2004a). It did not lead to major policy concessions from Democrats, since the budget that he signed on July 31 contained compromises on most key issues. But it did silence Schwarzenegger's Republican critics in Sacramento and set the tone for an election season in which he would side with the GOP in political battles while maintaining the moderate policy stances that had garnered him such high approval ratings.

The 2004 election season began on August 31, when Schwarzenegger addressed the Republican National Convention in a prime time slot and spoke passionately about the values that tied him to the party. He later campaigned for Bush in the swing state of Ohio and played an active role in legislative races across California (Talev, 2004b). He endorsed 49 Republican legislative candidates, attended six fundraisers on their behalf, campaigned with five candidates, and recorded phone massages and radio ads for Republicans (Vogel, 2004). However, when he judged whether or not to sign the bills that were passed that fall, Schwarzenegger was less reliably partisan. He did veto nearly a quarter of the bills that the majority-Democratic legislature sent to him, but this percentage was not quite as high as the peak percentage of vetoes that Gray Davis issued in the year 2000 (Detwiler, 2005). Looking for patterns in Schwarzenegger's vetoes, one journalist concluded that his policy stances "veer from right to left and back, and often contradict one another" (Talev, 2004b). He angered some business groups by signing a bill that mandated HMO coverage of child asthma, but pleased them by stopping measures that would have mandated maternity coverage and allowed the importation of prescription drugs from Canada. While the governor vetoed a bill that would have stopped job outsourcing, he also lobbied Congress to stop film productions from leaving the country (Talev, 2004b). He rejected a minimum wage increase, but signed a gun control bill and legislation to create incentives for buying hybrid vehicles (Talev, 2004c). Overall, he steered the same middle course of fiscal conservatism coupled with social and environmental moderation that his predecessors George Deukmejian, Pete Wilson, and even Gray Davis generally pursued.

Governor Schwarzenegger also stuck to a Sacramento tradition in the November election by taking positions on ballot measures that had been authored by other groups, sometimes waiting until after he had a chance to gauge their political appeal. Pete Wilson had done this with great success in 1994, hitching his reelection campaign to the fortunes of Proposition 187, which would have denied most social services to illegal immigrants (Lee, 2006: 139). Most of the initiative was overturned by the courts and never went into effect, but it was popular and helped to lift the previously unpopular Wilson to a comeback victory. Although Schwarzenegger was popular at this time and had two years until he faced reelection, he appeared to pursue a similarly careful strategy regarding the November 2004 ballot. While he led the fight against two tribal gaming propositions that would have weakened his bargaining position with casinos, his support for two other measures—Prop. 62's opening up of the state's primary elections and Prop. 71's stem cell research bond—came only after they appeared to be headed to victory. Endorsing both of them helped emphasize his moderate stances. Backing propositions that turned out to be winners, regardless of whether or not he was involved in crafting them, would help burnish his image as a powerful force in California direct democracy. As the election approached, the governor took public positions on a dozen propositions, and widely distributed a voter guide detailing his stances on 10 of them.

Table 9.1 reports Schwarzenegger's positions and lists the positions that the Democratic and Republican parties took on the measures. Because his role as a direct democracy kingmaker in this election has been heavily debated, it is worth looking closely at his record. Overall, the governor did very well, with a majority of voters taking the positions that he had recommended on 10 of the 12 propositions. But it is important to note that many of these measures were consensus issues upon which leaders of both parties agreed. Looking only at the measures over which he and the state Democratic Party issued conflicting endorsements, Schwarzenegger won four times, but the Democrats beat him twice. And if fewer than 1% of voters had decidedly differently on the health insurance referendum of Prop. 72, the governor and the Democrats would have been tied.

A closer look at Proposition 72 also sheds light on the implications that the "Two Constituencies" problem noted by Cain (1997, 337–40) has for direct democracy. Any governor's constituency is made up of the *voters* of California, because all of their votes have an equal weight in deciding who the next governor will be. By contrast, the legislature represents the constituency of the state's *residents*, because legislative districts are drawn to contain equal numbers of residents. These constituencies differ because not all residents become voters,

Table 9.1. Endorsements of Ballot Initiatives in 2004

	Content	Gov's Position	Dem Party Position	Rep Party Position	Yes Vote (%)
1A	Local Govt. Funding	Yes	Yes	Yes	**84**
59	Open Meetings and Records	Yes	Yes	Yes	**84**
62	Voter Choice Primary	Yes	No	No	*46*
63	Mental Health Tax	No	Yes	No	*54*
64	Limits on Lawsuits	Yes	No	Yes	**59**
66	Amend Three Strikes	No	Yes	No	**47**
67	Surtax on Cell Phones for ERs	No	No	No	**28**
68	Expand Gambling	No	No	No	**16**
69	DNA Collection	Yes	No	Yes	**62**
70	Tax Tribal Gaming	No	No	No	**24**
71	Stem Cell $3 Billion Bond	Yes	Yes	No	**59**
72	Healthcare Expansion	No	Yes	No	**49**

Notes: Governor's endorsements reported in "Governor Arnold Schwarzenegger's Ballot Proposition Voter Guide" and in Olney (2004). Party endorsement reported in Institute of Governmental Studies Library (2004), and support percentages reported in Secretary of State (2004b). For support percentages, boldface indicates that the side the Gov. Schwarzenegger endorsed won, while italics indicate that it lost.

and they differ systematically because voter turnout and eligibility is linked to race and class. For instance, the 52nd Assembly district in urban Los Angeles contains 41,354 voters, who get one representative in the Assembly (currently Mervyn Dymally). The much more affluent 4th Assembly District, located in Sacramento and the Sierra foothills, also gets one vote in the Assembly (Ted Gaines), but contributes more than three times as many voters (141,521) to gubernatorial elections. Overall, the median member of the legislature represents a constituency that is poorer, more liberal, and more ethnically diverse than the median voter in a governor's race (Kousser, 2005: 152).

Unfortunately for the legislature, the constituency in direct democracy contests looks just like the governor's constituency. Because votes are counted in initiative battles just as they are in gubernatorial contests, Arnold Schwarzenegger was effectively playing on home turf during the 2004 elections. He beat the legislature on many issues not because his personal charisma persuaded voters to change their minds, but because the rules for counting votes gave him an institutional advantage. Proposition 72 put a health care expansion that the legislature had passed up for voter approval, and the legislature's proposal narrowly lost. One interpretation of this result may have been that legislators got too far to the left of their constituents with this bill. Another possibility was that Governor Schwarzenegger turned the tide of public opinion against it. A look at district-by-district results shows that neither was the case; instead, the "Two Constituencies" added up to defeat for the bill. On its final vote in the Senate, SB 2 received support from 25 senators and was opposed by 15. In the November 2004 elections, a majority of voters in these same 25 Senate districts voted to support the bill, while majorities in the other 15 districts wanted to overturn it (Secretary of State, 2004b). The bill lost narrowly at the state level because fewer voters actually turned out in the many districts that backed it than in the few that opposed it. Governor Schwarzenegger succeeded with his 2004 propositions because of this dynamic and because he effectively linked himself to many popular initiatives, but he did not always swing voters to his side on more controversial measures.

An analysis of the state's legislative races shows that the governor failed, to the surprise of Republicans and Democrats alike, to influence voters in these contests. In 18 of the 48 Assembly seats held by Democrats, a majority of voters favored Gray Davis's recall. The Republican Party was able to recruit more candidates with prior elective experience in these districts than it normally would have, and Democrats recruited fewer (Kousser, Lewis, and Masket, 2004). In six of these districts, Schwarzenegger campaigned on behalf of Republican candidates.

On election day, though, none of these seats changed party hands. Democrats retained their 48–32 edge in the Assembly and their 25–15 edge in the Senate. The commotion of the recall election created no geographical realignment of the parties (Kousser, 2006). To many eyes, including those of many Republicans who thought Schwarzenegger's coattails would carry them to victory, nothing had changed in California politics. Yet an analysis of legislative voting patterns before and after the recall show that the governor who failed to swing voters succeeded in influencing their representatives. Democratic legislators moved toward the middle in their roll call voting behavior in 2004, especially those in districts that had backed the recall. These moves were statistically significant, substantively large, and unusual compared to previous sessions (Kousser, Lewis, and Masket, 2004). To us, it seems fitting that one of the strongest effects that Arnold Schwarzenegger had on California politics in 2004 was subtle, moderating, and visible only to Sacramento insiders.

Yet for a governor not known for his subtlety, this insider impact may not have been large enough. In part because of his frustration at not being able to

swing the vote in any legislative seat, and in part because of his principled dis-
agreement with a system that allowed legislators themselves to draw their district lines, Schwarzenegger began an attempt to redraw the political geography
of the state. His proposal to create an independent redistricting commission that
could, in time for the fall of 2006, create new and more competitive legislative
districts became part of his ill-fated package of "reforms" in 2005.

2005 State of the State Address:
Declaring War on Sacramento Interests

Disinclined to leave a legacy of subtle effects, Schwarzenegger began a bold
offensive in 2005, announcing his change of strategy by issuing a call to arms in
his January State of the State address. In martial tones, he announced an ambitious plan to reform California's governmental structure and set forth major policy initiatives that took on the very interest groups with whom he had made
peace in 2004. He proposed making deep spending cuts, shifting state employee
pensions into private accounts, basing teachers' pay on merit reports, eliminating 100 state boards and committees, and creating an independent commission
to redraw legislative districts (*San Diego Union Tribune*, 2005). Schwarzenegger clearly understood the risks of his new approach. In the speech, he predicted
that the "special interests" he targeted would soon "organize huge protests in
front of the Capitol" and "call me cruel and heartless" (Marinucci, 2005). But he
had faith that his popularity would insulate him against these attacks.

When he unveiled his budget plan later in January, Schwarzenegger gam-
bled that his approval ratings, still remarkably high, would give him the statewide clout to beat out some of Sacramento's most powerful interests. The state
still faced an $8.1 billion deficit, because the compromises reached in 2004 had
brought only temporary fixes. In 2005, the governor's budget proposal contained
$2.5 billion in borrowing, $1.3 billion in transportation funding cuts, shallow
cuts in nearly every budget area, and $2.2 billion less in education spending than
the state teachers union expected (Bluth, 2005). The last item was the most surprising and would cause Schwarzenegger the most trouble. The teachers union
accused him of reneging on the deal that had brought cuts to the education
budget the previous year in exchange for a promise of restoring the level of
spending guaranteed by a constitutional funding formula in 2005 (Delsohn,
2005). Though he would later accuse union leaders of "right-out lying" about
the deal, journalists backed up their interpretation (Skelton, 2005).

This action fit a pattern of actions by the governor that left Sacramento insiders feeling that they could not trust his promises. Public employee union
leaders expected the governor to steer clear of pension reforms when they acqui-
esced to cuts in 2004, and Latino legislators thought they had a handshake deal
with him to support a revised version of their drivers license bill (Delsohn,

2005). In any legislative body, honoring past commitments is the key to ensuring future cooperation, and these perceived reversals cost Schwarzenegger. During the spring of 2005, he also acquired a reputation for failing to follow through on policy proposals. In February, he withdrew his plan to eliminate the state boards and commissions (Rau, 2005). In April, Schwarzenegger's Youth and Adult Correctional Secretary announced that the governor's administration was scrapping plans to overhaul the state parole system by permitting alternatives to reincarceration (Furillo, 2005). By May, he abandoned his plan to reorganize the California Environmental Protection Agency (Rau, 2005). While it is unlikely that any of these policy reversals were noticed outside of Sacramento, all of them damaged his reputation with insiders.

2005 Special Election:
The Limits of Schwarzenegger's Populist Appeal

When he announced his bold goals for the year, Schwarzenegger had little hope that Democratic leaders in the legislature would acquiesce to them. As early as January, he began to set the stage for going around the legislature to move his agenda. "It will be the governor with his partners—the people of California—against the legislators," he told the press, framing himself clearly as a populist (Nicholas and Salladay, 2005a). His rhetoric also targeted interest groups. In December of 2004, when a group of nurses protested his decision to suspend a new law mandating nurse-to-patient ratios, he dubbed them "special interests" and said they were protesting because "I kicked their butt" (Marinucci, 2005). He had leveled similar charges against university students protesting a fee increase (Marinucci, 2005). By setting himself at odds with the interest groups that he had worked with earlier, he made enemies with deep pockets. Throughout the spring and summer of 2005, the nurses and the teachers began running television advertisements criticizing the governor (Weintraub, 2005).

As Figure 9.4 shows, these attacks corresponded with a dramatic decline in the governor's approval ratings statewide. Even more worrying for Schwarzenegger was that fact that his popularity dropped steeply in all areas of the state. Figure 9.5 shows parallel declines in all four of the regions identified by the PPIC. In an attempt to halt this decline, Schwarzenegger took his agenda directly to voters in the spring.

Leaving the capitol in a military Humvee with license plates that read "Reform 1," Schwarzenegger drove to a local Applebee's restaurant in March to gather signatures for three initiative petitions. One would shift public employee pensions to the private sector, one would create a redistricting commission, and one—representing a compromise version of his merit pay plan—would change teacher tenure rules (Nicholas and Salladay, 2005b). He may have simply been attempting to pressure the legislature, as he did with his workers compensation initiative. At the restaurant, the governor said, "As soon as we have those signatures, let's see if maybe that will wake up the politicians" (Mendel and Marelius, 2005). Yet many believed that this was simply a campaign warm-up for a fall special election that Schwarzenegger had the power to call. Even in January, Republican consultant Allan Hoffenblum said, "I have little doubt he has pretty much made up his mind that he is preparing for a November election" (Nicholas and Salladay, 2005a). A February poll showed that voters narrowly favored such an election and, by small margins, backed all of the governor's reform proposals (Field Poll, 2005). By May, Schwarzenegger announced that "We are going to call the special election no matter what" (Chorneau, 2005), and by August hopes of a compromise set of compulsory referendums had collapsed. The governor would use the initiative process to fight the dominant political party in the state and some of California's most powerful interest groups.

Across the board, Schwarzenegger failed in November. One of his proposals, the public employee pension measure, did not even make it to the ballot. He was forced to abandon it in April when the attorney general (Democrat Bill Lockyer) wrote a ballot summary stating that the hastily crafted law would deny death and disability penalties to police and firefighters (Morain, 2005). Schwarzenegger knew that his fight with interest groups could not survive a battle with the spouses and children of cops killed in the line of duty. In addition to the other two measures for which he collected signatures at Applebee's, Schwarzenegger added a measure that would prevent unions from spending their dues on politics without obtaining written approval from their members every year, and one that would cap the state budget and enhance the governor's veto powers.

These four measures, Propositions 74, 75, 76, and 77, became the governor's reform slate and unified his opponents. Schwarzenegger's ballot committees raised $60 million in support of his initiatives, but the campaigns to stop them raised $120 million (Davis, 2005). They spent much of their money attacking the governor and tying him to the measures. This strategy worked. As Figure 9.5 shows, by August 2005 the governor's approval ratings hovered at about 30% in Los Angeles and in the Bay Area, and only 40% in the more conservative parts of southern California and in the Central Valley. While the Schwarzenegger team did produce a voter guide with his picture on it, a similar pamphlet backing his propositions and prominently featuring John McCain never once mentioned the unpopular governor. Despite these efforts, all four initiatives failed, none of them capturing more than 46.5% of the vote (Secretary of State, 2005). The populist course that Schwarzenegger steered in 2005, compared to his traditional approach in 2004, brought him no policy success and serious political losses.

2006: Schwarzenegger Transforms into a "Postpartisan" Governor

Recognizing that his shift to the right and move toward populism had failed, Schwarzenegger transformed himself yet again in 2006. He easily survived his reelection battle by adopting a new ideological position while returning to the style that served him so well during his first year in office. The governor moved to the left, even outflanking his Democratic challenger on some issues, and again allied himself with the state's major interest groups. He began by hiring Susan Kennedy, a Democrat and former close advisor to Gray Davis, as his chief of staff. In his 2006 State of the State speech, he unveiled plans for an unprecedented $222 billion public works program that included much more state borrowing than even Democratic legislators had suggested (Nicholas, 2006). His budget proposal contained $1.7 billion more in education funding than the constitutional guarantee mandates, as well as funding increases for higher education and health care programs (Halper and Morain, 2006). In his most high-profile move, Schwarzenegger won national attention when he signed landmark legislation that put California at the forefront of efforts to reduce the emissions that contribute to global climate change (*New York Times,* 2006).

Just as important, his style shifted. When the "New Arnold" spoke at the 2006 Martin Luther King, Jr., breakfast in San Francisco, he never uttered the word "Republican," but instead praised his father-in-law (and former Democratic nominee for vice president) Sargent Shriver, and spoke positively about an ACLU-led lawsuit

After listening to the governor's speech, Democratic San Francisco Mayor Gavin Newsom observed that, "He's becoming a Democrat again. . . . He gets it, He's learned his lesson. . . . He's running back, not even to the center—I would say center-left" (Marinucci, 2006). By 2007, Schwarzenegger proclaimed himself the leader of a new "postpartisan" era, contrasting the progress he made in Sacramento with the gridlock in Washington, D.C. (Kondracke, 2007). Notably, he toned down his populist rhetoric, making no major threats to go over the heads of the state's political establishment by using the initiative process.

This new strategy clearly worked, assuring the governor's reelection, raising his position in polls, and even altering the geographic makeup of his support. Figure 9.4 shows that Schwarzenegger's popularity began to trend upward by early 2006, but Figure 9.5 demonstrates that it rose particularly sharply in the most left-learning areas of the state. In fact, a January 2006 poll found that while Schwarzenegger's new policy direction won him support among Democrats and independents early that year, he actually lost favor with Republicans (Survey and Policy Research Institute, 2006). Figure 9.5 shows that he eventually rebounded in California's Republican heartland, but that his support today is much more geographically dispersed than it once was. In January of 2005, when Schwarzenegger moved sharply to the right, his approval ratings in the "Other Southern California" region were 17 percentage points higher than they were in the Bay Area. By August 2006, after the governor shifted to the left in advance of his reelection contest, this gap had narrowed to five percentage points. Schwarzenegger's support is now distributed more broadly across California's political map. His wide appeal helped him to win a 56–39% victory over a Democratic opponent, Treasurer Phil Angelides, who was outspent and overmatched from the start.

A Paradox of Direct Democracy in California

Although he ran into temporary problems, Schwarzenegger's journey from Hollywood to the governor's office has been extraordinary in its speed and initial success. The key to Schwarzenegger's extraordinary career advancement lies in the interaction between the practice of direct democracy and his successful exploitation of his unique personal imagery. A political system with democratic institutions as open as those in California frees politicians—especially those with the visibility of Schwarzenegger—to pursue governing styles and policy directions that they would not be able to take up in environments stifled by strong parties or multiple checks and balances. But while the opportunities provided by direct democracy are great, so are the risks. In many ways, Schwarzenegger's rise and (at least temporary) fall point out an important paradox about the effects of direct democracy on California politics: While some of Hiram Johnson's institutions allow leaders to move toward the popular center of the political spectrum, other mechanisms can push them toward the edges and threaten to turn them out of office.

The presence of a recall provision in California allowed a political moderate like Schwarzenegger to avoid a Republican primary that might have led to his defeat or pushed him toward the right. As we note, Schwarzenegger considered running for governor through the traditional process in 2002. He did not, but watched his friend and fellow moderate Richard Riordan lose to the more conservative Bill Simon in the Republican primary. The recall replacement contest gave Schwarzenegger a unique opportunity to skip ahead to a general election without having to please the Republican base. The compulsory referendum mechanism that he used to great success in the spring of 2004 also had a moderating influence. The requirement that two-thirds of the legislators in each house support such measures guaranteed that Schwarzenegger was backed by a consensus and had allies in both parties during the proposition campaigns.

When he used the initiative to go around in the legislature in 2005, though, Schwarzenegger moved away from the center. Such extremism results from the strategic logic of the initiative process, since centrist measures preferred by the median legislator need not end up on the ballot at all (Kousser and McCubbins, 2005). Because of this, initiative measures are likely to be more controversial and further from the mainstream of California politics. Gathering funding for the intense campaigns that they generate requires alliances with one interest group or another, and most of these efforts fail (Lee, 2006). In 2005, Schwarzenegger learned the lesson that a majority of initiative authors are taught: Using this form of direct democracy frees them to propose an idea far from the position of the median legislator, but costs a lot and rarely leads to policy gains. In 2006, he largely abandoned the initiative process, instead working with the legislature to place a successful slate of infrastructure bonds on the ballot. This strategy returned Schwarzenegger to the mainstream of California politics, and for the first time he has begun to redraw the state's political map. As of 2007, his popularity spreads across the major parties and across California's often-divergent regions, a venture into new geopolitical territory.

References

Ainsworth, Bill. 2004a. "Governor's Charm Playing Well in Capitol." *San Diego Union Tribune*. February 22.

———. 2004b. "Governor's Tough Talk Criticized as Partisan." *San Diego Union Tribune*. July 21.

Alvarez, R. Michael, Melanie Goodrich, Thad Hall, D. Roderick Kiewiet, and Sarah M. Sled. 2004. "The Complexity of the California Recall." *PS* XXXVII, 1: 23–26.

Bluth, Alexa. 2004. "Governor Plans Sixth Budget Trip." *Sacramento Bee*. July 21.

———. 2005. "Governor to Offer 'Painful' Budget, Long-Haul Change." *Sacramento Bee*. January 10.

Bowler, Shaun, and Bruce Cain. 2004. "Introduction—Recalling the Recall: Reflections on California's Recent Political Adventure." *PS* XXXVII, 1: 7–9.

Cain, Bruce E. 1997. "Epilogue: Seeking Consensus among Conflicting Electorates." In *Governing California: Politics, Government, and Public Policy in the Golden State*, ed. Gerald C. Lubenow and Bruce E. Cain. Berkeley, Calif.: Institute of Governmental Studies Press.

Chorneau, Tom. 2005. "Governor Flatly Declares a Special Fall Election Will Happen." *San Diego Union Tribune*. May 20.

de Figueiredo, John M., Chang Ho Ji, and Thad Kousser. 2005. "Why Do Initiative Backers Waste Their Money? Revisiting the Research on Campaign Spending and Direct Democracy." Presented at *Direct Democracy in the American West: Historical Roots and Political Realities*, Stanford University, April.

Delsohn, Gary. 2005. "Critics: Governor Went Back on His Word." *Sacramento Bee*, January 17.

Detwiler, Peter. 2005. *How Often Do Governors Say No?* Sacramento, Calif.: Senate Committee on Local Government.

Field Poll. 2005. Release #2153: Voters Narrowly Back Governor's Legislative Districting Plan. San Francisco, Calif.: The Field Poll.

Furillo, Andy. 2005. "Parole Overhaul Scrapped." *Sacramento Bee*. April 12.

Gledhill, Lynda. 2005. "A Deal Unlikely on Ballot Measures." *San Francisco Chronicle*. August 15.

Halper, Evan, and Dan Morain. 2006. "Gov's Budget Cuts Welfare, Boosts Schools." *Los Angeles Times*. January 11.

Halper, Evan, and Peter Nicholas. 2004. "Governor's Allies Turn Budget Foes." *Los Angeles Times*. July 1.

Institute of Governmental Studies Library. 2003. "Hot Topic: Recall in California." Accessed at http://www.igs.berkeley.edu/library/htRecall2003.html in October.

———. 2004. "California Ballot Propositions: November 2, 2004 General Recommendations." Accessed at http://www.igs.berkley.edu/library/htBallotRec2004NOV.html" in October.

Kondracke, Mort. 2007. "Schwarzenegger's 'Post-Partisanship in Model for D.C." Real Clear Politics (www.realclearpolictics.com), March 1.

Kousser, Thad. 2005. *Term Limits and the Dismantling of State Legislative Professionalism*. New York: Cambridge University Press.

———. 2006. "Recalling the Realignment Literature: Did October 2003 Bring a Critical Election?" In *Clicker Politics: Essays on the California Recall*, ed. Shaun Bowler and Bruce E. Cain. Englewood Cliffs, N.J.: Prentice Hall.

Kousser, Thad and Mathew D. McCubbins. 2005. "Social Choice, Crypto-Initiatives, and Policy Making by Direct Democracy." *Southern California Law Review* 78: 949–84.

Kousser, Thad, Jeffrey B. Lewis, and Seth Masket. 2007. "Ideological Adaptation? The Survival Instinct of Threatened Legislators." *The Journal of Politics* 69: 828–43.

Lawrence, David G. 2004. *The California Governor Recall Campaign*. Belmont, Calif.: Wadsworth.

Lee, Eugene. 2006. "The Initiative Boom: An Excess of Democracy." In *Governing California: Politics, Government, and Public Policy in the Golden State*, ed. Gerald C. Lubenow. Berkeley, Calif.: Institute of Governmental Studies Press.

Legislative Analyst's Office. 2004. Overview of the 2005–05 May Revision. Accessed at http://www.lao.gov/2004/may_revision/011704_may_revision.htm in June.

Legislative Counsel, 2005. *Bill Information*. Accessed at http://www.leginfo. ca.gov/ in October.

Lubenow, Gerald C. (ed.). 2003. *California Votes*. Berkeley, Calif.: Berkeley Public Policy Press.

Marimow, Ann. 2004. "The People Who Have the Governor's Ear." *San Jose Mercury News*. February 22.

Marinucci, Carla. 2005. "Governor's Call to Arms Causing Deep Divisions." *San Francisco Chronicle*. January 9.

———. 2006. "'New' Schwarzenegger Gets Surprisingly Warm Welcome." *San Francisco Chronicle*. January 17.

Mendel, Ed, and John Marelius. 2005. "Governor Starts Drive to Get Agenda Before Voters." *San Diego Union Tribune*. March 2.

Morain, Dan. 2005. "Initiatives: Handle with Care." *Los Angeles Times*. April 12.

New York Times. 2006. "California: Schwarzenegger Signs Gas Emissions Act." September 28.

Nicholas, Peter. 2004. "Gov. Goes Along to Get Along." *Los Angeles Times*. June 30.

———. 2006. "Gov. Gets Earful from GOP." *Los Angeles Times*. January 12.

Nicholas, Peter, and Robert Salladay. 2005a. "Capitol Battle Lines Harden." *Los Angeles Times*. January 28.

———. 2005b. "Entrée Comes with Familiar Side of Governor." *Los Angeles Times*. March 2.

Olney, Warren. 2004. "Schwarzenegger Goes Against GOP on Initiatives." Background for October 19, 2004 airing of *Which Way L.A.?* accessed at http://www.kcrw.org/cgibin/db/kcrw.pl?show_code=ww&air_date=10/19/04 &tmplt_type=Show in March.

Rau, Jordan. 2005. "Governor Shelves Plan to Reorganize Cal/EPA." *Los Angeles Times*. May 4.

Sacramento Bee. 2003. "An Election Like No Other, the Recall Election." Special section of the *Sacramento Bee*. October 12.

Salladay, Robert, and Peter Nicholas. 2004. "Downsizing Arnold." *Los Angeles Times Magazine*. October 24, pp. 12–15, 27–28.

San Diego Union Tribune. 2005. "Gauntlet Thrown: Governor Vows to Pursue Major Reforms." *San Diego Union Tribune*. January 7.

Schrag, Peter. 2004. "Did CTA Eat Arnold's Lunch—And the Kids' Too?" *Sacramento Bee*. January 28.

Secretary of State. 2003a. "September 22, 2003 Report of Registration." Accessed at http://www.ss.ca.gov/elections/ror_092203.htm in November.

———. 2003b. "Statement of Vote: 2003 Statewide Special Election." Accessed at http://www.ss.ca.gov/elections/sov/2003_special/contents.htm in November.

———. 2004a. "September 3, 2004 Report of Registration." Accessed at http://www.ss.ca.gov/elections/ror_09032004.htm in March.

———. 2004b. "Statement of Vote and Supplement to the Statement of Vote: 2004 Presidential General Election." Accessed at http://www.ss.ca.gov/elections/sov/2004_general/contents.htm in March.

———. 2005. "Statement of Vote and Supplement to the Statement of Vote: 2005 Special Statewide Election." Accessed at http://www.ss.ca.gov/elections/sov/2005_special/contents.htm in March.

Sheppard, Harrison. 2004. "Arnold's First 100 Days Win Praise." *Los Angeles Daily News*. February 21.

Skelton, George. 2004. "Schwarzenegger Earns Respectable Marks, But Big Test Is Coming Up." *Los Angeles Times*. February 19.

———. 2005. "Governor is Digging Himself Deeper with Denial of School Funding Deal." *Los Angeles Times*. May 19.

Survey and Policy Research Institute. 2006. *Schwarzenegger's Statewide Approval Edges Upward Slightly*. San Jose, Calif.: Survey and Policy Research Institute at San Jose State University.

Talev, Margaret, 2004a. "Action Figure: Energetic and Charismatic, the State's New Governor has Earned High Marks from Across the Political Spectrum." *Sacramento Bee*. February 22.

———. 2004b. "Analysis: Flair for Surprise Keeps Him in the Catbird Seat." *Sacramento Bee*. November 14.

———. 2004c. "Gov. Schwarzenegger's First Year: 12 Defining Moments." *Sacramento Bee*. November 14.

Vogel, Nancy. 2004. "Schwarzenegger Star Power Fades for GOP in State Races." *Los Angeles Times*. November 1.

Weintraub, Daniel. 2004a. "First 100 Days: Three Out of 10 but Lots of Action." *Sacramento Bee*. February 24.

———. 2004b. "Arnold: Year One." *Sacramento Bee*. November 14.

———. 2005. "What We Have Here is a Failure to Communicate." *Sacramento Bee*. April 28.

Chapter 10

Sorting or Self-Sorting: Competition and Redistricting in California?

Bruce E. Cain, Iris Hui, and Karin Mac Donald

California's political geography is a product of both self-sorting and systemic sorting decisions. The state's east-west divide and its distinctive patchwork of racial and ethnic concentrations are the geographic expression of many individual residential decisions, driven in varying degrees by necessity and taste. This is the self-sorting component of California's political demography. District lines are then imposed on this demographic landscape in a process called redistricting that resets district boundaries to accommodate population changes measured in census tracts and blocks from one decade to the next. Districts are shaped to further various formal and informal goals: equal population first and foremost, but also communities of interest, respect for city and county boundaries, protection of minority communities under the Voting Rights Act, partisan "fairness," incumbency protection, and the like. Those who draw boundary lines in effect sort voters by districts subject to the constraints of contiguity, equal population, and sometimes compactness.

The issue of who gets to do the sorting and for what reasons has been controversial in California for many decades, but especially after the "one person, one vote" cases of the sixties and the amendment of the Voting Rights Act in

1982. Redistricting now as compared to the earlier period has to be more precise, open, and fair in the treatment of historically disadvantaged minority
groups. The courts have also expanded the scope of redistricting to cover all but
the smallest and most narrow local legislative bodies.

However, while the political system is "sorting" more regularly and in more
legally constrained ways, redistricting is still highly controversial. California's
2001 boundary plan provoked a level of outcry from the reform community and
the press that almost matched the controversy over the infamous "Burton" plan
in the eighties. Then, the problem was a partisan Democratic plan imposed by a
simple party-line majority vote and challenged by the Republicans in several
subsequent rounds of initiatives. Ironically, while the Democrats in 2001 could
have developed a partisan plan again, because they controlled all branches of the
state government, they chose not to, partly to avoid reigniting the previous bitter
partisan redistricting battles. Foregoing some small gains that could have been
carved out of the new census data, they negotiated the state's first post-*Baker v.
Carr* bipartisan plan.

Initially, there was a sigh of collective relief that the redistricting bill passed
without much partisan acrimony and the endless skirmishes of the eighties. But
after two election cycles, it became more obvious that the 2001 bipartisan deal
had a serious paucity of regularly competitive seats. Governor Arnold Schwarzenegger became particularly annoyed when his efforts to campaign for Republican state legislators in 2004 proved futile, leaving him to deal with a hostile
Democratic legislature. His call for redistricting reform to restore competition in
state legislative elections resonated with California's reform community, which
had tried and failed in the past to change the process. At the same time, the national reform community began to link redistricting publicly with the bitter partisanship in Washington. The governor called a special election in 2005 that
featured a measure, Proposition 77 that would have replaced the existing legislative redistricting with a commission of retired judges and forced a new mid-
decade redistricting. The voters soundly rejected Proposition 77, but the issue
remained a subject of lively debate in subsequent legislative sessions.

Whether or not changing from a legislative to a commission redistricting
system is a good or feasible idea, the general concern about electoral competition raises an important question: to what degree is the state's current lack of
partisan competitiveness is the result of politicians sorting voters into homogenous districts as opposed to voters self-sorting themselves into homogeneous
areas by residential choice? Self-sorting could be the explanation because socio-
economic characteristics (especially race) are correlated with political affiliations and attitudes. So areas that are homogeneously black and poor, for instance, lean heavily towards the Democratic Party and rural white areas towards
the Republicans. If the number of marginal seats is low, one reason might be
that areas are becoming naturally more homogenous. This natural sorting is am-
plified if politicians, seeking electoral safety, further increase the demographic

and political homogeneity of their districts on top of the voters' self-imposed socio-economic-racial homogeneity.

This chapter describes some map-drawing experiments intended to explore the possibilities of increasing competition from the levels we currently observe in California. It focuses on California's 53 congressional and 80 Assembly districts. Using a team of graduate and undergraduate students and one Geographic Information Systems (GIS) Specialist as our technical line-drawing team, we drew statewide plans for California's congressional and Assembly districts using specific sets of criteria. Some plans began with the existing majority minority districts, lines, i.e., the status quo; other plans were drawn "free-hand." Our team adhered to strict population equality, and drew contiguous districts that were at minimum as compact as the status quo, and in most cases more compact. We then varied three other criteria: maximizing the number of majority minority districts, minimizing the number of county and/or city splits and maximizing the number of competitive seats. Altogether we drew over 30 statewide congressional plans and 21 Assembly plans.[1] In the process, we considered multiple definitions of competitiveness and of majority minority districts. We used 2000 registration figures since those are the data the state used in its last redistricting.

Since an infinite number of plans can be drawn under even the simplest criteria, this experiment does not attempt to provide one answer to a question that has many. We also did not fine-tune our plans to the degree necessary to submit them as law. For instance, in some of the plans we did not clean up all the small census place splits. Census places often are noncontiguous and cleaning up a plan can add many hours to a line drawing exercise. We kept the population deviation under 1% but made no attempt to drive it down to one person. Rather, our plans were intended as heuristic devices, illustrating some key points about the trade-offs inherent in redistricting and the likely political effects of new districts. It should be noted that we did not use the community of interest criterion in our exercise because there is no widely shared definition of the term. We included the drawing of "square box"-type plans as one of our experiments, to simulate the kind of automated, stripped down redistricting process (compact, equally populated, and devoid of potential human/political interference) that some people have argued for over the years.

Our basic conclusion is that on average plans that respect all requisite federal legal guidelines will make about a fifth to a quarter of the districts competitive by historical standards. Even when making competitive seats is the primary goal, sacrificing other criteria at the expense of federal laws and traditional re-

---

[1] In addition to these, we also developed more than 20 other plans to examine other hypotheses, such as how the Costa criteria specified in the Prop 77 would affect the redistricting process. For this report, we concentrated on the 52 plans developed to examine trade-offs among constraints. Using these Assembly plans, we have tested different ways to nest two Assembly districts into one Senate district. Results on nesting will appear in a separate report.

districting criteria, less than half of the seats can be drawn to be potentially competitive. In short, sorting matters, but much of the noncompetitiveness in California is driven by self-sorting.

The remainder of this chapter describes the considerations that go into line-drawing that must be balanced against competition considerations. Then it considers the definition of a competitive seat, and using a historically based registration measure, assesses the potential for realizing various levels of competitiveness under different criteria scenarios, including pure boxes, an unconstrained maximum competitiveness model and a fully constrained plan. Finally, the chapter concludes with how various criteria trade-off with one another when they are implemented.

The Interplay of Various Redistricting Criteria

Line drawing is a matter of balancing various legal and political considerations. Some of these criteria are first-tier considerations, meaning they are required to have priority under federal law. The set of legally feasible districting plans is the intersection of the first three federal criteria: equal population, adherence to the Voting Rights Act, and contiguity.

Equal Population

Equalizing district populations is the basic rationale for changing district lines at the beginning of each decade. Districts are supposed to be equalized in population to further the "one person, one vote" principle. For example, if one district had 100 residents and another had 1,000, the residents of the first district would essentially have "more" representation than those of the second, and thus a vote in the first district would be valued differently than in the second.

The equal population criterion has been more and more stringently defined by the federal courts since 1965. Under current case law, congressional districts are held to "strict scrutiny" meaning that they cannot deviate from the ideal population[2] by more than a few people. For legislative districts, this criterion is not as narrowly interpreted, and most experts will advise to keep deviations below 10%, preferably much below that, to avoid claims of malapportionment. Big cities or counties are often split in order to adhere to the equal population requirement. San Francisco County had a total population over 776,000 according to the 2000 Census. Yet the ideal population for a congressional district is only

---

[2] The ideal population is computed by dividing the total population of the state by the number of districts.

639,088. Figure 10.1 shows that the county has to be split into two congressional districts, District 8 and 12.

The Voting Rights Act.

California is "covered" under Section 5 of the Voting Rights Act (VRA). This means that a redistricting plan has to be precleared by the Department of Justice (DoJ) before it can go into effect. The DoJ will evaluate plans for retrogression, i.e., they make sure that minority populations in four counties,[3] and in districts that are part of those counties, are not weakened in their potential political power under the new district lines. Line-drawers are severely limited in their creativity in those counties, and because these counties and their districts are necessarily part of the congressional plan, the entire state plan is affected and has to be precleared. A redistricting in California also has to take care not to run afoul of Section 2 of the VRA. The simplest explanation of the Section 2 nondilution standard is that in racially polarized areas in which minority groups constitute a majority in a district, groups should not be split up but rather kept whole.

Contiguity

Contiguity is the most basic of all redistricting criteria, but even it is subject to dispute. Consider that some districts are contiguous because they are connected by a bridge. As illustrated in Figure 10.2, the current Congressional District 7 spreads across Solano and Contra Costa counties and is connected via the Carquinez and Benicia bridges. The rule of thumb is that districts have to be connected in some way, and the more connected they are, the less controversial this criterion is.

Below the first tier are second-level redistricting criteria, which are those recognized in state law or referred to as "traditional redistricting" values by the federal courts. They include compactness, respect for city and county boundaries, and communities of interest.

Compactness

Compactness has been interpreted in many different ways. Currently at least seven different compactness measures are commonly used and are part of the

---

[3] The counties are Kings, Merced, Monterey, and Yuba

Figure 10.1. Map of San Francisco County and Congressional Districts 8 and 12

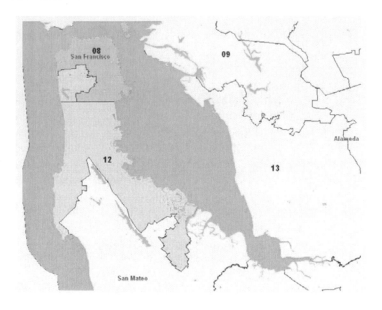

Figure 10.2. Congressional District 7

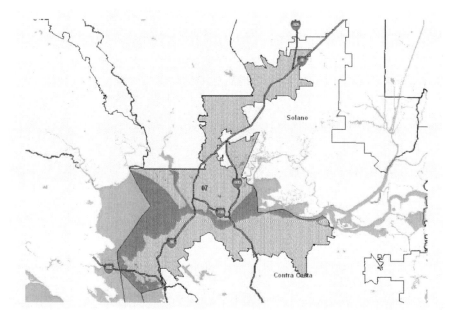

redistricting software we used for this study.[4] When our line-drawers were in-structed to draw compact districts, they would, in absence of any compactness measure, attempt to draw box-like districts that did not have too many edges or "fingers." Figure 10.3 shows some examples of our box-like districts in Los Angeles County that are more compact than the District 7 in the above diagram.

Respect for City and County Boundaries

This criterion seeks to minimize the number of times that district boundaries split local jurisdiction boundaries. A notable point is that many cities are actu-ally not contiguous. Figures 10.4 and 10.5 highlight the city boundary for Ba-kersfield and Fresno (shaded in darker gray). There are often outlying areas that redistricters need to pick up to keep a city whole. City boundaries can often not be very compact. California's counties, while more compact, are in many cases too large to be contained in one district. Some cities are equally subject to man-datory splitting to achieve equally populated districts. For the purpose of this study, as is commonly done in redistricting, we use census places to mean cities. Census place designations consist of cities and unincorporated areas. There are 1,081 census places in California.

Communities of Interest

This criterion is the most vaguely defined and is often the most important in its application when a decision has to be made about where to split a city or a county. At its highest level application, a community of interest could be a city or a county because of the common interest of a respective jurisdiction. It could also be a region, i.e. the central valley or coastal communities. On the smallest level, a community of interest might be a neighborhood, a redevelopment dis-trict or an area that encompasses a group of activists, advocating for a common goal. A community of interest is most often identified during the process of pub-lic hearings in which testimony is provided and areas are defined. Groups like the Asian Pacific American Legal Center and the Mexican American Legal De-fense and Educational Fund held workshops in communities throughout the state during the last redistricting process to collect information under this criterion. Elected officials are often helpful in providing information about existing com-munities of interest in their districts. In the absence of public hearings, testi-mony, and hence available data, this study did not have the benefit of being able to utilize this criterion. Rather than using our own biases to include only some

---

[4] Maptitude for Redistricting 4.7, by Caliper Corp.

Figure 10.3. Example of Compact, Box-like Districts

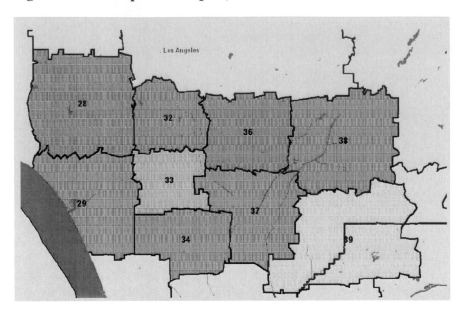

Figure 10. 4.　Map of the City of Bakersfield

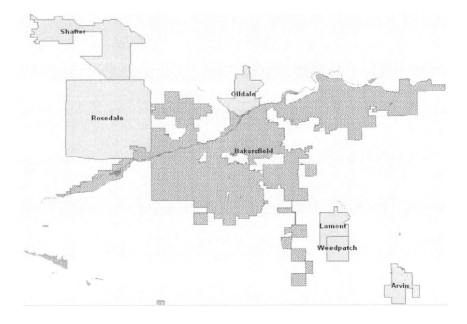

Figure 10.5. Map of the City of Fresno

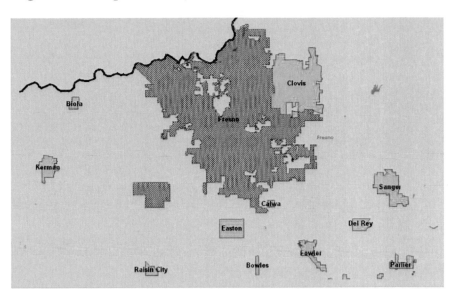

communities of interest with which we were personally familiar, we decided to exclude this criterion altogether.

Potential and Actual Competitiveness

Competition is the newest entrant into the second tier. Whether districts can indeed be drawn to be potentially competitive is a complex question that has as much to do with the electoral geography at hand as with the definition of what it means to have a competitive seat.

Often, the discussion of competition is grossly oversimplified and unnuanced. Many different measures of competition have been used in the past. Some evaluate a district based on the party registration of voters while others look at election outcomes. And then there is the question of cut-points; for example, is a district competitive within a 3, 5 or 7% spread of registration? Given that Democrats tend to have lower level of turnout, should Democrat registration be weighted differently than Republican? And how does the increasing number of voters that decline to state their party affiliation factor into the equation?

We focus on one measure of competition, the 0–3% Republican to 0–10% Democratic advantage registration range, or simply referred to as the 3–10 range. Using party registration data, we calculate the percentage of registered Democrats and Republicans by dividing the number of registered Democrats (or

Republicans) by the total number of registered voters in the district. Then we calculate the difference in party registration. For example, District 1 has 30% registered Republicans and 35% registered Democrats, the difference in party registration is five percentage points (35%–30%). In other words, the Democratic Party has a five percentage point party registration advantage in this district. Suppose District 2 has 40% registered Republicans and 38% registered Democrats, the Republican Party enjoys a two percentage point party registration lead. Therefore both districts fall into our 3–10 range. Looking at all the districts within a plan, we then count how many districts have a 0 to 10 percentage point Democratic advantage and how many districts have a 0 to 3 percentage point Republican advantage. This 3–10 measure emerged from an analysis of the congressional and state Assembly races in the 1990s in California, which showed that races within that range of registration were most likely (but still highly unlikely) to experience seat turnover.[5] We also evaluated other measures of competitiveness that proved to be less predictive. (See Appendix I.)

While party registration is the most common measure by which the balance of partisans is assessed, districts that look potentially competitive based on their registration figures do not necessarily predict competitive races. Many factors determine the outcome of elections, especially incumbency, which can add as much as a five- to seven-point advantage, but also the amount of money spent, the quality of the candidates, and the like. As a consequence, even seats with narrow registration margins do not frequently change party hands, and occasionally, seats with registration differences outside of what we have defined as the range of potentially competitive seats do.

Consider the record of the nineties, a decade in which congressional races were fought in districts drawn by the court masters. There were five cycles of 52 races between 1992 and 2000 for a total of 260 congressional contests. Of those, only 14 (5%) resulted in a change in party control. There were 37 races with registration differences of three points or less, and only six (16%) resulted in party change. Indeed, four of the seats (CD1: Hamburg-Riggs-Thompson; CD15: Mineta-Campbell-Honda; CD36 Harman-Kuykendall-Harman; and CD49 Schenk-Bilbray-Davis) accounted for eight of the party changes, and six others only changed once.

The other side of the coin is that seats that do not seem on paper to be competitive can sometimes experience a party turnover. A good example of this is CD1, which never had a Democratic registration advantage of less 13.5% for the Democrats, and yet, Dan Hamburg, a Democrat, lost to Frank Riggs, Republican, in 1994 and the seat was held by the Republicans until 1998 when Democrat Mike Thompson was elected. Here the factor was the division between the Democrats and the Green Party. A less dramatic example was Lynn Schenk's

---

[5] A seat turnover happens when the political party affiliation of the winner switches from one party to another in two consecutive elections.

victory in 1992 in a seat that was just outside the 3% Republican range (42.8 Republican to 39.12 Democratic) in the so-called year of the woman.

Because Assembly districts are smaller than congressional districts, candidates' personalities and political experience sometimes override advantages in political affiliation. Party registration difference becomes relatively less important in predicting the actual competitiveness of races. Out of the 400 races contested between 1992 and 2000 (80 districts by five election cycles), only 22 (6%) resulted in party switches. One would expect these party turnovers to have taken place in districts with razor thin party registration difference. The reality was contrary to such expectation. None of the turnover races occurred where party registration difference was less than three percentage points. Ten turnovers (45%) took place in districts with 0–3% Republican to 0–10% Democratic advantage registration range.[6] Some Republican candidates were able to win in districts with heavy concentration of Democrats. For example Bruce McPherson, a moderate Republican, was first elected to the State Assembly District 27 in left-leaning Santa Cruz in 1993. Brooks Firestone (AD35) won the seat in 1994 when the Democratic Party had a nine percentage point lead in registration and received over 65% of the votes in his second term.

Adding Competition — Congressional Level

The 2001 redistricting resulted in a bipartisan plan, meaning that the parties compromised and agreed to a fixed share of the seats. To ensure that the seat shares did not change, potentially marginal districts were made safer. This was accomplished by concentrating Democrats in districts held by Democrats and Republicans in districts held by Republicans, making all previously marginal seats safer. Figure 10.6 shows the distribution of seats by party registration margins. It clearly shows that the 2001 redistricting contained no seats in the range between 0 to 3% Republican advantage and 0 to 10% Democratic advantage.

What is possible in this potentially competitive range? Assume for the moment that one could legally do a minimal redistricting that drew only equally populated, highly compact box-like districts, ignoring all other federal and state considerations. Drawing five such plans, the averaged results from them are displayed in Figure 10.7. On average, these "random box" plans put 13 seats in the missing potentially competitive range. Another way of looking at this is that this random mapmaking created 40 safe Democratic and Republican seats: a

---

[6] AD24: Cunneen-R (1998) – Cohn-D (2000); AD25: Snyder-D (1992) – House-R (1994); AD35 O'Connell-D (1992) – Firestone-R (1994) – Jackson-D (1998); AD43: Rogan-R (1994) – Wildman-D (1996); AD44: Hoge-R (1994) – Scott-D (1996); AD54: Karnette-D (1992) – Kuykendall-R (1994) – Lowenthal-D (1998); AD61: Aguiar-R (1996) – Soto-D (1998); AD80 Bornstein-D (1992) – Battin-R (1994).

Figure 10.6. Existing District Party Registration Distribution

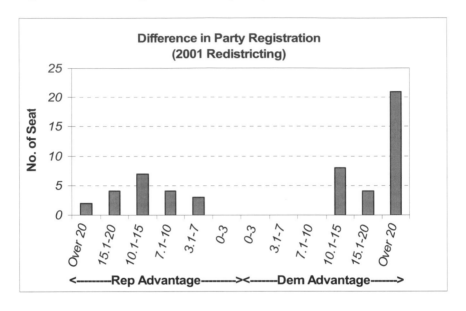

Figure 10.7. Random Plans Average Party Registration Distribution

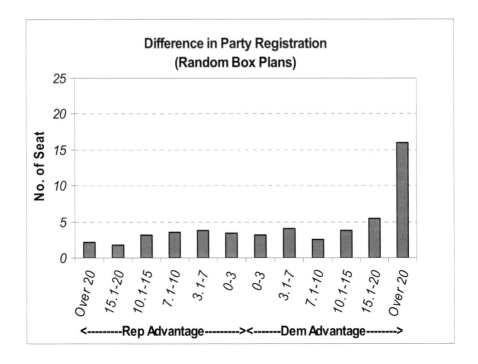

stark reminder that the political geography accounts for a large portion of the noncompetition in the state.

At the opposite end of the spectrum, we also drew a set of plans that maximized competition subject only to contiguity, equal population, and reasonable compactness. A map of this sort would not be legal (since it ignores Voting Rights issues), but it does suggest a potential upper bound on attempts to create more competitiveness. This is displayed in Figure 10.8. It shows that on average there were 20 seats in the potentially competitive range, or to put it another way, a plan that placed competitiveness above everything else still yielded 22 safe Democratic seats and 11 safe Republican ones.

The final illustration of the number of seats that can be created in the potentially competitive range is the fully balanced plan. These five plans took into account equal population, keeping the existing number of majority minority districts, reasonable compactness, minimizing county splits and maximizing the number of seats in the competitive range. Even with all these constraints, these seats averaged 13 districts in the missing 3 point Republican to 10 point Democratic range. See Figure 10.9.

Adding Competition—State Assembly Level

Although none of the Assembly districts had party registration differences within three percentage points in the bipartisan plan adopted in 2001, five out of 80 seats fell in the range between 3.1 and 10 point Democratic registration advantage. See Figure 10.10.

Again, we began by drawing highly compact districts of equal population without using any party registration data or considering any other redistricting criteria, producing four "random box" plans. These plans fared better than the 2001 bipartisan plan in terms of the number of potentially competitive districts. Refer to Figure 10.11, on average, 17 seats would fall into the 3 point Republican and 10 point Democratic registration range. The increase in the number of potentially competitive seats was made possible by reducing safe seats from both parties. Under the 2001 bipartisan plan, the Republican Party held 16 seats with at least 10 percentage point registration advantage, and Democrats had 46. Yet in these random box plans, the number of safe Republican and Democratic districts would be reduced to 13 and 40 respectively..

And as before, the second set of plans maximized the total number of potentially competitive seats, giving a good estimate on the upper bound one could achieve without considering legal ramifications. In contrast to the bipartisan plan, 10 seats could be added to the missing range within 3 point registration difference. Another 16 seats could have a Democratic registration lead of 3.1 to 10%. In other words, 26 seats could be in the potential toss-up range which might result in party turnover. See Figure 10.12.

Figure 10.8. Competitiveness Maximization Plans Average Party Registration Distribution

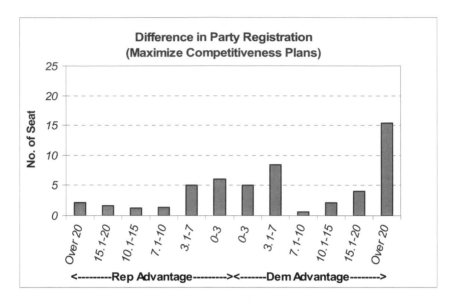

Figure 10.9. Fully Balanced Plans Average Party Difference Distribution

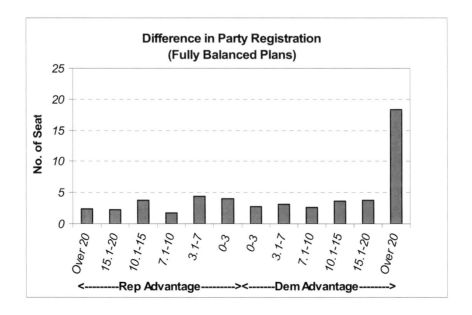

Figure 10.10. Existing State Assembly District Party Registration Distribution

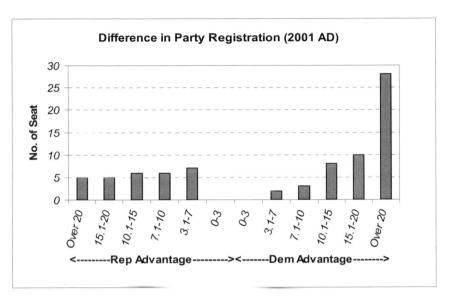

Figure 10.11. Random Plans Average Party Registration Distribution

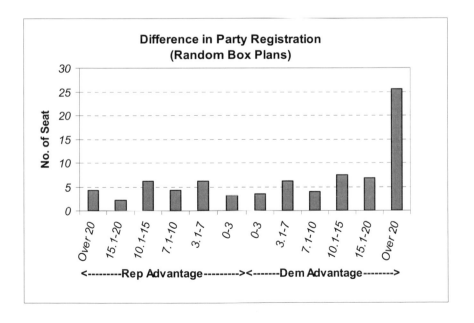

Figure 10.12. Competitiveness Maximization Plans Average Party Registration Distribution

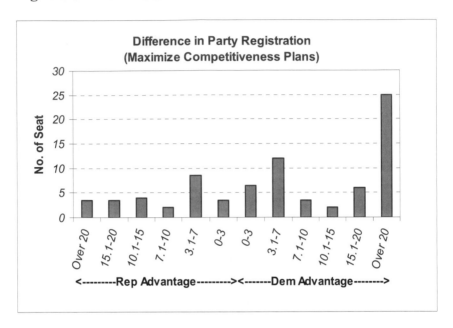

The last set of plans we produced was "fully balanced." Mappers first observed the federal redistricting criteria, namely equal population, contiguity, and Voting Rights Act. Then they attempted to draw compact and potentially competitive districts while minimizing county and city split. These plans on average produced 15 seats in the 3 point Republican and 10 point Democratic registration range. See Figure 10.13.

Discussion

There are some trade-offs of elevating one criterion over others, and multiple criteria interplay and have effects on each other and, consequently, on the outcome of a redistricting plan. In short, here are some of these trade-offs and constraints.

- A strict application of the equal population criterion is the single biggest constraint on keeping cities and counties whole. The more narrowly this criterion is applied, the more severe its effect will be on all other redistricting criteria, including those that we did not evaluate in this study specifically, such as preserving communities of interest within district boundaries.

Figure 10.13. Fully Balanced Plans Average Party Difference Distribution

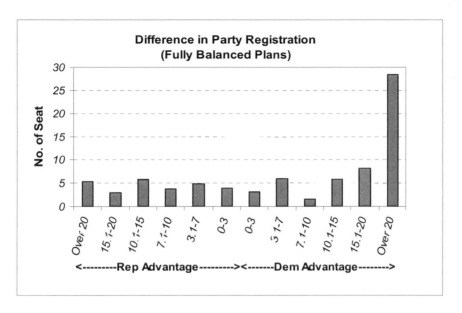

- California is covered under Section 5 of the Voting Rights Act. This means that districts that are completely or partially part of four counties must be drawn such that protected minority populations are not made worse off in terms of their opportunity to elect a candidate of their own choice after the redistricting than before. Any redistricting must take these seats into consideration in order not to violate federal law. No redistricting plan can go into effect until the Department of Justice has verified that no retrogression has taken place. In addition to those seats, there are additional majority minority districts currently in effect that redistricters should either preserve or add to.

- Voting Rights Act and majority minority districts are much more likely to be non-competitive than districts that do not preserve high concentrations of minority populations within the same district. They are also less likely to be very compact. To comply with federal law, any redistricting in California must allow for less compact and less competitive districts in these areas. Most importantly, there is a clear inverse relationship between the number of seats that could potentially be competitive and the number of majority minority seats.

- Preserving city and county lines constrains competitiveness. California's political geography is such that Democrats predominate in many urban areas and Republicans in suburban and rural areas. When city and county boundaries are kept intact, the consequence is a baseline of non-competitiveness in most areas.

Critics of the current, legal, California plan have described its districts as ugly or gerrymandered. In its most basic definition, a gerrymander is a district plan that is designed for either racial or political purposes. There is a tendency to decry every district that does not look like a box as a gerrymander. But our study shows that just because a district is noncompact does not mean it is a gerrymander. Redistricting criteria, especially the preservation of city and county boundaries, can place severe constraints on compactness because the boundaries of those jurisdictions are noncompact. Few cities in California are box-shaped. Furthermore, many cities have outlying, noncontiguous areas that have to be picked up to keep the respective cities whole. Thus the canvas on which districts are constructed is already biased toward noncompactness before one line has been drawn. Counties are, generally speaking, more compact than cities, but because their populations are often larger than the districts', splitting them cannot be avoided in many circumstances and they cannot be used as building blocks as readily as cities. Minority populations in California do not always reside in compact neighborhoods. More often than not, drawing legally required majority minority seats necessitates the drawing of noncompact districts.

Conclusion

In the current congressional plan, there are no districts in the range between 3% Republican and 10% Democratic. But it is important to understand that redistricting is limited in its capacity to create a heavily competitive state. The state's competition level is a function of both sorting and self-sorting. Due to the latter, even plans that ignore constitutional and good government criteria for the sake of maximizing competitiveness still leave well over half the state in safe seats. The sources of electoral safety to a greater degree lie in our choices to live with like-minded people and in socially homogenous areas.

Appendix I: Measuring Potential Competitiveness

Before we debate whether we should include competitiveness as one of the redistricting criteria, we need to pause and reflect on what does it really mean to draw a "competitive" district. Redistricting only happens at the beginning of each decade (unless there is a special Court order to do mid-decade changes). Mapmakers do not have crystal balls to look into the future. As discussed in the report, actual competitiveness of an election depends on an array of factors including partisan makeup of the district, incumbency, quality of candidates, national partisan tides, and campaign spending. No one can ever predict perfectly whether a race will have a narrow vote margin or not. Hence, there is a divergence between potential competitiveness and actual competitiveness. Line drawers can carve districts that may have a good chance of having a close race (potential competitive) but can never create an actual competitive district. Decision-makers can rely on (1) demographic data available after the release of the Bicentennial Census; (2) latest party registration data available from the secretary of state; and (3) their experience and knowledge about different regional politics and preferences during the redistricting process. The most challenging question remains: if we were to draw potentially competitive districts, what information or measure(s) could we rely on? How would our prediction change across measures?

We considered three measures, namely party registration, voting in previous statewide offices, and presidential election outcomes. Party registration, by far, is the most convenient measure. Individual-level party registration files are usually available through local county registrars. The Statewide Database, a nonpartisan data depository at the Institute of Governmental Studies (UC Berkeley), offers census block level data for the whole state of California. Users only need to load these registration data into their redistricting software and can immediately begin drawing. They can predefine potential competitiveness—for example, a district is deemed potentially competitive if the difference in party registration between the two major parties is within seven (or five or three) percentage points.[7] Users can aggregate registration data up to the district level and calculate the percentage of registered Democrats and Republicans out of the total number of registered voters. They can take the difference between the percentage of registered Democrats and Republicans and count how many districts fall into their predefined range. For our report, we picked the 3 point Republican, 10 point Democratic registration difference as our potentially competitive range based on our analyses of the actual races in the 1990s. For the report on Prop. 77 published by the Rose Institute in 2005, the authors extended the range to 5

---

[7] Note that these cut-off points are arbitrary in nature. These party registration difference ranges capture seats that may have a god chance of party turnover. Always bear in mind that actual party turnovers can occur outside these ranges.

point Republican, 10 point Democratic registration advantage.[8] Table 3a and 3b compare our indicator to the Rose Institute measure. Our fully balanced congressional plans would have on average 13 seats in the 3 point Republican, 10 point Democratic registration range, 15 if we extend the range to 5 point Republican. As for our fully balanced Assembly plans, stretching the range would capture 17 seats instead of 15.

One caveat about using party registration data—party registration can change noticeably between years. We drew our plans using 2000 party registration data (as these were used in the 2001 round of redistricting). Except a few outliers, almost all the congressional plans experienced reduction in the number of potentially competitive seats. For example, for our fully balanced congressional plans, the 2000 party registration data suggested we could expect 13 seats in the 3–10 range. Yet the number dropped to 12 if we re-analyzed these districts using 2004 party registration data.[9] This is partly due to a general realignment in partisanship in California. The coastal areas remain liberal-leaning while the inlands have turned increasingly conservative. In areas with new, rapid growing settlements, such as the Central Valley and Inland Empire, partisan realignment seems to tip towards the Republican Party. In other words, even if mappers intentionally created some potentially competitive districts, any narrow registration difference would probably be washed away as time goes by.

In addition to party registration, we constructed potential competitiveness measures based on previous vote outcomes. We created the "normal vote" measures by combining results for the six statewide races[10] in 1998 and 2002. As these statewide races tend to be less high-profile and voters usually vote along party line, the purpose of this measure is to estimate the underlying partisanship of districts. When we combined the six statewide races in two election cycles, we averaged the quality of the candidates, the differences in money raised, and other campaign-related factors. The pooled series also smoothed out fluctuations across time. Using this normal vote measure, our balanced criteria plans produced on average 11 congressional seats or 14 Assembly seats in the

---

[8] Douglas Johnson, Elise Lampe, Justin Levitt, Andrew Lee (2005), *Restoring the Competitive Edge: California's Need for the Redistricting Reform and the Likely Impact on Proposition 77,* The Rose Institute of State and Local Government, Claremont McKenna College.

[9] Results for Assembly plans were rather mixed. Out of the 21 Assembly plans, 12 of them experienced increase in the number of potentially competitive seats in the 3-point Republican, 10-point Democratic registration range if we were to use 2004 registration data instead of 2000. Ten plans experienced a reduction. The mixed results may be explained by the fact that Assembly districts are smaller, and hence regional partisan swing can result in bigger fluctuation in party registration. More qualitative analyses need to be done to better understand why some areas were susceptible to bigger partisan swing than others.

[10] The six races are lieutenant governor, secretary of state, attorney general, controller, treasurer, and insurance commissioner.

margin between 3% Republican and 10% Democratic registration advantage. Comparing registration differences with a normal vote score that combined statewide races shows that registration constitutes a good part of officeholding destiny. Party registration and normal vote are highly correlated. Our fully balanced congressional plans had 14, 11, and 7 seats within 7, 5, and 3 point registration margins. Using the normal vote measure, we got 14, 9, and 7 seats in the 7, 5, and 3 point range.

The third set of measures of potential competitiveness was constructed by using actual presidential election results in 2000. The 2000 presidential race between George W. Bush and Vice President Al Gore was one of the closest races in recent history. Despite the fact that party registration tends to overstate actual vote margin, the presidential vote in 2000 is generally close to the party registration distribution. In our balanced congressional plan, there were 11 districts with Bush vs. Gore margins of 7 or less, 9 with 5 or less, and 6 with 3 or less as compared to 14, 11, and 7 districts in terms of registration margins of 7, 5, and 3 points. Bush ran a little behind but voting seems to have followed party registration fairly well. As for our fully balanced Assembly plans, we observed a similar pattern. Based on 2000 party registration data, 18, 13, and 7 seats were in the 7, 5, and 3 registration margins, contrasted to 12, 8, and 6 seats in the 7, 5, and 3 presidential vote margins. In sum, by comparing the registration margins with the normal vote measure (i.e., the average margin of the statewide races below the governor) and the presidential vote in 2000, one can conclude that on average party registration is a pretty good predictor of vote margin.

Chapter 11

Has California Gone Colorblind?

J. Morgan Kousser

I. Introduction: Voting Rights and Political Reality

Despite the 1870 passage of the Fifteenth Amendment prohibiting denial or abridgement of the right to vote on account of race, the vast majority of African Americans in the southern United States were legally disfranchised by 1910, and most remained voteless in the Deep South in 1960. (Kousser, 1974; Lawson, 1976: 284) Because the timid 1957 and 1960 Civil Rights Acts proved ineffectual in the face of the refusal of adamantly discriminatory state and local officials to allow even the most obviously qualified blacks to register to vote, the Civil Rights Movement pressed for a more radical and comprehensive statute. In 1965, after the Selma-to-Montgomery March, Congress responded by passing the Voting Rights Act (VRA) (Landsberg, 2007). Although white southern obstruction of black voting registration swiftly collapsed in the late 1960s, leaders of the old racial order adopted another tactic to hang onto power: They instituted new electoral structures, redrawing lines of local and state election districts to give them safe white majorities or shifting from district to at-large elections to ensure that small geographic areas where African Americans were in a majority were submerged in larger, overwhelmingly white election territories (Parker, 1990). In the 1969 case of *Allen v. Board of Elections*, the U.S. Supreme Court ruled that the VRA could be employed to attack such discriminatory structures, and Congress effectively endorsed the Court's interpretation when leading members and key committee reports explicitly approved the *Allen* decision during the debate over the extension of key provisions of the VRA in 1970 (Kousser, 1999: 56, 61).

As the focus of voting rights litigation moved from outright *denial* of the individual right to vote to its effective *abridgement* through minority vote "dilution" by electoral structures, lawyers, Congress, and the courts faced a series of new questions: Did minority plaintiffs have to show that the challenged laws were specifically adopted with a racially discriminatory *intent*, or merely that they had a discriminatory *effect*? Since such laws would not prevent minorities from electing their preferred candidates unless a sufficient percentage of whites voted against those candidates through "racial bloc voting," how could one determine whether there was a high degree of racial bloc voting, and how high was illegally high? How large did a minority group legally challenging an at-large election or particular voting district lines have to be? Must minority voters be able to win an election in a district or a proposed district by themselves, or would it be enough if they could carry the seat with the help of sympathetic white voters? How should one measure whether the group was large enough, and how did partisanship in the electorate affect judgments on whether voting patterns were racial or were caused by other factors? Were redistricting authorities required to draw districts so as to make it possible for minority preferences to prevail with complete certainty, a lesser probability (if so, how much less?) or not at all (Kousser, 1999: 338–43, 373–77, 397–98)? Since all of these legal questions involved problems of measurement and empirical political science, political scientists and sociologists began to swap classrooms for courts.

This chapter investigates many of these questions for California in the 1990s. The most striking trend in California politics during that decade was the rise of Latinos to political power, especially in Congress and the state legislature. Did that trend occur because of an increased white willingness to vote for Latino candidates, stronger coalitions among Asian Americans, African Americans, and Latinos, or simply because of the growth of the Latino voting population? How should one gauge the ability of Latinos to be able to elect "candidates of their choice," in the words of the 1982 amendments to the VRA? Under what demographic and political conditions could Latinos in California elect candidates of choice, and did those conditions change over the course of the decade? Do Californians now vote for the person, not the ethnic group? Can national and state safeguards against racial discrimination in politics be relaxed without fear of ethnic strife and with confidence that all voters will have equal opportunities to elect the candidates that they most prefer?

II. Measures of Latino Political Success and Power

A. Who Represents Latino Voters?

The first step in answering these questions is to choose the most appropriate index of the success of minority voters. Since the beginning of minority ethnic politics in the United States, most famously with the massive Irish immigration to America in the 1840s and '50s, emerging minority ethnic groups have most preferred candidates from their own ethnic group (Kantowicz, 1980). This continued to be true in California in the 1990s, as the tables and figures in this paper imply. In California districts with the highest percentages of Latinos, where the choice of Latino voters is clearest, voters nearly always elect Latino candidates. So although not every Latino voter prefers to vote for a Latino candidate in every instance, not every Latino candidate considers himself or herself a representative of the Latino community, and many non-Latino officeholders are quite responsive to Latino interests, the election of Latino candidates is still the least complicated, least ambiguous measure of Latino political influence across districts and across time.

But should Republican, as well as Democratic Latino elected officials count in this index at this time in California? Let the data decide. Consider Table 11.1, which divides Assembly districts in the November 2000 election into six groups, depending on the party and ethnicity of the winning candidate, and spells out some ethnic and partisan traits of the groups of districts.[1] Three contrasts and one similarity are especially notable. First, note that African Americans comprised the majority of registered voters in the districts that elected black legislators, and Latinos comprised the plurality (the majority of the voting age population or VAP) in districts that elected Latino Democrats. In all other types of districts, Anglos accounted for at least 63.6% of the voters, rising to 79% in Anglo Republican districts. On average, Latinos and African Americans must control at least pluralities of the relevant electorates in districts that they seek to represent. Where whites controlled such pluralities, they elected Latinos in only one special case.

---

[1] The 2000 Assembly race was chosen because Latinos composed a higher proportion of winners in that contest than in any others for the Assembly, state Senate, or Congress from California from 1994 to 2000. There were no African-American or Asian-American Republicans elected to the California Assembly in the 2000 election. Black and white registered voter percentages were estimated by subtracting from the total number of registered voters in each district, by party, the estimates of Asian and Latino voters provided by the Statewide Database at the University of California, Berkeley. Assuming, on the basis of U.S. Census surveys, that the proportions of non-Hispanic black and white voting age citizens who registered to vote were approximately equal to each other, the non-Asian, non-Latino registered voter totals were then split into the same proportions as the black and white voting age populations in each district. Various sensitivity tests demonstrated that the black and white estimates do not vary much if one uses different assumptions about the black/white registration percentages.

Table 11.1. Not Colorblind or Nonpartisan—Partisanship and Ethnicity in the California Assembly Election of 2000

Traits of Average District		Party and Ethnicity of Winning Candidates, Nov. 2000		
		Latino Rep.	Latino Dem.	Black Dem.
Number of Districts		4	16	4
% of Registered Voters	Latino	16.1	41.8	20.8
	Black	5.1	9.9	55.3
	Asian	5.9	8.8	4.0
	Anglo	72.9	39.4	19.9
% Latino of Voting Age Population		25.2	55.7	45.9
% Latino of Citizen Voting Age Population		20.3	44.7	27.4
Democratic Registration Margin (D-R)		-7.4	29.1	60.5

Traits of Average District		Anglo Rep.	Anglo Dem.	Asian Dem.
Number of Districts		26	27	3
% of Registered Voters	Latino	12.3	13.3	10.1
	Black	4.4	7.6	17.7
	Asian	4.3	7.4	8.7
	Anglo	79	71.7	63.6
% Latino of Voting Age Population		20.7	20.7	17.4
% Latino of Citizen Voting Age Population		15.3	15.0	12.0
Democratic Registration Margin (D-R)		-10.2	22.6	20.4

That special case—Latino Republicans—highlights the second contrast, that between those districts that elected Latino Democrats and those that elected Latino Republicans. The Latino proportion of the registered voters was two and a half times as high in the sixteen Democratic as in the four Republican districts, and more conventional measures of voting strength, the proportions of the VAP and citizen voting age population (CVAP) that is Latino, were both 2.2 times as high.[2] Latino registered voters comprised 42% of the district of the average La-

---

[2] Note that the difference between the Latino VAP and the Latino CVAP was considerably greater in the districts represented by black Democrats than in each of the other groupings. The same was true of the difference between the Latino VAP and the percentage of Latinos who are registered. African Americans could control these districts not only because of their own strength, but also so many Latinos in the districts were not citizens and not registered to vote. This contrast also points out that the proportion of citizens among Latinos over 18 years old varied from place to place.

tino Democratic member of the Assembly, but less than half as high a percentage of the constituency of the legislators of any other ethnicity. They formed the core of the electorate for Latino Democrats, but not for Latino Republicans.

The third contrast is between the partisan groups. As I have shown elsewhere, statistical models based only on partisan registration percentages predicted nearly 90% of the outcomes of California Assembly and congressional races from 1970 through 1996 (Kousser, 1998). And the partisan registration percentages in the Democratic and Republican districts in Table 11.1 differed dramatically, regardless of the ethnicity of the successful candidates. In all of the Democratic groups of districts, Democrats outnumbered Republicans by an average of at least 20 percentage points, while in districts that elected Latino, as well as Anglo Republicans, Republicans outnumbered Democrats by seven or more percentage points.

This third contrast accents, as well, the key similarity in Table 11.1: The districts that sent Latino Republicans to Sacramento were much more similar to those that sent Anglo Republicans than to those of any other group. Since Latinos comprise a much smaller proportion of Republicans than of Democrats in California today, they necessarily have much less power in the Republican than in the Democratic party, and the conditions of that power are much less predictable. Consider one more statistic. The average Latino percentage of the Republican registration in the four districts that elected Latino Republicans to the Assembly in 2000 was only 10.2%, which was *below* the Latino percentage of the Republican registration of 12.7% in the 76 other districts in the state. That is, the Latino Republicans were elected from districts in which Latino Republican voters had *less* voting power in the Republican Party than in the average district in the state.

While knowledgeable political consultants might be able to draw districts that would be likely to elect particular Latino Republican politicians, it is much more difficult for political scientists to discover correlates of districts that would have a good chance of doing so. In the 1990s, there was just no easy way to differentiate such districts from other districts that were friendly to Anglo Republican candidates. The districts that elected Latino Republicans will therefore be excluded from the analyses in the rest of this paper. Even if they were included, it would make little difference, of course, because the party of Pete Wilson and Proposition 187 contained so few Latino elected officials.

B. Legal Standards for Political Opportunity

In order to determine whether minorities would have been able to elect their candidates of choice in a district, rather than an at-large electoral system or in one with different boundary lines between districts, federal courts and the U.S. Department of Justice began in the 1970s to try to determine what percentage it took to give minority voters that choice. In a Mississippi case, *Kirksey v. Board of Supervisors*, sociologist James Loewen, an expert witness for the African-

American plaintiff, suggested an *ad hoc* answer, which was adopted by the federal court and almost immediately applied by others to districts throughout the country—the "65% rule." In order to control the outcome in a district without relying on white votes for the black candidate, often called "crossover voters," Loewen guessed that Mississippi blacks needed to comprise 50% of the population, plus 5% for the fact that a smaller percentage of blacks than whites were over 18 years old, plus 5% more for the likelihood that the black registration rate lagged the white, plus a final 5% for the suspicion that African Americans were less likely to turn out to vote than whites (Brace et al., 1988: 44–46). In that year, 1977, the Justice Department employed the same rule of thumb in Brooklyn, New York, and the Supreme Court approved (*United Jewish Organizations,* 1977).

If actual data on registration rates, separated by race, had been available, the 65% rule would never have been proposed. Many lawyers, judges, and social scientists criticized the rule almost immediately, and a few went as far as to question whether minorities needed to be concentrated at all to elect candidates of their choice (Thernstrom, 1987; Swain, 1993; Butler, 1995) But social scientific research proved conclusively that in the South from the 1960s through the 1980s, extreme optimism about white "crossover" voting was without factual foundation (Davidson and Grofman, 1994).

A second, much less sanguine line of criticism agreed that there were *some* circumstances in which *some* whites would vote for certain African-American or Latino candidates. Social scientists tried to specify the conditions that made it possible to elect minority candidates of choice. Was there a particular percentage—if not 65%, then what?—that was generally necessary, and if so, how had this "effective majority" changed since 1965? Was it the same everywhere? Could different minorities properly be assumed to be more likely than whites to vote for other minority candidates, even if they were from different groups, such as blacks and Latinos? Could the failure of minority candidates be attributed not to racism, but to the more standard political factors of incumbency and partisanship (Brace et al., 1988; Bullock and Dunn, 1999)?

Judges used such discussions or their own instincts to answer related questions. Was there a "bright line" test, a single minority percentage that could be used to determine both whether there was a wrong and whether there was a remedy? In the leading case interpreting the 1982 amendments to the Voting Rights Act, *Thornburg v. Gingles* (1986), the U.S. Supreme Court adopted a test originally proposed in congressional testimony by lawyer James U. Blacksher, that, in Justice Brennan's words, "the minority group must be able to demonstrate that it is sufficiently large and geographically compact to constitute a majority in a single-member district" (*Thornburg v. Gingles,* 1985: 49). If no district that met that standard could be drawn, then the jurisdiction's failure to establish one had no discriminatory effect, and a lawsuit by minority plaintiffs challenging the redistricting would be dismissed. On the other hand, if there was evidence of discriminatory intent or effect, then the majority-of-a-minority or "majority-minority" rule would guide the judge in framing a remedy.

Although *Gingles* perhaps scrapped the 65% rule, it did not say how a "majority" was defined in practice, and lower court judges, lawyers, and social scientists continued over the next two decades to examine various definitions and to probe their consequences. Two questions became particularly important—whether voter registration, and not merely population data should be used as a measure of political power, and whether *Gingles*'s bright-line "majority" test should be relaxed when minority-favored candidates could reasonably expect to receive enough white crossover votes to win elections, even in districts where they did not comprise registration or population majorities. The Ninth Circuit Court of Appeals, the federal court that covers California and other western states, ruled in *Romero v. City of Pomona* (1988) that at least 50% of a potential district's citizens of voting age had to be members of a single minority group, and other circuit courts agreed. In 2003, however, a majority of the Supreme Court endorsed a relaxation of the majority-minority requirement in *Georgia v. Ashcroft*, and in 2006, in *LULAC v. Perry*, another majority of that Court treated registration data as superior to population figures as a guide to political opportunity.

C. What Was the Best Measure of Political Opportunity for Latinos in the 1990s?

As the federal court noted in the legal challenge to the 2001 California statewide redistricting, a 50% CVAP standard can be legally frustrating, because the U.S. Census Bureau does not release CVAP figures until long after decadal reapportionments and at least the initial lawsuits concerning them must take place (*Cano v. Davis*, 2002: 1234). For technical reasons, the CVAP data is also not easy to aggregate into voting districts, so that the Statewide Database in California had it available at the time this paper was written for both the 1992 and 2001 plans only for Assembly districts, not for state Senate or congressional districts.[3] Accordingly, only Assembly districts appear in Figures 11.1 and 11.2, which compare the number of districts, by deciles of the percentage Latino, for five different measures of Latino strength: population of all ages (hereafter POP), VAP, CVAP, total registration (hereafter REG), and Democratic registra-

---

[3] The lack of 1992 Latino registration data available on the Statewide Data Base at the time this paper was written precludes an analysis of that election at this time. Although the 1994 election was the high point of the decade for California Republicans, it does not seem to have had a major impact on Latino politicians' fortunes. No Latino incumbent lost, and the number of Latino Democratic nominees who were beaten in the general election was not out of line with the numbers from other elections during the decade.

Figure 11.1. What Percentage of a District Did It Take to Elect a Latino to the California Assembly, 1994–2000?

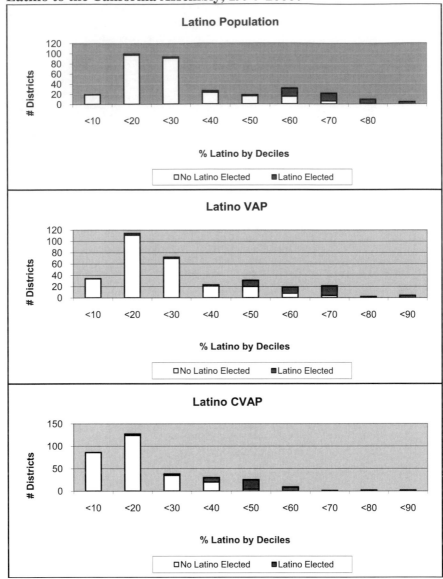

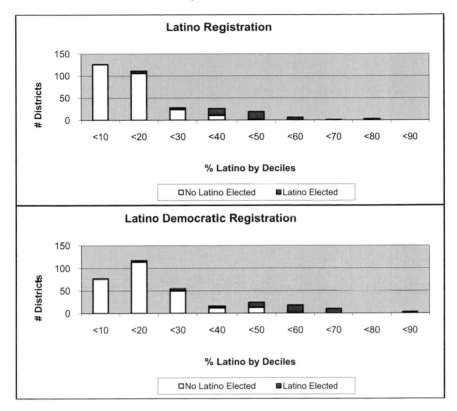

tion (hereafter DREG).[4] Each bar of Figure 11.1 shows the number of districts in the state in which, for example, the Latino population was below 10%, between 10 and 20%, between 20 and 30%, and so on. The white portion of each bar shows the number of districts that did not elect a Latino Democrat, the black portion, the number that did. In general, as one moves from left to right in each graph, the bars become shorter and darker.

---

[4] E.g., POP is the number of Latinos in a district/total population in the district, while DREG is the number of Latino Democrats in the district/total number of Democrats in the district. The registration figures are estimates available on the website of the Statewide Data Base, and they are widely used. They were compiled by comparing the names of every registrant with a Spanish-surname dictionary. The website contains district-level estimates of ethnicity by party (e.g., of Latino Democrats) for the Assembly, Senate, and Congress for 1994 and 2000, and of ethnic registration for 1994, 1996, 1998, and 2000. I calculated the proportion of Latino registrants who were Democrats for each district for 1994 and 2000, interpolated those percentages for 1996 and 1998, and multiplied the overall proportion of registrants who were Latino in 1996 and 1998 by the interpolated figures.

Figure 11.2. Five Indexes Compared: The Proportions of Latinos Elected in Districts Where They Had a Reasonable Chance

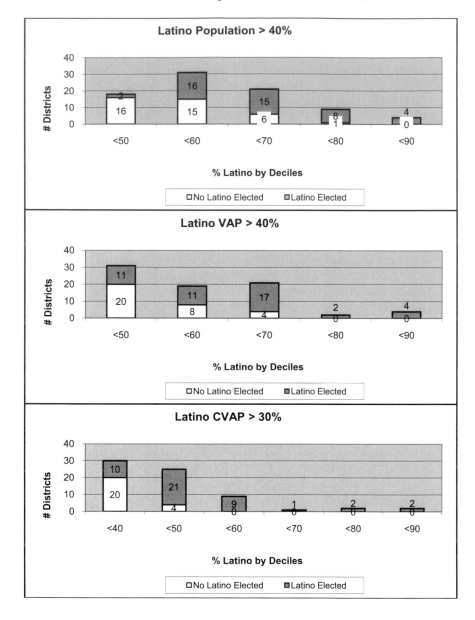

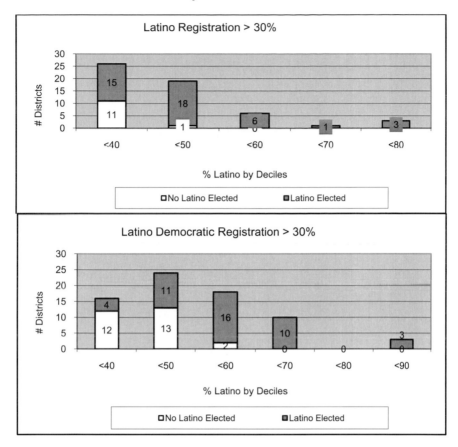

Three conclusions jump out of Figure 11.1. First, and most obviously, Latinos comprised less than 30% in from 66 to 83% of the districts, depending on which of the five measures is used, and almost no Latino Democrats (or Latino Republicans, for that matter) won general elections in those districts. Voters in the tall white columns, who were overwhelmingly white and who dominated the vast majority of districts in the state, only very rarely elected Latino Democrats. Second, the "bright line" point at which Latinos won every seat varied from measure to measure. It was 70% for POP and VAP, 50% for CVAP and DREG, and only 40% for REG. Such points cannot be defined mechanically, according to some rule of thumb. Bright lines sometimes shift and, on this evidence, they often wiggle. Third, drawing a bright line at 50% CVAP, as the Ninth Circuit did, would leave out a great many districts in which Latino Democrats, with the help of help of white or other crossover voters, won Assembly seats from 1994 to 2000. In districts that were 30–39% Latino CVAP, Latino Democrats won a third of the seats; in districts between 40 and 49% Latino CVAP, more than 80%. To set an absolute bright line, below which those who drew districts could slice and dice the Latino population any way they pleased, would be to rob Latinos of many opportunities to coalesce with non-Latino voters and elect candidates who represented the choice of the Latino community.

But can one of the five indexes be judged better than the others? Figure 11.2 compares the districts on the right-hand side of Figure 11.1, eliminating from Figure 11.1 those districts that contained few Latinos and rescaling the graphs so that comparisons are easier to see. What we are looking for is an index that separates out the most districts in which Latinos had approximately at least an equal chance with candidates from other groups to be elected. By that criterion, the POP and VAP measures seem inferior.[5] In the nearly 80% of the districts in which the Latino POP was below 50%, Latinos had almost no chance to be elected. In the 20% above 50% Latino POP, nearly two-thirds of the Latino Democratic candidates won. For VAP, there was a fairly strong break in the pattern of electing Latinos at a 40% concentration. Twenty-four percent of Latinos of voting age lived in districts that were at least 40% Latino VAP, but only 58% of those districts elected a Latino Democrat. Concentrating on Latino CVAP drives the break point down to 30%. Districts in which the Latino CVAP was at least 30% comprised 22% of the districts and were in 65% of the cases represented by Latino Democrats. But REG and DREG predict somewhat better than any of the population measures. In the 17% of the districts that were above 30% Latino REG, Latino Democrats won 78% of the elections, while in the 17% of the districts that were above 40% Latino DREG, Latino Democrats won 73% of the districts.

If we only compare REG and DREG, we can add in state Senate and congressional districts, for which data on registration is also available. Figure 11.3 shows the number of Assembly, Senate, and congressional districts represented by Latinos and others for each decile of the two Latino registration indexes. The

---

[5] Using the POP, VAP, and CVAP measures also neglect the fact that the numbers of Latinos registered to vote, as a percentage any population measure, varies widely from district to district. For the 2000 Assembly districts, for example, an average of 25% of the total Latino population, young and old, citizen and noncitizen, was registered to vote, but this ranged from 11% in one district to 46% in another, with a standard deviation (a measure of the average dispersion about the mean of a variable) of 6.5%. An average of 39% of the Latinos of voting age registered to vote in the 2000 Assembly districts, with a range of 19% to 61% from district to district and a standard deviation of 8.8%. An average of 66% of the Latino citizens of voting age registered to vote in the 2000 Assembly districts, but this ranged from 39 to 89% from district to district, with a standard deviation of 7.7%. Even within the Democratic Party, the proportion of the Latino CVAP that was registered varied widely from district to district. In 2000 Assembly seats, the maximum proportion of Latino citizens of voting age registered as Democrats varied from 24 to 57%, with an average of 40% and a standard deviation of 7.7%.

Figure 11.3. Two Registration Indexes Compared: Latino Democrats Elected in all Assembly, Senate, and Congressional Districts, 1994–2000

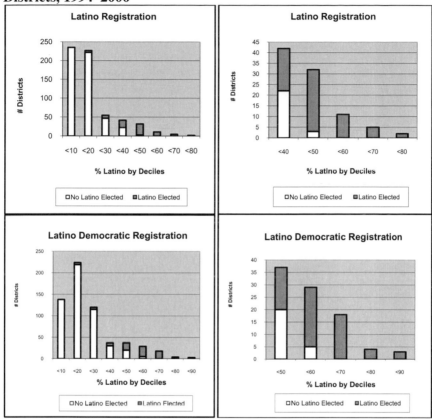

two graphs on the right-hand side of the figure are subsets of the graphs on the left, concentrating on the districts in which Latinos comprised at least 30% of the total and Democratic registration, respectively.[6]

The patterns of districts for the two indexes differed in two respects: There were more districts (128), in which Latino Democratic registration exceeded 30% than there were districts in which the overall Latino registration exceeded 30% (92). But while more Latino Democrats (73) won in the 128 DREG districts, a higher percentage (73%, compared to 57%) won in districts over 30% REG. If the cut-off point for DREG is raised to 40%, the total numbers of districts and the numbers represented by Latino Democrats are almost identical to

---

[6] To keep the number of columns the same in each graph, I have combined the small number of districts in which Latino Democratic registration exceeded 70%.

those where the Latino REG was more than 30%. By these measures, there is little reason to prefer one of the two registration indexes over the other.

But there are two other factors that counsel a concentration on DREG. An estimated 65.8% of Latinos in California in the year 1994 registered as Democ-rats, compared to 21.6% who registered as Republicans.[7] In a system of closed primaries or one in which few voters crossed party lines in the blanket primaries that were used in California during most of the 1990s, Latino voters could realistically hope to have a major influence only on the nominations of Democratic candidates. Second, there was substantial variation from district to district in the proportion of Latinos who registered as Democrats. In the 2000 Assembly, the mean (average) proportion of Latinos who were Democrats was 60%, but the standard deviation was 7.6%, and the range from district to district was from 41% to 73%. Using the overall Latino registration rate, rather than the Latino Democratic registration rate as an indicator of Latino voting power would underestimate the ability of Latinos to influence nominations in some districts and overestimate it in others. For the rest of this chapter, therefore, I will focus on DREG, the Latino percentage of Democratic registrants, as the best index of Latino voting power.

III. What Did It Take to Elect a Latino Democrat in California in the 1990s?

A. Rational Politicians Run Where They Can Win

Running for office is hard, lonely, often dispiriting work—mastering arcane policy issues, knocking on too many doors, asking for more and more money, accepting insults and uninformed questions and comments with unflappable good cheer. It is not something calculating politicians would take on if they knew from the outset that they had little chance to win. As Figure 11.4 demonstrates, Latino Democratic politicians were quite rational. In the 138 districts in which the Latino proportion of registered Democrats was below 10%, there were only seven districts in which there was any Latino candidate at all, and in none

---

[7] The general California trend away from registering with the two major parties continued in the 1990s. In 1994, 49% of all California voters registered as Democrats, while 37.2% registered as Republicans. By the 2000 election, the Democratic registration percentage had slipped to 45.4% and the Republican, to 34.9%. Latinos followed the same pattern as other Californians, only 61.8% of them registering as Democrats and 19.8% as Republicans in 2000.

Figure 11.4. Where Latinos Run, Where Latinos Win (Assembly, Congress, and Senate, 1994–2000)

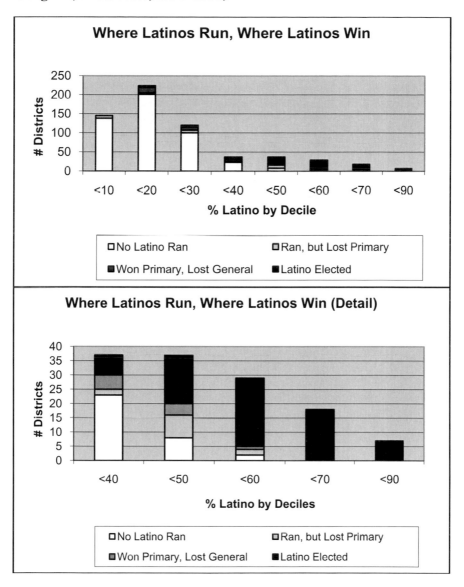

did these candidates win even the Democratic primary.[8] On the other hand, in the 37 districts where Latino DREG was between 40 and 50%, Latino candidates ran in 29, won the Democratic nomination in 21, and won the general election in 17. And in the 54 districts in which Latino DREG was more than half, Latino candidates ran in 52, won the Democratic nomination in 50, and won the general election in 49.

B. Increasingly Colorblind or Increasingly Latino?

The number of Latino Democrats elected to the California Assembly, Senate, and Congress rose from 18 in 1994 to 25 in 1998 (a more comparable year than 2000 because it was in the same four-year cycle of state Senate elections). Was this 39% gain the result of an increasing willingness of California voters, especially Anglo voters, to support Latinos, or just a rise in the percentage of Latinos in the electorate?

The Latino voter totals certainly rose dramatically. From 1994 to 2000, the Latino proportion of the population in California rose from 28.7% to 32.4%, an increase of 13.2%. But the Latino proportion of Democratic registration jumped from 16.1% to 22.1%, a 37.3% rise. The Latino population did not just grow. It politicized dramatically during the 1990s, especially from 1994 to 1996, in the aftermath of the controversy over Proposition 187, which was viewed by many Latinos as a racial issue.

This increased registration changed the political calculus in many legislative districts. In 1994, there were 29 Assembly districts in which the Latino proportion of the Democratic registration was in single digits; by 2000, only 15 districts. In 1994, there were nine Assembly districts in which Latinos amounted to 40% or more of the Democratic registration; in 2000, there were 15. And registration led to election: the number of Latinos in the Assembly rose from 10 in 1994 to 16 in 2000, with districts in which Latinos comprised 40% or more of the Democrats accounting for five of the six additional seats. Trends were similar in the state Senate and the congressional delegation.

Figure 11.5 summarizes the trends in all three bodies. It strongly implies that the increasing number of Latinos elected was a function of the increased number of Latino voters, not increasing ethnic crossover voting. If California voters were becoming colorblind over this period, we would see a shift in the composition of the columns in this chart. The dark portions at the tops of the columns would grow, indicating that Latino candidates found success in new

---

[8] Candidates not in serious contention for nominations, or candidates for parties that are in hopeless minority positions within districts are often barely mentioned in the press or remembered for very long by outside observers. Thus, in a good many cases, I was forced to rely on surnames to determine ethnicity. Although I made special efforts to separate Basque and Portuguese surnames from Spanish ones, I undoubtedly made some errors.

Figure 11.5. Trends in the Latino Democratic Registration and the Election of Latino Democrats in the Assembly, Senate, and Congress, 1994–2000

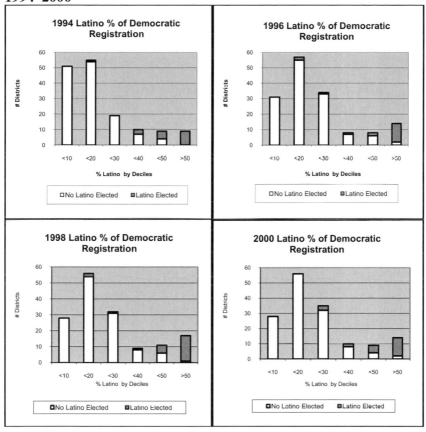

types of districts with fewer Latino registrants. We see no evidence of such a change. Instead, the heights of the columns change, showing that there are fewer and fewer all-white districts today. The jump in Latino registration was especially pronounced from 1994 to 1996, creating many more districts in which 20-30% of the Democrats were Latino and more districts with a Latino majority of Democratic registrants. Latino candidates succeeded in these districts at a constant rate throughout the decade. In other words, voting behavior did not change, but demographic trends created more districts that were hospitable to Latinos.

C. The Crossover Districts

Figure 11.5 shows that it was sometimes possible to elect Latino Democrats in the 12% of the districts in which Latino DREG was between 30 and fifty 50%. In fact, in 2000, 45% of the Latino Democratic members of the Assembly, Senate, and Congress were elected from districts in which Latinos comprised fewer than half of the Democrats. Latino districts between 30 and 40% Latino DREG were represented by Latino Democrats 19% of the time; in districts between 40 and 50%, 46% of the time. While these might have been considered "influence" districts—districts in which a minority community had the voting power to affect but not dictate electoral outcomes—during the 1991–92 round of redistricting, by the late 1990s, they were clearly "opportunity" or "crossover" districts. As the Latino population continues to diffuse within urban areas, such as the San Gabriel and San Fernando Valleys in Los Angeles County, and in northern Orange County, it is these ethnically mixed areas where Latino percentages are likely to experience the most growth in the immediate future. To focus on them is to study change and contingency, always interesting topics for political scientists. To exclude those voters from the protections of the Voting Rights Act or the Constitution is a mistake for judges, for it is to deny a large and growing population an equal opportunity to elect candidates of their choice.

Why did Latinos win in some districts in which their percentage of the Democratic registration was between 30 and 50%, but lose in others? If one were designing or evaluating the design of such districts, what other characteristics would encourage or discourage the success of Latino candidates? In particular, what difference did the partisan composition of the registrants, which has been shown to be an extremely potent predictor of electoral success in California, make to the prospects of Latino candidates in districts where they had to seek support from non-Latino voters?

Table 11.2 divides all of the Assembly, Senate, and congressional districts in the state from the 1994 through 2000 elections in which Latinos comprised between 30 and 50% of the registered Democrats into four groups—those that elected Latino, Anglo, or Asian Democrats, and those that elected Anglo Republicans. (There were no Asian or Latino Republican candidates elected from such districts.) Since each district counts once for each election, a district that, for example, sent the same Anglo Republican to Congress four times, is counted four times in the Anglo Republican totals.

Two contrasts are most significant. First, consider the Latino and Anglo percentages of registered Democrats in districts that elected Latino versus Anglo Democrats. In those that elected Latinos, the Latino Democratic percentage averaged 11 points higher than the Anglo Democratic percentage, while in those that elected Anglos, the Latino Democratic percentage averaged less than three points higher than the Anglo Democratic percentage. Apparently, in districts where Latinos had strong pluralities, enough African Americans and Asian Americans supported the Latino candidate in the primary to nominate him or her. Or perhaps for some reason there were more white crossovers in more

Table 11.2. Ethnic and Partisan Traits of Crossover Districts, 1994–2000 (Assembly, Congress, and Senate Districts where the Latino Percentage of the Democratic Registration is between 30 and 50%)

Traits of Average District		Party and Ethnicity of Winning Candidates			
		Latino Dem.	Anglo Dem.	Asian Dem.	Anglo Rep.
Number of Districts		24	22	2	25
% of Democrats	Latino	42.2	39.2	42.1	37.1
	Asian	3.9	3.2	25.4	3.1
	Black	22.9	21.1	14.8	12.9
	Anglo	31.0	36.4	37.8	46.9
% Latino of	Reg. Voters	33.2	30.5	31.3	24.9
	VAP	51.8	46.2	42.7	40.5
	Population	56.8	50.9	47	45.3
% Anglo of Voting Age Population		28	32.5	27	43.9
Democratic Registration Margin (D-R)		23.8	23.4	34.9	5.6

strong Latino plurality districts than in less strongly ones. In either case, the same conclusion follows straightforwardly: To nominate a Latino Democrat, create a district with a solid Latino plurality among Democrats.

But of course, nomination is not the same thing as election, and the second contrast defines the needle to be threaded. As in all 80 Assembly districts pictured in Table 11.1, above, there is in the subset of districts studied in Table 11.2 a stark contrast in the Democratic registration margin in districts won by Democrats of whatever ethnic group and Anglo Republicans. In districts won by Democratic candidates, the percentage of Democratic registrants exceeded that of Republican registrants by an average of 23% or more. In districts won by Republicans, the average difference was less than 6%. The vast majority of these Republicans were Anglos. In eight of the 25 contests in which Republicans won the general election, the Democrats that they beat were Latinos. But six of these nominations came in effectively overwhelmingly Republican districts, where no Democrat would have had much of a chance to win the general election. The second conclusion is therefore as obvious as the first: To elect any Democrat, make sure that the district has a fairly hefty Democratic registration margin.

Putting the two conclusions together defines the task: To draw Latino crossover districts, one needs enough non-Latino Democrats to elect a Latino Democratic nominee, but not so many as to deny a Latino primary candidate the nomination.

IV. Crossover Districts and the "Racial Gerrymandering" Cases

In the U.S. Supreme Court case of *Shaw v. Reno* (1993: 657–58), Justice Sandra Day O'Connor decried racial consciousness in redistricting as tending to "balkanize" or "segregate" voters by ethnicity, and the Supreme Court, usually by 5–4 margins, sought throughout the rest of the decade of the 1990s to outlaw prominority "racial gerrymandering" whether the districts were oddly shaped or not. By focusing on crossover districts, those who draw boundary lines in the future might reduce some of the Court's concerns, strengthening the redistricting plans against legal attacks. Because the Latino population has grown so much in the last generation, because there is still a substantial amount of housing segregation among Latinos, and because Latinos are concentrated in the Democratic party, it would take an almost unprecedented gerrymander to eliminate or even greatly reduce the number of legislative districts in which Latinos comprise a majority of the Democratic registrants. And as Figure 11.4 and other graphs show, those districts are extremely likely to elect Latino Democratic representatives. On the other hand, to increase the proportion of Latinos in such districts—to "pack" more Latinos into districts that Latinos can already easily win—would not only decrease the opportunity of Latino voters to elect more candidates of their choice, thus contravening Section Two of the Voting Rights Act, but it would also exacerbate the "apartheid" that Justice O'Connor decried in *Shaw v. Reno*.

Emphasizing crossover districts, on the other hand, obviates both difficulties. In districts in which Latinos are a plurality within the Democratic Party, they must obviously reach out to voters from other groups in order to be elected. As Justice Souter put it in *Johnson v. De Grandy* (1994: 1020), in such districts, minorities must "pull, haul, and trade to find common political ground." Voters in crossover districts are by definition not segregated or stereotyped, and the nature of the electorate cannot possibly cue elected officials to pay attention only to the majority ethnic group, for there is, among registered voters, no majority ethnic group, even within one political party. No member of any ethnic group in such a district can be guaranteed a seat; they can only be provided with an opportunity. All of these concerns that the Supreme Court mentioned in *Shaw v. Reno* and subsequent related opinions cannot apply to districts in which there is no ethnic majority of voters. Yet at the same time, as the figures from Table 11.2 demonstrate, crossover districts with certain traits in California in 2001 may avoid either overconcentration or dilution of Latino political strength, satisfying Section 2 of the Voting Rights Act by providing Latinos an opportunity to elect more of their most preferred candidates.

V. Real-World Validation and Legal Fiction

Political scientists are usually mere spectators at the game of politics. If their analyses are weak or their predictions, wrong, they may lose status, but not their jobs. Having more at stake, politicians and political operatives have more incentive than political scientists to reach a correct understanding of the brute facts of political reality. Therefore, when politicians' actions imply agreement with political scientists' analyses, we should have a bit more confidence in the validity of those analyses. The San Fernando Valley congressional district that was the chief focus of the major legal challenge to the 2001 California redistricting, *Cano v. Davis*, provides a good test for the assumptions and findings in this chapter.

From 1982 on, when he left the state legislature after a nearly-successful effort to become Speaker of the Assembly, Howard Berman had represented an eastern San Fernando Valley congressional district. From his early devotion to Cesar Chavez's farm worker movement to his political organization's sponsorship of rising Latino politicians to his cooperation with the Hispanic Caucus in Congress, Berman had repeatedly proven his devotion to Latino causes. Nonetheless, as the proportion of Democrats in his congressional district who were Latino mushroomed from 26% in 1994 to 38% in 1996 to 45% by 2000, Berman began to attract Latino opponents in the Democratic primary. In 1998, Raul Godinez, who raised only 5% as much money as Berman did, won 33% of the total primary votes and an estimated 76% of Latino votes against Berman. Rumors that more experienced Latino politicians who had greater name recognition and better access to campaign contributions were considering contesting Berman's seat after the 2001 reapportionment appeared in the authoritative *California Journal* (December 1998: 21).

Fortunately for Rep. Berman, his brother Michael was in charge of the 2001 congressional redistricting in California, and Michael reduced the Latino DREG in Howard Berman's district from 45 to 31%, while raising the Anglo DREG from 37 to 54%. What had been a Latino advantage of 8% became an Anglo advantage of 22%. The redistricting plan of the Mexican-American Legal Defense and Education Fund (MALDEF), which the legislature rejected when it adopted the Berman design, raised the Latino margin over Anglos among Democratic registrants from eight to 11 percentage points, which was just the statewide average of a crossover district won by a Latino Democratic candidate, as shown in Table 11.2.[9]

Illuminated against the demographic and political background of the 1990s, the 2001 redistricting of Rep. Berman's district supports the assumptions and conclusions of this paper—that Latinos strongly tended to vote for other Latinos

---

[9] The figures and analysis of this chapter were presented to the legislature in an earlier form as part of MALDEF's redistricting package. I had nothing to do with the drawing of any districts for MALDEF and did not know any details about any plan for the Berman district before formulating my paper for the legislative package.

for office, that voting in crucial areas was markedly racially polarized, that the growth of the Latino vote rather than Anglo crossover voting accounted for the rising success of Latino candidates over the course of the 1990s, and that Latino candidates had a real chance of success in predominantly Democratic districts where they enjoyed double-digit pluralities over Anglo Democrats. In a larger sense, the political experience of California Latinos in the 1990s and in the 2001 redistricting argues for a flexible, rather than a bright-line standard to gauge the ability of minorities to elect candidates of their choice. A 65% population rule or a 50% CVAP rule or any other arbitrary principle fails to capture changing political and demographic realities, fails to break down ethnic barriers in politics, and fails to move us closer to equal political opportunity.

References

Brace, K., B. N. Grofman, L. R. Handley, and R. G. Neimi. 1988. "Minority Voting Equality: The 65% Rule in Theory and Practice." *Law and Policy* 10: 43–62.

Bullock, C. S., III., and R. E. Dunn. 1999. "The Demise of Racial Districting and the Future of Black Representation." *Emory Law Journal* 48: 1209–53.

Butler, K. I. 1995. "Affirmative Racial Gerrymandering: Fair Representation for Minorities or a Dangerous Recognition of Group Rights?" *Rutgers Law Journal* 26: 595–624.

Cano v. Davis. 2002. 211 F.Supp.2d 1208.

Davidson, C., and B. Grofman (eds.). 1994. Quiet Revolution in the South: The Impact of the Voting Rights Act in the South, 1965–1990. Princeton, N.J.: Princeton University Press.

Grofman, B., L. Handley, and D. Lublin. 2001. "Drawing Effective Minority Districts: A Conceptual Framework and Some Empirical Evidence." *North Carolina Law Review* 79: 1383–1430.

Johnson v. De Grandy. 1994. 512 U.S. 997.

Kantowicz, E. T. 1980. "Voting and Parties." In *The Politics of Ethnicity*, ed. Michael Walzer et al. Cambridge, Mass.: Belknap Press of Harvard University, 29–68.

Kirksey v. Board of Supervisors of Hinds County, Mississippi 1977 554 F.2d 139.

Kousser, J. M. 1974. The Shaping of Southern Politics: Suffrage Restriction and the Establishment of the One-Party South. New Haven, Conn.: Yale University Press.

———. 1998. "Reapportionment Wars: Party, Race, and Redistricting in California, 1971–1992." In *Race and Redistricting in the 1990s*, ed. Bernard Grofman. N.Y.: Agathon Press, 134–90.

———. 1999. Colorblind Injustice: Minority Voting Rights and the Undoing of the Second Reconstruction. Chapel Hill, N.C.: University of North Carolina Press.

Lawson, S. F. 1976. *Black Ballots: Voting Rights in the South, 1944–1969.* New York: Columbia University Press.

Note. 2003a. "The Implications of Coalitional and Influence Districts for Vote Dilution Litigation." *Harvard Law Review* 117: 2598–2620.

Note. 2003b. "The Ties That Bind: Coalitions and Governance Under Section 2 of the Voting Rights Act." *Harvard Law Review* 117: 2621–42.

Romero v. City of Pomona. 1988. 883 F.2d 1418 9th Cir.

Shaw v. Reno. 1993. 509 U.S. 630.

Swain, C. 1993. Black Faces, Black Interests: The Representation of African Americans in Congress. Cambridge, Mass.: Harvard University Press.

Thernstrom, A. M. 1987. *Whose Votes Count? Affirmative Action and Minority Voting Rights.* Cambridge, Mass.: Harvard University Press.

Thornburg v. Gingles. 1986. 478 U.S. 30.

United Jewish Organizations of Williamsburgh, Inc. v. Carey. 1977. 430 U.S. 144.

Chapter 12

Is California Really a Blue State?

Morris P. Fiorina and Samuel J. Abrams

A Red to Blue Transformation

To a younger generation of political observers California is the quintessential blue state. California is Hollywood and San Francisco, medical marijuana and gay marriage, UC Berkeley, the self-esteem movement, tree-sitters, the first majority minority state—a long list of liberal symbols that raises the ire of conservative commentators. To an older generation of political observers, however, the Democratic turn in California is a relatively recent development.

The picture is clearest at the presidential level. Consider Table 12.1, which lists the post World War II presidential winners in the state. Harry Truman's 1948 victory was the last hurrah of the New Deal—he carried California by one-half of 1% of the vote. There followed a noteworthy string of 10 elections in which Republican candidates carried the state nine times, falling short only in the 1964 landslide of Democrat Lyndon Johnson. (In seven of the 10 elections a Californian was on the Republican ticket.)[1] In the 1980s national political commentators often discussed the Republican "lock" on the presidency, with Cali-

---

[1] Richard Nixon in 1952, 1956, 1960, 1968, and 1972, Ronald Reagan in 1980 and 1984.

Table 12.1. California Presidential Winners: 1948–2004

Truman
Eisenhower
Eisenhower
Nixon
Johnson
Nixon
Nixon
Ford
Reagan
Reagan
Bush
Clinton
Clinton
Gore
Kerry

Note: Republican winners are listed in bold.

fornia viewed as an important part of the lock.[2] The Democrats picked the Republican lock in California (as in the nation at large) in 1992, with help from Ross Perot who took almost 21% of the statewide vote. When more normal electoral conditions returned in 1996, however, the succeeding elections indicated that the Republican presidential era had ended: In the elections of 1996, 2000, and 2004 the Democratic margin has averaged almost 12% of the vote.

Gubernatorial outcomes present a similar picture of California elections in the last half of the twentieth century. Earl Warren first won office during World War II, won re-election twice (this was the preterm limits era), and served until he was nominated to the Supreme Court by President Dwight Eisenhower.[3] In the generation after Warren the only Democratic bright spots were the Edmund Browns, father and son. Since Warren's first election the Republicans have held the governor's mansion for 43 years compared to the Democrats' 21 years. Of course, until Arnold Schwarzenegger arrived on the scene in 2003, the post-1994 gubernatorial showings of Republican candidates were as poor as their presidential showings. See Table 12.2.

---

[2] A popular graphic of the era was a map depicting the Republican "lock" on the presidency—with California included in the lock. See, for example, the inside front cover of *The Election of 1988*, Gerald Pomper, ed. (Chatham House, N.J.: Chatham House, 1989).

[3] Pre-Warren the picture was even bleaker for Democratic gubernatorial candidates: between 1898 and 1942 they won only one election.

Table 12.2. California Governors: 1943–2006

1943–1954	**Earl Warren**
1955–1958	**Goodwin Knight**
1959–1966	Edmund Brown
1967–1974	**Ronald Reagan**
1975–1982	Edmund Brown, Jr.
1983–1990	**George Deukmejian**
1991–1998	**Pete Wilson**
1999–2003	Gray Davis
2003–2006	**Arnold Schwarzenegger**

Republicans: 43 years
Democrats: 21 years

Note: Republican governors are listed in bold.

Elections for U.S. senator showed a slightly less Republican tilt than presidential and gubernatorial elections, mainly because of one Democrat, Alan Cranston, who won four six-year terms. Even so, in the 48-year period between the elections of 1944 and 1992, Republicans occupied the California Senate seats for 54 senator years, compared to the Democrats' 42 senator years. Since 1992, however, the Republicans have been shut out by Democrats Dianne Feinstein and Barbara Boxer who will have held the state's two seats for a total of 32 years by the 2008 elections. See Table 12.3.

This brief electoral history suggests two conclusions. First, until quite recently Republicans were more than competitive in California statewide elections. Indeed, for most of the last half of the twentieth century California was, if not a red state, at least a reddish purple state.[4] Second, something happened in the decade of the 1990s that reversed party fortunes. The picture is crystal clear in the presidential and senatorial outcomes, and had it not been for the unusual recall election of 2003, the Republicans' recent gubernatorial record probably would look as bleak as their recent presidential and senatorial performances.

---

[4] The legislature is another matter. The legislature went Democratic in 1958 and has remained so since with only two brief two-year interruptions in the Assembly. The Democratic ascendancy in the legislature probably was related to the professionalization of the legislature in the early 1960s. See Morris Fiorina, "Divided Government in the American States: A Byproduct of Legislative Professionalism?" *American Political Science Review* 88 (1994): 304–16. "Professionalism, Realignment, and Representation," *American Political Science Review* 91 (1997): 156–62. For more on the Democratic advantage in legislative elections, see Chandler and Kousser's discussion of the "Two Constituencies" issue in Chapter 9 of this volume.

Table 12.3. California Senators: 1944–2008

California Senators: 1944–1992
(48 years x 2 senators = 96 senator years)
    Republicans: 54 years
    Democrats: 42 years

California Senators: 1992–2008
(16 years x 2 senators = 32 senator years)
    Republicans: 0
    Democrats: 32

To many observers the explanation for the reversal of party fortunes in the 1990s is quite simple: Republican Pete Wilson's 1994 gubernatorial campaign in which he backed Proposition 187, an anti-illegal immigrant initiative that passed overwhelmingly only to be set aside later by the courts. According to the conventional wisdom Wilson achieved his short-term goal of reelection at the cost of the long-term prospects of his party—the state's large and growing population of Hispanics reacted to Wilson's support of Prop. 187 by moving to the Democrats.

The hold of this conventional wisdom, not only in California, but nationally, became strikingly apparent in the spring of 2006 when political commentators focused their attention on the congressional battle over alternative immigration bills, especially provisions dealing with illegal immigration. A majority of congressional Republicans favored a strict immigration control bill dubbed "enforcement-only" (round 'em up and send 'em back, in the words of opponents). Congressional Democrats and President Bush favored an "enforcement-plus" bill that coupled immigration control with a path to citizenship for undocumented immigrants already in the United States (amnesty, in the words of opponents). Compromise proved impossible and no legislative action was taken. (Proposed legislation failed again in the summer of 2007).

The issue divided both parties. Democrats' traditional sympathy for minorities was in tension with studies showing that immigrants, especially illegal immigrants, put downward pressure on the wages of low-paid native workers, who tend to be Democrats. In addition immigrants' consumption of state and locally provided social services put Democratic officials on the fiscal firing line in immigration-impacted areas.[5]

But the lion's share of the commentary focused on tensions within the Republican Party. The divisions were partly about principle, especially respect for law and order; partly about material interests, notably the needs of various busi-

---

[5] The Democratic governors of Arizona and New Mexico declared states of emergency.

ness sectors for unskilled labor; partly about culture, especially nativist fears of a massive influx of third-world people, but especially about the conflict between opposition to immigration—whatever its basis—and pragmatic electoral considerations. As noted in the *Economist*,

> California's Republicans are still suffering because in 1994 they backed Proposition 187. . . . That prompted a . . . rise in Latino voter registration—and the shutting out of Republicans from power in the state legislature.[6]

Similarly, in an article entitled "Oh for Pete's Sake," the *Wall Street Journal* cautioned readers to remember the consequences of Wilson's support for Prop 187:

> [T]he results were disastrous for his party. By the end of the decade Democrats controlled every statewide elected office as well as both houses of the legislature.[7]

Presumably reporting the sentiments of the White House inner circle, David Broder, the dean of American political columnists, wrote:

> Wilson is blamed by many Republicans, including those around President Bush, for so alienating the growing Hispanic vote in California that the state's hoard of electoral votes has moved permanently into the Democratic column.[8]

And quoting a pollster who specializes in Latino issues, a *Washington Post* columnist nicely summarizes the conventional wisdom:

> The negative role model cited universally is former California governor Pete Wilson, who used the anti-illegal-immigration issue to win reelection in 1994 only to see his party suffer in subsequent elections. "California went from being a swing state to a solid Democratic state, mainly because of the overwhelming support of Hispanics," Bendixen said.[9]

---

[6] "More Marches, a growing backlash," *The Economist*, May 6, 2006, 30. A correction of the *Economist*'s history: the Republicans were essentially shut out of power in the California legislature in the 1958 elections. It seems unfair to attribute this development to something Governor Wilson did in 1994, especially because that election was the only one since 1968 when the Republicans managed to win a chamber (Assembly) in the California Legislature.

[7] Brendan Miniter, "Oh, for Pete's Sake," *WSJ.com*, July 25, 2006. Accesssed July 25, 2006.

[8] David Broder, "*GOP v. GOP* on Borders," *Washington Post*, June 15, 2006, A27.

[9] Dan Balz, "In Speech, A Balancing Act of Policy and Politics," *Washington Post*, May 16, 2006, A01.

The Conventional Wisdom Reconsidered

Conventional wisdom almost always exaggerates, but in this case, it turns out to be more wrong than right.[10] Of course, the importance of Latino voters in California has increased. The bottom line in Figure 12.1 shows that the proportion of registered voters who are Latino has approximately doubled since the early 1990s. In addition, exit polls indicate that the Latino tilt toward the Democrats in top-of-the-ticket races (top lines in Figure 12.1) has become more pronounced during the past decade. If a population group that supports your party is growing in size, and their tendency to support you in elections is increasing as well, then *other things being equal*, your party's electoral prospects are improving. The Field Poll has calculated the average Latino contribution to Democratic margins in recent elections. As reported in Figure 12.2, that contribution has increased from about four percentage points in 1994 to about seven percentage points today. So, there is no question that the Democrats have gained from the growing Latino vote. But given the size of Democratic margins in many recent statewide elections, the three percentage point or so gain provided by Latino voters clearly is only part of the story; a relatively small part, in fact.[11]

The explanation is that the "other things being equal" proviso noted in the preceding paragraph has not been met—far from it. Figure 12.3 plots the number (*not* the percentage) of registered voters in California from the end of World War II to the present. Since Wilson's 1994 reelection voter registration in the state has increased by about 1.4 million. Surprisingly, however, Democratic registration shows no net gain. Indeed, the number of registered Democrats was *higher* in 1994 than it has ever been—before or since. As *a matter of simple arithmetic, the gains Democrats made among Latinos since 1994 have been slightly more than offset by losses in other population groups*. At the same time the number of registered Republicans actually has marginally increased since 1994, so that the Democratic registration edge today is only a little more than three-quarters as large as it was in 1994. In sum, looking at either the absolute number of registered Democrats or at the Democratic advantage relative to Re-

---

[10] The authors wish to acknowledge the work of Josh Benson, whose 2003 undergraduate honors thesis, "From Reagan Country to Clinton Capital: The Political Transformation of California," provoked the senior author to think more seriously about the conventional wisdom. Among other things Benson found that levels or changes in the Latino population of California counties had little statistical relationship to levels or changes in the Democratic vote.

[11] A recent article in the professional literature makes a similar general point. Analyzing subjective party identification from Field polls, Bowler, Nicholson, and Segura argue that the effects of Prop 187 (and other 1990s propositions targeting minority populations must have affected voters outside the targeted groups, which were too small to account for the observed decline in Republican partisanship. Shaun Bowler, Stephen P. Nicholson, Gary M. Segura, "Earthquakes and Aftershocks: Race, Direct Democracy, and Partisan Change," *American Journal of Political Science* 50(2006): 146–59.

Figure 12.1. Latino Electoral Importance Is Growing

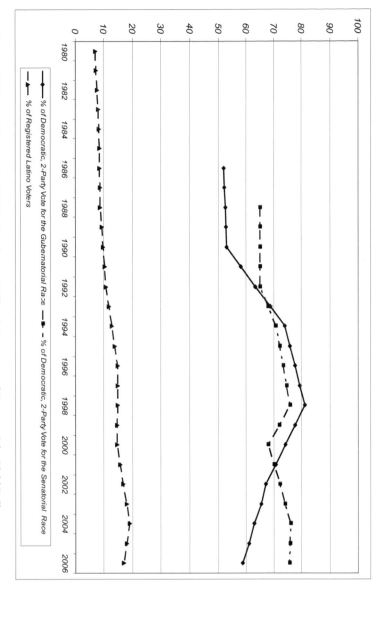

Source: US Census Bureau, the CPS Databank, the California Secretary of State, and the Field Poll.

Figure 12.2. But Not as Much as Often Assumed

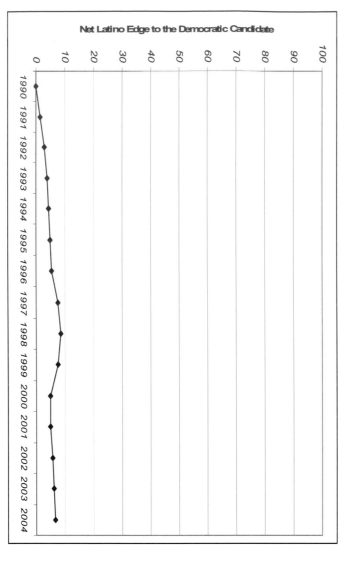

Net Latino Edge to the Democratic Candidate

Source: The Field Poll and their analysis of California Secretary of State.

Figure 12.3. California Voter Registration: No Democratic Gain Since 1994

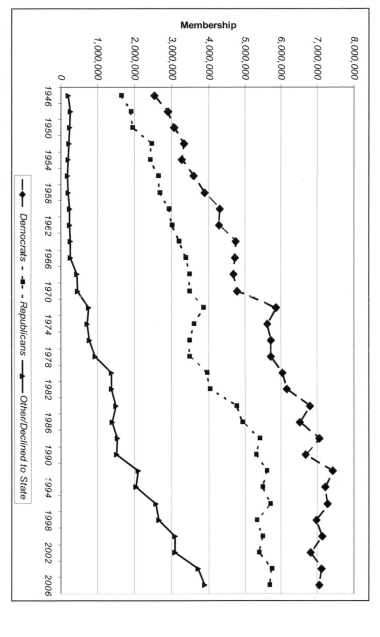

Source: California Secretary of State.

publican, the surprising conclusion is that in terms of voter registration the Democrats have lost ground since they began dominating statewide elections!

Where have the 1.4 million new registrants since 1994 gone? A few have
gone to established California minor parties such as the Libertarians, Greens,
and Peace and Freedom, but as the bottom line in Figure 12.3 shows, nearly
95% of the net gain in voter registration went to the "Other/Decline to State"
category—independents. Projecting these three lines provides the basis for Arnold Schwarzenegger's 2006 decision to reposition himself as a "postpartisan"
politician. If the trends from 1994 were to continue, the independents will catch
the Republicans in 2013 and the Democrats in 2016.[12] Such trends, incidentally,
are by no means unique to California. Twenty-five states that record voter registration by party report a surge in independent/nonpartisan registration between
2000 and 2004 averaging 21%. By comparison, Democratic registration increased about 7% on average and Republican registration 5–6%.[13] In such deep
blue states as Massachusetts and Connecticut, independents became the largest
category of registered voters some years ago.[14]

There is another, less obvious feature of Figure 12.3 that sheds light on the
main subject of this paper—the 1990s decline in Republican fortunes in California. Note that even during the long period when Republican candidates dominated the presidential voting and won senatorial and gubernatorial elections considerably more often than they lost, they never enjoyed a registration edge over
the Democrats. That is, Republican statewide victories were fashioned from
some combination of two factors: holding their own partisans at a higher rate
than the Democrats held theirs, and winning the bulk of the independent vote.
Given the numbers in the graph, the first consideration clearly was more important 40 years ago when independent registration was tiny, but the second grew in
importance as independent registration increased, and now appears to be the key
to Republican prospects in California for the foreseeable future.

To illustrate this point in dramatic fashion, consider the components of the
Republican vote at the peak of party fortunes with the components of their vote
at the nadir. Republican George Deukmejian won the 1986 gubernatorial election by a margin of 22 percentage points. Republican Dan Lungren lost the 1998
gubernatorial election by a margin of 20 percentage points. Table 12.4 contrasts
the components of the vote based on exit polls for the two elections.

---

[12] The regression equations are as follows:
Ind: $y = 292667(\text{year}) + 2E+06 \ (R^2 = 0.9622)$
Dem: $y = -34111(\text{year}) + 7E+06 \ (R^2 = 0.2337)$
Rep: $y = 28564(\text{year}) + 5E+06 \ (R^2 = 0.1329)$

[13] We thank Zachary Courser of Claremont McKenna College for calling these figures to our attention. The figures were originally gathered by Election Data Services.

[14] In the much publicized 2006 Connecticut primary election in which Ned Lamont
defeated incumbent Democratic Senator Joe Lieberman, few (if any) commentators noted
that Lamont's total primary vote in the (closed) Democratic primary amounted to less
than 6% of the voting age population of Connecticut.

Table 12.4. California Republican High vs. Low

	Deukmejian (61%)	Lungren (38%)
White	63	46
Black	12	11
Latino	31	17
Other	52	29
Democrat	27	7
Independent	53	35
Republican	91	79
Liberal	23	7
Moderate	54	32
Conservative	83	77
Union Member	46	25
< $12,500/$15,000	39	25
> $50,000/$75,000	68	43

Lungren's share of the Latino vote was 14 percentage points lower than Deukmejian's share (and as Figure 12.2 shows, the size of that vote had increased a bit). That much is consistent with the conventional wisdom. But far more important, Lungren's share of the much larger Anglo voter category was 17 percentage points lower than Deukmejian's share. Reading down the table, we see that Deukmejian held nine out of 10 Republican partisans, whereas Lungren held only eight of 10. But of greater numerical importance than a 10 percentage point difference in Republican support, Deukmejian induced more than a quarter of Democratic partisans to cross over, while Lungren attracted less than one out of 10 Democrats—a 20 percentage point difference in a larger voter category. And Deukmejian carried the independents in 1986 while Lungren barely attracted one-third of them—and the category was 50% larger by 1998.

The story for voter ideology is similar, but even more suggestive of the major source of Republican problems. Lungren fell only a little short of Deukmejian among self-identified conservatives, but whereas Deukmejian won almost a quarter of liberals, Lungren received less than one-third as high a proportion. And where Deukmejian carried the moderates, Lungren won less than one-third of their vote—and the size of the self-identified moderate voter category had reached almost 50% of the electorate by 1998.

The final figures in the table are perhaps the most striking: once overwhelming Republican support among affluent Californians has deteriorated to the point that a majority of them voted Democratic in 1998. The so-called "party of the rich" did not win a majority even among high income households.

While 1986 versus 1998 compares two extremes, the available exit poll data suggest that it captures the general pattern. Figure 12.4 graphs the proportion of political independents and ideological moderates who voted Republican for the gubernatorial and senatorial elections since exit poll data become available. A party that was winning the broad middle of the electorate as late as 1994 had been reduced to its partisan and ideological base by 1998.

Why the Republican Decline?

The conventional wisdom attributes the decline in Republican electoral fortunes in California to Latino reaction to the 1994 Republican campaign. Supposedly, a steadily growing Latino population has moved significantly toward the Democrats. While the evidence supports those propositions to some degree, Figures 12.1 and 12.2 indicate that the movement of Latinos to the Democrats has been neither sudden, nor massive in absolute terms, not is it nearly large enough to explain the observed turnabout in party fortunes. Rather, Republican statewide candidates in the past decade have performed much worse than previously among political independents and ideological moderates, and even among wealthy Californians. Pete Wilson was convicted of a political crime to which he was at most a minor accessory.

Why did a California electorate that had supported William Knowland, Thomas Kuchel, and Pete Wilson for senator, and Ronald Reagan, George Deukmejian, and Pete Wilson for governor change its partisan preferences in a relatively brief span of time? The most likely explanation is a change in the image of the California Republican Party and a change in the kind of candidate it nominates for statewide office. A generation ago the California Republican Party was a pragmatic, broad-based party that emphasized issues like taxes and spending of concern to the broad middle of the electorate (and even to many on the other side). It was a conservative party when conservative was defined largely in economic terms—low taxes, efficient public services, and limited government. Today the party is an ideological, narrowly based party that defines its conservatism by social and cultural issues like abortion and gay marriage that are of only secondary concern to most Californians; moreover, most Californians take more liberal views on such issues than California Republican activists do. The middle of the road in California runs through the economically conservative but socially tolerant quadrant of the ideological space.

Consider Table 12.5. The top panel lists the 10 counties in which Republicans suffered the smallest drop-off between the 1986 and 1998 elections (the

Figure 12.4. The Republican Collapse: 1994–1998

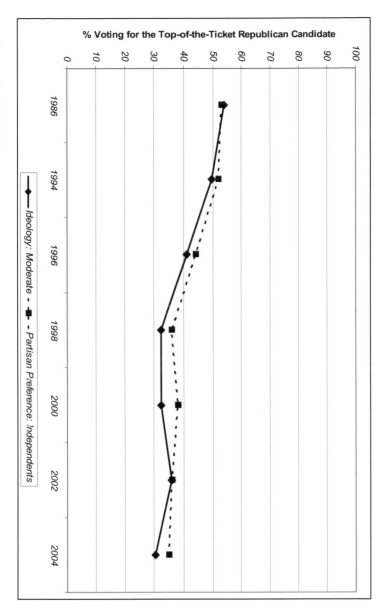

% Voting for the Top-of-the-Ticket Republican Candidate

Ideology: Moderate — Partisan Preference: Independents

Source: The Field Poll.

Table 12.5.
Counties with the Smallest Republican Drop-off, 1986–1998

County	Difference
Humboldt	13
Kern	13
Sierra	13
Madera	14
Fresno	16
Mariposa	16
Plumas	16
Shasta	18
Siskiyou	18
Tulare	18

Counties with the Largest Republican Drop-Off, 1986–1998

San Mateo	34
Napa	33
Lake	31
Sonoma	30
Solano	30
Marin	30
Contra Costa	30
Yolo	28
Santa Clara	28
San Benito	28

Republican vote fell in every one of the state's 58 counties). With the exception of fast-growing Kern and Fresno counties in the Central Valley, the counties showing the smallest declines in Republican support are sparsely populated mountain counties and far northern timber and cattle counties. The bottom panel of the table lists the 10 counties in which the Republicans have suffered their largest drop-off. Most of these counties lie in the San Francisco Bay area, extending northward to the wine counties of Sonoma, Napa, and increasingly Lake, eastward to Contra Costa County, and south to Santa Clara County (Silicon Valley). Many of these counties are densely populated, and becoming increasingly so. Moreover, their residents are highly educated, affluent professionals, the kind of people that used to constitute the core of the Republican vote.

It is a plausible surmise that the people who inhabit the former list of counties are more culturally conservative and therefore less likely to be put off by the contemporary Republican Party.[15] Evidence consistent with that surmise comes

---

[15] Also, in many of these counties the environmentalism of the Democrats probably is in conflict with local economic interests. Unfortunately, no major environmental initia-

from an examination of the relationship between the 1986–1998 fall-off in a county's Republican gubernatorial vote and its support for contentious social policy initiatives: the correlations indicate that the Republican vote dropped most sharply where the conservative side of the initiative fared most poorly:

Support for 1988 Prop. 102 (Quarantine HIV Positive Individuals) -.41
Support for 1996 Prop. 73 (Legalize Medical Marijuana) .46
Support for 2000 Prop. 22 (No Same-sex Marriage Recognition) -.43
Support for 2004 Prop. 71 (State Funding of Stem Cell Research) .52
Support for 2005 Prop. 73 (Parental Notification) -.45

The problem for the Republicans is that only one of the five initiatives—the same-sex marriage prohibition—won, by a strong 66% majority. The other four lost by majorities averaging more than 58%. Tellingly, the reversal in Republican fortunes is where we might least expect to see it if Californians were voting for or against Republicans on economic grounds rather than social grounds.[16] The wealthier the county, the larger the fall-off in Republican support—the correlation between the magnitude of the Republican decline and median household

---

tives were on the ballot during the period of the Republican collapse, so we can not investigate this factor further at this time.

[16] As noted above, Bowler, Nicholson, and Segura emphasize Republican Party support for ethnic/racial initiatives, namely 1994's Prop. 187, 1996's Prop. 209 outlawing racial preferences, and 1998's Prop. 227 banning bilingual education. Although they span an 11-year interval, county-level voting on all eight propositions is very highly correlated—a principal component analysis finds a single common factor that accounts for 86% of the variance. The factor loadings of the eight propositions are as follows:

Prop 187 (illegal immigrants) .978
Prop 22 (same sex marriage) .968
Prop 215 (medical marijuana) -.959
Prop 71 (stem cell research) -.926
Prop 102 (AIDS quarantine) .925
Prop 73 (parental notification) .908
Prop 209 (racial preferences) .891
Prop 227 (bilingual education) .860

Given such intercorrelations, it would take a much finer-grained analysis than this one (precinct-level, at least) to separate the racial/ethnic from the social/cultural impacts on Republican support. We think that given the actual voting outcomes, the social/cultural issues are dominant. That is, while Latinos and African Americans may have been motivated to move toward the Democrats by the racial/ethnic initiatives they perceived to be aimed at them, these three propositions were *approved* by an average margin exceeding 58%. Why would California Republicans be damaged by support for propositions that evidently were overwhelmingly popular among nonminorities? In contrast, of the five social/cultural initiatives only one (no same-sex marriage) was approved. The other four were *rejected* by the California electorate by an average margin of 58%. It seems more likely that the image of the California Republican Party was hurt far more by issues on which it took a clear minority position than on issues where it aligned with a clear majority.

income in 1998 is .45.[17] Evidently, middle- and upper-income Californians liked Republicans better a generation ago when they stood for "leave us alone" than today when they stand for "do as we say."

Conclusion

Ultimately, we conclude that Pete Wilson was framed. After his 1994 campaign both parties found it convenient to accept circumstantial evidence as conclusive and rush to judgment. They convicted Wilson on the basis of flimsy circumstantial evidence that does not stand up under close scrutiny. Why? For Democrats, attributing the Republican decline to alienated Latinos fits their stereotype of Republicans as bigoted, or at best unsympathetic to minority issues. Even better, Democrats could view the electoral losses subsequently suffered by Republicans as evidence that Republican callousness or prejudice had brought on just punishment.

But why would Republicans not search more carefully for the causes of their electoral misfortunes and meekly accept an ethnic explanation that they normally contest when advanced by Democrats? The simplest answer is that it shifted the blame. It is psychologically much easier for ideological activists to blame their defeats on demographic and historical factors over which they have little control ("there are more and more Latinos and they don't like us because of something that Wilson did in 1994") than to accept the fact that voters have looked at what they offer and rejected it.

More generally, what has happened in California appears to be the flip side of what has happened in national politics in the past few decades. The Reagan Revolution relied on a coalition of the economic and social branches of the conservative movement, and in its early years the former dominated, as social conservatives periodically complained.[18] Over time the balance shifted, however, until the public face of the party became dominated by social conservatism— anti-abortion, anti-gay, anti-stem cell research, as well as other minority positions like anti-environment.[19] More recently, the fiscal profligacy of the 2001–

---

[17] The correlations are all about .45 because the county rankings on both social initiative voting and various economic measures are very similar. Once again, the California pattern resembles the national pattern. A recent Pew survey reports that among voters whose household incomes fall in the top 10% of the income distribution, the ratio of Republican to Democratic party identification has fallen from 46:25 in 1995 (the year after the Republicans captured control of Congress) to 32:31 in early 2007. Nationally, Republicans and Democrats are now virtually dead even among the rich. See Michael Dimock, "Money Walks." http://pewresearch.org/pubs/451/money-walks.

[18] National defense was another important component of the Reagan coalition of course, but that is of less relevance to state elections.

[19] Political scientists Christopher Ellis and James Stimson report an examination of the policy views of respondents in the 2000 American National Election Study who clas-

2006 Republican Congress has blurred any lingering image of the Republicans as the party of economic conservatism.

One cannot deny the political benefits of this ideological evolution to the Republicans nationally. Most obviously, it contributed to the realignment of the south which finally eventuated in Republican congressional majorities in 1994.[20] But what some have called the "southernized" Republican Party has much less appeal in California, and more generally in the western United States, where a more libertarian brand of conservatism has historically been stronger. Indeed, there is now a serious ongoing argument that the Democrats should abandon efforts to compete for electoral votes in the south and concentrate instead on winning an Electoral College majority by peeling off several wavering states in the west.[21]

We suspect that in their underlying attitudes and policy views the California electorate of 2000 is not much different from the California electorate of 1990.[22] The reason statewide elections turn out so differently today is that the Republican Party offers voters a different kind of candidate for whom they have less enthusiasm. In our view California remains purple under its blue surface. Indeed, the Schwarzenegger phenomenon is evidence for that position. Rather than

---

sify themselves as conservatives or liberals. Of the 40% of the respondents who place themselves on the conservative side of the seven-point ideological scale, only one-fifth held conservative views on both social and economic issues. A little more than a quarter were social conservatives only and about one-seventh were economic conservatives only. The most surprising finding is that the largest category of conservatives—about one-third—did not hold conservative views on *either* economic or social issues. Christopher Ellis and James A. Stimson, "Operational and Symbolic Ideology in the American Electorate: The 'Paradox' Revisited," paper delivered at the 2005 annual meeting of the Midwest Political Science Association, Chicago, April 7–10.

[20] The political transformation of the South is a big topic, of course. The common view that racial issues largely account for the transformation has recently been challenged by Byron Shafer and Richard Johnson who argue that post-World War II economic development made class considerations a more important factor. Most observers also would note the resurgence of Evangelical political activism. Byron E. Shafer and Richard Johnston, *The End of Southern Exceptionalism* (Cambridge, Mass.: Harvard University Press, 2006).

[21] See Thomas F. Schaller, *Whistling Past Dixie: How Democrats Can Win Without the South* (New York: Simon & Schuster, 2006).

[22] Here we differ somewhat from Jacobson, who argues that the California electorate became much more polarized along partisan and ideological lines in the last three decades of the twentieth century. Near the end of his analysis he observes that the California Republican Party moved sharply rightward in the later years of this period, probably stimulating voters to follow suit. We agree, but we regard the relationships between Californians' ideological and partisan stances and their votes to be more contingent on the choices they are offered—if the Republicans gave them more Schwarzeneggers (and the Democrats more Steve Westlys), they would be less polarized in their voting. See Gary C. Jacobson, "Partisan and Ideological Polarization in the California Electorate," *State Politics and Policy Quarterly* 4(2004): 113–39.

an anomaly attributable to his Hollywood persona, Schwarzenegger illustrates the kind of Republican who can win in California. Consider that in the 2006 elections more than three-quarters of a million Californians voted for Arnold, but one line lower on their ballots, they declined to cast a vote for movement conservative Tom McClintock, the Republican candidate for lieutenant governor. If the Republicans were again to nominate candidates like Pete Wilson, Tom Campbell, Ed Zschau, and going back further—Ken Maddy and even Ronald Reagan, statewide elections would exhibit California's traditional purple hue. But it is not clear that the Republican Party today even contains many such potential candidates in its ranks, let alone is prepared to nominate them.

Chapter 13

The Antifederalist Moment in California Politics

François Vergniolle de Chantal

During the election cycle of November 2004, Californians were confronted with a most peculiar choice that pitted their local governments against the state government itself. Proposition 65 on the November 2, 2004 ballot would have required voter approval for any state legislation that reduces certain local government revenues. Even though it failed to pass, its mere existence is indicative of the high level of resentment from local governments as Sacramento increasingly used local revenues to pay for state-run programs. This is an additional illustration of the way California politics mirror national evolutions. Several chapters in this volume explore the growing east-west divide. Our emphasis here will be of a more institutional nature, highlighting the way Californians seem to have taken up the anti-centralization Republican rhetoric of the past 40 years. At the national level, Republicans have promoted a powerful political critique of the federal government that emphasizes views similar to the antifederalist ideas back in the late 18th century. This evolution, however, is not limited to the national level. It gradually trickled onto the state political stage in various degrees.

In California, this evolution reached a very high intensity level. Benefiting from a long tradition of autonomy—known as "home rule" since 1911—local subgovernments are also currently characterized by a wave of resentment and lack of trust versus state authorities. Our argument underlines the key part played by tools of direct democracy to account for this crisis. These two ele-

ments—decentralization and direct democracy—combine to support the idea of
an antifederalist moment in California politics that mirrors the national criticisms against big government.

Local government in the U.S. has no substantive political status: counties
for instance are creatures of the states. In other words, the comparison with the
relations between states and the federal government seems irrelevant: formally,
states are cosovereigns with the government in a dual federal system, as illustrated by the neofederalist decisions of the Rehnquist Court.[1] Furthermore, the
historical dimension of some states is known nationwide—say Massachussetts
and the War of Independence. No subgovernment can claim to have the same
level of recognition. The point of this chapter is, however, to analyze the relations between Sacramento and its subgovernments with a political perspective
that goes beyond the mere administrative dimension. The current configuration
between local units and the state government illustrates the power struggles
plaguing California: in a context of territorial competition analyzed elsewhere in
this volume, some subgovernments have increasingly relied on tools of direct
democracy to promote their interests at the expense of state's governability.

I will first make an overview of the national resentment against the government over the past decades in order to give substance to the claim of an antifederalist backlash. I will then move on to the institutional and political configuration of California by highlighting the tension between local governments and
Sacramento, as well as the larger context of distrust characterizing the Californian citizenry. Direct democracy tools will then be factored in. This will lead me
to emphasize the detrimental part they play: the initiative process, in particular,
nurtures the very ills it is supposed to remedy. Polarization in California thus
reaches a high level of intensity that turns the political stage into a battlefield
where entrenched contenders lose sight of the public interest.

"Government is not the solution to our problems . . . "

According to Reagan's famous statement in 1981, "Government is not the solution to our problems, government is the problem." The newly elected Republican president then successfully captured the mood of the time. As governor of
California in the late 1960s, he had supported Proposition 13 in 1978, and he
had a first-hand knowledge of how burdensome federal mandates could be. He
came to power with a decisivily antigovernment agenda. Spurred by the economic crisis of the 1970s, American public opinion was gradually becoming
suspicious of governmental intervention. National Elections Studies (NES)—
through the "Trust in Government index" used by the University of Michigan—
have repeatedly reported the reduced confidence in government, which first sur-

---

[1] Timothy J. Conlan, and François Vergniolle de Chantal, "The Rehnquist Court and
American Federalism," *Political Science Quarterly* 116:2 (summer): 253–75.

faced in national public opinion surveys in the late 1960s.[2] The Republican rhetoric is largely based on the criticism against "big government," its inability to meet the social and economic challenges of the time, the ballooning national debt, and the need to "starve the [federal] beast" in order to promote states as key policymaking actors in their own right.

Historians and political philosophers have largely documented that lack of trust in government is one of the basic characteristics of American political life since its very founding. This was especially true for the antifederalists. Their views in political theory were markedly suspicious of power in general and of the central government more specifically.[3] When it was created, the federal government was branded as a potential source of usurpation. It never wholly recovered from this initial suspicion. The building of an American state is thus highly peculiar by European standards, slow, and systematically criticized.[4] Considering this historical legacy, the extent of the federal reach in the 1960s combined with the popular support it had at the time is without equivalent. And it was contested right away. The antigovernment orientation first emerged nationally with the 1964 presidential campaign of the Republican candidate Barry Goldwater. Even though hints of the new positioning of the GOP were to be found during the 1920s and 1930s, as J. Gerring convincingly demonstrated, the campaign of 1964 remains the starting point of the antigovernment wave. Since then, all Republican candidates have committed themselves—at least rhetorically—to shift power back to the states.

This drive was so powerful that moderate Democrats themselves took up parts of the Republican argument, as illustrated by the Clinton Administration in the 1990s. "New Democrats" agreed on the need to streamline the government. Once in power, Clinton launched a national performance review under the supervision of his then Vice President Al Gore with precisely this objective in mind. Later, the 104th Republican Congress and Speaker Newt Gingrich were in a position to force Clinton further down the path of reforming the government. The 1996 welfare reform law is so far the most far-reaching piece of legislation that modified the balance of powers between the levels of government.

Ironically what is now roughly consensual was regarded as being way off the map when it was first initiated in 1964. The internal coup that led to the nomination of Barry Goldwater was a shock to moderates. As a candidate, Goldwater articulated a constitutional interpretation that emphasized states'

---

[2] The data is available at http://www.electionstudies.org/nesguide/toptable/tab5a_5. htm .

[3] On the views of the antifederalist movement, I refer the reader to the exhaustive work by Herbert J. Storring, *The Complete Anti-Federalist*, 8 volumes (Chicago: Chicago University Press, 1981). A more historical approach is the book by Saul Cornell, *The Other Founders: Anti-Federalism and the Dissenting Tradition in America*, (Chapel Hill, N.C.: University of North Carolina Press, 1999).

[4] Stephen Skowronek has aptly documented the developmental path of the American state in *Building a New American State: The Expansion of Administrative Capacities, 1877–1920* (Cambridge: Cambridge University Press, 1982).

rights against encroachments by the federal government, making heavy use of references to the founding fathers. Back then, no one was fooled by these appeals to lofty political ideals. To most Americans, these arguments were just a front for plain racism. States' rights was a code word to reject the Civil Rights Act and black emancipation. Goldwater was crushed by his Democratic opponent, Lyndon B. Johnson, who easily pictured Goldwater as both a war-monger and a racist, unfit for presidential office. But this defeat proved to be short-lived. Four years later, the Republicans finally captured the presidency: Richard Nixon was the first to successfully wield the antigovernment political weapon by supporting a new federalism. Nixon, however, proved to be a letdown for most advocates of governmental reforms. Contrary to his campaign promises, he could not get Congress to vote on significant changes in the field of federal-state relations. In many policy realms, he expanded the federal reach, notably in the field of the environment.

The two-terms of Ronald Reagan were different. Reagan also promised a new federalism but contrary to Nixon, he gave it a more substantive dimension. By then, the states' rights rhetoric was not understood as a coded racist language. Reagan gave both visibility and credibility to his neofederalist reforms by linking them to the tax issue. Federal tax cuts were successfully framed as political—and to some extent constitutional—issues by Reagan. By zeroing out budget lines, Reagan gave neofederalist policies an appeal that they still haven't lost. A few years later, the Republican "revolution" led in Congress by Newt Gingrich was based on Reaganite common sense: the government was widely considered responsible for all the wrongs in American society. In a new international context where the U.S. had no foreign enemy any longer, no communist threat to contain, the federal government itself had to pay a heavy price.

The Republican program—the Contract with America—turned government into the new enemy! A weakened Clinton was unable to resist this Republican impulse, as illustrated by his signing of the welfare reform legislation of 1996 that shifted many responsibilities back to the states. The mid-1990s were a time of unprecedeted antigovernment feeling that has not been surpassed yet. Accordingly, this was a time when antifederalist arguments were expressed in their clearest form. The Republican rhetoric was based on the denunciation of the standard one-size-fits-all federal policies. Regulations of all kinds were seen as encroachments on local powers—especially in the field of social programs, but also regarding environmental protection or gun control. The lack of representativity of federal officials was constantly emphasized, hence the drive for term limits. Federal taxes and the deficit were depicted as evidence of how wasteful the federal government could be. Republican leaders adamantly called for an amendment making deficits unconstitutional. To the Republican majority of the 104th Congress, citizens had a right to get their federal dollars back since the government was ill-suited to deliver on policy outputs.[5]

---

[5] Here are two references of political books written by key leaders of the time where the antigovernment argument is prominent: *To Renew America* by Newt Gingrich (1995)

Apart from welfare reform, the results of the 104th Congress were limited. For one thing, Clinton succeeded in using the Republican excesses to bounce back and be reelected as a moderate in 1996. The impeachment proceedings of 1998–99 finally led to the resignation of Newt Gingrich from the speakership. In 2000, Bush campaigned on a predictable platform for a Republican candidate, advocating smaller and more efficient government. But September 11 has convinced the American public that government has to be given the necessary powers to fight against external and domestic threats. The way the Republican administration has played the fear card—notably during the 2004 presidential election—proved successful in that regard. The trust in government regarding security issues is thus at its highest: ANES reports a level of trust toward government reaching 42% in 2002, to be compared with a low 27% in 1980. The Bush Administration had no difficulty in having Congress authorize the creation of the Homeland Security departement in 2002—the biggest government reorganization since the creation of the Departement of Defense in 1947. The Patriot Act (October 2001), and the executive order of November 2001 setting up military tribunals are also two landmarks in the way they grant sweeping powers to the executive in the field of domestic security.

Beyond the irony of a Republican president supervising a major centralization of power at the national level, three elements should be underlined to temper this initial reaction. First, a technical point about the new organizational structure meant to fight against terrorism. It does lead to an increase in both federal power and local power. The so-called first responders—firefighters, emergency squads among others—are in the forefront in case of an attack similar to 9/11, as well as National Guard units. The responsibility—and the funding—for these personnel fall within the scope of states' authority. In that sense, the new framework is not strictly speaking a centralizing decision. It is more adequately labelled as a concentration of governmental functions at both the state and the federal levels. Second, I would like to emphasize that G. W. Bush followed a very active fiscal policy that is largely reminiscent of Reagan's. Just like his predecessor, Bush Jr, pushed through Congress massive tax cuts, thus restraining the fiscal base of the federal government and considerably expanding the national debt. At the same time, Bush increased the defense budget and launched a costly military expedition in Iraq. The surplus of the Clinton era vanished within a few years. Economists, as well as Bush's father, usually refer to this behavior as voodoo's economics: what can possibly be the economic rationale for cutting federal taxes and increasing military spending?

For my part, I will emphasize the ideological dimension of it all. As a result of this economic policy, the federal government is obviously squeezed between conflicting pressures—less resources and more spending. The unique financial

---

or *Freedom Revolution* (1995) by Gingrich's ally in the House, Dick Armey. The antifederalist nature of Gingrich's ideas is further analyzed by William F. Connelly, Jr., "Newt Gingrich, Professor and Politician: The Anti-Federalist Roots of Newt Gingrich's Thought," *Southeastern Political Review*, vol. 27, no. 1 (March 1999): 103–29.

position of the U.S. makes it possible to borrow way beyond what would be possible to another country. There are, however, limits to this option as well. The conclusion is then the following: since the money has to be taken somewhere, especially for the funding of the defense effort, the only option left is to cut spending for other federal programs, notably social programs. What Bush has done is to build a structural incentive to weaken the federal government. The debt is an additional tool that pushes the country further down the path of a "leaner" government. Third, ever since the successful nomination of William Rehnquist as chief justice in 1986, a narrow majority of conservative justices has tried to give substance to the dual balance of the federal system. A series of decisions—*Lopez* in 1995 and *Printz* two years later being the most famous so far—articulated a constitutional reading reminiscent of the dual theory characteristic of the antebellum caseload. The death of Rehnquist and the retirement of O'Connor gave two openings to Bush: he succeedeed in appointing two new conservative justices whose credentials the Federalist Society would not contest. In other words, the recent appointments of Samuel Alito and John G. Roberts ensure that a restrictive reading of constitutional powers will still be favored by the Court's conservative majority.

What I would like to do now is to show that the national antifederalist mood has largely trickled down to state politics. State authorities themselves largely fell victim to the resentment voters have expressed over the past few decades. The state of California in particular is especially useful to understand what is currently at play. Two elements give a new visibility to antifederalist impulses in California: first, the extreme decentralization of its local subgovernments, largely necessitated by its sheer size in geographic and demographic terms; second, and more important, the widespread use of direct democracy, especially the ballot initiative. How do these factors interact with the antifederalist mood in California? It seems that local governments are caught in a fierce territorial competition where tools of direct democracy are used to bluntly assert their interests at the expense of the general welfare.

Local Governments and the Crisis of Political Trust in California

When the political scientist William Anderson wrote *The Nation and the States, Rivals or Partners*, back in the 1950s, he pointed out a basic element of American political institutions. Indeed, the tensions between all levels of government are a permanent fixture of American politics. It is eminently true for federal-state relations, but it is also a characteristic of state politics, especially in California, where the web of local governments is highly complex.[6] California

---

[6] An overview is available with the piece by Revan Tranter, "Cities, Counties, and the State: From Prop. 13 to 1A and the Future," in *Governing California*, ed. Gerald C. Lubenow (Berkeley: Institute of Governmental Studies Press, 2d ed. 2006), p. 107–27.

being a state that embody frontier values, there is hardly any surprise in that configuration: community, self-government, and rejection of hierarchical political orders all find their utmost expression in Californian local government. The so-called home rule option means that local entities can choose to be governed under the framework of the California government code or they can adopt a charter, which gives them more latitude in running their affairs. The larger cities and counties tend to be charter jurisdictions, ever since Los Angeles County pioneered home rule charters in 1913. This reform was supposed to come as an answer to the unresponsiveness of local governments at that time. It was thus part of the progressive agenda to modernize politics and update the state's political configuration. Since the early years of the twentieth century, Californian subgovernment has been in a position to develop its own idiosyncrasies.

Californian counties became the most prominent form of local government —largely because the regional distribution of population, spread sparsely over vast areas with towns scattered, contributed to it. One sign of this status is that there are relatively few regional bodies—with a planning or regulatory function addressing concerns beyond local city and county boundaries. Since these re gional bodies are few and far between, local subgovernments usually stick to local concerns while benefitting from a century-long tradition of autonomy that sets them apart, at least politically, if not legally, from being mere administrative creatures of the state.[7]

At first sight though, the Californian general framework remains similar to other states. Each of the 58 counties has a board of supervisors that is both the legislative and executive authority of the county; it also has quasi-judicial authorities. The county is subject to mandatory duties under state law to provide its residents with services like law enforcement, healthcare, road maintenance, and so on. These counties, subdivided into townships or towns, exist both for the implementation of the state government's policies and as local governments in their own right. Typically, the legislature delegates to the counties any of the functions that belong to the state; conversely, this means that the state may take back functions that it has delegated to counties. Counties have limited revenue generating authorities: they can tax local residents (mainly through sales or property taxes) and businesses, and they can incur public debt. They can also rely on eminent domain power. Finally, they have the power to raise a local income tax. The primary revenue sources for cities and counties are the property tax and the sales tax; the income tax is not significant. Property taxes account

---

The Californian Association of Counties also provides basic information at: http://www. csac.co unties.org/.

[7] Legally, it is quite difficult to establish a new county. In 1894 the state constitution was amended to require uniform laws concerning county creation. The California Government Code specifies the procedure: a favorable majority vote is needed both in the entire county affected and in the territory of the new county, an almost impossible task. As a result, no new county has been formed since 1907, when Imperial County was created from eastern San Diego County.

for the single most important revenue source for counties—30.6% of general revenue. The sales tax is the second most significant revenue source for counties, with counties collecting 14% of the general fund from this tax. Other taxes represent 13.6% of general fund revenues (these taxes include real estate transfer taxes, cable television franchise taxes, and hotel taxes). On the expenditure side, welfare, hospitals, and other general health-related issues comprise over 60% of total county government expenditure. Spending on education was second for counties.[8]

Next to counties, 478 cities are the second type of local government. Here again, cities are granted broad plenary powers to assert jurisdiction over just about anything. Cities actually have broader powers of self-government than counties—for instance, cities have broad revenue generating authority and counties do not. Cities cannot be abolished or merged without the consent of a majority of their inhabitants. The majority of these cities are within one of four metropolitan areas (greater Los Angeles, the San Francisco Bay Area, San Diego, and Sacramento). All of the state's 10 most populous cities are charter cities; San Francisco is unique in that it is the only consolidated city-county in the state.

Their broad municipal powers, however, are not the only specificity of city government in California. Another one is a major innovation that occurred back in the 1950s. In 1954 to be precise, the city of Lakewood pioneered what is now known as the Lakewood Plan, a contract under which a city reimburses a county for performing services that are more efficiently performed on a countywide basis. A city can thus incorporate a county on a partial basis for limited purposes. This system can also work the other way round and favor decentralization of fiscal and political responsibilities. Such contracts have become very popular throughout California, as they enable city governments to concentrate on particular local concerns through zoning. The second option especially—the idea of opting out of county control—has been taken to its logical extremes. The recent case of Los Angeless is especially relevant here: in 2002, Los Angeles faced the threat of losing its San Fernando Valley section, but residents voted down secession by a wide margin. Under this proposal the San Fernando Valley would have seceded and become an incorporated city of its own. Had the proposal passed, it would have created a new municipality of 211 square miles with about 1.35 million residents. The valley had already attempted to secede in the 1970s, but the state passed a law barring city formation without the approval of the city council.

In 1997, Assemblymen Bob Hertzberg and Tom McClintock gave the issue a new visibility. A grassroots movement to split the Los Angeles Unified School District (LAUSD) and create new San Fernando Valley-based school districts became the focal point of the desire to leave the city. Though the state rejected

---

[8] The data is taken from the Californian Association of Counties at http://www. csac.counties.org/. The following website also provides useful data: http://www.california cityfinance.com/. It is sponsored by the Californian League of Cities.

the idea of valley-based districts, it remained an important rallying point for Hertzberg's mayoral campaign, which ultimately proved unsuccessful. But the secession movement was still alive and well. Secessionists said the valley gave more money to Los Angeles than it receives back in services. This triggered a petition drive to put secession on the ballot. Measures F and H would decide whether the valley became a city; along with these measures, elections were held for 14 council members and a mayor.

Opponents asserted that secession was motivated by racist and class-based factors. Valley politicians such as State Senator Richard Alarcon and City Council President Alex Padilla opposed the initiatives. The leader of the LAUSD and former congresswoman and busing opponent Bobbie Fiedler campaigned against secession. The proposal passed with a slight majority in the valley, but was defeated by the rest of Los Angeles voters due to a heavily funded campaign against it led by Los Angeles Mayor James Hahn. The valley secession movement illustrates how far the competition between local governments can go. The high degree of decentralization paves the way for a constant struggle among subgovernments either to attract resources or to avoid externalities: local governments want to achieve a position where they can better attract sales tax generators like commercial malls or outsource developments they regard as detrimental. The increasing homogenization of specific districts documented elsewhere in the first section of this volume may lead to blunt assertion of local interests, as illustrated by the valley. It is especially relevant here to note that these NIMBY moves are pushed through tools of direct democracy.

Direct democracy provides subgovernments with all the legitimacy they need to push their financial interests through in a context of recurrent budget crisis. In the wake of Proposition 13, imaginative strategies have been necessary for localities to compensate for the lack of funds. Most California localities have sought their voters' approval for special assessments that would levy new taxes earmarked for services that used to be paid for entirely or partially from property taxes: road and sewer maintenance, school funding, street lighting, police and firefighting units, and penitentiary facilities. Sales tax rates have increased from 5% to 8% and beyond. California localities have taken measures such as using eminent domain powers and redevelopment laws to condemn blighted residential and industrial properties and convert them into sales tax generators.[9]

---

[9] Officials don't have much of a choice but to try and devise such sideways policies. Indeed, over 25 years later, Californian evidently still strongly supports Proposition 13 and its perceived effects. For instance, since the passage of Proposition 13, the state government has had the responsibility of dividing the property tax funds among the local governments that provide services. Some local government officials claim that this has taken away important local powers and has created a system that lacks fiscal responsibility. But most Californians disagree with this view. A majority favor the arrangement of having property taxes collected at the local level and then having the state legislature and governor be responsible for dividing the tax money among local governments. Some local government officials also argue that Proposition 13 makes it virtually impossible to pass local taxes and to raise revenues needed to provide local

But the overwhelming direct result of the initiatives expressing the taxpayer revolt of the 1970s and 1980s is the increased dependence of local governments on the state budget. Proposition 13 is paradigmatic here: it adversely impacted local finances—especially in the field of education—and led to some fiscal centralization at the state level. As an example, let's highlight the case of the monies counties receive from the state vehicle licensing fee (VLF). Unlike other states that allow counties and cities to levy separate taxes upon the ownership of motor vehicles, California has consolidated taxation of vehicle ownership into a single tax at the state level, but all vehicle license fee revenues must be allocated to cities and counties. This simplifies administration but also regularly leads to a flurry of fiscal emergencies in lean years when the state government withholds VLF revenue from local entities in order to balance the state budget.

This example shows that county governments are constantly struggling to achieve fiscal balance in a context where the state itself experiences revenue troubles. Local governments have thus resented the way Sacramento dips into what they consider their fiscal resources, whereas state authorities complain about the reluctance of local governments to take into account the needs of the larger Californian community. Misunderstanding is prevalent on both sides. In other words, the high level of institutional decentralization does not ease the tensions with Sacramento. On the contrary it seems to contribute to the deep crisis of trust that plagues Californian political life. Citizens feel that the main occupation of officials is to pass the buck from one level to the other, thus blurring the lines of financial accountability, at least in the short run. This promotes a political mood that is strongly suspicious of moves decided in Sacramento. The state's unresponsiveness toward local needs is regularly highlighted—for instance in the case of Proposition 65 in 2004. This has triggered a drive among the Californian citizenry to take the state government back. So far, however, the results of this popular *reconquista* have been mixed: the crisis of political trust has reached high levels and shows no sign of abating.[10] The state is perceived as a potentially obtrusive and unresponsive power. State authorities are victims of resentment that takes the same shape as the antifederalist movement on the national stage: some subgovernments rely on ballot initiatives to mobilize their inhabitants to limit the abilities of the state. In other words, state trends not only reflect the national discontent, but somehow deepen it.

California duplicates the national political struggle between states and the government at the local level. Its citizens have been quicker to express their pent-up frustrations in dramatic ways: specific groups and subgovernments

---

services to residents. Once again, average Californians have a different perspective. There is a widespread perception of this provision as being neutral or positive. Proposition 13 remains a formidable force in California politics.

[10] I refer the reader to a 1998 study on "government responsiveness" elaborated by the National Election Studies. Quoted in Mark Baldassere, *California in the New Millenium* (Berkeley: University of California Press, 2000). Numerous studies are available online at the website of the Public Policy Institute of California.

bluntly assert their interests through the initiative process. This is all the more significant now that ballot initiatives have become popular venues for policy-making. How then does direct democracy interact with the distrustful mood of Californian voters? This institutional option, far from providing a remedy for the ills supposed to plague state government, largely accounts for the high level of resentment people display toward their elected officials. To use an expression coined by Sidney Tarrow, the "structure of opportunities" in California has made it possible for the wave of resentment sweeping the American electorate to reach its ultimate consequences: the state is thus locked in a cycle of regressive moves. Indeed, the more citizens decide law by themselves, the more disillusioned they become with the state government's performances and motivations. The resulting discontent calls for even more direct action by the citizenry, thus paving the way for a decline of political trust. This is what I label the antifederalist moment" of California.

Direct Democracy and the Antifederalist Moment in California Politics

The political climate in California is such that it has become increasingly difficult for officials to reach consensus on an ever bigger set of topics. Contrary to other countries where tools of direct democracy are used—Switzerland for instance—the initiative process has turned California political life into a constantly polarized contest. It is hard to discern any of the positive outcomes that some legal experts and political scientists from all horizons have advocated. The least that can be said is that tools of direct democracy did not live up to expectations. Progressives of the 1900s would certainly be surprised to see how their institutional device has turned out. Hiram Johnson would have a hard time recognizing his brainchild.

In recent years, nowhere other than in California have there been so many controversial initiatives appearing on the ballot and so much money spent trying to pass or defeat them. The grassroots efforts have shaken the state government, its elected officials, and the political establishment to the core. This was made all the more easy because California endows laws enacted through the initiative process with a special, almost untouchable, legal status. In the 1970s and 1980s, the impulse behind initiatives was directly related to financial issues. In 1990, however, the voters turned their attention to the state legislators and constitutional officers, enacting term limits in an effort to eradicate career politicians and entrenched power in Sacramento. In 1994, in an angry mood about a depressed economy and severe budget crisis, they voted for Proposition 187, which required their governments to severely restrict the public services provided to illegal immigrants, such as social services, health care, and public education. It was ultimately declared unconstitutional by the courts, but since

1994, however, various laws and initiatives have sought to enact elements of Proposition 187.

Other examples of citizen-sponsored initiatives of a conservative flavor over the recent period are Proposition 209 in 1996 that ended affirmative action programs in local and state government; in the 1998 election, voters took school policy into their own hands by passing Proposition 227, restricting bilingual education programs in public schools.[11] Routinization of the initiative process is thus a fixture of Californian political life. But responsiveness is nowhere to be seen. The wide use of direct democracy in California generates a political, partisan, and institutional configuration that reinforces the very ills that initially led to the surge. Namely, it creates an unresponsive government that does not meet the expectations of the people—especially in budget terms. Thus, the tentative hypothesis is to say that antifederalism has both a higher degree of visibility and more consequences at the state level than on the national political stage, when tools of direct democracy are available. For clarity's sake, I would like to divide up these consequences in three categories: consequences on elected officials, on political procedures, and finally on policy outputs.

The first kind of consequences is oligarchical in nature: the initiative process creates a class of unreachable politicians. This new class resulting from direct democracy may be divided into two groups. At first, initiatives induce a lack of responsiveness from political institutions and officials that has been aptly described by Bruce Cain as creating risk-averse politicians. The gun behind the door metaphor illustrates this point: many elected officials resort to self-censorship so that they can avoid the political risks associated with an initiative or a recall. These tools may easily turn out to be out-of-control phenomena. But the gun metaphor quickly reaches its limits. Indeed, it turns out that the initiative is not the weapon of last resort of the lone virtuous citizen. The storybook version of how ordinary citizens, frustrated with legislative inaction, take matters into their own hands and write their own laws, and then return to their ordinary lives, is irrelevant. Some public figures may at times find direct democracy fitting for their own career. According to R. Ellis (2002), the number of initiatives on the ballot is determined not just by the demands of the people but by the suppliers of initiatives, who constitute the second part of this new class of politicians. In other words, the emphasis should not be exclusively on the mood of the voters but also on those who produce the initiatives.[12]

It is striking to witness the quick rise of political professionals who are activists of the initiative. Citizens' initiatives are not directly organized by political parties; most of the time, the initiatives are driven by interest groups or individuals that are not explicitly part of one of the two parties. These political actors have a strong tendency to use the threat of direct democracy in order to blackmail officials or competitors into meeting their demands. These activists

---

[11] This overview is taken from M. Baldassere, *California in the New Millenium,* 84.

[12] Richard J. Ellis, *Democratic Delusions. The Inititiative Process in America* (Lawrence, Kan.: Kansas University Press, 2002).

have turned into professionals belonging to a political elite that possesses skills, resources, experience, and influence that citizens typically lack. At the same time, these people are not held accountable by elections; in other words, citizens have no means of exerting a democratic control over initiative activists.

Ordinary interest groups have also increasingly entered the game. There is a "capture" process of the initiative by special interests such as labor unions, Indian tribes, and all sorts of corporate interests as well. Even wealthy individuals try to convert their economic resources into political power. The real, final problem, however, is not that the initiative process has been perverted by interest groups, activists, or even money, but rather that too many people are seduced by a populist rhetoric that insulates the initiative process from critical scrutiny. It paradoxically leads to a crisis of political accountability because it weakens the regular electoral process, the legislative branch, and forces the judiciary into stepping in.

Political procedures are clearly affected by the nearly constant use of direct democracy. State officeholders have themselves gained an increasingly prominent role in authorizing initiatives. Leaders can use direct democracy in the broader context of an institutional fight. Regularly elected officials now routinely reach for the initiative. It can be the weapon of choice for governors who find their bills stalled in the legislature or for legislatures who find themselves in the minority considering that the governor has no veto power over a decision taken by initiative. That tool is particularly attractive to candidates running for office who hope that a popular initiative may increase their visibility, help them raise money, and even increase turnout among political constituencies.

To circulate an initiative serves a political agenda and fulfills policy objectives. Direct democracy is thus an additional tool for the officials' repertoire of actions in a context of policy by other means as explained by B. Ginsberg and M. Shefter.[13] According to them, elections have become less decisive as mechanisms for resolving conflicts. Largely as a result of deadlocks in the electoral and legislative arenas, political struggles have come more frequently to be waged elsewhere and crucial choices more often made outside the electoral realm. Contending political forces have come to rely on such weapons of institutional combat as congressional investigations, media revelations, judicial proceedings, and, in the present case, tools of direct democracy.

One-shot initiatives provide credit-claiming possibilities for leaders and officials who find it convenient to appeal directly to the people to boost their career. Direct democracy may then be deemed worth their while by a sizeable number of office-holders. Over the recent period, the most prominent politician to use the initiative process in the 1990s was California Governor Pete Wilson, who authored or adopted as his own at least seven high-profile statewide initiatives—Proposition 187 being a prime example. To other politicians, however,

---

[13] Benjamin Ginsberg, Martin Shefter, *Politics By Other Means. The Declining Importance of Elections in America* (New York, Basic Books, 1999).

direct democracy may provide blame-avoidance opportunities since it makes it possible to by-pass legislative gridlock by sending the decision to the people.

In other words, direct democracy is far from being the voice of the people in its purest form. It also fits the political agenda of leaders in a timely manner and is to be analyzed accordingly as an instrument to gain political leverage or preserve political capital. This has deep consequences on public opinion: indeed, these types of initiative efforts have made voters even more cynical about elections. Instead of cementing the faith citizens should have in governmental institutions and electoral processes, initiatives seem to have the opposite effect. If needed, regularly scheduled elections can be bypassed to change the governorship, as illustrated by the 2003 recall election.

But there is another way by which regular elections are endangered. K. Miller and B. Cain rightly underlined that judicial review—the court's power to invalidate a law—is at the forefront of initiative politics.[14] The judicial process is turned into a surrogate of the political process. In other words, the irony of direct democracy is that the expansion of the initiative has made the political system more reliant on the judicial branch, meaning the branch that is most isolated from public pressure. In the name of enpowering the people, the initiative process leads to an increased reliance on the least democratic branch of government.

In California, as Ken Miller and Bruce Cain emphasize, nearly two-thirds of successful initiatives have been challenged in courts. Over half the time, the challenged initiative is struck down either in whole or in part. The catalyst for this increased reliance on courts has to do with the dangers inherent in the initiative process: the initiative process is more likely than legislatures to produce laws that adversely affect minorities. Since direct democracy is an efficient tool of grassroots political mobilization, it is often used to find easy scapegoats. Electoral sociology has it that political proficiency is a direct outcome of one's social status. In other words, low-income people with little cultural capital tend to exclude themselves from the political decision-making process. They regard themseves as being unable to correctly grasp the issues, and they tend to take refuge in nonvoting and derogatory comments on politicians.

On the opposite side of the equation, the turnout rate is much higher among affluent middle-class people. Needless to say, there is a racial ring to this social divide: whites are the core electorate of the initiative process. Specifically, while the state population is over 50% nonwhite, the state electorate is over two-thirds white. The present volume highlights the geographical dimension of this bias by emphasizing the self-sorting process at work in urban patterns. Considering this bias, minorities of all kinds tend to fall victim to decisions taken through the initiative process. This is all the more the case that marginalized groups are electorally silent, institutionally incompetent, thus devoid of ways to weigh in on

---

[14] Bruce Cain, and Kenneth Miller, "The Populist Legacy : Initiatives and the Undermining of Representative Government," in *Dangerous Democracy? The Battle Over Ballot Initiative in America*, ed. Larry J. Sabato, Howard R. Ernst, and Bruce A. Larson (Lanham, Rowman & Littlefield Pub., 2001), 33–62 .

officials. No surprise then in the overall trend of initiatives: against taxes, against immigration, against affirmative action, against bilingual education, etc. The common point of these decisions is that they adversely affect minorities: poor people, illegal aliens, blacks, Hispanics. Direct democracy may thus easily turn into a danger to the rights of minorities unless the courts are able and willing to protect these groups from attacks through direct legislation.

This configuration raises a deep and troubling question of political legitimacy. The judiciary is a counter-majoritarian institution by its very nature: unelected judges can nullify laws enacted by elected representatives. When applied against direct democracy though, judicial review becomes the most acute counter-majoritarian act. When a court strikes down a voter-approved initiative, it is not checking a branch of government; it is checking the people themselves. For populists, judicial review raises the specter of elitist, insular, activists judges overturning popular laws. Few acts are better calculated to breed popular frustration. This is especially troublesome because it is a direct threat to the judiciary's legitimacy. By entering ever deeper into the political debate, the judiciary becomes more vulnerable to partisan and ideological attacks. What is even worse is that reliance on the judiciary as a remedy often perpetuates the zero-sum, winner-take-all politics of the initiative process. It puts an end to the great art of legislative politics, namely to craft compromises and build consensus. The Supreme Court has held that it is irrelevant for the purposes of judicial review whether a challenged law has been enacted by a legislature or by the people directly.[15] There is no doubt that the confrontation between direct democracy and the judicial branch is profoundly pernicious for the political debate and the ultimate balance of democratic institutions in California.

Finally, I would like to highlight one last dimension of the antifederalist moment, which has to do with policy outputs delivered through the initiative process. Theoritically, direct democracy should improve the legitimacy of a given policy: the whole decision-making system should be better off since opposing voices are muted in advance. But the actual consequences are vastly different. Even before a law is enacted, tools of direct democracy prove to be inadequate. Particularly when a policy has complex and far-reaching consequences for government and society, the initiative is a poor law-making instrument. Backers of the initiatives typically convert complex policy issues into simple moral matters of right and wrong. Private individuals or groups draft the measures' language, usually with the help of private attorneys specializing in election law. Citizens sign petitions indiscriminately, without paying attention: this is far from a sign of democratic vitality but rather an abrogation of civic responsibility. The way signature-gatherers are paid for each signature they collect has led analysts to refer to this grassroots process as super-market democracy. The initiative process's paucity of opportunities for refinement, informed deliberation, consensus building, and compromise fuels litigiousness.

---

[15] *Citizens against Rent Control/Coalition for Fair Housing v. City of Berkeley*, 475 US 260, 1986.

To some extent, the recent multiplication of initiatives is a direct outcome of this paucity: after Proposition 13, a number of other initiatives were launched to adapt, reform, or reassert the basic drive of 1978. This led in turn to what came to be known as the overcrowding of public policy. An increasing number of expectations directed at the political system leads to a weakening of political legitimacy. Indeed, the political institutions, facing an increasing number of constraints and expectations, are unable to meet them. Direct democracy increasingly leads to a crisis of legitimacy in a political system unable to deliver in the context of an empowered citizery. Instead of building trust, the feeling of proximity between the people and their elected officials decreases. Insitutional gridlock becomes the norm because there are too many opportunities to contest decisions.

This status quo and institutional paralysis bring us back to square one: the first line of consequences I identified. Politicians appear to be out of touch, unresponsive, merely because they are risk-averse. From there, it is the same storyline all over again: increased reliance on direct democracy that weakens regular elections, which amplifies the overcrowding of public policy. A state like California thus shows that direct democracy breeds a self-nurturing antifederalism. The state seems to be locked in an antifederalist cycle. Taken together, the mix between the antifederalist mood and the wide use of direct democracy leads to a crisis of political accountability at the state level. By providing tools meant to increase responsiveness, the state government is less able to exercize its responsibility.

Conclusion

In a very famous sentence, Justice Louis Brandeis once described states as "laboratories of democracy" (*New State Ice Co v. Liebman*, 285 U.S. 262). The progressive reforms of the 1900s perfectly justified this assessment. California upgraded both its local government and its decision-making procedures. Counties were directly accountable and professionalized; new tools of direct democracy could help reform the legislature by balancing the influence of powerful interests. But the conservative national surge since the 1960s has given a new flavor to direct democracy.

What is unique to California is that the national political distrust is expressing itself in ways that have profound implications for how decisions are made about the state's future. The point of this chapter was to assess and qualify these implications. They can be labelled as an antifederalist moment" that mirrors the national antigovernment mood. Decentralization and direct democracy pave the way for a deep-seated resentment against Sacramento. Local governments now feel unable to deliver for their citizens, who, in turn, directly express their frustrations by multiplying increasingly agressive demands on their state government. State authorities are thus caught in confusing, sometimes opposing, expectations, which favor institutional inertia. The initial resentment is made even stronger by the very tools that were meant to be a safety. Far from abating, this trend is constantly on the rise, which means that the level of polarization in California now runs very high. People are strongly in favor of direct democracy and don't want to abandon what they see as their ultimate weapon. Plus, both the governor and legislators have incentives to leave the controversial decisions up to the voters and thereby avoid any political fallout. There is every reason to believe that the trend of relying on initiatives to shape public policy will continue, raising no less than the issue of the governability of the state.

References

Anderson, William. 1955. *The Nation and the States: Rivals or Partners?* Minneapolis: University of Minnesota Press.

Baldassare, Mark. 2000. *California in the New Millenium: The Changing Social and Political Landscape.* Berkeley: University of California Press.

Cain, Bruce, and Kenneth P. Miller. 2001. "The Populist Legacy: Initiatives and the Undermining of Representative Government." In *Dangerous Democracy? The Battle over Ballot Initiative in America,* ed. Larry J. Sabato, Larry J. Ernst, and Bruce A. Larson. Lanham: Rowman & Littlefield, Pub., 33–62.

Conlan, Timothy J., François Vergniolle de Chantal. 2001. "The Rehnquist Court and American Federalism." *Political Science Quarterly,* vol. 116, no. 2 (summer): 253–75.

Connelly, Jr., William F. 1999. "Newt Gingrich, Professor and Politician: The Anti-Federalist Roots of Newt Gingrich's Thought." *Southeastern Political Review,* vol. 27, no. 1 (March): 103–29.

Cornell, Saul. 1999. *The Other Founders: Anti-Federalism & The Dissenting Tradition in America.* Chapel Hill: University of North Carolina Press.

Ellis, Richard J. 2002. *Democratic Delusions. The Inititiative Process in America.* Lawrence, Kan.: Kansas University Press.

Gerber, Elisabeth R., Arthur Lupia, Mathew D. Cubbins, D. Roderick Kiewiet. 2001. *Stealing the Initiative: How State Government Responds to Direct Democracy.* Upper Saddle River, N.J.: Prentice Hall.

Gerber, Elisabeth R. 1999. *The Populist Paradox: Interest Group Influence and the Promise of Direct Legislation.* Princeton: Princeton University Press.

Gerring, John. 2001. *Party Ideologies in America, 1828–1996,* 2d ed. Cambridge: Cambridge University Press.

Gerston, Larry N., and Terry Christensen. 2003. *Recall! California's Political Eathquake.* Armonk, N.Y.: M. E. Sharpe.

Ginsberg, Benjamin, and Martin Shefter. 1999. *Politics by Other Means: The Declining Importance of Elections in America.* New York: Basic Books.

Goebel, Thomas. 2002. *A Government by the People: Direct Democracy in America, 1890–1940.* Chapel Hill: University of North Carolina Press.

Haskell, John. 2001. *Direct Democracy or Representative Government? Dispelling the Popular Myth.* Boulder: Westview Press.

Klinkner, Philip A. 1996. "Court and Country in American Politics: The Democratic Party and the 1994 Elections." In *Midterm: The Election of 1994 in Context.* Boulder: Westview Press, 61-79.

Lawrence, David G. 2004. *The California Governor Recall Campaign.* Belmont: Wadsworth.

Lubenow, Gerald C. (ed.). 2003. *California Votes.* Berkeley: University of California, Berkeley Public Policy Press.

———. 2006. *Governing California: Politics, Government, and Public Policy in the Golden State,* 2d ed. Berkeley: Institute of Governmental Studies Press.

Morone, James A. 1990. *The Democratic Wish: Popular Participation and the Limits of American Government*. New York: Basic Books.

Skowronek, Stephen. 1982. *Building a New American State: The Expansion of National Administrative Capacities, 1877–1920*. Cambridge: Cambridge University Press.

Schrag, Peter. 2004. *Paradise Lost: California's Experience, America's Future*, 2d ed. Berkeley: University of California Press.

Smith, Daniel A. 1998. *Tax Crusaders and the Politics of Direct Democracy*. Routledge: London.

Storing, Herbert J. (ed.). 1981. *The Complete Anti-Federalist*. Chicago: Chicago University Press.

Tarrow, Sidney. 1988. *Struggle, Politics, and Reform*. Ithaca: Cornell University Press.

Weaver, Kent R. 1986. "The Politics of Blame Avoidance." *Journal of Public Policy*, vol. 6, no. 4, 371–98.

About the Authors

Samuel J. Abrams is a Ph.D. candidate in government at Harvard University and a graduate fellow with the NSF Program on inequality and social policy. Abrams is a co-author of *Culture War? The Myth of a Polarized America* (with Morris P. Fiorina and Jeremy C. Pope) and the forthcoming book, *The Great Disconnect in American Politics* (with Morris P. Fiorina).

Gérald Billard is an assistant professor in urban geography and regional planning at the Université de Rouen (France). He holds a Ph.D. in urban and regional geography. Billard is the author of two books and a dozen articles on metropolitan planning and governance in the United States, Australia, and China.

Bruce E. Cain, Robson Professor of Political Science and director of the UC Washington Center, came to Berkeley in 1989 from the California Institute of Technology. A graduate of Bowdoin College and a Rhodes Scholar, he received his Ph.D. in political science from Harvard University. His writings include *The Reapportionment Puzzle; The Personal Vote*, with John Ferejohn and Morris Fiorina; and *Congressional Redistricting*, with David Butler. He received the Zale Award for Outstanding Achievement in Policy Research and Public Service and is a member of the American Academy of Arts and Sciences.

William M. Chandler is a professor of political science at the University of California, San Diego. He completed his undergraduate education at Cornell University and earned his Ph.D. at the University of North Carolina at Chapel Hill. His research has concentrated on comparative political analysis, with special interests in Canadian, German, French, and Italian governments and the European Union. Publications include *Public Policy and Provincial Politics, Federalism and the Role of the State* and *Challenges to Federalism: Policy-Making in Canada and West Germany*, plus numerous journal articles and book chapters on party government, Christian Democracy, party system change, European integration, and immigration policy.

Frédérick Douzet is an associate professor of geopolitics at the French Institute of Geopolitics of the University of Paris 8 and a graduate from the Graduate School of Journalism at UC Berkeley. She was a Fulbright scholar at the Institute of Governmental Studies at UC Berkeley for Summer 2005 and Spring 2006. She is a junior member of the Institut Universitaire de France and a member of the editorial board of the review of geopolitics *Herodote*. She has published *La couleur du pouvoir: Géopolitique de l'immigration et de la ségrégation à Oakland, Californie*, Belin, Paris, 2006.

Mark H. Drayse, associate professor of geography at California State University, Fullerton since 2001, received his B.A. in geography from Clark University, his M.A. in geography from the University of Toronto, and his Ph.D. in geography from UCLA. Drayse's current research interests include globalization and regional development, migration and ethnic labor markets, and welfare policy and urban poverty. He is collaborating with Raphael Sonenshein on an analysis of urban coalitions in an age of immigration, focusing on Los Angeles mayoral elections.

Morris P. Fiorina is the Wendt Family Professor of Political Science in Stanford's Department of Political Science and a senior fellow of the Hoover Institution. His current research focuses on the polarization of American politics. He has written or edited 10 books, most recently, *Culture War? The Myth of a Polarized America* (with Samuel Abrams and Jeremy Pope). A member of the National Academy of Sciences and the American Academy of Arts and Sciences, Fiorina has served on the editorial boards of a dozen professional journals in political science, law, and public policy.

Iris Hui is a doctoral candidate in the political science department at the University of California, Berkeley. Her research interests include redistricting, voting technology, contextual analysis, and race and ethnicity. She is a graduate of the University of Michigan.

J. Morgan Kousser is professor of history and social science at the California Institute of Technology and the author of *The Shaping of Southern Politics: Suffrage Restriction and the Establishment of the One-Party South, 1880-1910; Colorblind Injustice: Minority Vote Dilution and the Undoing of the Second Reconstruction;* and more than 40 papers and 70 book reviews. He has testified or consulted in over 30 voting rights cases, including the major challenges to congressional redistricting plans in California in 1992 and 2002. His most recent papers are on school segregation in Los Angeles and the history of Section 5 of the Voting Rights Act.

Thad Kousser is an associate professor of political science at the University of California, San Diego. He received a Ph.D. in political science from UC Berkeley, and an A.B. in government from Harvard. His publications include work on the initiative process, term limits, reapportionment, voting by mail, campaign finance laws, the blanket primary, health care policy, and European Parliament elections. His book, *Term Limits and the Dismantling of State Legislative Professionalism* (Cambridge University Press, 2005) won the Alan Rosenthal Prize, and he has worked in the California, New Mexico, and United States Senates.

Emmanuelle Le Texier, a political scientist, is a professor of American studies at the Université de Lille 3 in France. She focuses her research on political participation in urban enclaves. She conducted her research in San Diego during her

Fulbright visit to UCSD in 2002–2004. The result was a book entitled: *Quand les exclus font de la politique: Le barrio mexicain de San Diego* (Paris, Presses de Sciences Po, 2006). She has published several articles in Europe on Latino politics and immigration. She is affiliated with the Centre for Ethnic and Migration Studies (University of Liège, Belgium) and coordinates a project funded by the French National Science Foundation, entitled "The Cultural Politics of Race and Ethnicity: A Comparative Approach in the U.S. and the U.K., Post-1945."

Justin Levitt is currently a graduate student at the University of California, San Diego. A native of Seattle, Washington, he became interested in politics at an early age, serving as a page in the Washington state Senate. He graduated *cum laude* from Claremont McKenna College, earning his B.A. in philosophy, politics, economics, and Spanish. While at Claremont, he worked for the Rose Institute of State and Local Government, where he focused on demographics, redistricting, and political reform. He has also worked as a Jesse Unruh Assembly Fellow in the California State Legislature through California State University, Sacramento.

Karin Mac Donald is the director of the Statewide Database, the redistricting database for the state of California, and the Election Administration Research Center at the Institute of Governmental Studies at the University of California, Berkeley. She works and writes in the areas of redistricting, voting rights, political demography, local government, election administration, and electoral politics. She has served as consultant to many government, news, and nonprofit organizations and worked as a redistricting consultant for various local and regional entities, including the cities of San Diego and San Francisco in 2001 and 2002, respectively.

Kenneth P. Miller is an assistant professor of government at Claremont McKenna College. He received a B.A. from Pomona College, J.D. from Harvard, and Ph.D. in political science from UC Berkeley. His research and teaching interests are primarily in the areas of California politics, direct democracy, and constitutional law.

Raphael J. Sonenshein, professor of political science at CSU, Fullerton, received his B.A. in public policy from Princeton, and his Ph.D. in political science from Yale. His book *Politics in Black and White: Race and Power in Los Angeles* (Princeton University Press, 1993) received the 1994 Ralph J. Bunche Award from the American Political Science Association as the best book on racial and ethnic pluralism. Sonenshein served as executive director of the Los Angeles (appointed) Charter Reform Commission, described in his book, *The City at Stake: Secession, Reform, and the Battle for Los Angeles* (Princeton, 2004). In 2006, the League of Women Voters published his book, *Los Angeles: Structure of a City Government*. He is co-writing a book on urban coalitions in an age of immigration. He currently serves as executive director of the Los Angeles Neighborhood Council Review Commission.

François Vergniolle de Chantal is an associate professor at the University of Burgundy–Dijon, France. His latest book is "Le Fédéralisme américain en question" (Dijon, EUD, 2006) with a foreword by George A. Bermann (Columbia Law School). His current research deals with the U.S. Senate.

Dan Walters has written a daily newspaper column about California and its politics since 1981, first for the *Sacramento Union* and since 1984 for the *Sacramento Bee*. Walters, a journalist in California and Oregon since 1960, has written more than 7,000 columns. His column currently appears in the *Bee* and about 50 other California newspapers. He is the author of two books about California and its politics and is a frequent guest on national news programs and an even more frequent speaker before civic, academic, and business gatherings.

Ariane Zambiras is a Ph.D. candidate in sociology at the Ecole des Hautes Etudes in Paris. Her dissertation examines the connections between religion and politics in the United States, with an emphasis on the specificities of the religious framing of questions relating to the public good. Zambiras holds an M.A. from Sciences Po in Paris, and spent two years as a researcher with the Institute of Governmental Studies at UC Berkeley. She now teaches political sociology at the Institute of Political Science in Toulouse.